Kansai and the Asia Pacific

Economic Outlook : 2021-22

APIR ASIA PACIFIC INSTITUTE OF RESEARCH

About APIR

The Asia Pacific Institute of Research (APIR) was founded in 2011, with the aim of supporting sustainable development in the Asia Pacific region and Kansai/Japan.[1] In the rapidly globalizing economic environment, APIR has been conducting timely macroeconomic forecasts, as well as research in various fields, such as economy, finance, business, etc. We have also been actively providing academic insights into both domestic and global issues. APIR has extensive connections with the academia, government, and industry, especially in the Kansai area. Many leading companies, organizations and universities are supporting APIR's activities. We are constantly striving to expand our global network through collaborative research, seminars and cooperative activities.

---

1) Kansai is an area located in the center of Japan and has a huge market with a population of approximately 21.32 million and a GRP of approximately JPY 86,133 billion.

Mission:

As a problem-solving think tank, we develop solutions for problems faced by the Asia-Pacific region and contribute to the creation of new vitality and the advancement of sustainable development in both Japan and the Asia-Pacific region.

1. Research that provides logical and factual evidence for developing policies and business strategies.
2. Research, that is accumulating for future forecasts and is being used as a frame for identifying issues and making policy suggestions.
3. Research, the results and data of which are used as a public property and foundational research.

Based on research results, we make practical suggestions and provide information for the economic, academic, and governmental communities at the appropriate time. We also develop excellent human resources for the future.

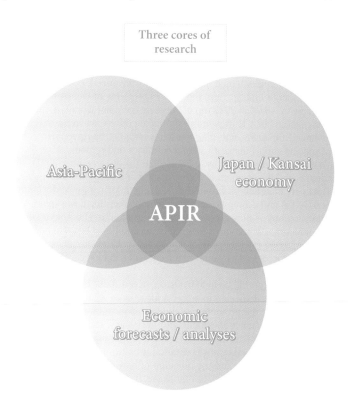

Three cores of research

Asia-Pacific

Japan / Kansai economy

APIR

Economic forecasts / analyses

MESSAGE FROM THE RESEARCH DIRECTOR

Asia Pacific Institute of Research
Research Director *MIYAHARA, Hideo*

The global economy was hit hard by the COVID-19 shock in 2020. The pandemic restricted face-to-face communication and constrained the movements of people and goods, thereby suppressing economic activities globally. As a result, the International Monetary Fund (IMF) estimates that the global economy (real GDP) contracted by –3.5% in 2020.

Efforts toward economic recovery from the COVID-19 crisis have been underway in each country. However, the level of recovery varies substantially across countries, depending on the infection rate and the government's choice of policies. In China, for example, the economy made a swift V-shaped recovery due to the thorough restrictions on mobility imposed immediately after the outbreak of COVID-19.

Along with the approval and roll-out of COVID-19 vaccines, economic stimulus measures have been implemented in many, mainly advanced, economies. As a result, positive signs began to emerge, and the IMF expects (as of October 2021) the world economy to grow by +5.9% in 2021 (up 0.7 percentage point from last year's forecast), and a further +4.9% in 2022. However, the significant difference in the vaccination rates between advanced and many emerging market economies has given rise to a new problem: that of vaccine supply disparity among countries and regions.

Japan's economy contracted by -4.5% in 2020 (as of December 2021). In the face of the pandemic, the government declared a state of emergency four times, but with serious efforts to maintain communication using information and communication technologies (ICTs) and economic activities by implementing a workplace vaccination program, the economy is now recovering, albeit gradually. The Tokyo Olympics and Paralympics held as a celebration of peace were an additional beam of hope. Currently, the COVID-19 infection rate keeps fluctuating, but it will eventually stabilize and subside. Therefore, it is necessary to analyze the current situation carefully and to prepare for the post-pandemic future.

The 2025 World Expo will be held in Osaka (Expo 2025 Osaka, Kansai). As part of it, Osaka and Kansai are expected to suggest ideas as to what the ideal future society should be. I believe that the promotion of digitalization will be a key theme. However, while digitalization is certainly inevitable and necessary, I am convinced that, rather than relying solely on digital technologies, making proper use of both digital and analog technologies will lead to an even more remarkable cultural progress. Expo 2025 Osaka will be a big event for Kansai, and the question of how digital technologies should be utilized in the future will be central. In that sense, the Expo will serve as a platform for analyzing the new lifestyles that appeared during the pandemic.

Remote work has become increasingly prevalent with the spread of the COVID-19, and it is here to stay. Making good use of office work and remote work will expand the possibilities for flexible workstyles. Such a change in workstyles might rectify the overconcentration of economic activity in Tokyo. As telework has already become widespread, an increasing number of people are moving out of Tokyo to areas offering more favorable living conditions.

Osaka is implementing a smart city project called "Umekita Phase 2", scheduled to open in 2024, in which the IoT (Internet of Things) will be utilized for medical care, education, and other purposes. The project embodies the environment needed for the Kansai economy to move toward a new development paradigm. Kansai is an economically diverse region attracting people who work in all sectors of the economy – not only in secondary and tertiary industries, but even in primary ones, such as agriculture. In order to make the most of this diverse environment, we would like to attract young people who can shape the future of Kansai and contribute to its dynamic growth.

In consideration of this, the *Kansai and the Asia Pacific Economic Outlook: 2021–22* consists of two main parts: "Part I: The Asia-Pacific Region: Current Politico-Economic Situation and Challenges" and "Part II: The COVID-19 Pandemic and Kansai's Economic Adjustment Process." In Part I, we address the recovery and adjustment of the Asia-Pacific region from the COVID-19 pandemic in 2021. We present various analyses that serve as stepping stones toward understanding the situation of post-pandemic Asia. These feature both national and international-level analyses, including the changing international trade order, and the issue of China's overseas lending.

In Part II, we analyze the impact of the COVID-19 pandemic in Kansai and the adjustment process by households and companies. We address issues such as population movement and medical supply systems, and we consider sustainable inbound strategies with a view to the post-pandemic future. We explain the current state of the tourism industry and challenges it is facing, including heightened expectations of DMOs (Destination Management/Marketing Organizations). As an extension of last year's issue, we have added an additional Part III, which summarizes the dynamics of the COVID-19 pandemic in Japan and other major countries.

Similar to past years, this year's *Economic Outlook* incorporates various perspectives on how to build a better future for everyone. I sincerely hope that this publication will be of use to all those who are passionate about the economic development of the Asia-Pacific and Kansai regions.

The Asia Pacific Institute of Research (APIR) will celebrate its 11th anniversary this year. We unwaveringly strive to translate our research findings into practice, and to serve as a front-runner contributing to the economic development of the Asia-Pacific region, including Japan and Kansai.

In closing, I would like to express my sincere gratitude to everyone who has contributed to the publication of this report.

February 2022

TABLE OF CONTENTS

About APIR ⸱⸱⸱ ii

Message from the Research Director ⸱⸱⸱⸱⸱⸱⸱⸱⸱⸱⸱⸱⸱⸱⸱⸱⸱⸱⸱⸱⸱⸱⸱⸱⸱⸱⸱⸱⸱⸱⸱⸱⸱ iv

Editors & Contributors ⸱⸱ viii

Preface: Back onto the Growth Track? ⸱⸱⸱⸱⸱⸱⸱⸱⸱⸱⸱⸱⸱⸱⸱⸱⸱⸱⸱⸱⸱⸱⸱⸱⸱⸱⸱⸱⸱⸱⸱ xii

Part I: The Asia-Pacific Region: Current Politico-Economic Situation and Challenges ⸱⸱⸱⸱⸱⸱⸱⸱⸱⸱⸱⸱⸱⸱⸱⸱⸱⸱⸱⸱⸱⸱⸱⸱⸱ 1

Chapter 1　Major Issues in the Asia-Pacific Region in 2021-22 ⸱⸱⸱⸱⸱⸱⸱⸱⸱⸱⸱⸱ 5

Section 1　The Process of Recovery and Adjustment of the World Economy from the COVID-19 Pandemic: The Three Main Points ⸱⸱ 5

Section 2　Comparison and Consideration of Fiscal Measures in Response to the COVID-19 Pandemic ⸱⸱⸱⸱⸱⸱⸱⸱⸱⸱⸱⸱⸱⸱⸱⸱⸱⸱⸱⸱⸱⸱ 24

Section 3　US Economy Aiming at a Stable Growth Path from Recovery ⸱⸱ 33

Section 4　The Rapidly Recovering Chinese Economy and Its Presence in the World ⸱⸱⸱⸱⸱⸱⸱⸱⸱⸱⸱⸱⸱⸱⸱⸱⸱⸱⸱⸱⸱⸱⸱⸱⸱⸱⸱⸱⸱⸱⸱⸱⸱⸱⸱⸱ 47

Section 5　China's Rise as the World's Top Creditor Nation: The Risks and the Outlook ⸱⸱⸱⸱⸱⸱⸱⸱⸱⸱⸱⸱⸱⸱⸱⸱⸱⸱⸱⸱⸱⸱⸱⸱⸱⸱⸱⸱⸱⸱⸱⸱⸱⸱ 58

Section 6　Turmoil in the World Trading Regime and Mega-FTAs in East Asia ⸱⸱ 70

Section 7　Labor Markets in Asia and the Informal Economy during the COVID-19 Pandemic ⸱⸱⸱⸱⸱⸱⸱⸱⸱⸱⸱⸱⸱⸱⸱⸱⸱⸱⸱⸱⸱⸱⸱⸱⸱ 80

Part II: The COVID-19 Pandemic and Kansai Economy's Adjustment Process ⸱⸱⸱⸱⸱⸱⸱⸱⸱⸱⸱⸱⸱⸱⸱⸱⸱⸱⸱⸱⸱⸱⸱⸱⸱ 93

Chapter 2　The Economies of Japan and Kansai: A Retrospective and Outlook ⸱⸱ 96

Section 1　The COVID-19 Pandemic and Household Responses: People's Flow and Household Consumption ⸱⸱⸱⸱⸱⸱⸱⸱⸱⸱⸱ 96

Section 2　The COVID-19 Pandemic and the Responses of Firms: A Deteriorating Revenue Environment and Employment Adjustment ·· 115

Section 3　The Japanese Economy: Recent Developments and Short-Term Forecasts ··· 131

Section 4　Kansai's Economy: Recent Developments and Short-Term Forecasts ·· 148

Chapter 3　Structural Changes in Kansai's Economy Due to the COVID-19 Pandemic ·· 165

Section 1　Migration Dynamics in Osaka Prefecture during the COVID-19 Pandemic ···································· 165

Section 2　The COVID-19 Pandemic and Problems in the Medical Care Provision System ································· 175

Section 3　The Utilization of DX in Kansai: Opportunities and Risks for Firms ··· 186

Chapter 4　Inbound Tourism in Kansai: A FY 2020 Retrospective and Outlook ·· 199

Section 1　A FY 2020 Retrospective: The COVID-19 Pandemic and Its Impact on Each Prefecture ······················ 200

Section 2　Kansai's Tourism Strategy: Current Situation and Issues Based on Surveys ··································· 216

Section 3　Future Roles and Challenges for DMOs: Examples from Kansai Case Studies ································ 234

Section 4　Analysis of the Tourism Industry Using the Tourism Satellite Account and Input-Output Tables ················ 252

Section 5　Impact of the COVID-19 Pandemic on Tourism Industry and the Effect of Policies to Generate Demand ··············· 269

Part Ⅲ: COVID-19 Chronology ································ 279

Part Ⅳ: Statistical Annex ····································· 305

Editors & Contributors

Editor in Chief	HONDA, Yuzo
Associate Editors	INOKI, Takenori; INADA, Yoshihisa; GOTO, Kenta
Production Editors	IMAI, Ko; ICHIMIYA, Masato; NOMURA, Ryousuke; YAMAMORI, Nobuhiro

Contributors

HONDA, Yuzo

Director of Research, APIR
Professor, Faculty of Economics, Osaka Gakuin University
Professor Emeritus, Osaka University
Ph.D. in Economics (Princeton University, 1980)
Preface; Chapter 1, Section 3

INOKI, Takenori

Research Advisor, APIR
Professor Emeritus, Osaka University;
Professor Emeritus, International Research Center for Japanese Studies
Ph.D. in Economics (Massachusetts Institute of Technology, 1974)
Chapter 1, Section 1

INADA, Yoshihisa

Director of Research & Director, Center for Quantitative Economic Analysis (CQEA), APIR
Professor Emeritus, Konan University
Ph.D. in Economics (Kobe University, 1992)
Chapter 1 Introduction; Part II Introduction; Chapter 2, Section 1, 3, 4; Chapter 4, Section 1, 2, 3, 4, 5

MATSUBAYASHI, Yoichi

Senior Research Fellow, APIR
Dean and Professor, Graduate School of Economics and Faculty of Economics, Kobe University
Ph.D. in Economics (Kobe University, 1991)

GOTO, Kenta

Senior Research Fellow, APIR
Professor, Faculty of Economics, Kansai University
Ph.D. in Area Studies (Kyoto University, 2005)
Chapter 1, Section 7

SHIBATA, Kenji

Former Chief Program Officer and Research Fellow, APIR
Sumitomo Mitsui Banking Corporation
MBA in Finance (Kwansei Gakuin University 2021)
Chapter 1, Section 1

FUJIWARA, Yukinori

Senior Research Fellow, APIR
Professor, Osaka University of Economics and Law
M.A. in Law (Osaka University, 1986)
B.A. in Economics (Osaka University, 1980)
Chapter 1, Section 2; Chapter 3, Section 2

KAJITANI, Kai

Senior Research Fellow, APIR
Professor, Graduate School of Economics, Kobe University
Ph.D. in Economics (Kobe University, 2001)
Chapter 1, Section 4

KIMURA, Fukunari

Senior Research Fellow, APIR;
Chief Economist, Economic Research Institute for ASEAN and East Asia
(ERIA)
Professor, Faculty of Economics, Keio University
Ph.D. in Economics (University of Wisconsin-Madison, 1991)
Chapter 1, Section 6

SHIMODA, Mitsuru

Director & Chief Researcher, Applied Research Institute, Inc.
Master of Economics (Tezukayama University, 1999)
Chapter 2, Section 3; Chapter 4, Section 4, 5

IRIE, Hiroaki
Associate Professor, Junior College Division, Kindai University
Ph.D. in Economics (Kwansei Gakuin University, 2012)
Chapter 2, Section 4

TAKABAYASHI, Kikuo
Senior Research Fellow, APIR
Professor, Faculty of Economics, Kwansei Gakuin University
Ph.D. in Economics (Kyoto University, 1989)
Chapter 4, Section 4

SHIMOYAMA, Akira
Professor, Faculty of Economics, Osaka University of Economics
Ph.D. in Economics (Kwansei Gakuin University, 2010)
Chapter 4, Section 4, 5

KARAVASILEV, Yani
Research Fellow, APIR
Assistant Professor, Kyoto Bunkyo University
Ph.D. in International Public Policy (Osaka University, 2017)
Chapter 1, Section 5

KINOSHITA, Yusuke
Program Officer & Research Fellow, APIR
Ph.D. in Economics (Kobe University, 2022)
Chapter 2, Section 1, 2; Chapter 3, Section 1; Chapter 4, Section 5

KUO, Chiu-Wei
Research Fellow, APIR
Ph.D. in Economics (Kyoto University, 2016)
Chapter 2, Section 2

OSHIMA, Hisanori
Chief Program Officer and Research Fellow, APIR
Seconded from DAIKIN INDUSTRIES, LTD
Chapter 3, Section 3; Chapter 4, Section 1, 2, 3

KOYAMA, Kenta
Program Officer & Research Fellow, APIR
Research dispatched from Kyoto Prefecture
Chapter 4, Section 3; Part III COVID-19 Chronology

SUGAMURA, Yurika
Staff, APIR
Part III COVID-19 Chronology

IMAI, Ko
Chief Program Officer and Research Fellow, APIR
Seconded from Resona Bank, LTD
Part I Introduction

ICHIMIYA, Masato
Chief Program Officer and Research Fellow, APIR
Seconded from MITSUI & CO., LTD
Chapter 4, Section 3; Part IV Statistical Annex

NOMURA, Ryosuke
Research Fellow, APIR
Part II Introduction; Chapter 2, Section 1; Chapter 3, Section 1; Chapter 4,
Section 1, 2, 3, 5
Part III COVID-19 Chronology

YAMAMORI, Nobuhiro
Program Officer & Research Fellow, APIR
Seconded from Takenaka Corporation
Part I Introduction; Part III COVID-19 Chronology; Part IV Statistical
Annex

(As of March 31, 2022)

PREFACE:
BACK ONTO THE GROWTH TRACK?

HONDA, Yuzo

As of December 30, 2021, the Delta variant is still raging around the globe. In addition, the new Omicron variant is increasingly spreading across the EU, the UK and the US, creating a great uncertainty in the future. The total number of deaths caused by COVID-19 exceeds 5.4 million globally. With more than 822 thousand deaths, the US is by far the most affected nation.

Despite the resurgence of the virus, the US economy is already recovering from the COVID-19 recession, thanks to the appropriate expansionary fiscal and monetary policies conducted by the US government and the Federal Reserve Board of Governors (FRB). Industrial production has surpassed its pre-pandemic level in February 2020. Both consumption and investment are recovering slowly but steadily.

Although the unemployment rate rose sharply to 14.7% in April 2020, hitting a record high since World War II, it rapidly declined to 4.2% in November 2021.

However, the issue with prices is becoming increasingly prominent. The 12-month percentage change in Consumer Price Index (CPI) stood at 6.8% in November 2021, much higher than the targeted 2%. There are at least three possible explanations for this increase. One is that consumption plunged sharply, leading to the lower prices at the beginning of the pandemic in 2020, making the inflation rate in 2021 appear higher when compared with the corresponding month of the previous year. Another explanation is that the disruption in the global supply chain due to the pandemic, together with the price hike in energy industries, has contributed to pushing up the overall price level. The third and most important factor, however, is that the FRB has been pumping a massive amount of base money into the economy to cope with the devastating consequences of the COVID-19 pandemic since March 2020.

In addition, in November 2021, President Biden signed into law the federal investment plan in infrastructure, the largest one in the past 14 years, and is also trying to pass another social safety net and climate change bill through the Congress. Although the infrastructure bill is in balanced budget and neutral to the economy in the long run, it is designed to be expansionary in the short run to support the fight against the recession.

Some economists argue that the scale of the expansionary fiscal and monetary stimuli by the government and the FRB are too large considering the current stage of recovery. At first, the government and the FRB interpreted the high inflation rate as transient, but have now admitted the increasing threat of persistent galloping inflation in the future, and have decided to shorten the tapering period and to eventually end it by the end of March 2022.

The US economy seems to be on the right track, but COVID-19 still remains the greatest risk. The number of new daily infections is on the sharp rise again, and is now more than 300 thousand.

All these developments in US affect the Japanese economy in real time through stock prices, exchange rates, interest rates, and other variables.

The Japanese economy was already in downturn around the middle of 2019, partially due to the trade war between the US and China, and partially due to the domestic consumption tax hike from 8% to 10% in October 2019. On top of these head winds, the COVID-19 dealt a blow to the Japanese economy in March 2020. Production plummeted sharply, but rebounded quite quickly to its pre-pandemic level by the middle of 2021. However, the fifth wave of the pandemic started to wash over the Japanese economy around the beginning of July, and peaked at the end of August, roughly coinciding with the summer Olympics and Paralympics held in Tokyo. Production dropped again in September 2021 as the virus raged throughout the country.

As a result of the pandemic, the unemployment rate rose from 2.2% at the end of 2019 to over 3% by the end of 2021 and remained high until November 2021, hovering around 2.8%.

Prices have kept declining since the beginning of 2020, largely due to lack of spending in the service sector, including transportation, hotel accommodations, retails, and other service industries. In 2021, however, there were two exogenous shocks to the Japanese economy, which counteracted the deflationary pressure. One was the sharp rise in energy prices, the other was the rise in import prices. As a result, the 12-month percentage change in headline CPI stood at 0.6% as of November 2021.

Overall, the economic recovery in Japan is weaker and slower than that in the US. The fifth wave has now subsided, and the number of new infections is limited for the moment. However, it is yet to be seen how damaging the impact of the Omicron variant will be. The Japanese economy is facing a bumpy recovery process.

Part I of this year's Economic Outlook discusses the economic status quo in the major countries along the Pacific Rim, which surround Japan. Part II outlines the performance of the Japanese economy in general, as well as that of the Kansai area in particular. The fact that the coronavirus is threatening our lives and the global economy alike is a recurring theme throughout this volume. For your convenience, we have added a chronology of events related to the COVID-19 pandemic in Part III this year too. Although this Economic Outlook is an abridged English-language version of the original Economic Outlook 2021 published by APIR in Japanese, some of the authors have updated their manuscripts in order to provide readers with the latest information.

Part I

THE ASIA-PACIFIC REGION: CURRENT POLITICO-ECONOMIC SITUATION AND CHALLENGES

IMAI, Ko; YAMAMORI, Nobuhiro

Part I outlines the process of recovery and adjustment from the COVID-19 pandemic in major countries around the world. Since the start of the COVID-19 pandemic, the leaders of major countries and regions, such as Japan, the US, and the EU, have changed. These changes are attracting global attention. As the world is moving toward the post-pandemic era, efforts are being made to address climate change in parallel with efforts to deal with COVID-19. We analyze these efforts and their impact. We pay special attention to such efforts and policies in major countries in the Asia-Pacific region, and we elucidate the challenges they face in their recovery. Furthermore, we explain the various issues of the world economy's adjustment in response to the COVID-19 pandemic, including the international trade order (mega-FTAs), changes in the labor market, and the impact of China's overseas lending. These analyses serve as an important background for analyzing the economies of Japan and Kansai in Part II.

Section 1, entitled "**The Process of Recovery and Adjustment of the World Economy from the COVID-19 Pandemic**," serves as an introduction to this year's Economic Outlook. It discusses developments in three dimensions. The first one is the economic impact of COVID-19, including how fiscal policies influenced the behaviors of consumers and firms in the US, and how the pandemic affected industries and regions in Japan. The second one is the vaccine rollout, inducing the cause of its delay in Japan, and overview of the vaccine distribution strategies of major countries. The third one is climate change, as it has become a top priority for governments around the world, in addition to the COVID-19 pandemic.

Section 2 presents an international comparison of the financial measures of major countries' responses to COVID-19, based on the analysis in the Fiscal Monitor, published by the International Monetary Fund (IMF) in April and October of 2021. It examines the challenges to achieving fiscal soundness. While such discussions are not on the official agenda in the government and the Diet in Japan yet, in Western countries strategies for achieving fiscal soundness, which had deteriorated while responding to COVID-19, are in full swing. The section stresses the need to consider such measures in Japan while paying close attention to discussions and trends in other countries.

Section 3 outlines the impact of the COVID-19 pandemic on the US economy and examines how the US government and Federal Reserve Board of Governors (FRB) are responding to it. The section also explains the intentions behind of the US government's the "American Rescue Plan", the "Infrastructure Plan", the "American Family Plan" and FRB's expansionary monetary policy. It discusses the current trends in the US economy as well as the controversy over the scale of economic policies. Lastly, it provides an outlook on the policies by the Biden administration and analyzes its impact on the Japanese economy.

Section 4 examines the recovery of the Chinese economy from the COVID-19 pandemic. It outlines China's anti-COVID-19 measures and its economic recovery policies, with a special focus on fiscal policy. It also discusses the economic challenges that China is expected to face in the future, noting that the Chinese economy, which achieved a V-shaped recovery in the wake of the pandemic, is changing its strategy from "great international circulation" represented by the Belt and Road Initiative (BRI) to the "great domestic circulation," which aims to develop the Chinese domestic market. Finally, it discusses the future direction of US-China frictions as well as China's increasing presence.

Section 5 is an analysis of the increasing dependence of developing countries on Chinese loans – a trend exacerbated by the COVID-19 pandemic, which made debt servicing a major challenge in many nations. The section outlines the historical background and the characteristics of Chinese overseas lending, focusing on the difference between its reported and its actual extent. It discusses the determinants and geographical distribution of Chinese lending, and provides an outlook for the future, touching on the roles of developed countries and international institutions in dealing with developing countries' increasing dependence on China.

Section 6 looks at the challenges faced by the "middle powers," the countries sandwiched between the U.S. and China, whose relationship has escalated from a trade war to a major power confrontation. The section discusses the impact of COVID-19 and of the US-China decoupling on GVCs, and explains the role and significance of RCEP. It addresses the necessity to maintain the international trade order, and discusses the role for international trade policies, including mega-FTAs, in addressing the consequences of the U.S.-China conflict in the areas of politics and security.

Section 7 outlines the labor market during the COVID-19 pandemic, with a special focus on the informal economy. It presents the trends in labor markets in Asia and the actual state of the informal economy. It then explains the impact of the pandemic on the informal economy. It notes that the recovery of people living in the informal economy is a precondition for a full-fledged recovery of the global economy as a whole, and discusses future challenges and prospects.

INTRODUCTION

INADA, Yoshihisa

Almost two years have passed since the first COVID-19 infection. Due to the lack of sufficient data related to COVID-19, in last year's Economic Outlook we mainly presented a theoretical framework (Chapter 1, Section 1) and conducted analysis based on it, while this time, a certain amount of data for analysis was available.

The global economy rapidly deteriorated due to the spread of COVID-19 infections and the resulting states of emergency and lockdowns. This unprecedented and therefore unpredictable deterioration reached its nadir in the second quarter of 2020. Since then, the recovery has been uneven across countries and industries.

Figure 1.0.1 shows the real GDP growth rate of major economies. In 2020 Q1, Japan, the U.S., the EU and China all entered recession, with China's economic decline (-9.5% QoQ) being the largest, strongly influenced by the strict

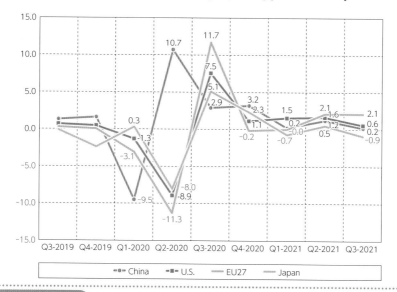

Figure 1-0-1 The impact of COVID-19 on economic growth (QoQ % change)

Source: OECD

lockdown and production shutdown in Wuhan[1]. As a result of the strict virus containment policy implemented by the Chinese government, the economy recovered by +10.7% in 2020 Q2, making up for the decline in the previous quarter. Since then, China's economy has maintained positive growth, albeit at a slower pace. On the other hand, the economies of Japan, the U.S., and the EU hit the bottom one quarter later than China, in 2020 Q2. The substantial differences in the recovery phases of Japan's main trading partners (the U.S., the EU, and China) to a certain extent influenced the economic recovery of Japan and Kansai too[2].

The U.S. economy has already recovered to its pre-pandemic level, logging five consecutive quarters of positive growth as of 2021 Q3. The EU economy registered near-zero growth in 2020 Q4 and 2021 Q1, but returned to positive growth starting 2021 Q2. On the other hand, Japan's economy has gone through a series of fluctuations since the beginning of 2021, logging a negative -0.7% QoQ growth in Q1, followed by a positive +0.5% in Q2, and a negative -0.9% in Q3. The reason for Japan's poor recovery is the delay in vaccination. As vaccination progresses, consumer sentiment is expected to improve, boosting the flow of people. As a result, consumer demand, which had been pent up, is expected to surge. Vaccination is expected to be a game changer for the future direction of the economy[3].

---

1) Japan's real GDP shrank in 2019 Q3 due to the consumption tax hike in October 2019. The modest positive growth that followed in 2020 Q1 was essentially a reactionary increase, which means that 2020 Q1 can already be regarded as a recession.
2) Chapter 2, Sections 4 and 5 provide more information on the relationship between Japan and Kansai and their trading partners.
3) For information on vaccination, see Chapter 1, Section 1. The relationship between vaccination rates and consumer sentiment is discussed in Chapter 2, Section 4.

Chapter 1

MAJOR ISSUES IN THE ASIA-PACIFIC REGION IN 2021-22

Section 1
THE PROCESS OF RECOVERY AND ADJUSTMENT OF THE WORLD ECONOMY FROM THE COVID-19 PANDEMIC: THE THREE MAIN POINTS

SHIBATA, Kenji; INOKI, Takenori

Issues the World Economy Will Be Facing

According to the International Monetary Fund (IMF), fiscal policies implemented by governments in response to the economic hardship caused by the novel coronavirus (COVID-19) pandemic are estimated to be worth USD 16.0 trillion as of April 2021[1]. It is believed that the impact of the deterioration of the fiscal balance of economies will impose strong limitations on economic management in the future.

Today, a year and a half after the arrival of COVID-19, some countries such as the US and China are beginning to enter a recovery phase and are posting positive economic growth rates. Even by industry, there is a clear division between industries that were hardly hit at all and those that were forced into severe recessions. We must be careful not to generalize, because the circumstances are specific to each country in terms of the policies that were or were not effective.

In the near future when this pandemic subsides, the world economy is expected to face various issues and enter a new phase. Many issues need to be studied, including 1) how each country will deal with the accumulating public debt resulting from fiscal spending that was expanded for COVID-19 measures, 2) under what kind of economic and trade structures will emerging countries aim for economic growth, and what will be the impact of rising resource prices

---

1) Estimates from IMF, *Fiscal Monitor*, April 2021.

on emerging countries, 3) what kind of economic and technological relation-ships will be established between emerging countries and technological hege-monies such as the US following the accelerated spread of digital technologies under the pandemic, 4) what changes did the pandemic cause to the income gap between nations in the global economy, as well as to income gaps within nations, and 5) what changes can be observed in trends in trade in goods and in services, and in direct investment.

Structure of This Section

Regarding this wide range of issues, in this section we will go over some of the things we know now about the issues in the process of recovery and adjustment from the COVID-19 pandemic. In the first part of this section, rather than a mac-roeconomic effectiveness perspective of the fiscal policies, we will introduce a US study that used big data to examine the impact of policies on the economic behaviors of consumers and firms, as well as to determine which policies were effective. For Japan, we will look at the impact of COVID-19 on effective demand by industry and region.

In the second part that follows, we will present vaccine measures according to data, the cause of their delay in Japan, and a glimpse of the strategies of the leading nations with regards to their distribution. We will discuss the issues around the development, production, and distribution of the COVID-19 vac-cines, whose speedy rollout and administration is desired.

In the final third part, among the global environmental problems that nations worldwide must tackle continuously and as a priority, we will briefly summarize the climate change issues that are being addressed fully on a global scale. Some are of the view that climate change and the COVID-19 pandemic are not entirely unrelated. This is because the possibility cannot be ignored that environmental changes due to climate change caused an imbalance in the ecosystem for which the virus serves as a medium, resulting in the arrival of a new virus.

1. Examination of the Effectiveness of COVID-19 Measures

(1) Example of a US Study

Simply measuring the amount and content of fiscal spending as well as its im-pact on consumption and employment as macro variables is not sufficient to accurately estimate the causal relationship between policy and effects. In recent studies, methods using anonymized so-called "big data" of personal information, such as credit card company, bank account, and salary data, as well as sales data of retailers, etc., gathered by private firms, are becoming mainstream. As an informative study, Chetty, Friedman, Hendren, Stepner, The Opportunity Insights Team (2020) obtained some interesting results, which we will summarize and introduce[2].

What kind of policies were implemented on what timing, and what changes did those policies bring to the behaviors of consumers and firms? Monthly, quarterly, and annual data from official statistics cannot detect policy effects that change by day and by week. What distinguishes the study by Chetty et al., is that it uses granular data (so-called big data) gathered by private firms to uncover the impact of COVID-19 on consumer spending, income, employment, etc.

This approach integrates data collected by credit card processors and human resources companies that manage salaries or data recorded by financial transaction service firms into a single publicly accessible data set over a short period of time (about seven days) and connects it to existing national statistics to create and edit data by region (county), industry, and income class, and it has advanced these studies dramatically. In the US, a system that can track data that has been broken down by region, industry, and income class at high speed is being built jointly by industry, government, and academia.

By analyzing such data, the study by Chetty et al., first reveals the following three points. 1) A decrease in consumer spending among the high-income class due to health reasons (fear of becoming infected), 2) a decrease in income among small and medium-sized firms in the service sector, such as food deliveries targeting the high-income class, and 3) a worsening of the employment situation among low-income employees in the delivery industry, in particular, verifying the increase in the unemployment rate in high-income areas.

The following are worth noting:

1) High-income households (top 25%) accounted for more than half of the decrease in spending between January and May. On the other hand, spending in low-income households (bottom 25%) saw no significant decrease or change.
2) This decrease in spending is not due to a decrease in income. Decline in spending due to a "fear of infection" is notable in industry sectors that are based on face-to-face transactions, such as food services and transportation.
3) The pattern of the decrease in spending is different from depressions in the past where decreases in spending in durable goods (such as furniture and automobiles) were prominent.

---

2) Chetty, Friedman, Hendren, Stepner, The Opportunity Insights Team (2020). See also the New Version (27431) by the same authors from November 2020 published after this paper.

Part I

Part II

Part III

Part IV

4) The impact of the decrease in consumer spending on restaurants and small local businesses was significant.

5) In areas where the wealthiest households live (determined by zip code), there were many deliveries of meals to wealthy households. However, due to COVID-19, the income of small businesses decreased by more than half.

6) Loss of employment in small businesses was significant in wealthy areas.

7) Businesses in which income declined were forced to lay off employees. In areas where the wealthy live, more than 50% of the low-income workers in small businesses were laid off within two weeks of the start of the COVID-19 pandemic. Meanwhile, in areas with the lowest rent, job creation was less than 30%.

Next, as to which types of policy contributed to mitigating the economic impact of the pandemic, the effects of 1) orders by state governments to resume economic activities, 2) stimulus payments for households, and 3) loans for small firms, were examined and were found to lead to the following notable results.

1) Orders to resume economic activity had only a small effect. Some states resumed so-called non-essential businesses on April 20, while others waited until May. Comparing these two groups, spending and income increased very little as a result of the order to resume.

2) The effect of the CARES Act (Corona virus Aid, Relief, and Economic Security Act) stimulus payments

They had the effect of increasing spending particularly among the low-income group. When the payment was received on April 15, spending among the low-income group immediately increased. However, they were not effective for the businesses hit hardest by COVID-19, nor did they help increase employment.

This spending was aimed at durable goods that do not require face-to-face transactions. The increase in income was relatively small among businesses hit hardest by COVID-19 and small businesses in wealthy areas.

The effect on employment takes longer to appear than the increase in spending. Employment in wealthy areas is weak and no recovery effect from the stimulus payment has been observed.

3) A small business loan is a loan that firms with 500 employees or less are eligible for that does not require repayment if employment is maintained at the same level as prior to the crisis. But this loan system has had hardly any effect on employment.

As described above, the study by Chetty et al., shows results that can be useful for Japan as well. Of note is that it points out that the recovery of economic activity is difficult without strong measures against the virus.

Of the three policies discussed above, the stimulus checks were effective in increasing spending among the low-income group but did not lead to additional spending for businesses hit hardest by COVID-19. Small business loans also are not leading to employment. For short-term effects, stimulus payments should be used to compensate for the loss of income in order to stop the decline in consumer spending, while consumer confidence is restored through public health policies, leading to increased spending.

We would also like to note that the study by Chetty et al., emphasizes the possibility of the COVID-19 shock hurting the economy in the long run. The problem is education. In low-income areas where equipment for online education is not widely available, the numbers of users of the educational app platform for math (Zearn) used in remote classes remain at low levels, below the 50% baseline. These numbers indicate the possibility of a decrease in social fluidity and stagnation in human capital development in the low-income group.

(2) Example of a Japanese Study

As a high-quality Japanese study, we would like to introduce an analysis using the inter-prefectural input-output table to study how final demand (particularly household consumption, accommodation, and exports) changed with the COVID-19 shock, and its impact. Ochiai, Kawasaki, Tokui, and Miyagawa (2021) used various data to analyze the impact of the spread of the novel coronavirus on the economy in 2020[3].

First, they used the 2005 Inter-Prefectural Input-Output Table to ascertain the changes in household consumption, accommodation, and exports by month and by prefecture and measured how these exogenous demand shocks spread across prefectures to all areas. Since this COVID-19 shock mainly originated in industries close to final demand and spread to upstream industries, they used backward linkage analysis from downstream to upstream.

1) Regarding household consumption, they explained based on the monthly prefectural data of the Ministry of Internal Affairs and Communications (MIC) Family Income and Expenditure Survey that while there are industries heavily damaged by consumer lifestyle changes during the COVID-19 pandemic, there are industries where new consumer demand has been created. The study looked at the decline in consumption by dividing the expenditure into

---

3) Written and edited by Miyagawa, T. (2021), *Economics of the COVID-19 Shock* (Japanese title: *Korona Shokku no Keizaigaku*), Chuokeizai-sha (RIETI's research results), Chapter 4 "Industrial and Regional Impacts of the COVID-19 Shock" (Korona Shokku no Sangyomen, Chiikimen eno Eikyo)

more detailed items.

Food expenses decreased year-on-year in April and May of 2020, by 4.6% and 3.4% respectively. These are not big decreases, but when broken down to meals outside the home and others, meals outside the home decreased significantly by 64.8% in April and 58.9% in May, while "Food expenses other than meals outside the home" increased year-on-year, indicating that the decrease in opportunities to eat out due to the COVID-19 pandemic converted consumption to cooking at home and deliveries. Likewise, breaking down "Transportation & communication" expenses into transportation expenses and communication expenses, transportation expenses significantly decreased year-on-year, while communication expenses roughly increased, showing that communication expenses increased in place of the decrease in transportation expenses. This is more or less the same as the results of the US study mentioned earlier.

2) For accommodation, the Overnight Travel Statistics by the Japan Tourism Agency were used to explain the impact on accommodation at the destination. Hotel occupancy nationwide was around 70% in 2019 but dropped to in the 10% range in April and May 2020 during the state of emergency. In July when "Go To Travel" was launched, the occupancy rate rose to around 30% and then to in the 40% range when Tokyo was added in October, but it has not reached 50%.

The study also points out that the biggest factor behind the difference in occupancy rate by prefecture is the ratio of international guests. Prefectures such as Kyoto where the ratio of international guests is high saw a significant drop in the number of guests, while prefectures such as Fukushima where the ratio of international visitors has always been low only saw a small drop in the number of guests. Additionally, based on the Report on Prefectural Accounts by the Cabinet Office, Ochiai, Kawasaki, Tokui, and Miyagawa (2021) point out that when comparing the share not only of accommodation businesses, but also accommodation and restaurant service businesses including restaurant businesses in the local economy, tourism prefectures such as Okinawa, Yamanashi, and Nagano had a large share of international visitors, and therefore require more time for an economic recovery.

3) Exports were already weak with Japan's total exports decreasing 5.6% year-on-year in 2019 according to Trade Statistics due to the US-China trade conflict, and then the COVID-19 crisis spread globally and caused them to plunge. The double-digit year-on-year decrease continued until August in manufacturing products, which account for most of the exports, delivering a serious blow to the domestic economy.

Next, what has been the ripple effect of the impact of the COVID-19 shock on household consumption, accommodation, and exports? Results from an analysis using the inter-prefectural input-output table is introduced to explain this point. First, the monthly value-added based ripple effects up to September for all industries nationwide are broken down into domestic demand and foreign demand (exports), and domestic demand is further separated into intraregional and extraregional. As a result, comparing the intraregional effect and the extraregional effect of domestic demand, we can see that in general, the impact on intraregional effect was greater. For exports, May was the peak of the impact due to the worldwide chaos, but since then, a decrease in the negative effect has continued.

How about when compared by industry? The top industries whose value added were negatively impacted between March and September were industries led by domestic demand such as textiles, petroleum and coal products, services (private and non-profit), and transportation and communication. Transportation equipment also saw its largest drop in early May, but export-led transportation equipment disappeared from the top decline spot in September due to improved exports.

Lastly, Ochiai, Kawasaki, Tokui, and Miyagawa (2021) explained the impact by prefecture in the order of impact on domestic demand (intraregional and extraregional) and foreign demand (exports) as of May. In May, the boost from exports was significant and prefectures impacted by exports were at the top in terms of the overall size of the impact. For the prefectures most impacted based on the change in value adjusted according to the economic size of each prefecture, the overall impact was most significant in Tokyo, Aichi, Osaka, Kanagawa, and Saitama in that order; for domestic demand, Tokyo, Osaka, Kanagawa, Aichi, and Saitama; and for exports, Aichi, Tokyo, Kanagawa, Shizuoka, and Osaka.

In conclusion, the following points were revealed as a result of the careful analysis by Ochiai, Kawasaki, Tokui, and Miyagawa (2021). The biggest downturn of the Japanese economy due to the COVID-19 shock was observed in May 2020, and while half of this was due to the impact of domestic activities being suppressed under the state of emergency, the remaining half of the impact was due to the level of economic activity being reduced via domestic input-output because of the significant drop in exports. Subsequently, the drop in exports became smaller, with foreign demand factors mostly removed after September and domestic demand factors remaining.

Additionally, an analysis of the breakdown of consumable items related to domestic demand showed that demand for some items grew due to teleworking during the COVID-19 pandemic and from demand related to "nesting" (staying at home), while demand for other items such as those in the field of clothing dropped significantly, resulting in a stark divide.

Furthermore, since the suppressing effect on consumption is mainly occurring in the services field and where input-output is likely to complete within each prefecture, the intraregional effect is believed to exceed the extraregional effect, which supports the validity of making decisions on the balance between infection control and economic activity on a regional basis.

2. Current State of the COVID-19 Vaccinations and Outlook for the Economic Recovery

(1) Current State of Vaccine Development in Japan

In Japan, vaccinations began on February 17, about two months after in Europe and the US. The following description is based on information as of the end of May 2021.

Table 1-1-1 shows the state of the COVID-19 vaccine development by the major pharmaceutical companies (firms selected for the Urgent Improvement Project for Vaccine Manufacturing Systems) as of March 2021. They are all in the clinical study phase. On the other hand, the COVID-19 vaccines currently administered worldwide, including in Japan, were approved by regulators for administration to humans in less than a year. For example, the phase I trials[4] for the mRNA vaccine jointly developed by Moderna and the National Institute of Allergy and Infectious Diseases began on March 16, 2020, only nine weeks after the Chinese government published the base sequence of the virus causing COVID-19 on January 11. In Europe and the US, vaccine development began immediately after the COVID-19 pandemic began, with authorization for emergency use obtained in the US in December. In Japan, AnGes and Shionogi have finally started their phase I/II trials.

Thus, COVID-19 vaccine development in Japan lags behind that in other countries and the following factors have been indicated.

(i) Scale of R&D Expenditure

Vaccine R&D requires facilities that can accommodate the large volume of vaccines required for clinical study following development. The Ministry of Health, Labour and Welfare (MHLW) launched the Urgent Improvement Project for

---

4) Vaccine development is carried out in three steps: the basic research, the non-clinical study, and the clinical study. There are three phases in the clinical study, of the phase I trial to the phase III trial.

Table 1-1-1 State of vaccine development by major pharmaceutical firms in Japan

(As of March 2021)

Developing firm	Vaccine type	Basic information	Clinical study status	Prospect of manufacturing system
Shionogi, National Institute of Infectious Diseases (NIID), UMN Pharma	Recombinant protein vaccine	Viral protein (antigen) is produced using genetic modification technology and administered to humans.	Phase I/II trials started (Dec 2020)	- Aims to build a manufacturing system for 30 million people by the end of 2021 - JPY 22.3 billion subsidy provided by the Ministry of Health, Labour and Welfare (MHLW) under the Urgent Improvement Project for Vaccine Manufacturing Systems
Daiichi Sankyo, The Institute of Medical Science, The University of Tokyo (IMSUT)	mRNA vaccine	mRNA of the virus is administered to humans and viral protein (antigen) is synthesized inside the human body.	Phase I/II trials started (Mar 2021)	- JPY 6.03 billion subsidy provided by MHLW under the Urgent Improvement Project for Vaccine Manufacturing Systems
AnGes, Osaka University, Takara Bio	DNA vaccine	Virus's DNA is administered to humans and viral protein (antigen) is synthesized inside the human body from the DNA via the mRNA.	Phase I/II trials started (Osaka City Univ., Osaka Univ.) Phase II/III trials started (eight facilities in Tokyo and Osaka) (Nov 2021)	- Planned to be manufactured by Takara Bio, AGC, Kaneka, etc. - JPY 9.38 billion subsidy provided by MHLW under the Urgent Improvement Project for Vaccine Manufacturing Systems
KM Biologics, IMSUT, NIID, National Institute of Biomedical Innovation, Health and Nutrition (NIBIOHN)	Inactivated vaccine	Cultured virus, which are processed so that infectivity and pathogenicity are lost, is administered to humans as an inactivated virus (conventional vaccine).	Phase I/II trials started (Mar 2021)	- JPY 6.09 billion subsidy provided by MHLW under the Urgent Improvement Project for Vaccine Manufacturing Systems

Note: Takeda Pharmaceutical Company, a firm not chosen for the Urgent Improvement Project for Vaccine Manufacturing Systems, signed a contract to develop and distribute the COVID-19 vaccines developed by Moderna and Novavax for Japan.

Source: Compiled by the author based on the MHLW website (https://www.mhlw.go.jp/stf/seisakunitsuite/bunya/0000121431_00223.html)

Part I

Part II

Part III

Part IV

Vaccine Manufacturing Systems[5] aimed at improving the manufacturing systems for biopharmaceuticals, including for new types of vaccines. Six firms were chosen in the first selection in June 2020 and a total of JPY 90 billion in subsidies for domestic manufacturing of COVID-19 vaccines is expected.

Meanwhile, in the US, development subsidies from the Biomedical Advanced Research and Development Authority were announced one after another from February to July 2020 to Johnson & Johnson (J&J) (USD 456 million), Moderna (USD 483 million), AstraZeneca-University of Oxford (USD 1.2 billion), Novavax (USD 1.6 billion), etc. under the Department of Defense's special project Operation Warp Speed (OWS)[6].

A simple comparison shows that the amount of support per firm and the speed with which the measures were taken affect vaccine development.

(ii) Vaccine Development System

A difference between the key nations that are leading in vaccine development and Japan is whether the idea that "vaccines are a pillar of security" exists. The governments of countries such as the US, UK, Germany, France, China, and Russia, which have the leading vaccine manufacturers, position vaccines as an important strategic item to prepare for infectious disease risks when sending their troops overseas. Protecting their people from a pandemic is the first goal, but vaccines are positioned as a tool for national defense and diplomacy, not as a COVID-19 emergency support measure, and the market is managed under a national policy as part of security. Differences in the national development system are also clear depending on whether daily life is viewed as in peacetime or in a time of emergency.

(iii) Differences in Vaccine Development Technologies

The vaccines developed by major countries that are being administered worldwide today are shown in Table 1-1-2.

Focusing on the types of these vaccines, we can say that development of the following three types was rapid: mRNA vaccines from Pfizer (US) and Moderna (US), viral vector vaccines from AstraZeneca (UK) and J&J (US), and recombinant protein vaccine from Novavax (US). There is no infrastructure for developing these vaccines in Japan, and the fact that Japan is only equipped with the

---

5) The Urgent Improvement Project for Vaccine Manufacturing Systems is a project for the early development of a system for actual manufacturing (large-scale manufacturing) of biopharmaceuticals including the COVID-19 vaccine in Japan, and it is aimed at promoting the early supply of the COVID-19 vaccine in Japan.

6) A project that the US started to accelerate the development and manufacturing of COVID-19 vaccines. Around USD 10 billion (around JPY 1.2 trillion) was invested, with the Centers for Disease Control and Prevention (CDC), Department of Defense, Department of Energy as well as private firms participating.

Table 1-1-2	Major COVID-19 vaccines developed worldwide	

Pharmaceutical firm/ Vaccine type	Date approved for use in key countries	Initial forecast for manufacturing/ supply
A	Pfizer (US) *mRNA vaccine	UK: 12/02/2020 Emergency US: 12/11/2020 Emergency EU: 12/21/2020 Conditional JP: 02/14/2021	Plans to manufacture up to 50 million doses by the end of 2020 and up to 2 billion doses of the vaccine by the end of 2021.
B	AstraZeneca Oxford University (UK) *Viral vector vaccine	UK: 12/30/2020 EU: 01/29/2021 Conditional JP: 05/21/2021	Plans to supply for 2 billion people worldwide, 300 million people in the US, 100 million people in the UK, 400 million people in EU, and 1 billion people in emerging countries.
C	Moderna (US) *mRNA vaccine	US: 12/18/2020 Emergency EU: 01/06/2021 UK: 01/08/2021 JP: 05/21/2021	Plans to supply 500 million to 1 billion doses per year worldwide. Plan to supply 20 million doses within the US by the end of Dec 2020.
D	Johnson & Johnson (Janssen) (US) *Viral vector vaccine	US: 02/27/2021 Emergency EU: 03/11/2021 Conditional UK: 05/28/2021 JP: 05/24/2021 Approval application	Aims to start mass supply (gradually up to around 1 billion people per year worldwide) in 2021.
E	Sanofi (FR) *(i) Recombinant protein vaccine (ii) mRNA vaccine	(i) Phase IIb trials under way since Feb 2021 in the US, etc. (ii) Phase I/II trials under way since Mar 2021.	Announced that a recombinant protein vaccine is expected to be put to practical use in 2021 Q4, if things go well.
F	Novavax (US) *Recombinant protein vaccine	Phase III trials under way in the UK since Sep 2020. Phase III trials under way since Dec 2020 in the US, etc.	Overseas, the production goal is 100 million doses per year by late 2020.

Source: Compiled by the author based on materials on MHLW website and reports from each firm

traditional technology of inactivated vaccines[7] is another reason for the delay in development. Additionally, since the new vaccines developed overseas were found to be effective, Japanese pharmaceutical manufacturers that are lagging behind in development may be having a hard time conducting clinical trials.

In Japan, Shionogi is developing a vaccine using a recombinant protein technology with the goal of manufacturing vaccines domestically. We look forward to the manufacturers of such domestic vaccines applying for approval soon, and also as a measure for addressing the worldwide vaccine shortage.

(2) Current State of Vaccine Production in the World and the Challenges

Next, we will explain about the overseas vaccine production systems, listing

---

7) An inactivated vaccine is a traditional method where viruses are grown in eggs and inactivated.

Table 1-1-3   Countries developing vaccines and their manufacturing sites

Country	Developer	Vaccine name (vaccine approved by WHO)	Manufacturing sites (example)	Scale
US	Pfizer /BioNTech	(mRNA type vaccine) Product name: Comirnaty Dec 2020 Emergency Use Authorization	Pfizer - US (Chesterfield, Missouri) - US (Andover, Massachusetts) - US (Portage, Michigan) - Belgium (Puurs) BioNTech - Germany (Marburg) *China (Fosun): Manufacturing, sales	Manufacturing capacity scheduled to expand to 2.5 billion doses by the end of 2021 (As of Mar 30, 2021)
UK	AstraZeneca /Oxford University	(Viral vector vaccine) Product name: Covishield, Vaxzevria, etc. Feb 2021 Emergency Use Authorization	Manufacturing - UK (Oxford, Keele) - India (Pune: Serum Institute of India) - Netherlands (Leiden) - Korea - Japan (JCR Pharmaceuticals) Vial filling and packaging - UK (Wrexham)	Annual manufacturing target is 3 billion doses (As of Feb 21, 2021)
US	Moderna	(mRNA type vaccine) Moderna COVID-19 vaccine Apr 2021 Emergency Use Authorization	Manufacturing (Contract with Lonza Group) - US (Portsmouth, New Hampshire) - Switzerland (Visp) Vial filling and packaging - US: Catalent - Spain: Laboratorios Farmacéuticos Rovi	- Manufacturing scheduled for 2021: 800 million to 1 billion doses - Manufacturing scheduled for 2022: 3 billion doses (As of Apr 29, 2021)
US	Johnson & Johnson	(Viral vector vaccine) COVID-19 vaccine Mar 2021 Emergency Use Authorization	Manufacturing - US (Bloomington, Indiana) large-scale manufacturing - Italy (Anagni): Catalent facility - US (Grand Rapids, Michigan) - Spain (Barcelona) - France (Marcy-l'Etoile): Support, infrastructure provided - Japan (Takeda Pharmaceutical Company announced manufacturing support plan, March 16, 2021)	Up to 3 billion doses scheduled for manufacturing in 2022
China	Sinopharm	(Inactivated vaccine) BBIBP-CorV May 2021 Emergency Use Authorization	Manufacturing - China (Beijing, Wuhan) Manufacturing site: plan (i) UAE: New plant in operation in 2021 (ii) Serbia: Manufacturing scheduled to start in October (iii) Egypt: Agreed to manufacture vaccines locally (iv) Bangladesh: Local manufacturing approved	Expected to manufacture amount for 1 billion doses in 2021 (As of Feb 26, 2021) (i) Up to 200 million doses scheduled for manufacturing per year (ii) Up to 24 million doses scheduled for manufacturing per year
China	Sinovac Biotech	(Inactivated virus COVID-19 vaccine) CoronaVac Jun 2021 Emergency Use Authorization	Manufacturing - China (Beijing) First plant: Beijing (Jul 2020) Second plant: Beijing (Feb 2021) Third plant: Beijing (Apr 2021) - Indonesia: Plans to expand manufacturing of Sinovac vaccines Manufacturing site: plan (i) Brazil: Began construction of manufacturing facility for 100 million doses/year (Scheduled for completion in Sep 2021) (ii) Malaysia: Obtained approval for vaccine "filling/finishing" (iii) Turkey: Obtained manufacturing license (iv) Hungary: Manufacturing plan exists	As of beginning of April 2021, 100 million doses are expected to have been administered worldwide. The Chinese government manufactured 10 million doses for COVAX thus far and plans to manufacture 3 billion doses by the end of the year

Source: Compiled by the author based on press releases from each firm
Compiled by the author based on articles of each firm for which the source is the English version Wikipedia (https://en.wikipedia.org/wiki/COVID-19_vaccine#Efficacy)

some examples from the major countries developing them. Table 1-1-3 summarizes the manufacturing sites and manufacturing scale of the COVID-19 vaccine developers approved by the World Health Organization (WHO) based on press releases from each firm, etc. It shows that each developer has manufacturing sites overseas and that they are aiming to establish a stable manufacturing system for domestic and international supply.

Such developments around manufacturing sites are also linked to political aspects referred to as vaccine diplomacy. For example, India was expected to become a key export base for COVID-19 vaccines, but on the start of the COVID-19 pandemic, supply problems occurred such as export restrictions. Additionally, China is actively engaging in vaccine diplomacy in the Indo-Pacific region, including with the Philippines with which it is in conflict over territorial rights and maritime interests in the South China Sea, and it is attempting to increase its influence. Furthermore, China is pursuing diplomacy that capitalizes on vaccine inequity by promoting vaccine distribution to middle-income countries such as Mexico and Brazil.

There is the harsh reality in international politics that vaccine distribution not only helps to save lives, but it is also being used as a diplomatic tool with the

| Table 1-1-4 | Cumulative number of infected persons and the vaccination status |

(As of July 29, 2021)

Country	Number of infected persons (1,000)	Number of vaccinations administered per 100 people	Total number of vaccinations administered (1,000)
World	196,630	52.27	4,074,032
China	93	112.5	1,619,218
US	34,751	102.88	344,072
India	31,572	33.05	456,034
Brazil	19,839	65.88	140,029
UK	5,828	124.82	84,738
Germany	3,772	109.43	91,688
France	6,142	107.64	72,728
Italy	4,337	111.86	67,631
Russia	6,139	41.17	60,086
Indonesia	3,331	24.11	65,959
Japan	904	68.5	86,641
United Arab Emirates	678	168.62	16,677
Israel	869	128.77	11,146

Note: The total number of vaccinations administered is the number of vaccines administered and is different from the number of people to whom a vaccine has been administered.
Website last viewed on August 6, 2021.
Source: Compiled by the author based on "Our World in Data, ONS, and UK government website"

post-COVID period in sight.

However, needless to say, to mitigate the risk of the COVID-19 pandemic, each country must promote vaccinations systematically, build manufacturing plants domestically for vaccines that have been approved overseas, and act swiftly for a domestic supply and exports to neighboring countries. In Japan, there are developments, such as JCR Pharmaceuticals announcing it will build a new plant for the AstraZeneca COVID-19 vaccine stock solution, while establishing a vaccine supply chain in all parts of the world is also an urgent issue.

(3) Issue of Vaccine Distribution in the World

Table 1-1-4 shows the cumulative number of infected persons and the vaccination status by country as of July 2021. Key countries developing vaccines and countries with deep economic ties with these developer countries show higher numbers of vaccines administered. We can also assume from this table that vaccine distribution to developing countries is not progressing well.

To respond to this situation, the World Health Organization (WHO) is working on supplying vaccines to countries around the world through the COVAX Facility[8]. COVAX is aiming at supplying at least two billion doses of the vaccine in 2021 and since its first international transportation to Ghana on February 24, it has delivered vaccines to more than 100 countries in 42 days. The number of doses exceeded that of the 38 million doses provided by AstraZeneca, Pfizer-BioNTech, and Serum Institute of India (SII)[9]. However, Serum Institute of India (SII) which was the largest vaccine supplier under COVAX, subsequently stopped its exports in March due to a sudden increase in infections in India, and the issue of achieving a fair supply of vaccines has not been resolved.

As seen above, the divide between developed countries and developing countries in terms of vaccination status is clearly growing. In Japan, vaccines needed for domestic vaccinations are being secured with supplies from Pfizer, AstraZeneca, and Moderna. The development of a domestic manufacturing system as soon as possible is desired.

3. Is the Pandemic Unrelated to Climate Change?

Thus far, we have discussed the relationship between the pandemic and eco-

---

8) COVAX Facility is a framework led and launched by the World Health Organization and the United Nations Children's Fund (UNICEF) for the procurement and equal distribution of vaccines in the world.
9) From the website of Japan Committee for UNICEF (https://www.unicef.or.jp/news/2021/0087.html).

nomic policy and the issues Japan faces with the vaccine rollout. What should be noted is that because of the arrival of COVID-19, it was a year in which interest in the other important issues faced by the world economy and in people's lives has faded.

COP26 that was scheduled for October 2020 was postponed by one year to the fall of 2021. This is not surprising, since the urgent issue now is how to end this pandemic. However, this does not mean we can view climate change and the novel coronavirus pandemic as totally unrelated mutual phenomena. Simply put, some experts say the COVID-19 pandemic occurred when the balance in the ecosystem was lost via the virus due to environmental changes caused by climate change. We must not allow our awareness and interest in climate change to fade while focusing our attention solely on issues at hand, such as poverty, famine, health, and hygiene.

Below, we will briefly describe the most recent measures against climate change in major countries and their greenhouse gas (GHG) reduction targets.

Climate Change Policies and Numerical Targets of Major Countries

1) Japan

In light of Prime Minister Suga's declaration in October 2020 of achieving a carbon neutral and decarbonized society by 2050, the Cabinet decided on December 8 of the same year on support funds for developments of technologies for carbon neutrality. Since approximately 85% of greenhouse gas emissions in Japan are energy-derived CO_2, the realization of a hydrogen society, including switching to green electricity, was announced. This policy can be seen as mostly aligned with those in Europe and the UK. The "Green Growth Strategy Through Achieving Carbon Neutrality in 2050" formulated mainly by the Ministry of Economy, Trade and Industry (METI) specifies the current challenges and future actions in each of the 14 priority fields[10] and formulates action plans covering various policies.

---

10) For further details, see materials for the Growth Strategy Council on the METI website (the 14 priority fields are listed below).
  1. Offshore wind power industry 2. Fuel ammonia industry 3. Hydrogen industry 4. Nuclear power industry 5. Automobile, storage battery industries 6. Semiconductor and ICT industries 7. Shipping industry 8. Logistics, people flow and infrastructure industries 9. Foods, agriculture, forestry and fishery industries 10. Aircraft industry 11. Carbon recycling industry 12. Housing/building industry, next generation solar power industry 13. Resource circulation industry 14. Lifestyle-related industry

Part I

Part II

Part III

Part IV

2) The US

As soon as President Biden was sworn in in January 2021, the US rejoined the Paris Agreement, and announced its target of reaching net zero GHG emissions by 2050. Climate change measures are positioned as a central issue for the administration and an executive order was issued aiming to conserve at least 30% of federal lands and ocean territories by 2030. Specific policies include the announcement of an "infrastructure and clean energy investment plan," which will invest USD 2 trillion over the four years of the administration's first term to increase environmental investment in areas such as automobile, public transportation, and power. However, it is worth noting that this policy is exercised through executive (presidential) privilege and may be cancelled by a future president.

3) China

Decarbonization in China, the country with the world's largest CO_2 emissions, is important to meet the global goals for tackling climate change. China is developing decarbonization technology industries such as EV and FCV and allocating large subsidy budgets for new energy vehicles (JPY 450 billion in FY 2020).

In "The 14th Five-Year Plan for Economic and Social Development of the People's Republic of China (2021–2025)" passed by the National People's Congress in March 2021, plans to continue addressing climate change were presented with a goal set of reducing carbon dioxide emissions per unit of GDP by 18% during the period. However, while the transition period from peak carbon emissions to carbon neutrality is said to be around 50 to 70 years in Japan, the US, and Europe, the transition period in China is only 30 years (2030 to 2060). Considering that coal-fired thermal power plants are being newly constructed in China even today, we can assume that transitioning from an energy ratio centered on coal will take much time and face many problems.

4) Europe

European nations including Germany, the UK, and France that identify themselves as environmentally advanced countries have a longer history of working on this issue than other developed countries. In 1994, the European Environment Agency was established as an agency of the European Union (EU) with jurisdiction over environmental issues, and in 2005, the EU was the first in the world to start a carbon dioxide (CO_2) emissions trading system for its 25 member states.

A new European Commission started on December 1, 2019, and on the 11th

Table 1-1-5		Greenhouse gas reduction targets for the major countries	

Country/ region	Greenhouse gas reduction target		Share of CO_2 emission in the world (2018)
	Medium-term target	Long-term target	
US	-50% to -52% in 2030 (compared to 2005)	Become carbon neutral by 2050	14.7%
Japan	-46% in FY 2030 (compared to 2013)		3.2%
EU	-55% in 2030 (compared to 1990)		9.4%
UK	-78% in 2035 (compared to 1990)		
Canada	-40% to -45% in 2030 (compared to 2005)		1.70%
China	- -65% or more in 2030 in CO_2 emissions per GDP (compared to 2005) - Peak out CO_2 emissions by 2030	Become carbon neutral by 2060	28.40%
India	-33% to -35% in emissions per GDP in 2030 (compared to 2005)	No remarks at this time	6.90%
Russia	-30% in 2030 (compared to 1990)	No remarks at this time	4.70%

Note: Regarding India's "per GDP" target, if GDP grows more than the emissions by the target year, it is possible that emissions are increasing.
Note: Red characters are items whose target has been raised and added due to the climate summit held in April 2021.
Source: Compiled by the author based on materials published by JETRO

of that month, they announced the European Green Deal[11]. The new European Commission reached a provisional agreement on the European Climate Law on April 2021 to write into legislation their goal of becoming the first "climate neutral continent" by 2050.

The UK amended its Climate Change Act[12] in June 2019 to set the policy goal of net zero carbon dioxide emissions by 2050.

Table 1-1-5 shows the greenhouse gas reduction targets and the timing on which carbon neutrality will be achieved for the major countries.

To achieve carbon neutrality by 2050, each country has set a greenhouse

---

11) The European Green Deal is a set of action plans, such as raising the EU climate target for 2030 and reviewing related regulations accordingly, with the goal of the EU achieving "climate neutrality" with net zero greenhouse gas emissions by 2050.

12) A law enacted in the UK in 2008 as the first in the world to stipulate climate change measures for the next 50 years. It aims to improve carbon management and to promote the UK's transition to a low-carbon economy, as well as to enable the UK to demonstrate leadership for global reductions in emissions based on international agreements.

Part I

Part II

Part III

Part IV

gas reduction target for 2030, but the base years have not been unified, making side-by-side comparisons of the level of contribution difficult. For example, the Biden administration announced that it would reduce greenhouse gas emissions by half, but its emissions per capita as of 2030 are higher than other countries with high emissions that also have reduction targets set for 2030. Additionally, China and India set their emission reduction targets not in terms of total emissions, but in terms of emissions per GDP.

In other words, countries have set reduction targets in different ways, and there is no denying the fact that the targets are in some way convenient for themselves. However, there is no doubt that 2030 will serve as a milestone year in determining how serious the countries are about achieving carbon neutrality by 2050.

Lastly, we will touch on nuclear power generation, which is unavoidable when countries address climate change and consider energy alternatives to coal that is the source of greenhouse gas emissions.

Some countries, including Japan, are beginning to review their energy policies in the direction of reducing their dependence on nuclear energy. However, there are many countries that are not reviewing their positions on nuclear power generation. Rather, some say we need to consider the idea that depending to what extent climate change is addressed, dependence on nuclear power generation is unavoidable. Furthermore, some predict that nuclear power generation in emerging countries and developing countries will increase dramatically in the future. It is undeniable that how the global energy supply system will change in the future is an important issue for industries, as well as for the daily lives of people.

References

Cabinet Secretariat, Growth Strategy Council (6th), Material 2: "Green Growth Strategy Through Achieving Carbon Neutrality in 2050"

Hara, M. (2021), *The Speedy Development of the Novel Coronavirus Vaccine* (Japanese title: *Shingata Korona Wakuchin wa Ikani Jinsokuni Kaihatsu Saretaka*), Kokusai Shogyo Publishing.

IMF, *Fiscal Monitor*, April 2021
https://www.imf.org/en/Topics/imf-and-covid19/Fiscal-Policies-Database-in-Response-to-COVID-19

Ministry of Health, Labour and Welfare (MHLW) website, "Vaccine Development and Outlook"
https://www.mhlw.go.jp/stf/seisakunitsuite/bunya/0000121431_00223.html

Nikkei Business, April 26,2021

Nikkei Business Online Edition (March 30, 2021)
   https://business.nikkei.com/atcl/gen/19/00005/032600173/

Nikkei Business Online Edition (May 20, 2021)
   https://business.nikkei.com/atcl/NBD/19/world/00369/

Our World in Data COVID-19 Data Explorer (viewed July 29, 2021)

Raj Chetty, John Friedman, Nathaniel Hendren, Michael Stepner, The Opportunity Insights Team, "How did COVID-19 and Stabilization Policies affect Spending and Employment? A New Real-Time Economic Tracker based on Private Sector Data," NBER Working Paper 27431 (First Version) (June 2020)

Raj Chetty, John Friedman, Nathaniel Hendren, Michael Stepner, The Opportunity Insights Team, "The Economic Impacts of COVID-19: Evidence from a New Public Database Built Using Private Sector Data," NBER Working Paper 27431 (New Version) (Nov. 2020)

Toyo Keizai (February 6, 2021)

Written and edited by Miyagawa, T. (2021), *Economics of the COVID-19 Shock* (Japanese title: *Korona Shokku no Keizaigaku*), Chuokeizai-sha.

Part I

Part II

Part III

Part IV

Section 2
COMPARISON AND CONSIDERATION OF FISCAL MEASURES IN RESPONSE TO THE COVID-19 PANDEMIC

FUJIWARA, Yukinori

1. Introduction

Following the rapid spread of the novel coronavirus (COVID-19) worldwide from the beginning of 2020 (certified as a pandemic by the World Health Organization), national governments have been implementing large-scale fiscal measures to mitigate the economic damage, including increasing direct fiscal spending, tax cuts, and support for private sector funding.

These extraordinary fiscal measures have been positively evaluated because they have prevented an escalation of economic stagnation and an increase in job losses, but at the same time, they have significantly increased fiscal deficits and government debt to unprecedented levels, resulting in a tough fiscal outlook.

In this section, I compare the fiscal measures taken in selected economies in response to the COVID-19 pandemic and discuss fiscal consolidation issues based on the analyses in the Fiscal Monitor reports[1] released by the International Monetary Fund (IMF) in April and October 2021.

2. Status of Fiscal Measures in Response to the COVID-19 Pandemic

(1) Scale of Fiscal Measures in Response to the COVID-19 Pandemic

According to the IMF, the scale of fiscal measures implemented in response to the COVID-19 pandemic by national governments was estimated to be USD 16.9 trillion (16.4% of nominal GDP) globally as of October 2021. Figure 1-2-1 illustrates the scale of the fiscal measures taken in selected economies (as percentages of nominal GDP) based on the IMF's country classifications[2]. The comparison shows that there is a large difference between countries in terms of their ability to increase government expenditure.

---

1) The Fiscal Monitor is a report prepared and published twice a year by the IMF Secretariat on each country's latest fiscal conditions and medium- to long-term fiscal projections.
2) The IMF has classified global economies into advanced economies, emerging market economies, and low-income developing countries, which are also used in this report.

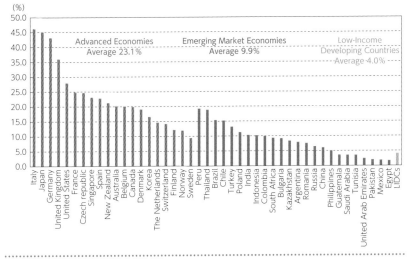

Figure 1-2-1   Scale of fiscal measures in selected economies (percentage of GDP)

Note: The classifications of advanced economies, emerging market economies, and low-income developing countries are based on the definitions of the IMF. Ratios are percentages of nominal GDP.

Source: IMF, Database of Country Fiscal Measures in Response to the COVID-19 Pandemic

The scale of fiscal measures is the largest in advanced economies with strong economic power (23.1% on average), followed, although with a large difference, by emerging market economies (9.9% on average), while the scale is generally small in low-income developing countries (4.0% on average).

Among the top five advanced economies, Italy is the highest at 46.2% as a percentage of nominal GDP, followed by Japan (45.1%), Germany (43.1%), the UK (36.0%), and the US (27.9%).

The top emerging market economies are Peru (19.2%), Thailand (18.8%), Brazil (15.4%), Chile (15.2%), and Turkey (13.1%). China, which contained the outbreak of COVID-19 infections at an early stage, stood at a low 6.1% relative to its economic scale.

The IMF classifies the contents of fiscal measures into measures within a budget (additional spending and forgone revenues such as tax cuts) and off-budget measures (equity, loans, and guarantees by the government sector). Off-budget measures are support by financing from private sources. Figure 1-2-2 and Figure 1-2-3 show international comparisons of the scale of fiscal measures as percentages of nominal GDP in advanced economies and in emerging market economies based on the classifications.

Regarding fiscal measures, which is the larger of the within-budget and off-budget measures differs depending on the country. Generally speaking, ad-

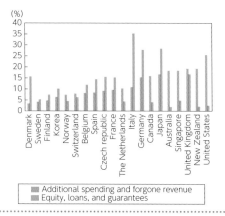

Figure 1-2-2 Scale of fiscal measures in advanced economies (percentage of GDP)

Note: Ratios are in percentages of nominal GDP.
Source: IMF, Database of Country Fiscal Measures in Response to the COVID-19 Pandemic

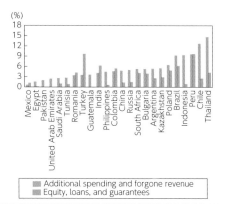

Figure 1-2-3 Scale of fiscal measures in emerging market economies (percentage of GDP)

Note: Ratios are percentages of nominal GDP.
Source: IMF, Database of Country Fiscal Measures in Response to the COVID-19 Pandemic

vanced economies with larger government debt compared to the pre-pandemic levels have implemented larger off-budget measures (Spain, France, Italy, and Japan). In Germany as well, which maintains strict fiscal discipline, off-budget funding support measures account for a larger percentage. On the other hand, in the US, which provided direct benefits to individuals three times and a large amount of additional unemployment insurance benefits, the additional spending within the budget accounts for a much larger percentage.

In emerging market economies, unlike advanced economies where the

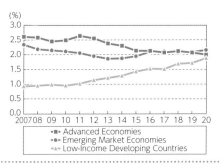

Figure 1-2-4 Changes in interest payment costs of general governments (percentage of GDP)

Note: Ratios are percentages of nominal GDP.
Source: IMF, Fiscal Monitor, April 2021

types of fiscal measures differ from country to country, the higher the stage of economic development, the more flexibly fiscal measures have been taken, and many economies rely more on additional spending within their budgets.

It can be said that the reason why such extraordinary large-scale fiscal measures were taken in advanced economies and some emerging market economies is because the COVID-19 pandemic, which emerged rapidly, and its serious impact prompted quick responses. As the IMF points out, in the background to this lies central banks' large-scale monetary easing measures, including reductions in their policy interest rates and purchases of government bonds, that allowed the fiscal authorities of each country to finance their huge fiscal deficits by issuing government bonds at low interest rates.

As shown in Figure 1-2-4, in the continued low interest rate environment, interest payment costs as percentages of nominal GDP of the general governments of advanced economies and emerging market economies have remained at low levels (1.9% to 2.6%) for the past 10 years. Although interest payment costs have been trending upward in low-income developing countries, the ratio still remains at the low level of less than 2.0% as a percentage of GDP.

But recently, long-term interest rates have been trending upward. The US 10-year government bond interest rate increased from around 0.7% in September 2020 to around 1.5% in November 2021. The Federal Reserve Board (FRB) decided on a policy of gradually reducing quantitative easing from November 2021. Long-term interest rates may continue to rise in the future, coupled with inflationary concerns due to the expansion of demand associated with the huge fiscal stimulus package under the Biden administration. It should be noted that if the rise in interest rates spreads to advanced economies, there is the risk that this will increase interest payment costs in each country.

(2) Outlook for the Fiscal Balance and Government Debt

Large-scale fiscal measures in response to the global spread of COVID-19 have significantly worsened each country's fiscal balance. The IMF projects a sharp deterioration of fiscal balances in 2020 (Table 1-2-1). When looking at the ratio of the fiscal deficit to nominal GDP in 2020, the average was 10.8% for advanced economies, 9.6% for emerging market economies, and 5.2% for low-income developing countries.

The IMF predicts that fiscal deficits will shrink in most countries in 2021 because COVID-19-related support measures will end or decrease. Although each country's fiscal deficit is currently well above their pre-pandemic levels, the IMF predicts that the deficits in most countries will return to their pre-pandemic levels by 2026.

Large-scale fiscal measures in response to COVID-19 have become a factor

| Table 1-2-1 | | | | | | Changes in general governments' fiscal balances (percentage of GDP) | | | | | |

(Percent of GDP)	2016	2017	2018	2019	2020	Projections					
						2021	2022	2023	2024	2025	2026
World	-3.5	-3.0	-3.0	-3.6	-10.2	-7.9	-5.2	-4.2	-3.8	-3.6	-3.5
Advanced Economies	-2.7	-2.4	-2.5	-3.0	-10.8	-8.8	-4.8	-3.6	-3.2	-3.1	-3.0
Canada	-0.5	-0.1	0.3	0.5	-10.9	-7.5	-2.2	-0.5	-0.1	0.2	0.4
France	-3.6	-3.0	-2.3	-3.1	-9.2	-8.9	-4.7	-3.9	-3.6	-3.4	-3.4
Germany	1.2	1.3	1.9	1.5	-4.3	-6.8	-1.8	-0.4	0.0	0.5	0.5
Italy	-2.4	-2.4	-2.2	-1.6	-9.5	-10.2	-4.7	-3.5	-2.9	-2.6	-2.4
Japan	-3.8	-3.3	-2.7	-3.1	-10.3	-9.0	-3.9	-2.1	-2.1	-2.1	-2.2
United Kingdom	-3.3	-2.4	-2.2	-2.3	-12.5	-11.9	-5.6	-3.6	-3.2	-3.1	-2.9
United States	-4.3	-4.6	-5.4	-5.7	-14.9	-10.8	-6.9	-5.7	-5.2	-5.3	-5.3
Emerging Market Economies	-4.8	-4.1	-3.7	-4.7	-9.6	-6.6	-5.8	-5.2	-4.8	-4.4	-4.1
China	-3.7	-3.8	-4.7	-6.3	-11.2	-7.5	-6.8	-6.2	-5.6	-5.0	-4.5
India	-7.1	-6.2	-6.4	-7.4	-12.8	-11.3	-9.7	-8.8	-8.3	-8.1	-7.8
Russian Federation	-3.7	-1.5	2.9	1.9	-4.0	-0.6	0.0	0.2	0.1	-0.2	-0.5
Brazil	-9.0	-7.9	-7.1	-5.9	-13.4	-6.2	-7.4	-6.4	-5.4	-4.8	-4.4
Mexico	-2.8	-1.1	-2.2	-2.3	-4.5	-4.2	-3.5	-3.2	-2.9	-2.8	-2.8
Saudi Arabia	-17.2	-9.2	-5.9	-4.5	-11.3	-3.1	-1.8	-1.4	-1.1	-0.6	0.1
South Africa	-3.7	-4.0	-3.7	-4.8	-10.8	-8.4	-7.0	-6.4	-6.2	-6.5	-6.8
Low-Income Developing Countries	-3.8	-3.6	-3.4	-3.9	-5.2	-5.4	-5.0	-4.5	-4.3	-4.1	-3.9

Note: Ratios are percentages of nominal GDP.
Source: IMF, Fiscal Monitor, October 2021

Table 1-2-2	Changes in general government debt (percentage of GDP)										

| (Percent of GDP) | 2016 | 2017 | 2018 | 2019 | 2020 | Projections | | | | | |
						2021	2022	2023	2024	2025	2026
World	83.2	82.0	82.3	83.6	98.6	97.8	96.9	97.0	96.9	96.8	96.5
Advanced Economies	105.6	103.2	102.7	103.8	122.7	121.6	119.3	119.3	119.1	118.8	118.6
Canada	91.7	88.8	88.8	86.8	117.5	109.9	103.9	100.2	96.9	93.4	89.7
France	98.0	98.3	98.0	97.6	115.1	115.8	113.5	114.6	115.4	116.2	116.9
Germany	69.3	65.0	61.6	59.2	69.1	72.5	69.8	68.0	65.9	63.4	60.9
Italy	134.8	134.1	134.4	134.6	155.8	154.8	150.4	149.4	148.6	147.5	146.5
Japan	232.5	231.4	232.5	235.4	254.1	256.9	252.3	250.8	251.0	251.3	251.9
United Kingdom	86.8	86.3	85.8	85.2	104.5	108.5	107.1	109.4	110.5	111.2	111.6
United States	106.9	106.0	107.1	108.5	133.9	133.3	130.7	131.1	131.7	132.5	133.5
Emerging Market Economies	48.4	50.5	52.4	54.7	64.0	64.3	65.8	67.1	68.2	69.0	69.8
China	48.2	51.7	53.8	57.1	66.3	68.9	72.1	74.5	76.6	78.5	80.1
India	68.9	69.7	70.4	74.1	89.6	90.6	88.8	88.1	87.3	86.3	85.2
Russian Federation	14.8	14.3	13.6	13.8	19.3	17.9	17.9	17.7	17.8	17.5	17.5
Brazil	78.3	83.6	85.6	87.7	98.9	90.6	90.2	91.7	92.4	92.6	92.4
Mexico	56.7	54.0	53.6	53.3	61.0	59.8	60.1	60.5	60.9	61.2	61.5
Saudi Arabia	13.1	17.2	19.0	22.8	32.5	29.7	30.8	30.4	29.5	28.4	27.2
South Africa	47.1	48.6	51.6	56.3	69.4	68.8	72.3	74.9	77.4	80.2	83.0
Low-Income Developing Countries	39.5	42.1	42.7	44.2	49.9	50.2	49.8	49.0	48.5	48.0	47.3

Note: Ratios are gross debts' percentages of nominal GDP.
Source: IMF, Fiscal Monitor, October 2021

behind the record accumulation of government debt[3], as well as the worsening of fiscal balances (Table 1-2-2). When looking at the ratio of the government debt of general governments to nominal GDP in 2020, the average was 122.7% for advanced economies, 64.0% for emerging market economies, and 49.9% for low-income developing countries.

The ratio of each country's government debt to nominal GDP is expected to remain at a high level until 2021, and in advanced economies, it is expected to slightly decline towards 2026. There may be some emerging market economies and low-income developing countries in which it will continue to increase due to development factors. International aid may need to be expanded to support low-income developing countries.

The ratio of Japan's government debt to nominal GDP is the highest among

---

3) Government debt here refers to gross debt or the total amount of debt that requires payments of the principal and interest. Gross debt data are used in this report because net debt data on some emerging market economies and low-income developing countries are not available from the IMF's Fiscal Monitor. There is no difference in data trends between gross debt and net debt.

Part I

Part II

Part III

Part IV

advanced economies at well over twice the level of pre-pandemic GDP, which is progressively increasing to respond to COVID-19. For Japan, which faces structural challenges such as increasing social security spending and government debt with the progress of the aging population, the risk of rising interest rates has become even greater. If government debt has a negative impact on long-term economic growth, there is the concern that Japan could be most seriously affected.

The IMF also mentions risks to the fiscal outlook. A scaling up of vaccine production and delivery, especially to emerging market economies and low-income developing countries, would improve the economy and limit further fiscal deterioration. On the downside, new variants of the virus and low vaccine coverage could increase pressure and inflict new damage on public budgets. The realization of contingent liabilities from guarantee programs may also lead to unexpected increases in government debt. In short, the longer the pandemic, the bigger the financial problems.

3. Challenges for Fiscal Consolidation in the Future

During the COVID-19 pandemic, the unprecedented size of the fiscal response has saved people's lives and jobs. Although the current fiscal measures are appropriate, the increased government debt will remain high for many years.

The IMF points out that commitment to fiscal sustainability is important for future fiscal management. Governments can signal their commitment to fiscal discipline to the public and to the markets, while also addressing the ongoing crisis, in various ways, including by reducing structural fiscal deficits or by adopting strong fiscal frameworks into which deficit reduction in the future is embedded. The IMF points out that if the market trusts the government's commitment to fiscal discipline, financing deficits becomes easier.

Looking ahead to the post-pandemic environment, I believe the situation is in line with IMF's recommendations for future financial management. Advanced economies with an extraordinarily large amount of government debt may need a common commitment to fiscal sustainability with a view to the post-pandemic era and a clear path to fiscal consolidation.

Unfortunately, in Japan the government and the Diet have not yet started full-fledged discussions, but studies and discussions on concrete measures for the consolidation of the fiscal situation that has deteriorated due to the responses to COVID-19 have already started in Europe and the US.

In the US, the Democratic Party announced on August 9, 2021, a USD 3.5 trillion budget plan over a 10-year period for measures to achieve growth by investing in the fields of infrastructure, education, medical care, and childcare. As the financial resources for this, raising the corporate tax rate for large companies and raising the maximum income and capital gain tax rates are being discussed.

The UK's finance minister Rishi Sunak has stated the need for fiscal consolidation in line with the announcement of the 2021 budget, and as a measure to that end, announced a corporate tax hike for the first such hike in nearly half a century. The current uniform corporate tax rate of 19% will be raised to a maximum of 25% from April 2023 depending on corporate profits (the bill was passed on June 10, 2021).

In Germany, the Basic Law for the Federal Republic of Germany requires the federal government to maintain balanced finances and limits its borrowing to no more than 0.35% of GDP. The borrowing limit may be exceeded in the case of natural disasters or unusual emergency situations following the adoption of a resolution by the Bundestag, the German federal parliament, accompanied by a redemption schedule. According to the redemption schedule, the excess borrowing for COVID-19 measures (EUR 41.9 billion for 2020, EUR 216.4 billion for 2021) will be repaid by 2042.

In France, the report released on March 18, 2021, by the Committee for Future Finance set up by Prime Minister Jean Castex clarifies the policy of ensuring fiscal sustainability by keeping the government expenditure growth rate lower than the revenue growth rate over the long term. The 2022 budget bill (submitted by Parliament on September 22) stipulates that COVID-19 related debt (EUR 165 billion) will be repaid by 2042.

The European Union will finance the Next Generation EU Program by issuing common bonds, whose repayment schedule until 2058 has also been determined. Introductions of new taxes and levies are being discussed as sources of redemption funds.

In this way, major advanced economies have begun discussing measures to secure financial resources, including tax hikes, and for fiscal consolidation in light of the deterioration of fiscal conditions.

The Japanese government should also flexibly implement the necessary fiscal measures to respond to the COVID-19 crisis without hesitation, but it should not leave the loose fiscal discipline unattended. It is crucial for Japan to discuss and consider what kind of measures should be taken for fiscal consolidation after the ongoing emergency has ended in the near future.

Whatever the case, I expect the Japanese government to urgently discuss measures to be taken for fiscal consolidation and present the discussion process and proposals to the public in an easy-to-understand manner.

Part I

Part II

Part III

Part IV

References

IMF, Fiscal Monitor, April 2021
IMF, Fiscal Monitor, October 2021

Section 3
US Economy Aiming at a Stable Growth Path from Recovery[1]

HONDA, Yuzo

1. Introduction

The COVID-19 pandemic, which has caused more than 3.55 million deaths worldwide and more than 590,000 in the US alone, is still rampant all over the world and has not settled down yet. In the US, however, the once out-of-control surge of COVID-19 is rapidly subsiding thanks to the mandatory wearing of face masks and the incredible speed of the vaccine roll out by President Biden who took office on January 20, 2021. As of June 2, 2021, about 41% of adults over the age of 18 have completed the full two doses and about 61% have received at least one dose, and the total number of vaccinations has reached 297 million. As a result, the number of newly infected people, which once exceeded 200,000 per day, has now decreased to 20,672 (two-week average) and the declining trend is continuing. With the decline in infection cases, people's economic activities are becoming active and the expectation for normalization is rising.

The first feature of the COVID-19 recession in the US is that it is a combined recession caused by an infectious disease. Above all in such a case, the infectious disease (COVID-19) itself has the greatest impact on the economy, but there are interactions between the spread of the disease and people's behaviors, which in turn produce the combined economic outcomes. Unless the infectious disease subsides, a full-fledged economic recovery cannot be expected. If the impact of COVID-19 were temporary, the adverse effects on the economy may have been similar to those of natural disasters, such as a hurricane, but the adverse effects are different from natural disasters in that they are not a one-shot phenomenon but a series of results that interact with human activities.

The second feature of the COVID-19 recession is the size of its impact. It is the worst recession for the US economy since World War II with an impact as massive as the Global Financial Crisis (GFC) in 2008. However, the major difference from the GFC is that the starting point of the recession was an enormous decrease in autonomous consumption, which had an immediate impact on the entire economy.

1) I would like to thank Prof. Kazuhiko Nishina and Dr. Karavasilev Yani for their helpful advice on this report. However, any possible remaining errors are my own.

This report provides an overview of the impact so far of the still ongoing COVID-19 pandemic on the US economy, and of how the US government and the Federal Reserve Board of Governors (FRB) have been responding and how the US is trying to rebuild its economy.

The organization of this report is as follows. The next section 2 provides an overview of the impact of COVID-19 on the US economy and its features. Section 3 briefly explains the American Rescue Plan (ARP; $1.9 Trillion Stimulus Package), the Infrastructure Plan, and the American Family Plan (AFP) by the US government as well as the expansionary monetary policies by the FRB. Section 4 describes the current state of the US economy as a combined result of the impact of COVID-19 and the policies by the US government and the FRB. Section 5 introduces the hot debate over the scale of the current policies adopted by the government and the FRB. The last section 6 explains the outlook for the Biden administration's policies and their impact on the Japanese economy.

2. Impact of COVID-19 on the US economy

First, in order to understand the scale and nature of the COVID-19 pandemic, let's compare the current COVID-19 recession with the previous GFC.

2-1. Comparison of the COVID-19 Recession with the Global Financial Crisis in 2008

(1) Production

Figure 1-3-1 shows the monthly production index data during the COVID-19 recession and the GFC. While there might be a few different views on when the GFC began, Figure 1-3-1 sets the starting date of the GFC as December 1, 2007, when production began to decline after the housing bubble burst. The starting date of the COVID-19 pandemic is set to February 1, 2020, just before the wide spread of COVID-19 in the US. The graph compares the production time line for the COVID-19 recession with that for GFC.

First of all, Figure 1-3-1 shows that production plunged in both recessions, to slightly higher than 80% of the level just before these incidents. They are the two worst recessions in the US since World War II.

Secondly the bottom of GFC was 19 months after its starting month, while the bottom of the COVID-19 recession was in April 2020, only 2 months after its starting month. GFC was triggered by the burst of the housing bubble in the summer of 2006, leading to a turmoil in financial markets, which in turn widely spread to the real economy by September 2008. The impact of the turmoil in the financial markets on the real economy was so devastating that it took more than

Figure 1-3-1   Global Financial Crisis and the COVID-19 Recession: Production

Source: Federal Reserve Bank of St. Louis

six and a half years for production level to fully return to normal.

In contrast, production experienced a sharp and significant drop in the COVID-19 recession immediately after the wide spread of the disease, but it soon recovered to 94% of the pre-pandemic level and to 97% by April 2021, 1 year and 2 months after the start of the recession. Of course, this rapid recovery is, as described later, mainly attributable to the fiscal and monetary policies implemented by the government and the FRB.

(2) Unemployment rate

Figure 1-3-2 uses monthly index data to make a comparison on unemployment rates between the COVID-19 recession and GFC. Comparing the size and depth of economic damage, the unemployment rate spiked in April 2020 to 14.8% in the COVID-19 recession, just 2 months after February 2020 when COVID-19 began to spread widely. Although 14.8% is much higher than the worst unemployment rate of 10.0% in GFC, it rapidly recovered to 6.1% in April 2021.

The COVID-19 pandemic brought about not only an increase in unemployment, but also a reduction in labor force participation, an increase in temporary leave from work, and a decrease in working hours. Such trends are most notable in socially vulnerable populations (Bloom et al.(2021)).

2-2. Long-term effects[2]

In addition to the short-run impacts on the current economy, including on production and the unemployment rate, the long-run impacts of the COVID-19 pandemic cannot be overlooked. Unlike ongoing short-term effects, however,

---

2) Much of this subsection relies on Arthi and Parman (2021).

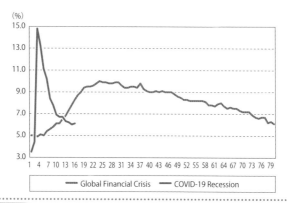

| **Figure 1-3-2** | Global Financial Crisis and the COVID-19 Recession: Unemployment Rate |

Source: Federal Reserve Bank of St. Louis

it is difficult to identify the long-term effects, since objective and clear evidence is hard to obtain now. For this, Arthi and Parman (2021) adopted a historical approach and considered long-term effects. Recognizing that the COVID-19 pandemic is an extremely severe infectious disaster that caused an economic depression, they discussed the long-term effects of the COVID-19 pandemic on health, the labor force, and human capital by obtaining insights into the pandemic from history on the 1918 Spanish Flu pandemic, and the 1930s Great Depression. The former provides the information on the nature of a devastating infectious disease, and the latter its impacts on the economy, respectively. The following outlines the issues relating to long-term effects in line with the discussion by Arthi and Parman (2021).

The authors discussed the long-term effects of infectious diseases by dividing them into (1) direct effects on health and (2) the corresponding economic effects (indirect effects).

(1) Direct effects on health

First, it is natural that reducing the death toll from infectious diseases is a top priority issue. It is known that the elderly and those with underlying disease are prone to death. From the past cases, infectious diseases are also known to have a large adverse impact on health, including morbidity and mortality. They adversely affect low-income people and other socially vulnerable populations, mainly women and racial minorities. The spread of infectious diseases also reduces the number of marriages and live births, further affecting the population and its composition in the country. It is statistically known that those who were infected but survived also suffered from various adverse effects in their subsequent lives.

The 1918 Spanish Flu pandemic is known to have caused reductions in high school completion rates, wages, and socioeconomic status, alongside increases in the probability of living in poverty, the receipt of welfare payments, the likelihood of incarceration, miscarriages, stillbirths, and infant mortality rates. It is also known that those who were exposed to the Spanish flu pandemic in their mother's womb are likely to have suffered from various health problems later in life compared with other generations, ranging from basic functional limitations, such as hearing, speaking, lifting, and walking, to increased probability of experiencing diabetes and strokes. In Japan, it reduced boys' and girls' heights by 0.28 cm and 0.14 cm, respectively.

In the case of the COVID-19 pandemic, it has been reported that in addition to the impact on physical health, there is an increased risk of mental health disorders due to limited interactions with other people.

(2) Economic effects (indirect effects)

Those who were in their mother's womb during a pandemic suffer a great socioeconomic handicap even after they grow up. A decrease in household income has direct economic adverse effects, lowering their college completion rates and lifetime earnings, and raising their rates of later-life poverty. These adverse effects are more pronounced in poorer areas.

Other problems arising from the economic impacts are the long-term adverse effects on labor markets and human capital acquisition. In the Great Depression, it was markedly the less-educated workers, who entered the labor market in the 1930s, and those born in areas adversely affected by the depression that incurred the larger reduction in their incomes. It has also been reported that many younger workers reluctantly accepted the jobs that they otherwise might not have accepted in better economic times because of their current dire need for work, or competition with older workers, or both of these factors.

So far, we have discussed the long-term effects of infectious diseases by dividing them for convenience into (1) the direct effects on health and (2) the economic effects (indirect effects). However, in reality, there are some aspects in which health problems cannot be separated from economic problems. Infectious diseases have adverse effects on all people, but how and to what extent such effects will emerge are different, and they tend to be stronger among socioeconomically vulnerable populations. The reason why socioeconomic status matters is because it is closely related to occupation, living standards, and access to medical care. As a result, it is said that the adverse effects of infectious diseases are not uniform across a society , and even exacerbate existing socio-economic disparities. It has also been reported in the media that COVID-19 has caused greater damage to socioeconomically vulnerable populations.

The following points are important as the implications for policies from a long-term perspective. Infectious diseases create long-term adverse effects on both health and economic aspects (human capital formation), which is highly costly in the long run. The sooner the human capital investment is made, the more productive it will become. Therefore, it suggests that implementing government relief measures now, such as cash transfers, can create larger long-term benefits in terms of costs-benefits from a long-term perspective.

In the next subsection, we will review what measures the US government and the FRB have taken for the above-mentioned serious pandemic disaster.

3. Fiscal and monetary policies by the government and the FRB

COVID-19 affects both production and spending in the economy at the same time. If people stop traveling or going out for meetings, it will decrease travel-related consumption, accommodation use, restaurant- and transportation-related sales, etc., to reduce total economic spending (or demand).

If COVID-19 infections break out in a factory or a production supply chain, production may be disrupted. If disruption spreads widely, supply will decrease in the entire economy. Thus, COVID-19 can logically reduce both aggregate demand and aggregate supply. However, when observing the real economy, we see the impact on aggregate supply has been limited up until today, while a decrease in aggregate demand has had a significant impact.

If a decrease in autonomous spending is left unattended, it will cause a negative chain reaction of declining consumption, generating negative multiplier effects that further curtail aggregate spending and incomes. Therefore, stopping this negative chain reaction by taking all possible fiscal and monetary policy measures is a top priority issue. When COVID-19 began to spread widely in February 2020, the then Trump administration and the FRB immediately increased government spending and implemented monetary easing policies. These policies are standard economic policies taught in modern macroeconomics.

3-1. Expansionary fiscal policy 1: American Rescue Plan (ARP; Biden's $1.9 Trillion Stimulus Package)

Regarding fiscal policies, after a series of rescue packages by the former Trump administration, the ARP proposed by the new President Biden amounting to about

USD 1.9 trillion was approved by Congress in March 2021. The additional measures by the Biden administration focused mainly on household support and consisted of cash transfers of USD 400 billion, unemployment benefits of USD 250 billion, COVID-19 measures of USD 400 billion, and other items of USD 850 billion.

Despite the lack of cooperation from the Republican Party, President Biden's USD 1.9 trillion COVID-19 rescue plan was approved and implemented in May 2021 with the support of the Democratic Party, which has voting majorities in both the upper and lower houses of the US Congress.

3-2. Expansionary fiscal policy 2: Infrastructure Plan and American Families Plan

On March 31, 2021, President Biden proposed a plan for infrastructure development and job creation (hereinafter, the "Infrastructure Plan") worth USD 2.3 trillion over eight years. The plan is to invest in infrastructure such as roads, bridges, and schools to boost productivity. The program is to be financed by raising corporate tax from 21% to 28% over 15 years.

On April 28, 2021, President Biden made his first policy address after taking office at a joint session of Congress, where he presented another USD 1.8 trillion, 10-year American Families Plan (AFP). This AFP together with the above USD 2.3 (or 2.2) trillion Infrastructure Plan announced on March 31 makes a total of USD 4.1 trillion government spending and tax cuts.

The Infrastructure Plan consists of four pillars: (1) the improvement of transportation networks such as roads, bridges, ports, railways, and airports, (2) the improvement of water and sewage, public schools, childcare facilities, public facilities such as community colleges, and buildings ("infrastructure" is defined in a broader sense than the conventional one, including high-speed broadband and clean energy development such as solar power generation), (3) systems development to support people with disabilities and the elderly, and (4) support for technological innovation, the domestic manufacturing industry, etc., to create high-quality domestic employment opportunities. Through the above-mentioned large-scale infrastructure development over eight years, the plan aims for a high economic growth rate by creating high-quality domestic employment opportunities and raising the level of the domestic middle class.

The AFP addresses the following four challenges: (1) providing various programs to support access to a good education, such as education support for children (three and four years old) and two years of free community college, (2) providing access to quality and affordable childcare, (3) providing up to 12 weeks of paid leave for family-related leave and medical leave, and (4) extending tax credits under the USD 1.9 trillion ARP that passed Congress in March.

Part I

Part II

Part III

Part IV

Biden wants to finance the Infrastructure Plan with a corporate tax increase over 15 years and a part of the AFP with a tax increase for high income earners, respectively. Additional spending for the Internal Revenue Service Agency is also proposed to eradicate tax evasion and to increase revenue. The Biden administration is currently discussing the Infrastructure Plan with the Republican Party in Congress to pass a bipartisan bill.

These policies have at least the following two major objectives; one is the improvement of productivity through infrastructure development, while the other is the creation of high-quality domestic jobs. The trickle-down theory (or trickle-down economics: a theory that claims that if the rich get richer, the benefits will trickle down to everyone else) in the previous policies did not work because it only increased the profits of giant companies like GAFA (Google, Amazon, Facebook, Apple), whose huge profits boosted only the wealth of a few capitalists, and the income of the middle class was taken by foreign countries such as China. These are some observations lying behind the above new policies.

3-3. Expansionary monetary policies

The FRB also implemented expansionary monetary policies one after another. On March 3, 2020, immediately after the wide spread of COVID-19, the FRB lowered the federal fund rate (FFR) (i.e., money market rate) by 0.5% to a range from 1.00% to 1.25%, and on March 15, it further cut it by 1.00% to a range from 0.00% to 0.25%. The FRB decided to purchase US Treasuries worth at least USD 500 billion and mortgage-backed securities (MBS) worth USD 200 billion per month and launched a new quantitative easing policy. On March 23 of the following week, the FRB introduced various programs to provide abundant liquidity, including an emergency liquidity supply program to maintain the stability of financial markets, as the liquidity of the entire economy was expected to contract rapidly if left unattended. As of May 2021, the FRB is continuing a policy to lead the money market rate to almost 0% and to supply a large amount of high-powered money to the economy through a quantitative easing policy to fight against the recession.

So far, we have explained the impact of COVID-19 on the economy and the measures taken by the government and the central bank to address this impact. In the next subsection, we will explain the resulting state of the US economy as of May 2021.

4. Current state of the US economy

(1) Production

Figure 1-3-3 shows the production index from January 2000 to April 2021. The production level rebounded sharply from the decline in March and April 2020, partly due to the effects of the bold and seamless expansionary fiscal and monetary policies started immediately after the wide spread of COVID-19. But since February 2021, the pace of recovery has somewhat slowed down.

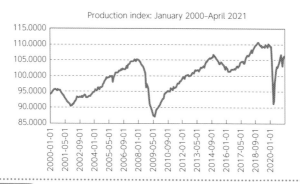

Production index: January 2000–April 2021

Figure 1-3-3   Production index: January 2000–April 2021

Source: Federal Reserve Bank of St. Louis

Unlike natural disasters such as hurricanes, floods, earthquakes, and wildfires, the economic impact of the infectious disease is not transient, but persistent. If people in society protect themselves using defensive measures such as social distancing, mask wearing, and vaccinations, the negative impacts on the economy will be reduced. But if economic activities are resumed with insufficient protection, the infection will spread again and the impact could be significant. The figures on production activity represent the results of the conflict between the COVID-19 pandemic and human society. The slowdown in the recovery after February 2021 is taken to be largely due to the counterattack by the infection. Since progress is being made in the vaccination roll out, the recovery trend is expected to strengthen after May 2021.

(2) Unemployment rate

Similarly to the production index, the unemployment rate hit a peak of 14.8% in April 2020, the worst in the post-war period, and then quickly recovered to 6.1% as of April 2021 due to the successful expansionary fiscal and monetary policies. However, there still remains a considerable gap to reach 3.5% in February 2020, the rate before the spread of COVID-19.

(3) Prices

For the consumer price index (CPI) in April 2021, the headline CPI increased by 4.2% and the core CPI, excluding food and energy, by 3.0% compared to the same month of the previous year, both significantly exceeding the target of 2%. However, all of these indices have risen sharply since March 2021, partly reflecting the impact of the sharp decline in the indices in the same month in the previous year due to the rapid spread of COVID-19. The FRB is maintaining its policy stance of continuing monetary easing, judging that the price increase of more than 2% in recent months is only transient. The expansionary monetary policy by the FRB has been effective in raising housing prices, stock prices, commodity prices, and personal consumption, and depreciating the US dollar, which shows that expansionary monetary policy strongly supports the real economy from a financial perspective.

The above is an overview of the current state of the US economy. It seems that the most important factor in the outlook is still whether or not COVID-19 can be completely contained.

5. Are fiscal and monetary policies too expansionary?[3]

As seen above, the expansionary fiscal and monetary policies taken after the surge in COVID-19 cases have helped prevent a sharp economic downturn. This achievement by the government and the FRB cannot be denied. However, some economists have warned the government and the FRB about continuing the fiscal and monetary policies even now for more than a year from the wide spread of COVID-19. One such economist is Lawrence H. Summers, a professor at Harvard University, who advised the president on economic policies during the Clinton and Obama administrations. For example, he criticized the USD 1.9 trillion ARP, which was enacted by the Biden administration, for being too large a budget and that it could overheat the economy, leading to excessive inflation in the future[4]. He also expressed his concerns about the possibility of excessive inflation in the future, arguing against the FRB's explanation that the current surge in inflation is only transient.

---

3) I would like to thank Kazuhiko Nishina for drawing attention to Krugman's editorial (2021b) for this section.
4) Barry Eichengreen (2021), a professor at the University of California, Berkeley, also wrote that concerns about economic overheating due to excessive government spending could not be dispelled.

On the other hand, Paul Krugman, a professor at Princeton University, is one of the economists who support the government's and the FRB's view. His take is that the economy has recovered significantly, as seen from indicators such as the production index and the unemployment rate, but the labor market is still far from full employment. Hence the current expansionary fiscal and monetary policies should be continued for the time being. In response to Summers' claim that the budget size of the USD 1.9 trillion ARP package is too large, Krugman argues, using Figure 1-3-4, that if it turns out to be too large, monetary policy may be tightened at the appropriate timing.

Figure 1-3-4 reproduces the figure drawn by Krugman published in the New York Times. It is assumed that the US economy is currently at the point P where the IS curve 1 intersects with the ZLB (zero lower bound) line. There is an output gap between the actual GDP and the potential GDP at the full employment level.

The FRB can usually stimulate the economy by lowering interest rates during a recession, but there is a limit to how low it can go; namely, the "zero lower bound (ZLB)." The ZLB does not necessarily mean that the interest rate has the lower bound exactly at 0%, but rather it means that the interest rate is bounded at some value close to zero. If the ZLB is not low enough for the real economy, the economy is stuck in a liquidity trap. In such a case, the interest rate cannot be lowered below the ZLB by an expansionary monetary policy. However, an expansionary fiscal policy is still effective in achieving full employment. The IS curve 2 in Figure 1-3-4 shows a case where the fiscal stimulus is excessive and the policy goes too far. Krugman explains that if the output gap (the difference between potential GDP and real GDP) disappears as shown in the figure, the FRB should use monetary policy to curb economic overheating, adding that the US economy has a track record of successful monetary tighten-

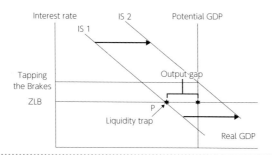

Figure 1-3-4   When an Expansionary fiscal policy Goes Too Far

Source: Krugman (2021b)

ing in the mid-1980s and mid-90s without causing dangerous recessions.

6. Outlook for the US economy and its implications for the Japanese economy

Finally, in this subsection, I would like to discuss the outlook for the US economy and its impact on the Japanese economy.

6-1. Recovery from the COVID-19 recession

In response to a recent media question, President Biden declared that "America is back." The Biden administration, which started on January 20, 2021, has made a good start so far. Immediately after taking office, President Biden succeeded in greatly suppressing COVID-19, which had been out of control, by procuring sufficient vaccines and guiding people to get vaccinated, as well as by making it mandatory for 100 days for people to wear face masks.

The fight against COVID-19 is the most important factor for the US economy in the short run. President Biden has set a goal of administering at least one vaccine shot to 70% of Americans by July 4. If the US government firmly maintains a direction of suppressing COVID-19 to completely control the pandemic in the future, there are currently no other major factors that would hinder the future growth of the US economy[5]. In that case, a gradual recovery from the deep recession will continue. On the other hand, if the control of COVID-19 is delayed for some reason, the future economic recovery will also be delayed. Considering that the government and the FRB have firmly implemented counter-pandemic measures, we can fully expect that they will take promising measures to address the pandemic in the future as well.

The recovery of the US economy is also extremely important for the Japanese economy. First, the US economy and its policies have a significant and immediate impact on the Japanese economy through stock prices, exchange rates, and interest rates. Also in the real economy, the US is not just Japan's second-largest trading partner. Since the US is the world's largest economy, its economic recovery will lead to a global economic recovery, which in turn indirectly improves the Japanese economy through its trade volumes and overseas business activities. Due to these reasons, the US's early exit from the COVID-19 pandemic is vitally important for the Japanese economy as well.

---

5) However, it is necessary to pay close attention to the recent surge in housing prices.

6-2. Medium- to long-term issues

For the medium to long term, the Biden administration announced a USD 2.3 trillion Infrastructure Plan in March 2021 and USD 1.8 trillion American Family Plan in April 2021. With regards to the Infrastructure Plan, as of May, the Democratic Party is seeking a compromise with the Republican Party. The Infrastructure Plan is based on the ideas of orthodox economics. It aims to improve productivity and income for the middle class by developing infrastructure, including renovations of old bridges and roads, and securing employment for the middle class. The plan is to get the budget balanced in multiple years, as it will take 15 years to cover the cost of the 8 years of spending[6]. The policies are designed to help the recovery from the current recession, as spending comes first in the short run.

Only 4 months have passed since the Biden administration took office in January (as of the time of writing this report in May 2021), but the launch of the new administration is having an extremely large impact on the world economy, including the Japanese economy. President Biden had consistently insisted on aiming for a clean energy society even before the presidential election. President Biden has decided to return to the Paris Agreement on the first day of his inauguration, while the former President Trump repeatedly defended the fossil fuel industry in which the US has a comparative advantage and withdrew from the Paris Agreement immediately after taking office. President Biden says he plans to switch from fossil fuels to new clean energy sources, creating new industries and jobs in the process.

In Europe, the trend towards clean energy has already progressed. This trend is now further accelerated worldwide by the start of the Biden administration. Global warming countermeasures and conversion to clean energy sources will change the regulations on exhaust gas emissions in each country, which will in turn change the rules of competition for the development of new world-class technologies. It is a shift in competition rules under which companies compete with each other in making good products at competitive prices. The shift in competition rules will have a broad impact on the automobile industry, the financial industry, and the energy industry, including electric power.

This new trend is now widely and deeply affecting Japanese society. It has been reported that six related laws, including the revised Industrial Competi-

---

6) Krugman (2021a) calls for an increase in government spending funded by deficit financing for the post-pandemic US economy. His policy prescription differs from the Biden administration's Infrastructure Plan in that it does not presuppose a fiscal balance.

tiveness Enhancement Act that promotes corporate efforts to combat climate change, were passed and enacted in the House of Councilors plenary session on June 9, 2021. These new trends are expected to continue and even intensify in Japan as well, at least as long as the Democratic Party takes the initiative in the US.

References

Arthi, V., and J. Parman(2021) "Disease, Downturns, and Wellbeing: Economic History and the Long Run Impacts of COVID-19", Working Paper 27805, National Bureau of Economic Research, USA.

Bloom, N., R. S. Fletcher, and E. Yeh(2021) "The Impact of COVID-19 on US Firms", Working Paper 28314, National Bureau of Economic Research, USA.

Eichengreen, B. (2021), "Unable to Dispel Concerns about Overheating (Japanese title: Keiki Kanetsu no Kenen Fusshoku Dekizu)", Nihon Keizai Shimbun (morning edition), Keizai Kyoshitsu, June 22. (in Japanese)

Krugman, P(2021a)" The Case for Permanent Stimulus(Wonkish)", New York Times, March 7.

Krugman, P(2021b)" Krugman Wonking Out: Braking Bad? When the Fed Fights Inflation", New York Times, May 7.

Section 4
THE RAPIDLY RECOVERING CHINESE ECONOMY AND ITS PRESENCE IN THE WORLD

KAJITANI, Kai

1. The Chinese Economy and Its Recovery from the COVID-19 Pandemic

(1) COVID-19 Measures Supported by Utilitarianism

In *China: A Happy Surveillance Nation* co-authored with Mr. Kota Takaguchi, I evaluated China's governance system as a "happy surveillance nation" based on the combined philosophies of paternalism and utilitarianism. The nation provides its citizens with convenience and economic benefits using big data, and at the same time, it aims to stabilize society and to improve public safety using this data (Kajitani and Takaguchi, 2019). Such a governance system appeared even more clearly in 2020 from the COVID-19 measures taken by the Chinese government and society during the COVID-19 pandemic.

The Chinese government thoroughly deployed paternalistic intervention in people's lives when taking counter-measures against the novel coronavirus. Specifically, the government blockaded Wuhan City, rapidly constructed isolation hospitals, mobilized medical staff from all over the country, and enforced facial mask production. It also implemented thorough quarantine and isolation measures using personal data collected through smartphones, including contact information with others (Uragami, 2020).

The decisions made in accordance with utilitarianism are also effective in specifying and isolating infected persons with the full use of the surveillance technology. In the COVID-19 pandemic, China used the Health Code, which was developed through the extension of the previous technologies. The Health Code uses colors to indicate the infection risk of each person by using a combination of information, such as smartphone location information data collected through the applications of major IT companies like Alipay and WeChat Pay, movement records by public transportation providers, and people's health information. When the possibility of being infected is identified, the Health Code turns yellow or red depending on the degree of possibility of infection, and in such a case, the use of many facilities including restaurants becomes prohibited. It is already well-known in Japan that the Chinese government has been advancing such a quarantine system by thoroughly controlling personal information.

Part I

Part II

Part III

Part IV

(2) Suppressed Direct Benefits

China ensured surveillance and isolation with the skillful use of IT technology, as well as through physical and human mobilization, and controlled the infection. But what economic measures did China take to support an economic recovery? We will explain them below, focusing particularly on fiscal policies.

In November of last year, the IMF published data on how much each country has increased expenditure on COVID-19-related financial affairs and measures. Based on this data, Figure 1-4-1 compiles each country's financial support and additional fiscal support.

The Figure indicates that as of September of last year, European nations were prominent particularly in terms of financial support. For additional fiscal support, Japan recorded around 10% of GDP, which is quite high, and the US undoubtedly recorded the highest. The US took fiscal action with spending of about USD 2.2 trillion or about 9.3% of GDP, including cash benefits, by March 2020 during the Trump Administration period. In April, the Congress decided on an additional economic measure of USD 484 billion. Further, it signed-off on a plan for an additional economic measure for USD 1.9 trillion including a cash benefit of a maximum of USD 2,000 per person on March 11, 2021, after the start of the Biden Administration.

Meanwhile, China's additional government spending was about 4.5% of GDP. It consisted of expenditure of CNY 147 billion on the medical area (e.g. preventing and controlling the epidemic, improving the public sanitation emergency management system, etc.) and CNY 3.1 trillion on non-medical areas including providing funds for municipalities' employment initiatives, enlarging the applicable ranges of minimum life security and benefits, and expanding the social support program for poor households. While the amount itself does not look so

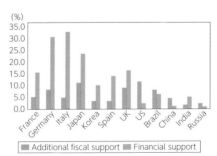

| Additional fiscal support ■ Financial support |

Figure 1-4-1 COVID-19 related fiscal & financial support measures by major governments (GDP ratio)

Source: Database of Country Fiscal Measures in Response to the COVID-19 Pandemic
Note: The values are as of September 11, 2020.

small, this additional government spending includes CNY 1.6 trillion to increase the authorized limit of special municipal bonds issued as financial resources for infrastructure investment. That is to say, more than half of the additional government spending is allocated for the implementation of industrial policies such as subsidies for purchases of new-energy vehicles and capital investment in the construction of new infrastructure such as 5G.

But this does not mean that China allocates no government spending to workers who were made unemployed and to businesses that were forced to close. For example, the additional government spending includes refunds for social insurance premiums paid in 2019 by the companies that did not make employees unemployed or that minimized dismissals. It also includes the payments of unemployment allowance or minimum life security made to migrant workers who returned home. Further, a financial burden of CNY 1.5 trillion was also reduced. This includes the exemption or postponement of social security payments for small and medium-sized companies and the exemption or reduction of value-added tax payments, mainly for companies in Hubei Province. It also includes a corporate income tax reduction by implementing an investment allowance of 100% for companies whose businesses were affected by the COVID-19 pandemic. So it is noteworthy that support was provided in the form of exempting or deferring social insurance premiums and tax burdens in all cases, but hardly at all in the form of directly distributing benefits to individuals and businesses.

That is, direct benefits provided to individuals and businesses seem to have been extremely suppressed compared to in the US and Japan. Instead, low-paid workers who lost their jobs were encouraged to subsist through conducting self-help efforts, of becoming stallholders or performing gig-work. For instance, when Prime Minister Li Keqiang visited Yantai City in Shandong Province in May 2020, he praised the robustness of stallholders, commenting that he expected that "the street stall economy" or the informal sector would provide unemployed persons with temporary employment opportunities.[1]

---

1) "100,000 People Found Jobs in One Night! Hot Street Stall Economy! Praised by Prime Minister! Night Market in Hubei Attracting a Large Crowd" dated June 3, 2020, the Chinese Central Government's Official Web Portal (http://gov.cn/xinwen/2020-06/03/content_5516900.htm), accessed on May 31, 2021

2. Issues Faced by the Chinese Economy

(1) A Growth Strategy Emphasizing the Supply-side

As stated in the previous subsection, China promptly resumed economic activities and achieved a V-shaped recovery in the second half of 2020. The nation did so by thoroughly controlling the infection, tracking people's movements with the full use of digital technology such as the Health Code, and conducting careful examinations and isolating those with a high infection risk (Figure 1-4-2).

According to the official statistics, the real GDP growth rate in 2020 was 2.3%. In terms of the growth rate in 2021, the IMF forecasted that the real GDP growth rate would be 7.9%. On the other hand, the targeted real GDP growth, which was shown in the government activity report at the National People's Congress 2021, was at least 6%, which is fairly modest compared to the forecast.

What direction will the Chinese economy aim for? As early as March 2020, the Communist Party of China had released a document entitled Opinions on the More Complete Arrangement System of the Production Factor Market and the Establishment of its Mechanism. This document shows important points when seeing the future trends of economic development announced by the Chinese government (Research Office for China, Research and Advisory Department, 2020).

The document emphasizes the directions of the five main production factors: land, labor, capital, technology and data. That is, the Chinese government will 1) realize a highly-effective arrangement in line with the market mechanism, and 2) eliminate systematic causes that hinder the smooth movements of

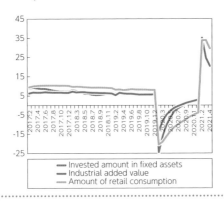

Figure 1-4-2   Changes in various economic indices

Source: Website of the National Bureau of Statistics of China: http://www.stats.gov.cn/
Note: All values are cumulative values from the beginning of the year.

factors and facilitate the establishment and development of the production factor market. In the backdrop to this is the implementation of supply-side reforms that bring about industrial shakeouts that reduce excess production capacity. It seems that the government is attempting to effectively provide jobs to unemployed people, who are overflowing due to the shakeouts, by changing the labor market.

Another significant point when predicting the Chinese economy's trends in the future is the term "domestic general circulation." The government addressed this term as a replacement of overseas capital expenditure typified by the Belt and Road Initiative or international general circulation, which the government had focused on.

The term "domestic general circulation" was used when a policy based on a new growth framework was released in the Political Bureau of the Communist Party of China (CPC) Central Committee Meeting held in July 2020. The policy aims to facilitate domestic and international dual circulation, particularly focusing on domestic general circulation. In addition, domestic general circulation was defined in the proposal of the 14th Five-Year Plan, which was approved in the fifth plenary session of the 19th CPC Central Committee held in October of the same year. It was defined as "to break down industrial monopolization and regional protection in each segment of the domestic market, production line, allocation, distribution and consumption, and to bring about the favorable circulation of the national economy." With this definition, the nature of domestic general circulation became clear; namely, that the government intends to punish regional governments' protectionism and to facilitate supply-side reforms through the marketization of production factors.

In other words, domestic general circulation appears to inherit the trend of aiming for a different growth pattern from rough growth by facilitating supply-side reforms or flowing production factors. The Chinese government had been addressing supply-side reforms as a long-term economic development policy since 2014. At the same time, the government had addressed active overseas investment, as typified by the so-called Belt and Road Initiative, as one of the new economic growth models. It is expected that overseas investment will be toned down, and that economic growth will be driven by the effective rearrangement of production factors such as land, the labor force and capital, as well as by decarbonization businesses like new-energy vehicles.

(2) Future Issues for the Chinese Economy

Next, we will look at some of the issues that the Chinese economy might face.

The first issue is the recurrence of the debt problem. As seen in the BIS

Part I

Part II

Part III

Part IV

statistics showing the debt-to-GDP ratio of each country, the ratio of the corporate sector had been curbed to the level of 149.3% of GDP at the end of 2019 through the so-called deleverage policy. The ratio had increased to 163.1% at the end of September 2020 due to an increase in borrowing by companies whose businesses were directly affected by the COVID-19 pandemic. Under such circumstances, it is actively argued that the corporate sector's excess debt problem may recur.

As if confirming the argument, it was revealed that the Tsinghua Unigroup, a large public semiconductor manufacturer, experienced difficulties in funding in early November 2020. In 2021, it was reported that China Huarong Asset Management, a bad-debt disposal company that is 60% owned by the Ministry of Financing, had fallen into credit uncertainty. As such, it was repeatedly reported that the financial positions of large public companies were deteriorating. According to a news report on May 13 by *The Nikkei*, the amount of corporate bonds maturing in three years up to 2023 will reach a total of USD 2.14 trillion or over JPY 230 trillion, 1.6 times larger than in 2018 through 2020.

When faced with the severe economic turmoil brought about by the COVID-19 pandemic, the US took expansionary economic measures without caring about an increase in sovereign debt. In contrast, the Chinese government took such measures in a suppressive manner, which caused the corporate sector's debt to expand. That is, if the Chinese government considers the expanded corporate sector's debt as a true crisis, it can shoulder the debt by actively issuing treasury bonds, and the nation's finances possess sufficient strength to do so. In this respect, I believe that this issue is not as big of a crisis as is widely argued at the moment.

The second issue for the Chinese economy is the employment situation. China's surveyed unemployment rate peaked at 6.2% in February 2020 and continued to fall thereafter. Meanwhile, it has been pointed out that the value of this rate does not necessarily reflect the reality. An especially important point is that it does not count the number of migrant workers from rural areas. According to an expert's estimate, the number of unemployed people in urban areas was 70 to 80 million people when the employment situation was at its most severe in the fiscal year ended March 2020, which resulted in the unemployment rate reaching about 20% (Zhang, 2020).

The unemployment rate has been declining thereafter. However, it became apparent that small and medium-sized companies, particularly in industries such as the service industry that have experienced a demand shock, survived the crisis by reducing their employment of low-skilled peripheral workers, because these companies receive no support from the government. Even after the unemployment rate declined, issues such as the employment of new college graduates and stagnant wages have been identified, although the employment situation has recovered. Considering that the economic recovery from the COVID-19 crisis was supported by the unstable employment of peripheral workers like migrant workers and gig-workers, there is no doubt that stable employment will be one of the most important points for the Chinese economy going forward.

The third issue is constraints on private-sector platformers, as typified by the Alibaba Group. This issue arose when the IPO of Ant Group, an affiliated financing company in the Alibaba Group, was suddenly suspended in November 2020.

Large platformers like Alibaba have risen to prominence under a protection policy that restricts the activities of the leading US IT companies named GAFA (Google, Apple Facebook, Amazon) and have the characteristic of being the products of industrial policies. Meanwhile, Alibaba's activities are about to be heavily restricted at present, because its presence and influence on society and economy have become too large. It is still fresh in our minds that Alibaba was fined as much as CNY 18.228 billion in April 2021 for the so-called "one out of two" measure, which prohibited competitors from opening e-commerce stores and impeded fair transactions.

The Alibaba Group is not the only target of restrictions. On November 10, 2020, the Chinese government disclosed its draft antimonopoly guidelines for the internet platform economy. In December of the same year, antimonopoly measures and the prevention of unplanned capital expansion were emphasized at the Central Economic Work Conference. With this policy, other major IT companies, including Alibaba's competitors such as Tencent, also become investigation targets based on the application of the Antimonopoly Act.

As the reason that the government strengthened restrictions imposed on Alibaba, it is pointed out that the public banking sector is concerned that the aggressive financial services by Ant Financial, an Alibaba Group company, will put pressure on banking businesses. The opinion of Prof. Fujio Kawashima of Kobe University is that the intimate relationship between the government and the platformers is over. This is evidenced from the fact that the People's Bank of China can collect consumer information through its digital-CNY initiative without depending on the settlement services of platformers such as Alipay, and that the policy possibly reflects the intention of the financial authority to emphasize this regulation (Kawashima, 2021).

These platformers' funding ability has largely supported innovation in China's high-tech area until now. If the enforced regulation hinders this momentum, it will become a major challenge for Chinese companies' continuous innovation going forward.

3. Direction of the US-China Friction and China's Rising Presence

I assume few people object to the idea that the largest issue for the Chinese economy is the friction with the US. There is no doubt that the US-China tariff battle, which occurred in 2018 under the Trump Administration, significantly impacted China's domestic economy.

Figure 1-4-3 indicates the trend of the economic policy uncertainty index, which indexes uncertainty about economic policies and rising anxiety about the economic outlook in the future due to the involvement of these policies, based on the frequency of economic terms being used in each country's newspaper reports.

As is clear from the trend of the index, amid concerns that the intensifying conflict between the US and China will increase uncertainty in the global economy, in the trade talks on January 15, 2020, the US and Chinese governments reached a partial agreement called the Phase One agreement.

The Phase One agreement is limited to areas such as import tariff reductions and the enforced protection of intellectual property. Areas like industrial subsidies, which are hard for China to compromise on, have been postponed to the Phase Two agreement.

The hurdle for future trade negotiations between the two nations is the abolition of industrial policies by the Chinese government, particularly in the high-tech area, which was shelved in the Phase One agreement. The US has asked China to abolish industrial subsidies, particularly those provided by the

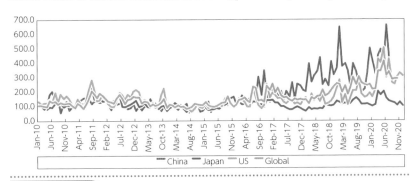

Figure 1-4-3   Changes in economic policy uncertainty

Source: Economic Policy Uncertainty (http://www.policyuncertainty.com/index.html)

central and regional governments, because the subsidies provide an advantage for Chinese high-tech companies. But China would not agree to the condition of abolishing subsidies provided by regional governments, and this makes an agreement between the two nations difficult.

A large hurdle for the trade negotiations between the US and China is the Chinese government's direct support for Chinese companies through industrial policies, particularly its so-called industrial subsidies. However, not many industrial subsidies are directly paid from government spending. Instead, what has had an increased presence in the support for the "new industries" in recent years in China are the investment funds in which the government is involved in some way.

In parallel with the rapid expansion of venture capital, various sovereign investment funds have also been established. From the perspective of facilitating innovation, "industrial investment funds (government guidance funds)" have increased their presence. These funds invest in government projects and support the optimization of industrial structures, such as through corporate fundraising and mergers with funds collected from lenders like government agencies, financial institutions, corporations, PE funds and public pensions. For instance, an industrial investment fund, which was established to support the integrated-circuit (IC) industry in September 2014, was larger in scale than the government subsidies. It has been noted that the government reinforced its influence on the advanced IC industry through this fund.

Nevertheless, it is difficult to judge whether these investment funds, particularly those established by regional governments, are "bad industrial policies" that distort markets and damage fair competition due to government intervention, as the US claims.

For instance, not all China's government guidance funds are so-called national policy funds like the National Integrated Circuit Industry Investment Fund and the Advanced Manufacturing Industry Investment Fund that targets an asset size of CNY 50 billion or over, which the US considers to be a problem. According to the Research Report on the Development of China Government Guidance Funds 2019 issued by pedata.cn, government guidance funds are roughly classified into three groups. The largest group is mother funds; that is, mother funds themselves that do not directly invest in companies, and funds under the umbrellas of mother funds that invest in companies. The next largest group is funds established by regional governments that directly invest in specific companies. The last group is funds in a PPP fund format that collect money from the private sector and invest it in infrastructure projects led by the regional government. Among the government guidance funds, the overwhelming majority are small and medium-sized funds targeting an asset size of CNY 10 billion or less. Funds targeting asset sizes of CNY 1 billion or less and between CNY 1 and 10 billion comprise 43.2% and 36.8% of all funds, respectively.

The regional governments established many of these small-sized funds to support local companies, to secure employment, and to promote the regions. This is the way that the Chinese government has continued to provide backing with policies since the 1980s, so that the regional governments support local companies. It seems difficult for the government to accept the complete termination of such a traditional method.

Conclusion

In recent years, industrial policies have attracted economists' attention more and more. Aiginger and Rodrik point out that the reasons behind this are the requests for changes to the industrial structures in developing nations, the prolonged deterioration of the labor markets and the financial crises in advanced nations, and the significant changes in technologies (Aiginger and Rodrik, 2020). A notable point is that they mentioned China's presence as a factor involved in all of the above reasons.

In the first place, standard economic theory suggests that investment decisions should be left to the private sector as long as market failure does not occur. Since the beginning of the 21st century, however, various industrial policies have been implemented and the effects have been evaluated on the grounds of "knowledge spillovers" due to stagnant technological progress and sluggish research and development costs.

It cannot be said that the industrial policies that the Chinese government is advancing are totally based on the philosophy of state capitalism and distorting markets, as some argue. In fact, considering the current trend in economics, many of those policies can withstand a full evaluation.

So far, China's industrial policies have fully pursued economic efficiencies and the implementation methods have also been sophisticated, ascertaining global trends including in Western nations. Keeping these facts in mind, we should pay close attention to developments in China in the future.

References

Aiginger, K. and Rodrik, D. (2020), "Rebirth of Industrial Policy and an Agenda for the Twenty-First Century," Journal of Industry, Competition and Trade Vol. 20, pp. 189–207.

Kajitani, K. and Takaguchi, K. (2019), *China: A Happy Surveillance Nation* (Japanese title: *Kofuku na Kanshi Kokka Chugoku*), NHK Shuppan Shinsho.

Kawashima, F. (2021), "Policy Competition, Aiming at Mega IT" (Japanese title: *Kyoso Seisaku, Kyodai IT ni Shojun*), *The Nikkei*, February 18, 2021.

Research Office for China, Research and Advisory Department (2020), "China Starts Marketization Reform for Production Factor Arrangement – the Smoothened Factor Movements as New Driving Force for Economic Growth" (Japanese title: *Chugoku de Seisan Yoso Haichi no Shijoka Kaikaku ga Kaishi – Sumuzuka Sareru Yoso Ido ga Keizai Seicho no Aratana Gendoryoku ni*), *MUFG Bank (China), Weekly Economic Report* No. 452, May 12, 2020.

Uragami, S. (2020), Novel Coronavirus VS 1.4 billion Chinese People (Japanese title: Shingata Korona VS Chugoku 14 okunin), Shogakukan Shinsho.

張斌(2020)「政治局会議首提"六保"背后: 就業市場巨大圧力如何緩解？」 『新浪財経』2020年4月19日

https://finance.sina.com.cn/money/smjj/smdt/2020-04-19/doc-iircuyvh8683143.shtml, accessed on May 31, 2021

Part I

Part II

Part III

Part IV

Section 5
CHINA'S RISE AS THE WORLD'S TOP CREDITOR NATION: THE RISKS AND THE OUTLOOK

KARAVASILEV, Yani

1. Introduction

The COVID-19 pandemic caused the sharpest contraction of global output since WWII. Its impact on developing countries has been disproportionately large—as many as 150 million people have been driven into extreme poverty (World Bank, 2021a). While the governments of developed countries have been able to finance robust counter-cyclical fiscal responses to the crisis, the governments of developing countries, which face higher interest rates, are either struggling to service their debt or are directing finance that could be used to support health and social sectors toward repaying debt. Recent reports by the World Bank and influential economists alike have emphasized the huge role of China in the accumulation of that debt, and have warned that developing countries' dependence on China might and limit their policy options and thereby complicate their recovery from a COVID-19-related debt crisis.

Considering the global importance of this issue, this article first elucidates China's increasingly big role in official overseas lending by outlining the history of Chinese lending, its characteristics, its extent and geographical distribution. The article then outlines the concerns related to Chinese lending, including fears that China might resort to debt-trap diplomacy or cause a debt crisis in developing countries. Finally, the article evaluates the possibility for these concerns to materialize.

Since the focus of this analysis is official lending, i.e., lending to governments rather than firms or individuals, this article focuses exclusively on long-term public and publicly guaranteed debt (PPG), also called government debt. As of 2019, PPG debt ($3.1 trillion) represents more than half of the long-term external debt ($5.8 trillion) of the 120 developing countries covered by World Bank statistics, the remaining part being private sector non-guaranteed debt (Figure 1-5-1).

Of PPG debt, one-third ($1.1 trillion) is owed to official creditors, including multilateral creditors (like the World Bank) and bilateral ones (like China). The latest debt statistics by the World Bank show that about 35% of the $439 billion bilateral official PPG debt owed by all developing countries is owed to China (36% if China is excluded). This ratio more than tripled between 2010 and 2019

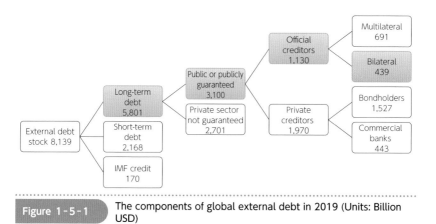

Figure 1-5-1 The components of global external debt in 2019 (Units: Billion USD)

Source: Based on "International Debt Statistics 2021" by the World Bank

(Figure 1-5-2).

Although the amount owed to China might seem minuscule compared to the total amount of long-term debt (less than 3%), the speed with which it has risen has raised serious concerns, as it might have far-reaching geopolitical consequences. What has aggravated these concerns even more is a recent influential study by Horn, Reinhart & Trebesch (2019), which shows that more than half of PPG debt to China goes unreported, and suggests that China is the single largest creditor to developing countries. Reading this, one wonders how China became the epicenter of international official lending.

2. The rise of China as a top creditor nation

After WWII, many developing countries tried to industrialize. This required large-scale investment, which was funded mainly by external borrowing from commercial banks in developed countries. Banks in rich countries were eager to lend, as at the time it was believed that governments arc too big to default. However, the oil crises in the 1970s caused major changes in the global financial system, due to which of developing countries' external debt increased to unsustainable levels.

The end of the Bretton Woods system in 1971 led to a shift in economic policy making in the United States and the United Kingdom, whereby interest rates started to be increasingly utilized as a means to control inflation. With prices expected to rise sharply as a result of the oil shocks, interest rates were increased significantly in an effort to contain inflation. The increase was particularly steep during the second oil crisis in 1979.

Part I

Part II

Part III

Part IV

Rising oil prices combined with high interest rates meant that poor countries were faced not only with higher debt as oil importers, but also with higher debt interest payments. To make matters worse, funding from the Soviet Union, which had often lent to developing countries as part of the Cold War, started to decline. All this led to a debt crisis in many developing countries in the 1980s (Hurt, 2021).

During that period, the World Bank and the International Monetary Fund (IMF) became key players by offering conditional loans and advice to help manage the debt of developing countries. The conditions of the loans, however, were often too strict from the perspective of developing countries. Some of those conditions severely limited borrower countries' policy options, and have received much criticism.

In the 2000s, however, China emerged as a major global economic power, and it proactively started providing loans free of those strict conditions, which made them very popular in developing countries.[1] In particular, African governments rapidly increased their borrowing from China, as they sought to end their dependence on the IMF and the World Bank, who demand market liberalization in exchange for loans—conditions that China does not impose.

The Global Financial Crisis accelerated the global expansion of Chinese investment and lending, due to the divergence in the economic trajectories of the West and China. Declining economies made western nations more inward looking and busy dealing with their own economies. China, whose economy was thriving, took the opposite direction.

In 2009, the China Banking Regulatory Commission (CBRC) reported that five large commercial banks had set up 86 branches outside of China in order to tap the opportunities provided by international financial markets. Since then, the extent of China's overseas lending has surpassed that of the World Bank and the IMF (HRT, 2019). In 2016, China (including Hong Kong) surpassed any other nation in terms of net international investment (NIIP)[2], and replaced Japan as the world's biggest creditor nation.

The culmination of China's global engagement was the famous Belt and Road Initiative, unveiled by Chinese leader Xi Jinping in 2013 and eventually

---

1) In the late 1990s the Chinese government announced a new strategy aimed at encouraging Chinese enterprises to invest abroad. The Chinese government started actively promoting Chinese investments abroad—an effort that culminated with the establishment of the "Go Out Policy" (走出去战略). China's accession to the WTO in 2001 effectively incorporated the country into the global economy.

2) A positive NIIP value indicates that a nation is a creditor nation, while a negative value indicates that it is a debtor nation.

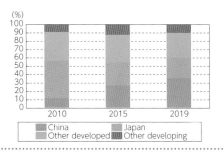

Figure 1-5-2 Creditor composition of debt owed to bilateral by all developing countries

Source: Based on "International Debt Statistics 2021" by the World Bank

incorporated into the Constitution of China in 2017. Being arguably the largest infrastructure investment project in human history, it is also perhaps the most controversial. Several Western governments have accused the Belt and Road Initiative of being neocolonial, ensnaring many countries into China's sphere of influence through the means of debt-trap diplomacy. These concerns have become especially conspicuous since the onset of the COVID-19 pandemic, when the economies of almost all developing countries contracted, which gave rise to fears of a looming debt crisis.

3. The COVID-19 pandemic and the DSSI initiative

In view of the debt crisis that could be triggered by the COVID-19 pandemic, the World Bank and the International Monetary Fund urged G20 countries to establish the Debt Service Suspension Initiative (DSSI). The purpose of the DSSI was to provide a temporary suspension of debt-service payments owed by 73 particularly vulnerable countries to their official bilateral (but not multilateral) creditors, thereby helping them concentrate their resources on fighting the pandemic and safeguarding the livelihoods of their poorest citizens. The suspension period took effect on May 1, 2020, and was set to end in December 2021.

As part of the effort to support the DSSI, the World Bank recently published the specific debt statistics of these 73 countries. The data highlighted the huge extent of China's lending to DSSI countries—close to 60% of their official bilateral PPG debt is owed to China, almost double the ratio officially owed by all 120 developing countries (35%, Figure 1-5-2 above).

In the case of debt service payments, which include newly accumulated interest, and have to be dealt with more urgency in the short-term than debt stock, the ratio is even higher. Of DSSI countries' debt service payments due in 2021, an astonishing 64% was due to China. The 2022 ratio is even higher (Figure

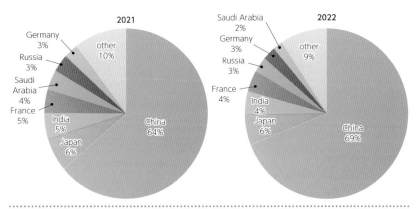

Figure 1-5-3   Debt service payments due by DSSI counties to creditor countries in 2021 and 2022

Source: Based on World Bank (2021b) data

1-5-3).

This data, however, is only the tip of the iceberg, as DSSI countries are only 73 of the 120 developing countries, and the remaining 50, for which no bilateral data has been disclosed, include some of China's largest borrowers. Indeed, the official bilateral PPG debt stock owed by DSSI countries ($178 billion) is only about 40% of the official bilateral PPG debt owed by all 120 developing countries ($439 billion, see Figure 1-5-1).

While there is no bilateral data for each of the remaining 50 countries, the World Bank does publish aggregate data, which shows that the ratio of official bilateral PPG debt stock owed to China by all 120 developing countries more than tripled between 2010 and 2019, reaching about 35% (or 36% if China's debt is excluded, Figure 1-5-2). However, according to an influential and widely cited 2019 by Horn, Reinhart & Trebesch, (hereafter HRT), this number is vastly underestimated.

HRT collated details on almost 5,000 loans and grants extended by the Chinese government and state-owned creditor agencies to more than 150 countries worldwide, with total commitments of $520 billion.[3] A main insight from the data is that over half of Chinese official bilateral lending remains unreported. HRT estimate that the real amount was about $350 billion in 2017, meaning that

---

3) HRT (2019) rely on data Institutes like the China Africa Research Initiative (CARI) and Aid-Data, which collect information about Chinese loans from a wide range of public sources. However, those numbers show only China's loan commitments, and it is difficult to know how much of those commitments have been actually disbursed and repaid.

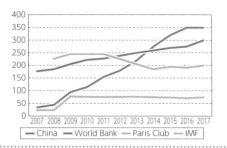

Figure 1-5-4   External debt stock owed to China versus multilateral creditors (Units: Billion USD)

Source: Based on Horn, S., Reinhart, C. M. & Trebesch, C. (2019)

China has effectively become the largest official creditor, easily surpassing the World Bank and IMF (Figure 1-5-4).

The estimate implies a ratio of indebtedness of developing countries to China closer to 57% rather than the above-mentioned 36%, if China's debt is excluded. According to their estimates, in some countries the ratio of indebtedness to China is over 80% of total (bilateral and multilateral) PPG, a ratio which is far higher than the World Bank figure of 60% for the DSSI countries' bilateral PPG. Such are the cases of Laos and the Maldives* in Asia; Angola*, Djibouti*, the Republic of Congo*, South Sudan and Zambia* in Africa; Fiji* and Tonga* in the Pacific; and Venezuela and Ecuador in Latin America (DSSI countries are marked with an asterisk).

According to the authors, the main reason why official data does not reflect the true extent of Chinese lending is the secretive nature of China's overseas lending mechanism. The next section sheds some light on its specificities.

4. Why is China's overseas lending so opaque?

Unlike other major economies, almost all of China's overseas lending is official, meaning that it is undertaken by the Chinese government, state-owned companies, or the state-controlled central bank. The two most important overseas creditors, by a large margin, are China's two state-owned policy banks: China Export-Import Bank and China Development Bank. Both operate under the direct ownership and supervision of the Ministry of Finance and the State Council.

The Chinese government does not disclose data on its lending activities, and the fact that China's lending is entirely official means that it is not accounted for by rating agencies like Moody's or Standard and Poor's who monitor sovereign borrowing from private creditors only. Commercial providers, such as Bloomberg or Thomson Reuters, do not keep track of China's official overseas loans either. The Paris Club does not either, as China is not a member of the club and is therefore not subject to the standard disclosure requirements. In addition, China does not divulge data on its official flows with the OECD's Creditor Reporting System, and it is not part of the OECD Export Credit Group, which provides data on long- and short-term trade credit flows. The financial industry does not monitor China's state-driven cross-border lending flows either. China did join the list of countries reporting to the Bank for International Settlements (BIS) in 2015, but the Chinese government has not agreed to publicly release any bilateral data.

On the other hand, the use of state-owned policy banks means that the credits are rarely de facto borrowed bilaterally, i.e. government-to-government. While the Chinese government provides credit mostly through two state-owned policy banks, the recipients also tend to be state-owned enterprises rather than governments, meaning the transaction is essentially the same as company-to-company lending. As such, it is often not collected by the statistical offices of recipient countries. Low-income countries are particularly bad at accounting for such transactions. As a result, the debtor countries themselves have an incomplete picture on how much they have borrowed from China and under what conditions.

Another characteristic of Chinese lending is what HRT describe as a "circular" lending strategy that minimizes the risk of default. For risky debtors, China's state-owned policy banks often choose not to transfer any money to accounts controlled by the recipient. Instead, the loans are disbursed directly to the Chinese contractor firm that implements the construction project abroad. The loans thus remain within the Chinese financial system, making it harder for recipient countries to misuse the money. Because this type of overseas loan is not actually transferred abroad, there is no cross-border flow to report.

Last but not least, an analysis by Gelpern et al. (2021) found that Chinese lending contracts contain unusual confidentiality clauses that prevent borrowers from revealing the terms, or even the existence of their loans. Chinese contracts before 2015 rarely contained such clauses but virtually all contracts signed after 2015 did. Chinese financial institutions tend to seek more favorable terms than other creditor countries and international financial institutions, using collateral arrangements such as lender-controlled revenue accounts, as well as promises not to engage in collective restructuring. Gelpern et al. argue that this limits the sovereign debtor's crisis management options and complicates debt renegotiation.

The characteristics of Chinese lending have therefore raised concerns that heavy borrowers of Chinese money might become China's geopolitical hostages. To shed more light on these concerns, the next section outlines the circumstances of the most indebted countries, and the potential risks they are facing.

5. Are nations borrowing from China at risk?

Figure 1-5-5 shows the geographic distribution of China's lending based on the estimates by HRT (2019). Clearly, the heaviest borrowers of Chinese money (by percentage of GDP) are concentrated in Africa. In Asia, low-income countries around China stand out, including Pakistan, Laos, Cambodia, Kyrgyzstan, and Tajikistan. In Latin America, it is oil-rich Venezuela and Ecuador.

China's overseas lending is evidently highly correlated with the abundance of natural resources[4] and China's geopolitical interests. In addition, many of the countries that borrow heavily from China have authoritarian regimes and high levels of domestic instability, and are often subject to sanctions imposed by Western countries, making bilateral borrowing from rich countries difficult. Loans from the World Bank and IMF, which demand political reforms such as democratization and economic liberalization, are also inaccessible to such countries. This makes loans from China, which impose no such conditions, enor-

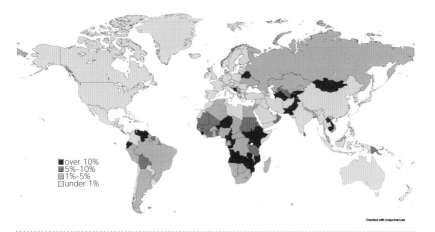

over 10%
5%–10%
1%–5%
under 1%

Created with mapchart.net

Figure 1-5-5   Debt owed to China by country (% of GDP)

Source: Based on Horn, S., Reinhart, C. M. & Trebesch, C. (2019)

---

4) The reason often cited for this is that China does not have enough natural resources to meet its own industrial demand.

Part I

Part II

Part III

Part IV

mously attractive.

An example of natural resource-backed lending is Venezuela, which has been ruled by an authoritarian socialist government since the Bolivarian Revolution in 1999. The oil-rich country has been plagued by a severe socio-economic crisis. Diplomatic ties with the United States were severed, and instead the Venezuelan government established very close political and economic ties with presumably ideologically similar China, which provides easy loans in return for oil. Very similar is the case of African countries, where the lending conditions imposed by the World Bank and the IMF have arguably led to currency devaluation, lower growth rates and widespread dissatisfaction. As a result, many African governments, especially of countries like oil-rich Angola, copper-rich Zambia, and of metal, mineral and timber-rich countries in central and eastern Africa, have resorted to raising funds in other ways, with Chinese lending presenting itself as an easy alternative.

On the other hand, an example of geopolitical interest-driven lending is Pakistan, China's strategic ally against India. China supplies Pakistan's defense forces with a variety of modern weapons and supports Pakistan's stance on Kashmir. In turn, Pakistan supports China on the issues of Xinjiang, Tibet, and Taiwan.

Concerns about China's practice of lending to distressed countries culminated in 2018, when the US Trump administration accused China of engaging in "debt-trap diplomacy," citing unpayable debt in places of geopolitical interest to the Chinese government and in low-income resource-rich countries (Trump White House, 2018).

The main concern is that by using debt as a political tool, China may place various restraints on the policies of the debtor countries, or that the debtor countries might even fall under the effective control of China. Specifically, the Trump administration cited the case of Venezuela repaying its debt to China with oil, and the case of Sri Lanka, which transferred more than 6,000 hectares of land around the Hambantota port to China on a 99-year lease, as it was unable to repay its debt. There are now concerns about Chinese control of similar port projects in Gwadar in Pakistan[5], Kyaukphyu in Myanmar, Mombasa in Kenya, and Piraeus in Greece.

Such developments are far from being a historical precedent. China's foreign lending shares many characteristics with the foreign lending of France, Germany, and Britain in the 19th century. Another historical analogy is the lend-

---

5) Pakistan has already given China exclusive rights and tax exemptions to operate the Gwadar port for the next 40 years, giving China 91% of the port's revenue.

ing boom to developing countries in the 1970s, which resulted in a debt crisis. This analogy raises serious concerns about a debt crisis similar to that in the 1980s, especially in view of the COVID-19 pandemic.

6. Is Chinese lending going to cause a debt crisis?

At present, there is limited evidence to claim that Chinese lending could cause a debt crisis in developing countries. In the past, China has provided debt relief to various countries on multiple occasions, and most importantly, it is currently participating in the DSSI initiative outlined above. According to a Johns Hopkins University study (Acker et al., 2021), as of March 2021, China has already provided relief to 23 DSSI countries, and is also negotiating with heavily indebted poor countries in Africa on debt restructuring.

These developments are a good omen, and it is believed that China may expand the scope of the suspension of debt repayment. Another positive sign was a speech Chinese leader Xi Jinping delivered on June 17, 2020, in which he encouraged Chinese financial institutions to comply with the DSSI initiative and to hold consultations with African countries to work out arrangements for commercial loans with sovereign guarantees.

However, China's approach to debt restructuring is not standardized across countries, and the fact that debt relief is handled on a case-by-case basis makes the outlook less certain. In addition, China is unlikely to resort to debt cancellation. According to Kratz et al. (2020), debt write-offs are mostly limited to small zero-interest loans, and are less likely for large loans. Past and present examples suggest that deferral (rescheduling principal repayments and sometimes excluding interest payments) is the preferred solution for the Chinese government. This means that China is unlikely to wipe away bilateral debt in exchange for control of strategic assets. In other words, it is improbable that China will resort to debt-trap diplomacy.

7. The outlook

In the short term, especially in view of the COVID-19 pandemic, it seems likely that China will limit its overseas in the face of unsustainable debt repayments by borrower countries. More importantly, however, China's lending seems highly unlikely to recover in the medium-to-long term either.

The main reasoning behind this forecast is the fact that China's external lending is fundamentally motivated by internal factors, not external ones. HRT (2019) find that the standard push factors of capital flows identified in the aca-

Part I

Part II

Part III

Part IV

demic literature have limited explanatory power with regard to Chinese lending. Rather, its main drivers appear to be China-specific push factors, in particular China's economic growth. Therefore, the future of China's external lending will most likely depend on China's growth performance, and virtually all current economic, political and demographic trends[6] point to the inevitable slowdown of the Chinese economy. All major institutions, including the Chinese government itself, have already downgraded their forecasts for China's future GDP growth. The Chinese Academy of Social Sciences and the People's Bank of China estimate China's potential growth rate to be about 5.5% in 2022. While most analysts expect GDP growth of around 5%, some have even lower expectations, with Nomura Securities forecasting a modest 4.3% in 2022.

In addition to this, the following three trends also suggest that Chinese overseas lending has already passed its peak: (1) China's foreign exchange reserves have been decreasing since their peak in 2013–2014; (2) China's current account surplus as a percentage of GDP keeps declining; (3) China is turning inward, as exemplified by the government's new economic plan, which envisions China's future growth as largely based on domestic consumption and aims to reduce China's reliance on international trade and foreign investment.[7]

Finally, considering the fact that most developing countries began borrowing from China in the first place precisely because they were unable to raise funds from traditional sources (rich countries and international institutions), one might speculate that the future of China's overseas lending will also depend on whether developed countries and international financial institutions will be willing to extend loans and aid to developing countries on looser terms.

References

Acker, K., Brautigam D. & Wang Y. (2021) "Global Debt Relief Dashboard: Tracking Chinese Debt Relief in the COVID-19 Era." China Africa Research Initiative (CARI), Johns Hopkins University School of Advanced International Studies.

Gelpern, A., Horn, S., Morris, S., Parks, B. & Trebesch, C. (2021) "How China Lends: A Rare Look into 100 Debt Contracts with Foreign Governments."

---

6) Short-term factors include the recent disruption in global supply chains, semiconductor and commodity shortages, and the unfavorable climate in the Chinese real estate sector exemplified by Evergrande's near-bankruptcy. Long-term factors are centered around the rapid and inevitable aging of the Chinese population and ensuing shrinkage of the workforce.

7) China's 14th Five-Year Plan was drafted during the fifth plenum of the 19th Central Committee held from 26 to 29 October 2020.

Center For Global Development.

Good Governance Africa (2017) "China vs. the IMF." 19 April 2017.
    <https://gga.org/china-vs-the-imf/>

Hurt, S. R. (2021) "Third World debt." Encyclopedia Britannica,
    <https://www.britannica.com/topic/Third-World-debt >

Horn, S., Reinhart, C. M. & Trebesch, C. (2019) China's Overseas Lending. Kiel
    Working Paper No. 2132—updated April 2020. (In-text reference: HRT)

Horn, S., Reinhart, C. M. & Trebesch, C. (2021) "China's Overseas Lending:
    A Response to Our Critics." May 7, 2020, Center for Global Development.

IMF (2018) "IMF Data: Balance of Payments and International Investment Po-
    sition Statistics (BOP/IIO)." <https://data.imf.org/?sk=7A51304B-6426-
    40C0-83DD-CA473CA1FD52>

Kratz, A., Mingey, M., D'Alelio, D. (2020) "Seeking Relief: China's Overseas
    Debt After COVID-19." Rhodium Group.

Trump White House (2018) "Remarks by Vice President Pence on the Adminis-
    tration's Policy Toward China." October 4, 2018. <https://trumpwhitehouse.
    archives.gov/briefings-statements/remarks-vice-president-pence-adminis-
    trations-policy-toward-china/>

World Bank (2021a) "COVID-19 to Add as Many as 150 Million Extreme Poor
    by 2021"
    <https://www.worldbank.org/en/news/press-release/2020/10/07/covid-
    19-to-add-as-many-as-150-million-extreme-poor-by-2021>

World Bank (2021b) "International Debt Statistics 2021" <https://data.world-
    bank.org/products/ids>

Part I

Part II

Part III

Part IV

Section 6
TURMOIL IN THE WORLD TRADING REGIME AND MEGA-FTAs IN EAST ASIA

KIMURA, Fukunari

1. Standpoint of Middle Powers

The US-China confrontation has changed its nature from a trade war or a tariff war at first to a confrontation between superpowers. At the same time, the interpretation of the key words "national security" and "sensible technologies" has also broadened. The scope of US policy toward China was not just the rule-breaking tariff policy, but it has also expanded to a series of measures imposed on Huawei, export regulations, foreign investment regulations, inward investment regulations, government procurement restrictions, and "clean network" construction. After the Biden Administration was established, issues have broadened further to those that are difficult to compromise on, such as human rights and democracy. On the other hand, Chinese diplomacy has become aggressive not only toward the US, but also toward other nations. In addition to a series of assertive policies called "wolf worrier diplomacy," China has also announced various arbitrary policies symbolized by the Export Control Law enacted in December 2020.

Japan's stance on China is identical to the US's in many aspects. There are many issues on which Japan basically shares common values with the US, such as protection of intellectual property, state-owned enterprises, data flows, national security, democracy, and human rights. On the other hand, regarding the arbitrary interpretation of national security and sensible technologies, there are some aspects on which Japan cannot easily agree. Japan and Japanese firms want to maintain favorable economic relations with both the US and China. International trade relations differ from security relations in nature and do not necessarily see a distinction between friends and enemies. Even with some aspects where the same values cannot be shared, it is possible to establish trade and investment relations. Further, the US does not expect complete decoupling with China. Currently, many American firms continue Chinese businesses particularly in the financial and high-tech areas, and American consumers enjoy great benefits brought from the economic relations with China. In fact, China's exports to the US have grown significantly.

The nations sandwiched between the US and China—Japan, South Korea, Taiwan, ASEAN, Australia, New Zealand and India—will be called "middle powers" hereinafter. Each middle power maintains a different political and psychological distance with the US and China, but they all have a deep economic connection with both nations.

What fears do middle powers have? The first fear is to be urged to choose between the US and China and forced to stand at the forefront of unreasonable confrontation. Middle powers want the scope of decoupling to be clarified, but superpowers have some incentives to leave it ambiguous. The second fear is that superpowers will form agreements that are convenient only for themselves. For example, the Phase One agreement signed in January 2020 includes commitments that may damage third countries, such as the compulsory quotas imposed on imports from the US by China. In fact, the modeling and simulation of the agreement shows a result that many third countries will obtain negative welfare effects[1]. The third fear is that the rule-based trading regime will weaken. If rules are loosened by the confrontation between superpowers, an incentive for nations to restrict themselves with the rules will diminish, especially for superpowers. For that reason, a danger of superpowers imposing forbidden trade policies on nations that will never retaliate against them will increase, depending on the political situation at that moment. No rule keeper fluctuates the norms of the whole world.

Under these circumstances, it is unfortunate that middle powers have no means of completely controlling the confrontation between superpowers. In particular, what international trade policies can do is limited, but this does not mean that they can do nothing. What we should aim for using international commercial policies are to stabilize the global trade order as much as possible and to establish a trade policy system to achieve a rule-based trading regime in every way possible. Working on this challenge requires the formation and utilization of mega-Free Trade Agreements (FTAs).

2. The Current Situation of Factory Asia

(1) The Pivotal Role of ASEAN

Firstly, we will look at the current situation of Factory Asia, as the background.

East Asia, which includes Northeast Asia and Southeast Asia, has led the world in international production networks (IPNs) or the second unbundling, particularly in the machinery industry, and has established Factory Asia since the 1990s[2]. Emerging and developing nations have actively adopted develop-

---

1) Refer to, for example, Freund, Maliszewska, Mattoo, and Ruta (2020).
2) Refer to Ando and Kimura (2005), Baldwin (2016).

ment strategies with active participation in IPNs, and multinational firms such as Japanese firms have contributed to the expansion and deepening of IPNs. In the backdrop to this has been the long-lasting peace and the rule-based trading regime in East Asia.

ASEAN's commitment to Factory Asia is strong. China's presence has steadily grown in East Asia since it joined the World Trade Organization (WTO) at the end of 2001. Looking at the trends in the trade of machinery, the large volume of China's exports is conspicuous. However, China's machinery exports are mostly to the rest of the world, and the ratio of exports to East Asia is small. That is, IPNs including China take the form of strong ties with nations other than those in East Asia. In contrast, ASEAN has close import and export relations with Japan, China and South Korea. Although the relative weight against China has been shrinking, ASEAN has continued to function as the IPNs' hub.

To maintain its status as the hub, ASEAN established the ASEAN-plus-one FTAs network in addition to the economic integration of ASEAN itself. Further, it has played an active role in the conclusion of the East Asia Regional Comprehensive Economic Partnership (RCEP). Why has ASEAN particularly promoted the RCEP? It does not make sense for ASEAN to have considered only tariff elimination with the RCEP. Tariffs within ASEAN are already almost nil without exception. With ASEAN-plus-one FTAs completed by 2010, ASEAN already concluded FTAs with six neighboring nations. The nations newly tied with FTAs based on the RCEP are all non-ASEAN countries: Japan-Korea and Japan-China, as well as India-China, Australia and New Zealand at the time when India was participating in the negotiations. Therefore, unless tariff elimination between ASEAN and non-ASEAN countries is advanced much more than in ASEAN-plus-one FTAs, ASEAN may suffer from a negative trade diversion effect because an increase in trade between non-ASEAN countries would push down ASEAN's exports. Nevertheless, the leaders of ASEAN have promoted the RCEP because they expect a positive trade creation effect produced by the whole Factory Asia being activated by the RCEP, in addition to other effects such as rules of origin (ROOs) and trade facilitation rather than tariff elimination. Further, they expect that ASEAN can secure its centrality in the economic integration in East Asia.

We, however, should note that the degree of each ASEAN country's participation in IPNs is significantly different. This means that such a situation has the potential risk of weakening ASEAN's centrality. When considering the direction of not only ASEAN, but also the whole Factory Asia, the important point is how to maintain the solid ties within ASEAN. In particular, it is essential that Indonesia, which accounts for 40% of ASEAN's economy and population, will continue its commitment to free trade and investment and lead ASEAN.

(2) COVID-19

Amid the outbreak of COVID-19 in China followed by the pandemic, concerns over the vulnerability of global value chains (GVCs) arose. Some journalists argued that the era of GVCs was over and that factories in emerging and developing countries should return to home countries (reshoring). In contrast, another insisted that facilitating the decentralization of production bases even further would raise the robustness of supply chains and that the excess concentration of production in China should be avoided. In addition, there was also an argument suggesting that firms should improve risk management because we are entering an era of "just-in-case" rather than "just-in-time." However, in the end supply chains in East Asia, especially IPNs, have been retained as they were. Looking back now, it seems that these arguments slightly overreacted to the initial shock in some aspects.

Three factors are responsible for these overreactions[3]. Firstly, COVID-19 accompanied by city lockdowns and social distancing was a shock to supply chains, and the nature of the shock was not properly perceived. Unlike global financial crises and the Great East Japan Earthquake in the past, this time three kinds of shocks occurred on different timings and in different places: negative supply shocks, positive demand shocks, and negative demand shocks. Negative supply shocks first occurred in February 2020 in the form of imports of intermediate and final goods from China being disrupted, and then occurred in various other countries as the infection spread. However, imports from China rapidly recovered in the following month, and the shocks in other nations settled down in a relatively short time. Meanwhile, facial masks and medical related products were hit by positive demand shocks. When concerns over the supply of so-called essential goods including foodstuffs, not just medical products, temporality increased, confusion spread because some countries restricted exports, prioritizing their own citizens (this is perceived as negative supply shocks by the other nations). However, the excess demand was resolved relatively quickly, except for the current vaccination issue.

Rather than these two kinds of shocks, the most worrisome was actually the third shock of negative demand shocks caused by the depressed global economy[4]. However, the unprecedented mitigation policies implemented by each nation have kept the financial sector sound and the asset market has also not collapsed, meaning that the situation will not worsen so much. In the recovery process, positive demand shocks occurred concerning teleworking and stay-at-

---

3) The following is an argument by Ando, Kimura and Obashi (2021).
4) Kimura (2020) noted the risk that negative demand shocks would be prolonged.

home related products such as telecommunication equipment and dishwashers that were needed when working remotely. This supported economies, but it is a so-called k-shaped recovery because the impact differs depending on the type of industry and business.

Secondly, empirical studies on the Asian Currency Crisis, the global financial crises and the Great East Japan Earthquake have proven that IPNs, which are particularly sophisticated among GVCs, are robust against various supply and demand shocks[5]. This fact, however, was not generally well recognized. IPNs could certainly be a channel to transmit shocks, but relationship-specific transactions, which are established through investments based on a medium- to long-term outlook, are not easily interrupted (robust) and are quick to recover even if interrupted (resilient) compared to normal transactions in a spot market. This means that IPNs can play a role as a built-in stabilizer in a time of crisis. As a matter of course, firms designed and operated IPNs before the COVID-19 crisis, considering a trade-off between the efficiency brought by the decentralized location of a business base and the risk associated with it. Even though firms may review IPNs with newly acquired information, there will be no change to them continuing to operate IPNs down the road.

Thirdly, it can be pointed out that the deterioration of the US-China relationship caused overreactions toward the decoupling movement. The voices insisting that business bases in China should leave became stronger, especially in Japan, because the negative supply shocks that initially started from China and the positive demand shocks that hit medical-related products were connected with an alert against China. Labor-intensive processes have been relocated to third counties for several years due to soaring wages in China. In addition, the relocations of sensitive technologies and rare earth-related production bases have also been observed to some extent. But for many Japanese firms, Chinese operations are important and large-scale withdrawals from China have not happened yet. We should continue to pay close attention to the decoupling movement going forward.

To make IPNs more robust and resilient, it is necessary to expand and deepen them by refining the investment environment and improving connectivity. Although the form that the manufacturing industry should take will significantly change amid the digital transformation, task-by-task specialization is unlikely to lose its superiority for a while. On considering complementarity with digital technologies, the advantages of Factory Asia should be used for the time being.

_____

5) Refer to Ando and Kimura (2021).

3. Japan's Mega-FTAs Strategies

The mega-FTAs strategies, which Japan has been working on since 2013, reached a turning point when the RCEP was signed in November 2020. Once the RCEP comes into effect down the road in January 2022, Japan will be tied to almost all its major trade partner nations based on FTAs. If Japan seeks new FTA partners, they will be the Common Market of the South (MERCOSUR), Brazil, and South Africa, but these FTAs are unlikely to produce significant economic effects. However, Japan should not lose interest in FTAs, and on the contrary, it is important for Japan to deal with the new phase by using the characteristics of mega-FTAs as "living agreements."

Table 1-6-1 complies the status of recent Free Trade Agreements (FTAs) negotiations involving Japan. Japan's participation in the negotiation of the Trans-Pacific Partnership Agreement (TPP) has come up in conversation since the administration period of the Democratic Party of Japan. Around the time when the second Abe administration was inaugurated in December 2012 and Japan officially announced its desire to participate in the TPP negotiations in March 2013, the formation of mega-FTAs between major nations and the participation by many nations have become fully fledged. Japan's participation in the TPP negotiations also greatly stimulated the start of the Japan-EU Economic Partnership Agreement (Japan-EU EPA) and the RCEP negotiations. Although the US withdrew from the TPP soon after the Trump Administration was established in January 2017, the Comprehensive and Progressive Agreement for Trans-Pacific Partnership (CPTPP) was finalized under Japan's initiative. Currently, the CPTPP has come into effect in eight nations. The Japan-EU EPA also reached agreement and came into effect in February 2019. Despite the prolonged negotiations, the RCEP was finally signed by 15 nations excluding India in November 2020 and will be in effect in January 2022 among countries that have completed domestic clearance.

For the past five years, international trade and investment have been exposed to a great risk. While rule-based trading regime has weakened and the US-China confrontation has intensified, the formation of mega-FTAs has rather been accelerated. In the backdrop to this has been a change in the expected role of mega-FTAs.

The roles previously assigned to mega-FTAs were first, further liberalization and second, international rule making. The WTO should have played these roles as the negotiation forum since its establishment in 1995, but it has hardly functioned for this because it faced opposition from major developing nations on every occasion. Meanwhile, economic globalization has steadily progressed,

Part I

Part II

Part III

Part IV

| Table 1-6-1 | Recent Free Trade Agreements Involving Japan |

	Start of negotiations	Signed	Came into effect	Participating countries
Trans-Pacific Partnership Agreement (TPP)	Jul. 2013 (Japan participated in the negotiations)	Feb. 2016	Not in effect (US withdrew in Jan. 2017)	Australia, Brunei, Canada, Chile, Japan, Malaysia, Mexico, New Zealand, Peru, Singapore, the US and Vietnam
Comprehensive and Progressive Agreement for Trans-Pacific Partnership (CPTPP)	→	Mar. 2018	Dec. 2018	Mexico, Japan, Singapore, New Zealand, Canada, Australia, Vietnam, Peru (already effective in all of the above), Brunei, Chile and Malaysia
Japan-EU Economic Partnership Agreement (Japan-EU EPA)	Apr. 2013	Jul. 2018	Feb. 2019	Japan and 28 EU nations (27 nations in Jan. 2020 due to Brexit, the UK being included until the end of 2020 as a transition period)
Trade Agreement between Japan and the US and Agreement between Japan and the US Concerning Digital Trade	Apr. 2019	Oct. 2019	Jan. 2020	Japan and the US
Japan-UK Comprehensive Economic Partnership Agreement (Japan-UK EPA)	Jun. 2020	Oct. 2020	Jan. 2021	Japan and the UK
East Asia Regional Comprehensive Economic Partnership (RCEP)	May 2013	Nov. 2020 (excl. India)	Jan. 2022	10 ASEAN nations, Australia, China, Japan, South Korea, and New Zealand (in effect only with countries that have ratified it)

and the level of liberalization and the coverage of international rules based on the WTO have become totally insufficient. Impatient major nations decided to step into liberalization and international rule making with mega-FTAs, although they are fully aware that it is the second-best choice. The significance of these two roles is not lost.

In addition to these roles, the third role was recently added to mega-FTAs, which is to maintain the rule-based trading regime. The vulnerability of the rule-based trading regime increases the risk that each nation will deviate from the trade rules and norms that are usually trusted. The policy risk emerging from it will be a great hindrance for international businesses.

There are incentives, especially for superpowers, to use arbitral trade policies depending on their political motivation at that time without fear of retaliation. The US-China confrontation creates exactly a political environment that encourages this. Further, the WTO's function for settling disputes has notably weaken, because the Biden Administration, following on from the Trump Administration, has been blocking the appointment of the WTO's Appellate Body members. If that is the case, it is unavoidable that nations other than superpowers will also easily deviate from the existing norms. Even mega-FTAs cannot completely cut off the bad flow, but they are expected to be a deterrent to a certain extent.

Looking at Japan's recent FTAs from such a viewpoint, it is apparent that the third role has strongly been perceived. The CPTPP shows high-level liberalization and new standards for international rule making, and at the same time, it clearly intends that the middle powers sandwiched between the US and China will unite and protect the rule-based trading regime as much as possible. The UK decided to start accession negotiations in June 2021. Not limited to the UK, the CPTPP is also expected to develop as a forum for the middle powers that will unite and aspire to free trade and investment. The conclusion of the Japan-EU EPA was also accelerated, aiming to jointly protect the trade order disturbed by the Trump Administration. The Trade Agreement between Japan and the United States alone was hurriedly concluded not to aspire to free trade, as symbolized by the word "free" being omitted, but mostly to avoid the US's rule-breaking trade policies. The Japan-UK EPA was also concluded using the Japan-EU EPA as a model in order to stabilize Japan-UK economic relations after Brexit.

4. The Significance of the RCEP

The RCEP was finally signed in November 2020 and will be in effect in January 2022 among signatories with ratification. What role can the RCEP play? We can see its significance from the aspect of three roles. The first role, liberalization, receives a harsh evaluation. The tariff elimination rate based on the number of items, including those being gradually eliminated, stands at 91% for all participating nations, which is almost at the same level as existing East Asia FTAs. However, the rate is low for partners newly tied with FTAs; that is, the rates of Japan toward China and South Korea are 86% and 81%, and of China and South Korea toward Japan are 86% and 83%, respectively. It is also unusual for a different tariff elimination schedule to be set by a partner nation. Considering that the tariff elimination rate required for mega-FTAs by the CPTPP are set at 99–100% (95% only for Japan to protect the agriculture), the RCEP should endeavor to raise the degree of liberalization, using opportunities such as the fifth-year re-view after coming into force.

Meanwhile, rules of origin (ROOs) are more trade-friendly than the CPTPP, and the aspects of custom procedures and trade facilitation can also be highly evaluated. Regarding trade in services, the RCEP tried to adopt a negative-list approach (listing services on hold for liberalization). The nations that did not complete the approach are about to progress the transition procedure from a positive-list approach (listing services to be liberalized). For investments, ROOs have promised a liberalization with a negative-list approach and have also stipulated royalty regulations and the prohibition of performance requirements, including technology transfer requirements. As we have seen, the RCEP have many aspects that are more advanced than the existing ASEAN plus one FTAs. Once an agreement comes into force, it will bring certain economic effects.

The second role, international rule making, is highly evaluated on the point that it comprehensively covers various policy modes. The major policy modes that are included in the CPTPP but not in the RCEP are only state-owned enterprises, labor, and environment. However, there are only a few rules asking for strong commitments, such as significant changes in each nation's domestic policy. Instead, the RCEP can be positioned as the starting point for negotiations when trying to involve China in international rules down the road.

Attention is being considerably focused on intellectual property (Chapter 11), e-commerce (Chapter 12), and government procurement (Chapter 16). For intellectual property, the RCEP has made a stronger commitment to trademarks than the WTO's Agreement on Trade-Related Aspects of Intellectual Property Rights (TRIPS). Regarding e-commerce, the three principles of the CPTPP are free cross-broader data flows, the prohibition on data localization requirements, and the prohibition on forced disclosure of source code, and the RCEP specifies the former two even though their effectiveness remains doubtful. Government procurement has not been included in the previous FTAs in East Asia that much and its contents are limited to transparency, promotion of cooperation, and future outlook, but it has taken a step forward.

We should pay attention most to the third role, the contribution to the maintenance of the rule-based trading regime. It is extremely meaningful that the nations where Factory Asia is being developed, including China in East Asia, show their rule-oriented stance, being tied with one trade agreement. In addition, Chapter 18 stipulates that the RCEP Ministerial Meeting and the RCEP Joint Committee shall be held annually, and that four subordinate committees and an administration office shall be established. Although this is an imitation of ASEAN's progressive economic integration model, ordinarily it can deepen the agreement step by step and function as one of the stable communication channels when a dispute occurs. It does not mean that the RCEP will solve all issues, but it is expected that the establishment of such a forum including China will be effectively used. Unfortunately, India dropped out in the middle of the negotiations, but it should definitely come back to the RCEP if it wishes to join Factory Asia down the road.

5. Conclusion

The US-China confrontation and the conflict between liberalist nations and China in the political and security arenas do not seem likely to settle down easily. However, the economic relations created through trade and investment are continuing and the conflict does not mean that both the US and China intend to completely cut off their economic relations. Although international trade policies, including mega-FTAs, will not solve all issues, it is necessary to continue to strive in order to maintain the rule-based trading regime. We should start with what we can do to begin with.

References

Ando, Mitsuyo and Fukunari Kimura. (2005), 'The Formation of International Production and Distribution Networks in East Asia', in T. Ito and A. Rose (eds.), International Trade in East Asia (NBER-East Asia Seminar on Economics, Volume14), Chicago: University of Chicago Press, pp.177-216.

Ando, Mitsuyo and Fukunari Kimura. (2012), 'How Did the Japanese Exports Respond to Two Crises in the International Production Networks? The Global Financial Crisis and the Great East Japan Earthquake', Asian Economic Journal, 26 (3), pp.261–87.

Ando, Mitsuyo; Kimura, Fukunari; and Obashi, Ayako. (2021) "International Production Networks Are Overcoming COVID-19 Shocks: Evidence from Japan's Machinery Trade." Forthcoming in Asian Economic Papers.

Baldwin, Richard. (2016) The Great Convergence: Information Technology and the New Globalization, Cambridge: Belknap Harvard University Press.

Freund, Caroline; Maliszewska, Maryla; Mattoo, Aaditya; and Ruta, Michele. (2020) "When Elephants Make Peace: The Impact of the China-U.S. Trade Agreement on Developing Countries." Policy Research Working Paper 9173, The World Bank.

Kimura, Fukunari. (2020) 'Exit Strategies for ASEAN Member States: Keeping Production Networks Alive Despite the Impending Demand Shock', ERIA Policy Brief, No. 2020-03 (May).

Section 7
LABOR MARKETS IN ASIA AND THE INFORMAL ECONOMY DURING THE COVID-19 PANDEMIC

GOTO, Kenta

Introduction

2020 was a turbulent year, shaken badly by COVID-19 that had spread across the globe. The coronavirus was first identified in Wuhan, China, in December 2019, and it quickly propagated beyond Hubei Province in January 2020, affecting other regions throughout China. The Chinese government had responded with city lockdowns accordingly. However, the virus had already been transmitted globally, and the World Health Organization (WHO) declared a pandemic in March 2020. As of the time of writing this report in May 31, 2021, the cumulative number of people infected with COVID-19 has reached 170 million, and the death toll has exceeded 3.5 million worldwide.[1]

This COVID-19 pandemic has had a significant impact on the world economy. According to the World Economic Outlook released by the International Monetary Fund (IMF) in April 2021, the world economy shrank by 3.3% in 2020, while the impact was greater in countries that depend on tourism and exports of primary products (i.e., mostly developing countries). It has been clear that the pandemic has also had severe adverse consequences on world poverty, with an additional 95 million people being expected to have entered the ranks of the extreme poor in 2020 compared with the estimation before the pandemic. However, the report also refers to some signs of a recovery. For example, while the impact of the pandemic on the industrial sectors greatly differs depending on the country and the industry, production levels have generally returned to pre-pandemic levels and a similar trend can be observed in the trade of goods (IMF 2021).

Looking at global labor markets, the impact of the COVID-19 pandemic is still significant, and the rates of unemployment and underemployment remain high. In labor markets in Asia, it has been noted that phenomena such as an increase in unemployment and a decrease in the labor force participation rate are biased toward industries in which many women and young people work (UN et al. 2021; IMF 2020; IMF 2021).

In this report, we will first provide an overview of the impacts of the

---

1) https://coronavirus.jhu.edu/map.html (Access date: May 31, 2021)

COVID-19 pandemic on labor markets in the world and in Asia, and we will then focus on the informal economy in Asia. As described later, more than half of the global workforce make their living in the informal economy, rather than in the so-called formal economy that constitutes the norm in developed countries such as Japan. Economic integration has connected Japan closer today with Asian countries where the informal economy is dominant. The dynamics of the informal economy will have important implications in understanding future development trajectories of local economies in Asia.

At present, data on labor markets during the COVID-19 pandemic are still limited, and this is particularly acute for the informal economy. Therefore, this report is mainly based on data and analyses from relevant institutions such as the International Labour Organization (ILO) and others.[2]

The COVID-19 Pandemic and Labor Markets in Asia

First, let's take a look at the trends in the global and Asian labor markets during the COVID-19 pandemic. An ILO report published in January 2021 states that the global labor markets have experienced unprecedented disruption due to COVID-19 (ILO 2021a). According to the report, 8.8% of global working hours were lost in 2020, relative to 2019 Q4, which corresponds to 255 million full-time equivalent (FTE) jobs (assuming a 48-hour working week). The disruption was about four times greater than that witnessed during the global economic and financial crisis of 2009. These working-hour losses include both employment losses of about 114 million jobs and working-hour reductions within employment. It has been shown that the impact was particularly large on women, young people, the self-employed, and low-skilled workers.

Seventy-one percent of global employment losses translated mainly into rising inactivity rather than unemployment. Behind this is the fact that many people gave up on looking for jobs due to lockdowns as containment measures and to economic downturns. In monetary terms, global labor income fell by 8.3%, which amounts to USD 3.7 trillion, or 4.4% of global gross domestic product (GDP). Employment declined in many industries, and the particularly hard-hit sectors were accommodation, food services, retail trade, and construction. In contrast, employment increased in information and communication, and finance and insurance. It has become clear that the impact of the COVID-19 pandemic significantly varies across industries, countries, and regions, which raises con-

---

2) The data and analyses in this report are based on the information available as of May 31, 2021.

cerns about widening inequalities.

The impact of the COVID-19 pandemic was also remarkable in labor markets in Asia,[3] and the annual decline in working hours was 7.9% in 2020, which corresponds to 140 million FTE jobs, and labor income decreased by 6.6%. The Asian subregions present very heterogeneous losses, with East Asia the lowest at 4.2%, and China at 4.1%. This is followed by Southeast Asia and the Pacific at 8.2% (Southeast Asia alone at 8.4%), and South Asia the highest at 12.7%. India in particular recorded a serious loss of 13.7%. In the Asia region, the impact of the pandemic occurred with a regional time lag. The East Asian labor market was most heavily affected during 2020 Q1, registering a total loss of working hours of 11%. The two regions of Southeast Asia and the Pacific, and South Asia, experienced the largest losses in 2020 Q2. South Asia in particular exhibited this trend, registering a loss of 34.5% (ILO 2021a).

What is the Informal Economy?

Next, let's look at the informal economy. The informal economy is a concept that covers economic activities of companies that are not registered, not subject to taxation, and whose work falls outside the frameworks of social security systems and labor laws. The informal economy has long been regarded as a phenomenon specific to developing countries that would disappear along with economic growth. Although nearly half a century has passed since its discovery, it still occupies a large part of the global economy. It has also been reported that new forms of informality are expanding even in developed countries (Jütting and Laiglesia, 2009).[4] Therefore, the informal economy has recently been attracting attention (see Box 1 at the end of this report for supplementary explanation of the concept of the informal economy).

The informal economy is very diverse in terms of its forms and characteristics, and in certain countries or regions it has often developed against the backdrop of the factors unique to them. The characteristics of informality also tend to differ depending on the specific local institutional environment and the attributes of companies and workers. Therefore, it is difficult to effectively define the concept at the global level. As such, this report discusses the current situation based on the ILO's definition that depicts it as a matrix with the con-

---

3) See Material 1 for details of the regional classifications of Asia and countries in each region.
4) A particular concern in developed countries (high-income countries) is informal employment in the formal sector, such as by irregular workers, which has been increasing recently.

ventional enterprise-based "sector concept" on one axis and the "employment concept" on the other, because this would enable a focus on employment and labor dimensions of informality (Hussmanns, 2004; Endo and Goto, 2018).

The Reality of the Informal Economy

In Japan, the informal economy is rarely reported on by the media, and therefore, the level of recognition of it may be low. However, it is a very important economic sector that accounts for about 30% of global economic output.[5] According to the estimates of the World Bank, the informal economy's share of total global output has been declining year by year. For example, it declined from 20.4% in 1990 to 17.4% in 2018 in high-income countries, while it remained at the high level of 31.7% as of 2018 in low- and middle-income countries (Ohnsorge and Yu, 2021).[6]

On the other hand, the informal economy has an even greater presence in terms of employment. According to the ILO's report, as of 2016, 61.2% of the global employed population aged 15 years and above made their living in the informal economy (ILO 2018). The share in Asia was 68.2%, which was slightly higher than the world average (the highest was 85.8% in Africa). Excluding agricultural workers, the share of informal employment worldwide has dropped to 50.5%, but it is still high in Asia at 59.2%.

In general, there is a correlation between the economic level and formality of a country, so the share of informal employment in developed countries tends to be relatively low. For example, the share of informal workers in Japan is 18.7%, which is almost the same as the average of developed countries, while the share in developing countries in Asia (low-income countries and middle-income countries) is 71.4% (62.8% excluding agricultural workers), which is obviously higher than that of developed countries. Table 1-7-1 summarizes the informal economy in Asia in terms of output and proportion of informal workers.

Informal employment exists in the informal, formal (officially registered enterprises), and household sectors, and nearly 85% of the world's informal workers work in the informal sector, while 11% of informal workers are employed in the formal sector and 4% in the household sector. Globally, informal work is a greater source of employment for men (63.0%) than for women (58.1%). Despite

5) The global average from 1990 to 2018 was 31.8%.
6) In the World Bank's report, the informal economy used for measurement was defined to include only "self-employment." Therefore, readers should note that it is not necessarily consistent with the reports of the ILO and OECD.

Table 1-7-1   Size of informal economy in Asia

	Share of informal economic output (2010–2018 average)	Proportion of informal workers	
		Total employment	Non-agricultural workers
Thailand	46.2	55.8 (*)	37.6 (*)
Cambodia	40.0	93.1	89.8
Philippines	36.4	n.a.	n.a.
Myanmar	29.2	85.7	82.3
Malaysia	28.1	n.a.	n.a.
Laos	23.6	93.6	78.5
Indonesia	16.3	85.6	80.2
Vietnam	12.6	76.2	57.9
China	9.6	54.4	53.5
Japan	n.a.	18.7	16.3

Note 1: Data regarding employment for each of the countries are from the following years: Thailand (2017), Cambodia (2012), Myanmar (2015), Laos (2010), Indonesia (2016), Vietnam (2008), China (2013), and Japan (2010).
Note 2: "n.a." = Data is not currently available.
Sources: Output = Ohnsorge and Yu (2021); Employment proportion data = ILO (2018), except for Thai data, which is based on WIEGO (2019).

this, women are more often to be found in the more vulnerable categories of work, and the lower their income level, the higher their share of informal employment. Thus, there is a strong gender aspect involved in issues related to the informal economy (ILO 2018).

Impact of COVID-19 on the Informal Economy

Next, let's take a look at the trends in the informal economy during the COVID-19 pandemic.[7] Figure 1-7-1 shows total employment, informal workers, and the proportion of informal workers significantly impacted by the COVID-19 pandemic as of the end of April 2020. This suggests that almost 1.6 billion, or 76%, of informal workers worldwide, have been highly impacted by the pandemic. Looking at this by national income level, the proportion of informal workers is higher in low-income countries, but the proportion of informal workers affected by the COVID-19 pandemic is as high as over 75% in all income levels, except for

---

7) It should be noted that most of the data in this report were released around 2020 Q2 when each country began to implement strict COVID-19 containment measures, such as lockdowns, and information and analyses were also limited to those that were available at that time.

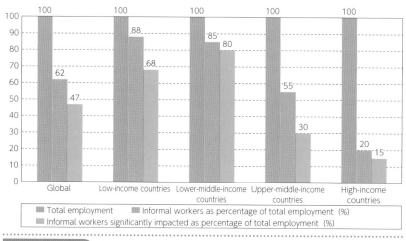

| Figure 1-7-1 | Proportion of informal employment significantly impacted by the COVID-19 pandemic (April 2020) |

Source: ILO (2020a), p. 8, figure 3

upper-middle-income countries.[8]

The COVID-19 pandemic has also significantly affected the incomes of informal workers. Comparing the median earnings of informal workers with the estimates of "earnings in the first month of the crisis," earnings are expected to decline by about 60% globally. The level of decline significantly differs depending on the income level of the country; 28% in upper-middle-income countries, 82% in lower-middle and low-income countries, and 76% in high-income countries. By region, the expected decline is largest in Africa and Latin America (81% respectively), while in Asia, the median earnings of informal workers was USD 549 (2016 PPP USD) before the COVID-19 pandemic, which fell to USD 430 after the pandemic, a decrease of about 22%. Compared with pre-pandemic levels, relative poverty among informal workers (those with earnings below 50% of the median earnings) increased by 34 percentage points globally; in particular, by around 52 percentage points in high-income countries and 56 percentage points in lower-middle- and low-income countries. In Asia as a whole, it is estimated to have increased by about 14 percentage points (ILO 2020b).

It is generally understood that employment adjustments are easier in the

---

8) The World Bank classified the world's economies into the following four income groups following a revision in July 2020: (1) low-income countries: less than USD 1,036, (2) lower-middle: USD 1,036–4,045, (3) upper-middle: USD 4,046–12,535, and (4) high: USD 12,536 or more.

informal economy than in the formal economy. Workers in formal sectors who are given various protections through their wage employment contracts are overwhelmingly in the minority in developing countries. Therefore, when an external shock such as COVID-19 occurs, many people maintain their livelihood while taking on multiple informal jobs, rather than spending time looking for a formal job, and as a result, the unemployment rate rarely fluctuates significantly. Actually, many informal workers are own-account workers, so it is relatively easy for them to start or stop working. For these reasons, job losses have been greater in the informal economy than in the formal economy, while working-hour losses tend to be smaller in the informal economy than in the formal economy (ILO 2021b).

The impact of the COVID-19 pandemic on the informal economy also depends on the characteristics of each sector. Taking the impact of the pandemic on economic output as an employment risk, the ILO classifies the sectors into five categories according to the size of the impact based on the International Standard Industrial Classification (ISIC rev. 4) as shown in Table 1-7-2 (ILO 2020a).[9] In this classification, (1) Accommodation and food service activities, (2) Real estate activities; Administrative and support service activities; Professional, scientific and technical activities, (3) Manufacturing, (4) Wholesale and retail trade; repair of motor vehicles and motorcycles are identified as the high-risk sectors, and 1,245 million people (37.5% of the total employment) in these high-risk sectors are most seriously affected. Among these, the largest number of people, of over 480 million, are employed in (4) Wholesale and retail trade; repair of motor vehicles and motorcycles.

Table 1-7-3 summarizes the employment status of informal workers by the level of risks associated with the sectors. This suggests that 75% of informal workers are working in small units of less than 10 workers (own-account workers and workers in small firms with 2 to 9 workers), and nearly half of these are own-account workers. As mentioned earlier, 76% of informal workers have been highly impacted by COVID-19, but the share increases to almost 90% if limited to high and medium-high risk sectors. Furthermore, although this is not represented in the table, 42% of female informal workers work in high-risk sectors, compared to 32% of male workers (ILO 2020b).

The COVID-19 pandemic has had a particularly strong impact on youth

---

9) The risks posed to individual sectors due to the exogenous shocks from the COVID-19 crisis are evaluated using the estimation model using data based on the following three axes: (1) global firms' output indices, (2) investment in fixed assets, domestic trade, and foreign trade, and (3) business expectations (ILO 2020a).

Table 1-7-2	Economic sectors classified by risk level

Risk level	Economic sector (based on ISIC rev. 4)	Total employment (thousands)	Sector employment as percentage of total employment (worldwide) (%)	Percentage of women (%)
Low	Education	176,560	5.3	61.8
	Health and social work	136,244	4.1	70.4
	Public administration and defense; compulsory social security	144,241	4.3	31.5
	Electricity, gas, steam and air conditioning supply; Water supply; sewerage, waste management and remediation activities (*1)	26,589	0.8	18.8
Low–Medium	Agriculture, forestry and fishing	880,373	26.5	37.1
Medium	Construction	257,041	7.7	7.3
	Financial and insurance activities	52,237	1.6	47.1
	Mining and quarrying	21,714	0.7	15.1
Medium–High	Arts, entertainment and recreation; Other service activities	179,857	5.4	57.2
	Transportation and storage; Information and communication	204,217	6.1	14.3
High	Accommodation and food service activities	143,661	4.3	54.1
	Real estate activities; Administrative and support service activities; Professional, scientific and technical activities	156,878	4.7	38.2
	Manufacturing	463,091	13.9	38.7
	Wholesale and retail trade; repair of motor vehicles and motorcycles	481,951	14.5	43.6

Note 1: "Utilities" in the ILO report were translated as in (*1) above in accordance with the Japanese version of the International Standard Industrial Classification of All Economic Activities (ISIC).
Source: ILO (2020a), Table 2, pp. 4–5 (Japanese translation by author)

(aged 15 to 24). According to ILO, 77%, or 328 million of the world's young workers (in Asia, 84%, or 183 million of its young workers) are in informal jobs. Almost 40% of total employment (about 178 million people) in this age group work in high-risk sectors, and three-quarters of them are informal workers (ILO 2020c).

There are many difficulties in developing and implementing public support programs through fully identifying these informal workers (CGAP 2020), but some countries are providing them with support. For example, in Thailand, the government provided 5,000-baht monthly handouts to informal workers. It was originally intended to cover 3 million workers, but 22 million people ended up registering for those informal worker benefits. China, the Philippines and Viet

| Table 1-7-3 | Number and percentages of informal workers by at-risk group of sectors |

	Risk level					Total
	High	Medium-High	Medium	Low-Medium	Low	
Total employment (millions)	1,245	384	331	880	484	3,324
Informal workers (millions), of which:	712	213	213	795	128	2,060
Own account workers (%)	43	44	43	57	12	47
2-9 workers (%)	26	31	28	31	22	28
10-49 (%)	10	6	11	4	11	7
Over 50 (%)	22	19	18	8	56	18
Highly impacted informal workers (millions)	626	194	176	515	54	1,564
% highly impacted	88	91	83	65	42	76

Source: ILO (2020b), Table A3, p. 15. (Japanese translation by author)

Nam have integrated COVID-19 testing into their health insurance packages, which have been made available to informal workers as well (ILO 2020d). Despite these measures, the impact of COVID-19 on the informal economy has been large, and its recovery is likely to take some time.

Conclusion

This report has provided an overview of the impact of the COVID-19 pandemic on labor markets both worldwide and in Asia, based on data and information available as of end of May 2021, which is when this report was prepared. It had become clear that its impact was extremely large. However, it should be noted that some of these evaluations may include the direct, physical, and short-term effects of robust restrictions on movements, such as strict lockdown measures. The COVID-19 pandemic has not yet subsided, and more comprehensive and detailed data are needed to examine its long-term and structural impact on labor markets. Analyzing labor markets from these perspectives will require the incorporation of important individual market characteristics according to contexts based on country, industry, and informality.

In addition, there has been increased interest in the emerging forms of work and employment due to increased use of digital technologies during COVID-19. The long term impacts this could bring in terms of fundamental changes in the labor market, and how it would play out in relation to the informal economy, are probably new issues that need to be addressed in the future as well.

In 2020, several vaccines for COVID-19 were developed, and their rollout started at the end of the year in developed countries, led by the US. Japan, which has not yet entered the practical application stage of its homegrown vaccine and depends on imports for its vaccine supply, is proceeding with inoculations, although it has lagged behind other developed countries. On the other hand, the supply of vaccines has generally been much slower in developing countries. Given this, there is no question about the importance of the COVAX Facility, which is a global initiative whose main purpose is the joint purchase and distribution of COVID-19 vaccines using both public and private funds from developed countries.

For the highly integrated global economy to achieve a full-scale recovery, it is essential that developing countries, which are dominated by people living in the informal economy, quickly recover from the COVID-19 pandemic. How international communities can cooperate to address the COVID-19 pandemic will be the key to the sustainable development of the world in the future.

Box1 From the Concept of Informal "Sector" to Informal "Economy"

Underemployment has been regarded as one of the major contributing factors in discussions related to the roots of poverty. Under this approach, the reason why people in developing countries are poor is mainly attributed to the fact that they tend to be employed in traditional sectors that are pre-modern, and therefore much less productive. In addition, as an excessive number of workers share a limited amount of work, this is resulting in a low (or almost zero) marginal product of labor (employment insufficiency).[10] Such a condition is called disguised unemployment because people appear to be employed but in reality they remain effectively unemployed.[11] Therefore, addressing disguised unemployment by expanding productive modern sectors through the accumulation of capital and absorbing surplus workers were considered key to reduce poverty.[12]

---

10) In developing countries, generally the concept of underemployment is often considered more appropriate to capture the reality than the concept of unemployment. In fact, recent empirical studies using micro data show that the labor productivity of people who are considered redundant in developing countries is often positive, rather than zero (even with large variations), which means many people are underemployed in reality (Gollin, 2014).

11) The term 'disguised unemployment' is often used in the context of labor markets in developing countries. This concept was first introduced by the British economist Joan Robinson during the US Great Depression in the 1930s in an effort to make Keynes's theory more applicable. He defined involuntary unemployment as enforced idleness, but Robinson pointed out that, in reality, many of the unemployed worked in whatever ways they could, living hand-to-mouth (Benanav, 2019).

12) As an extension of this argument, an idea that became famous later is that of the unlimited supply of labor as proposed by Arthur Lewis. For the significance of this theory today, see Gollin, 2014.

Part I

Part II

Part III

Part IV

Unlike in developed countries, however, workers in formal wage-based employment relationships constitute a minority in developing countries. In addition, the weak social security systems in these countries do, in general, not provide those people the option to remain completely unemployed. As such, they typically juggle different types of informal work, making continuous transitions between employment and unemployment. This situation has made it difficult to establish an operational definition and measurement tools that are useful for policy intervention, that has led to a re-focusing towards the statistically obscure informal sector (Benanav, 2019).

This informal sector concept was first discussed in the ILO report on employment in Kenya, published in 1972 (ILO 1972).[13] This concept is basically an enterprise-based concept focusing on economic entities that operate outside legal frameworks, such as those that are unregistered. With the introduction of this informal sector concept, a view also emerged that informal economic activities, that had previously been regarded as something to be reduced in discussions of underemployment, should be positively evaluated as income generating opportunities (Endo and Goto, 2018). Such informalities have nevertheless been considered as a phenomenon unique to developing countries, that would decrease and disappear along with economic development.

However, in the 1980s, when many developing countries were hit by a debt crisis and entered an era of structural adjustment, the momentum for labor market deregulation (flexibility) increased globally. This shift shed light on the limitations of the informal sector approach as informal economic activities, which should have disappeared with economic development, began to expand rather than contract (Benanav, 2019). In relation to this, informality, which was previously thought to be a problem unique to developing countries, was expanding in developed countries as well through irregular forms of employment (Jütting and Laiglesia, 2009). As a response, the ILO adopted the concept of the informal economy, incorporating the employment axis (informal employment) to cover informalities in the formal sector in addition to the informal sector, in 2003. There was a clear shift from the traditional and dualistic sector (enterprise)-based understanding of formality and informality towards a more comprehensive approach to the informal economy by focusing on the informality of employment (ILO 2018; Endo and Goto, 2018).

---

13) The term 'informal sector' is considered to have been first used by Keith Hart in his research report on Ghana from the Institute for Development Studies (IDS) at Sussex University.

Note: This section is partially supported by JSPS Grants-in-Aid for Scientific Research 19H00553.

References

Benanav, Aaron. 2019. "The origins of informality: the ILO at the limit of the concept of unemployment" *Journal of Global History*, 14 (1), 107–125.

CGAP, 2020. Relief for informal workers: Falling through the cracks in the COVID-19 crisis. COVID-19 Briefing, Washington DC: CGAP.

Endo, T. and Goto, K. (2020), "Informalizing Asia: the other dynamics of the Asian economy" in Goto, K; Endo, T; and A. Ito (eds.) *The Asian Economy: Contemporary Issues and Challenges*. London and New York: Routledge, 169-187.

Gollin, Douglas. 2014. "The Lewis Model: A 60-Year Retrospective." *Journal of Economic Perspectives* 28 (3), 71–88.

Hussmanns, Ralf. 2004. *Measuring the informal economy: From employment in the informal sector to informal employment, Working paper No. 53*, Policy Integration Department, Bureau of Statistics, Geneva: ILO.

International Labour Organization. 1972. *Employment, incomes and equality: a strategy for increasing productive employment in Kenya*. Geneva: ILO.

International Labour Organization. 2018. *Women and men in the informal economy: a statistical picture (third edition)*, Geneva: ILO.

International Labour Organization. 2020a. *ILO Monitor: COVID-19 and the world of work. Second edition*. Geneva: ILO, January.

International Labour Organization. 2020b. *ILO Monitor: COVID-19 and the world of work. Third edition. Updated estimates and analysis*. Geneva: ILO, April.

International Labour Organization. 2020c. *ILO Monitor: COVID-19 and the world of work. Fourth edition*. Geneva: ILO, May.

International Labour Organization. 2020d. *Extending social protection to informal workers in the COVID-19 crisis: country responses and policy considerations*. Geneva: ILO, September.

International Labour Organization. 2021a. *ILO Monitor: COVID-19 and the world of work. Seventh edition*. Geneva: ILO, January.

International Labour Organization. 2021b. *Asia-Pacific Employment and Social Outlook 2020: Navigating the crisis: towards a human-centred future of work*. Bangkok: ILO.

International Monetary Fund. 2020. *Regional economic outlook update. Asia and Pacific: navigating the pandemic: a multispeed recovery in Asia*. Washington, DC: IMF, October.

International Monetary Fund. 2021. *World Economic Outlook: Managing Diver-*

gent Recoveries. Washington, DC: IMF, April.

Jütting, Johannes P. and Juan R. de Laiglesia. 2009. *Is Informal Normal?: Towards More and Better Jobs in Developing Countries*. Development Centre Studies, Paris: OECD.

Ohnsorge, Franziska, and Shu Yu (eds.). 2021. *The Long Shadow of Informality: Challenges and Policies. Advance Edition*. Washington DC: The World Bank.

United Nations, Asian Development Bank, and United Nations Development Programme. 2021. *Responding to the COVID-19 Pandemic: Leaving No Country Behind Bangkok*. Thailand: United Nations.

WIEGO. 2019. "Informal Workers in Urban Thailand: A Statistical Snapshot." *WIEGO Statistical Brief* No 20, September.

Material 1 Regional classification of Asia and countries in each region

East Asia	China, Hong Kong, Macau, Japan, South Korea, North Korea, Taiwan
Southeast Asia	Brunei, Cambodia, Indonesia, Laos, Malaysia, Myanmar, Philippines, Singapore, Thailand, East Timor, Vietnam
Pacific Islands	American Samoa, Australia, Cook Islands, Fiji, French Polynesia, Guam, Kiribati, Marshall Islands, Federated States of Micronesia, Nauru, New Caledonia, New Zealand, Niue, Norfolk Island, Northern Mariana Islands, Palau, Papua New Guinea, Samoa, Solomon Islands , Tokelau, Tonga, Tubal, Vanuatu, Wallis and Futuna
South Asia	Afghanistan, Bangladesh, Bhutan, India, Iran, Maldives, Nepal, Pakistan, Sri Lanka

Part II

THE COVID-19 PANDEMIC AND KANSAI ECONOMY'S ADJUSTMENT PROCESS

INADA, Yoshihisa; NOMURA, Ryosuke

Having discussed the major issues facing the Asia-Pacific region in Part I, in Part II we shift the focus to the Kansai region and Japan. We analyze the impact of COVID-19 and the adjustment of the economy to the pandemic from various angles. The following is a summary of the contents of each chapter in Part II (Chapters 2 to 4).

Chapter 2 consists of four sections.

In Section 1, we discuss the characteristics of the adjustment of the household sector to the pandemic. As a state of emergency was declared in April 2020 in response to the increasing number of COVID-19 infections, consumer spending declined significantly. We analyze this decline using high frequency data on human flows and household consumption.

In Section 2, we examine the adjustment of the corporate sector. We focus on the deterioration of corporate earnings and on employment adjustments. In Kansai, employment in accommodation and food services had been increasing due to the strong demand by inbound tourism. However, the pandemic caused a major employment adjustment, particularly affecting women many of whom work as non-regular workers in these industries.

Sections 3 and 4 provide a retrospective overview of economic conditions for fiscal years 2020 to mid-2021, followed by our forecasts for FY 2021 to FY 2023.

Section 3 focuses on Japan, whose recovery has been slower than that of other major economies. We present our forecast for the economy, which incorporates the second official advance GDP estimate for 2021 Q3, as well as our latest assumptions concerning exogenous variables, such as fiscal and monetary policies and variables related to the global economy. Our real GDP growth forecast for Japan is +2.7% in FY 2021, +2.6% in FY 2022, and +1.7% in FY 2023. A baseline assumption in our forecasts is that although the possibility of a pandemic caused by the new Omicron variant is increasing, both the number of deaths and the severity of the condition of infected people are likely to be curbed considerably due to progress in vaccination. The highlights of our forecast are the expected rapid increase in consumption due to forced savings by households on the one hand, and the impact of supply constraints on industrial production on the other.

Section 4 focuses on Kansai, where the economic impact of the emergency states in FY 2020 was greater than in other regions, and the recovery of many economic indicators was delayed substantially. Our real GDP growth forecast for Kansai is +2.8% in FY 2021, +2.8% in FY 2022, and +1.8% in FY 2023.

Chapter 3 analyzes the major issues in the Kansai economy, which crystalized in the wake of the pandemic.

Section 1 examines the dynamics of migration movements during the pandemic, focusing on Osaka Prefecture. The disappearance of demand by inbound tourism affected many employees in their 20s, especially those from western Japan, who had moved to Kansai to work in tourism-related industries.

Section 2 deals with the issues of healthcare service provision. The COVID-19 pandemic revealed the vulnerabilities of Japan's healthcare system, and it necessitated an analysis of the measures that need to be taken so that the system can respond more quickly and flexibly in the event of an emergency.

Section 3 provides an overview of the digital transformation (DX) of Japan and Kansai, emphasizing that a global perspective and a focus on sustainability are essential in order to boost the effectiveness of DX investments. Ensuring security on the one hand, and addressing the ethical, legal, and social issues (ESLI) associated with the introduction of new technologies on the other, will play important roles in increasing the sustainability of DX investments.

Chapter 4 provides an overview of the tourism industry in Kansai in FY 2020, and analyzes its strategies and *status quo*. We conduct a quantitative analysis of the influence of the tourism industry on the economies of Japan and Kansai based on Input-Output tables.

In Section 1, we analyze trends in inbound demand that evaporated due to the COVID-19 using major statistics. In addition, we review the trends of domestic tourism, and discuss the impact of the "Go To" travel campaign, a government measure to stimulate demand. As a background to the analysis in the next section, we review the analytical framework necessary for the success of future inbound tourism strategies, including brand power, innovation, regionalization and the "safety, security, comfort" concept introduced in last year's Economic Outlook.

In Section 2, we interview the tourism departments of Kansai prefectures about the situation of inbound tourism and the state of tourism administration. We find that the tourism promotion strategies differ greatly by prefecture, both in terms of scale and strategies. Considering this diversity of tourism strategies, we emphasize the importance of Destination Management /Marketing Organizations

(DMO).

Section 3 builds on the previous section by discussing the activities of DMOs in the prefectures of Kansai. We conclude that a successful post-pandemic strategy should be focused on marketing and public relations and based on the culture and history of the region.

Section 4 provides a quantitative overview of the tourism industry in Japan based on the travel and tourism satellite accounts. In addition, we conduct an original analysis of the tourism industry using the extended 2017 Input-Output table. We clarify the position of the tourism industry in the national economy in terms of the employment and income it generates, and of its impact on other industries. Finally, we compare the impact of the COVID-19 pandemic on the economies of Kansai prefectures.

In Section 5, we conduct an inter-industry relationship analysis of the pandemic impacts on the tourism industry in 2020. We estimate the decrease in consumption by foreign visitors as well as the decline in domestic travel, including the ripple effect of the "Go To" travel campaign. Our analysis shows that the campaign mitigated of the decline in consumption by foreign and domestic visitors by about 8%.

Chapter 2

THE ECONOMIES OF JAPAN AND KANSAI: A RETROSPECTIVE AND OUTLOOK

Section 1
THE COVID-19 PANDEMIC AND HOUSEHOLD RESPONSES: PEOPLE'S FLOW AND HOUSEHOLD CONSUMPTION

INADA, Yoshihisa; KINOSHITA, Yusuke; and NOMURA, Ryosuke

Sections 1 and 2 of this chapter describe in detail the adjustment process of households and businesses from the COVID-19 disaster. In the first half of Sections 3 and 4, we outline the current state of the Economies of Japan and Kansai, respectively, and in the second half we present our economic forecasts for FY2021 through FY2023.

Two years have passed since the outbreak of the COVID-19 pandemic, and as we approach the end of 2021, the movement of people is returning to its pre-pandemic level, basking in a temporary sense of freedom from the COVID-19 pandemic, while being acutely aware of the risk of a sixth wave of infections and prolonged supply constraints. Japan's economic recovery from the pandemic has not been smooth, and the degree of recovery has been slower than that of other major countries.

As the possibility of a new variant (Omicron) pandemic increases, countries around the world are rushing to provide booster vaccines. Based on the experience so far, even if the rapid spread of the new variant is inevitable, both the number of deaths and the condition of those infected are likely to be considerably less severe. This assumption is reflected in our forecasts for the economies of Japan and Kansai. Other important assumption in our forecast is the rapid increase in consumption due to the accumulation of forced savings by households, as well as the impact of supply constraints on production by companies. Our forecasts were made while paying special attention to these factors.

1. Insights from high-frequency data

Two years have passed since the start of the COVID-19 pandemic, and people's lifestyles have changed significantly. During this period, household consumption behavior has also changed significantly because people have been forced to avoid the Three Cs (crowded places, close contact settings, and closed spaces) to ensure thorough social distancing. Figure 2-1-1 shows the number of new infections for COVID-19, people's flow trends by purpose (retail and recreation, groceries and pharmacies), and changes in daily consumption. In particular, under the first state of emergency in April 2020, individual consumption decreased because people's flow was sharply curtailed alongside the increase in the number of new infections. During the second and subsequent states of emergency, there still seemed to be a close relationship between the number of new infections, people's flow, and individual consumption, although it was not as clear as during the first state of emergency.

| Figure 2-1-1 | Infection situation and changes in people's flow and consumption expenditure |

Note: shows seven-day moving average. Shaded areas indicate periods of a state of emergency.
Source: Open data by MHLW, the Family Income and Expenditure Survey by MIC and the Community Mobility Report by Google LLC

The relationship between people's flow and consumption has so far been analyzed in terms of transportation policies and trade area analysis for companies, but the scope has been limited. After the start of the COVID-19 pandemic, statistical data became available as open data, so in this section, we analyze trends in people's flow and household consumption by using people's flow and other data in the COVID-19 Community Mobility Report by Google and high-frequency data, such as on daily consumption, in the Family Income and Expenditure Survey by the Ministry of Internal Affairs and Communications (MIC).

The structure of this section is as follows. Subsection 2 summarizes all of the four states of emergency that have been declared so far to confirm people's flow characteristics by purpose and time slot during these declaration periods. In subsection 3, based on the analysis in the preceding subsection, household consumption trends are discussed by item by dividing the pandemic period into three phases. Of particular interest is household consumption trends during the states of emergency. Subsection 4 estimates how much the GRP in the Kansai region's six prefectures decreased due to the decline in household consumption during the periods of the first and second states of emergency. In addition, to mitigate the impact of the pandemic, the Go To Campaign project was implemented from late July 2020 with the aim of stimulating tourism demand, and subsection 5 confirms the movements of related items in daily consumption. Lastly, Subsection 6 describes the outlook for the future.

2. Declarations of a state of emergency and people's flow

(1) Declarations of a state of emergency

Following the start of the COVID-19 pandemic, various infection prevention measures have been taken to reduce contact between people. The pillars of the measures are as follows: 1) requests for commercial facilities (restaurants, department stores, theaters, etc.) and public facilities to suspend operations or shorten business hours, 2) requests for people to refrain from going out unnecessarily, expecting them to exhibit voluntary restraint for outings, and 3) encouragement of teleworking and staggered work hours.

Table 2-1-1 summarizes the restrictions imposed by the declarations of state of emergency. The first declaration of a state of emergency was issued for seven prefectures on April 7, 2020, which was expanded to all prefectures on April 16. On entering May, it was decided to extend the declaration period to the end of May, but in prefectures where the infection situation had calmed down, the declaration was lifted on May 14 and it was lifted nationwide on May 25. Following the resurgence of the infections (the third wave) from November, the second declaration of a state of emergency was issued for Tokyo and three other prefectures on January 8, 2021, and seven prefectures were added on January 14. Then the declaration was gradually lifted, and finally the Tokyo metropolitan area's state of emergency was lifted on March 21.

However, after lifting the second declaration of a state of emergency, the number of new infections increased again (the fourth wave) at a faster pace than the third wave. As the situation in the medical care provision system became

| Table 2-1-1 | | State of emergency periods and restriction details |

	Period	April 7–May 25, 2020	January 8–March 21, 2021	April 25–June 20, 2021	July 12–September 30, 2021
Restrictions	Request to close schools	○	×	×	×
	Request to suspend operations	Entertainment facilities, athletic and amusement facilities, theaters, commercial facilities, etc.	×	Entertainment facilities, athletic and amusement facilities, theaters, commercial facilities, restaurants serving alcoholic beverages, etc.	Entertainment facilities, athletic and amusement facilities, theaters, commercial facilities, restaurants serving alcoholic beverages, etc.
	Request to shorten business hours	Restaurants (until 8 p.m.) (Serving alcoholic beverages: until 7 p.m.)	Restaurants (until 8 p.m.) (Serving alcoholic beverages: until 7 p.m.)	Restaurants not serving alcoholic beverages (until 8 p.m.)	Restaurants not serving alcoholic beverages (until 8 p.m.)
	Encouragement to shorten business hours	×	Entertainment facilities, athletic and amusement facilities, theaters, commercial facilities, etc. (until 8 p.m.)	×	Entertainment facilities, athletic and amusement facilities, theaters, commercial facilities, etc. (until 8 p.m.)
	Request to refrain from holding events	○	× (Strict requirements must be met to hold events)	×	× (Strict requirements must be met to hold events)
	Self-restraint on going out	Going out unnecessarily	Going out unnecessarily (Strictly refraining from going out after 8 p.m.)	Going out unnecessarily (Strictly refraining from going out after 8 p.m.)	Going out unnecessarily (Strictly refraining from going out after 8 p.m.)
	Restrictions on commuting to work	Encouragement of teleworking and staggered work hours (70% teleworking target)	Encouragement of teleworking and staggered work hours (70% teleworking target)	Encouragement of teleworking and staggered work hours (70% teleworking target)	Encouragement of teleworking and staggered work hours (70% teleworking target)

Source: Compiled by the author.

tighter, the third declaration of a state of emergency was issued on April 25. In the third declaration, stronger measures were applied compared to the second declaration, such as requests to large-scale commercial facilities, entertainment facilities, and restaurants, including those serving alcoholic beverages, to suspend operations. As a result, the number of new infections decreased, and the fourth wave moved toward convergence (Figure 2-1-1). So the government lifted the third declaration of a state of emergency for nine prefectures excluding Okinawa Prefecture on June 20. The state of emergency in seven prefectures such as Tokyo and Osaka was changed to the Priority Measures for Prevention of Infection Spread for the period from June 21 to July 11[1].

After that, to address the resurgence of infections (the fifth wave) by highly infectious variants (the alpha and delta variants) and to secure the medical care provision system, the fourth declaration of a state of emergency was issued in Tokyo on July 12. In addition, it was decided to extend the period of the Priority Measures for the Prevention of Infection Spread for the four prefectures (Saitama, Chiba, Kanagawa, and Osaka Prefectures) until August 22. Even so, the spread of infections did not stop, and the government additionally designated seven prefectures as the target areas for the state of emergency for the period from August 20 to the originally scheduled expiry of September 12, which was later extended to September 30.

(2) Declarations of a state of emergency and people's flow

Have the declarations of a state of emergency affected people's flow? Next, we will confirm changes in people's flow during the periods of the declarations of a state of emergency by dividing people's flow data into two types: i) by purpose and ii) by time slot.

i) Changes in people's flow by purpose

The COVID-19 Community Mobility Report by Google announced people's flow trends in six categories (retail and recreation, groceries and pharmacies, parks, transit stations, workplaces, and residential) (Table 2-1-2). The report shows how visits (and lengths of stay) at these six places changed compared to the baselines (the median values for the corresponding day of the week during the 5-week period Jan 3–Feb 6, 2020) using high-frequency daily data.

People's flow trends change depending on calendar holidays (Golden Week, summer vacation, consecutive autumn holidays, year-end and new year holidays, etc.), but the trends are also greatly affected by the infection situation and the anti-infection measures (Figure 2-1-2).

As shown in Table 2-1-2, the places in the six categories above, except for parks with substantial people's flow fluctuations, can be divided into the three types: 1) places with decreased people's flow due to the COVID-19 pandemic, 2)

---

1) When infections surged once again after the second state of emergency was lifted, the Act on Special Measures against Novel Influenza, etc. was partially amended on February 3, 2021, and the Priority Measures for Prevention of Infection Spread were newly implemented. The first issuance was on April 1 for Miyagi Prefecture, Osaka Prefecture, and Hyogo prefectures, and each prefectural government designated the target municipalities and requested that the relevant businesses suspend operations and limit alcohol service hours.

| Table 2-1-2 | Place categories and target places |

Category	
Retail and recreation	Restaurants, cafes, shopping centers, theme parks, museums, libraries, movie theatres, etc.
Groceries and pharmacies	Grocery stores, food wholesalers, fruit and vegetable markets, luxury grocery stores, drug stores, pharmacies, etc.
Parks	Local parks, national parks, public beaches, marinas, dog parks, plazas, gardens, etc.
Transit stations	Public transportation bases (eg subway, bus, train stations), transfer stations, etc.
Workplaces	Workplaces
Residential	Residences

Source: the Community Mobility Report by Google LLC

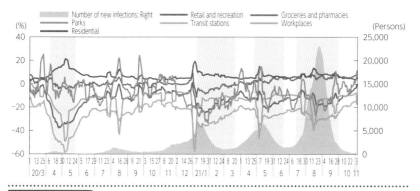

| Figure 2-1-2 | Changes in the number of new infections and people's flow by purpose |

Note: shows seven-day moving average. Shaded areas indicate periods of a state of emergency.
Source: the Community Mobility Report by Google LLC

places with no significant change in people's flow, and 3) places with increased people's flow. Retail and recreation, transit stations, and workplaces fall under type 1), groceries and pharmacies under type 2), and residential under type 3).

Figure 2-1-3 shows the average people's flow trends during each declaration period for the above three types. Looking at this figure, retail and recreation, transit stations, and workplaces categorized as type 1 (places with decreased people's flow) showed a significant drop in people's flow under the first state of emergency, but the decline rate gradually declined during the second and subsequent states of emergency, alongside the diminished effects of restraint on going out as people became accustomed to the pandemic and the states of emergency.

Next, groceries and pharmacies categorized as type 2 (places with no

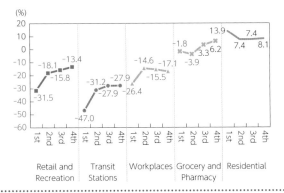

Figure 2-1-3   Changes in people's flow during each state of emergency period

Source: the Community Mobility Report by Google LLC

change) experienced no significant change in people's flow under the first state of emergency, while people's flow decreased under the second state of emergency. It is considered that consumers hoarded medical supplies due to product shortages during the first state of emergency, but since the supply shortages were resolved thereafter to some extent, people refrained from going out during the second period. The effects of the restraint on going out diminished during the third and fourth emergencies.

Lastly, residential categorized as type 3 (people's flow increase) saw an increase in people's flow (length of stay) to places of residence during the first period because people in households refrained from going out. People's flow to places of residence also increased during the second and third periods, but the flow of people's rate was lower compared to in the first period as people started to go out more. The number of new infections hit a record high due to the highly infectious delta variant during the fourth emergency period. Compared to the second and third periods, people's flow to places of residence somewhat increased as people in households refrained from going out, fearing the risk of infection.

Summarizing the above, it can be said that the effects of refraining from going out were generally large during the first state of emergency, but the effects gradually diminished from the second state of emergency onwards.

ii) Changes in people's flow by time slot

Next, we will confirm the mobile population by time slot. Figure 2-1-4 and Figure 2-1-5 show the percentage changes in the mobile population by time slot compared to in the same week of 2019 nationwide and in the Kansai region's six

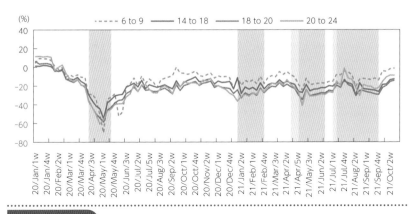

Figure 2-1-4   Changes in the mobile population nationwide by time slots

Note: Orange shaded areas indicate periods of a state of emergency. Yellow shaded areas indicate periods of designated areas for pre-emergency measures.
Source: V-RESAS by Cabinet Office

prefectures.

When looking at nationwide trends in Figure 2-1-4, people's flow was reduced in all time slots under the first state of emergency. On the other hand, during the second state of emergency, although people's flow after 18:00 was reduced, the reduction effect in the early morning and daytime time slots was diminished. This is because as seen in Table 2-1-1, unlike the first declaration when requests to suspend operations were widely made for entertainment facilities, schools, etc., measures under the second state of emergency were mainly to restrict the nighttime operations of restaurants with a high infection risk, while entertainment facilities where a large number of people gather in the daytime were only requested to shorten their business hours. In addition, people's flow between 6:00 and 9:00 (the commuting time slot) also increased from the first declaration, which shows that the people's flow reduction effect was diminished[2]. In the third declaration, people's flow after 20:00 somewhat decreased compared to the second declaration as a result of the strict restrictions, including requests for restaurants serving alcoholic beverages to suspend operations and requests for facilities such as department stores and theaters to shorten their business hours, but no significant change was seen in other time

2) According to the Worker Awareness Survey by the Japan Productivity Center, the teleworking rate of companies has been declining: 31.5% (May 2020), 20.2% (July 2020), 18.9% (October 2020), 22.0% (January 2021), 19.2% (April 2021), and 20.4% (July 2021). Thus, people's flow reduction effects on companies have diminished.

slots. From late July, people's flow after 20:00 increased compared to during the third state of emergency, and there were concerns about resurgence of infections. In the fourth state of emergency, people's flow gradually decreased due to the measures taken, such as requests to refrain from visiting crowded places in target areas and limits on the number of people permitted at large-scale commercial facilities where clusters (groups of infected people) occurred frequently.

Next, we will check people's flow in the Kansai region's six prefectures (Figure 2-1-5). This figure shows that people's flow decreased in the same way as nationwide people's flow in all time slots during the first state of emergency, but the rate of decline after 18:00 was smaller than the national rate. The same phenomenon was observed during the second state of emergency. During the third state of emergency, people's flow decreased to the same level as national people's flow[3]. After that, the Priority Measures for Prevention of Infection Spread were implemented but the effects were limited, and people's flow increased again. However, in the fourth emergency, people's flow decreased significantly compared to the national level, partly because Osaka Prefecture requested that department stores halve the number of visitors to the basement food floor.

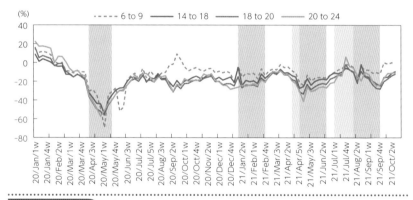

Figure 2-1-5   Changes in the mobile population in the Kansai region's six prefectures

Note: Orange shaded areas indicate periods of a state of emergency. Yellow shaded areas indicate periods of designated areas for pre-emergency measures.
Source: V-RESAS by Cabinet Office

---

3) The Ministry of Health, Labour and Welfare's COVID-19 Advisory Board Data Analysis Team (2021) reported that in Osaka Prefecture, the second state of emergency and priority measures did not reduce the de-facto population, but the third state of emergency contributed to the reduction in the de-facto population in all time slots. In addition, Komaki (2021) showed that during the third state of emergency, the effects of the restraint on going out were higher in metropolitan areas where stronger requests were made.

3. Declarations of a state of emergency and household consumption

As seen in Figure 2-1-1, changes in people's flow to commercial facilities, such as retail and recreation and groceries and pharmacies, are closely related to people's consumption trends. Next, we will discuss changes in household consumption and characteristic expenditure items by dividing the COVID-19 pandemic period into three phases—the initial outbreak and the declaration of a state of emergency period (January–June 2020), the recovery period after hitting bottom (July–December 2020), and the resurgence period (January–September 2021)—based on the daily household consumption data from the Family Income and Expenditure Survey by the MIC, while taking into account the analysis of the people's flow data in the preceding subsection (Figure 2-1-6, Figure 2-1-7)[4].

(1) The initial outbreak and the declaration of a state of emergency period: January–June 2020

Looking at Figure 2-1-6, we see that in March 2020 when the number of new infections of COVID-19 increased, services expenditure, such as on food (mainly dining out) and package tours, decreased significantly because many people started to stay at home (decrease in face-to-face services expenditure). Expendi-

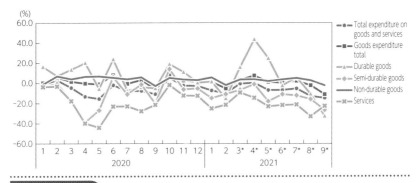

| Figure 2-1-6 | Changes in expenditures by category (nationwide) |

Note: *relative to the same period of 2019.
Source: the Family Income and Expenditure Survey by MIC

---

4) Consumption expenditures in the Family Income and Expenditure Survey include pocket money (of which, the detailed uses are unknown), social expenses, and remittance. The analysis here was made based on expenditures on goods and services excluding these items.

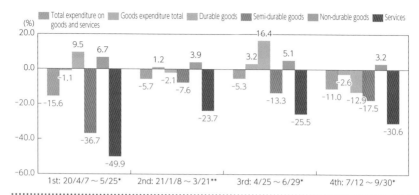

Figure 2-1-7   Changes in expenditures by category during the periods of the declarations of a state of emergency (nationwide)

Note: *relative to the same period of 2019. **relative to 2020/1/8-2/28, 19/3/1-21.
Source: the Family Income and Expenditure Survey by MIC

ture on semi-durable goods such as clothes also decreased. On the other hand, due to rising demand from people staying at home, expenditure on durable goods such as game consoles and software increased.

Goods and services expenditures decreased by 15.6% year-on-year since the first declaration of a state of emergency on April 7 (Figure 2-1-7). While goods expenditure showed only a slight decrease by 1.1% year-on-year, services expenditure significantly dropped by 49.9% year-on-year. Expenditure on non-durable goods increased by 6.7% year-on-year due to an increase in demand for home-cooked meals, but expenditure on semi-durable goods, consisting mainly of non-essential items such as clothes, significantly decreased by 36.7% year-on-year. Also, a noteworthy characteristic is that expenditure on durable goods such as TVs and personal computers increased by 9.5% year-on-year due to increased demand from people staying at home and teleworking.

In June, the rate of decline of goods and services expenditures decreased. This can be attributed to the normalization of economic activities following the lifting of the declaration of a state of emergency on May 25 nationwide and the pent-up demand generated by special cash payments and the last-minute demand before the expiry of the cashless consumer return project that boosted consumption. When looking at expenditures by item, a characteristic is that expenditure on durable goods increased significantly due to the provision of special cash payments.

(2) Recovery period from the bottom: July–December 2020

Next, we confirm the amount of expenditure on goods and services for July–December 2020 (Figure 2-1-6). This period is positioned as the recovery period after the first state of emergency.

In July, the decline rate of household consumption increased from the previous month due to the end of the pent-up demand generated by special cash payments and the reactionary decline in demand following the expiry of the cashless consumer return project. In August, the decline rate of services expenditure, such as recreation and dining out, slightly increased from the previous month due to people's restraint on going out amid an increase in the number of new infection cases (the second wave of infections).

It is difficult to judge the results for September and October because there was last-minute demand in September 2019 prior to the consumption tax hike and a reactionary decline in October 2019. Looking at Figure 2-1-2 above, it seems that people's flow recovered with the improvement in the infection situation, which somewhat mitigated the consumption decline. Also, thanks to the policy support, such as the Go To Campaign project, services expenditure, whose recovery was delayed compared to goods expenditure, showed some signs of picking-up[5].

Since mid-November, semi-durable goods and services expenditures declined due to people's restraint on going out with the resurgence of infections. The decline rate of services expenditure increased in December.

(3) Resurgence period: January–September 2021

Finally, we will look at the consumption trends from January to September 2021 (Figure 2-1-6).

In January, services expenditure decreased, impacted by the shortened business hours due to the reissue of the state of emergency and the suspension of the Go To Travel Campaign. Although still under the state of emergency, in February people's flow increased as the number of new infections decreased. Although the impact of restraint on going out seemed to have been mitigated, the decline rate of consumption was larger compared to in February 2020 that had one more day as it was a leap year.

The data for March and subsequent months were compared to the data of two years ago when there was no negative impact of COVID-19. The decline rate in services expenditure was mitigated in March and April with an increase in people's flow, but the decline became larger again in May and June due to the declaration of the third state of emergency on April 25. Goods consumption

---

5) According to the Additional Table for MIC's Family Income and Expenditure Survey, hotel charges in October 2020 increased by 31.8% year-on-year.

Part I

Part II

Part III

Part IV

showed a relative recovery, but service consumption remained weak, as it faced strong downward pressure due to the fourth declaration of a state of emergency on July 12.

We will also look at the trends in goods and services consumption expenditures during the three state of emergency periods (Figure 2-1-7). Total goods and services expenditure decreased by -15.6% year on year during the first state of emergency, but the impact remained relatively minor at -5.7% during the second and -5.3% during the third state of emergency. Then during the fourth state of emergency when the number of infections increased sharply, the decline rate of total goods and services expenditure increased to -11.0%. Services expenditure recorded a large decline of -30.6%, though not as large as during the first state of emergency.

4. Estimating economic losses caused by the declarations of a state of emergency

In the previous subsection, we estimated the impacts of the states of emergency on household consumption based on daily data. During this period, households were forced to reduce non-essential consumption among their consumption expenditure items by refraining from going out, etc. In this subsection, we will look at the calculations of the impacts on household consumption in each prefecture in the Kansai region caused by the declarations of a state of emergency by focusing on non-essential consumption.

Below, we will first confirm the declines in household consumption during the two state of emergency periods based on the non-essential consumption decline estimation flow in Inada, Kinoshita, and Nomura (2021). Then, based on that information, the levels of consumption decline in each prefecture in Kansai will be estimated.

(1) Consumption decline estimation flow
As described in Figure 2-1-8 Non-essential consumption decline estimation flow, the ultimate decline in non-essential consumption is estimated by multiplying the base household consumption as the benchmark by the three parameters of (1) non-essential consumption ratio, (2) decline rate, and (3) period[6]. These three parameters are explained below.

---

6) See Inada, Kinoshita, and Nomura (2021) for detailed estimation methods.

Figure 2-1-8 Non-essential consumption decline estimation flow

Source: Compiled by the author.

(2) Non-essential consumption and parameter explanations

The Family Income and Expenditure Survey by the MIC classifies expenditure items into basic expenditures and selective expenditures[7]. Under the states of emergency, it is assumed households reduce non-essential consumption among their selective expenditures.

The share of non-essential consumption (full year 2019) to the total goods and services expenditure (the first parameter) was 29.3%. The point to focus on here is how much non-essential consumption, which accounts for less than 30% of household consumption expenditure, was actually reduced by the declaration of a state of emergency.

Table 2-1-3 shows the decline rates of non-essential household consumption (the second parameter) from the daily data of consumption expenditure from the Family Income and Expenditure Survey.

The total decline rate during the first state of emergency was -41.1%, but the decline rates were very high for some items, such as public services (-91.8%), entertainment (-73.1%), and dining out (-68.0%). While semi-durable goods also showed a decline of about 40%, expenses for durable goods increased (+9.4%) probably due to demand from people staying at home. During the second state of emergency, the total decline was -19.7%, a reduction by half from the first time. Above all, expenditure on durable goods turned to a decline, which is consistent with the people's flow trends (residential) (see Figure 2-1-3 above).

Finally, the state of emergency periods as the third parameter assume people in the three prefectures in the Kansai region, and the estimations were made for the first period of 44 days from April 7 to May 21, 2020, and the second period

7) Basic expenditures here are regarded as daily necessities, mainly including food, rent, utilities, and health and medical services. Selective expenditures are regarded as expenditures on luxury goods, including household appliances, durable goods for education and recreation, clothing, monthly fees, etc.

Part I

Part II

Part III

Part IV

Table 2-1-3   Non-essential consumption decline rate comparison

(Unit: JPY, %)

Item	Item of expense	First SoE (20/4/7~5/25)		Second SoE (21/1/8~3/21)	
		Expenditure	YoY change	Expenditure	YoY change
Durable goods	Cars, household electric appliances, furniture, etc.	18,574	9.4	30,937	-2.1
Semi-durable goods	Clothes, bags, jewelry, etc.	17,983	-41.3	37,161	-11.2
Non-durable goods	Food, consumables, etc.	10,013	-3.4	13,592	-1.1
Public services	Rail fares, highway fares, etc.	392	-91.8	1,890	-65.4
Dining out	Dining out	6,247	-68.0	15,642	-39.5
Entertainment	Travel fees, facility admission materials, monthly fees, etc.	5,972	-73.1	14,733	-41.8
Others	Parking fees, rent-a-car fees, etc.	6,081	-5.1	9,927	-5.3
	Total	65,263	-41.1	123,882	-19.7

Source: Estimated by the author.

of 45 days from January 14 to February 28, 2021.

The benchmarks for the consumption decline estimations are nominal private household final consumption expenditures for FY 2019 in Kansai taken from Prefectural Economic Calculations (Cabinet Office). Since the FY 2018 figures are the most recent, advanced estimations of real gross regional products (GRP) in Kansai prefectures by APIR were used to estimate the FY 2019 nominal private household final consumption expenditures[8].

(3) Consumption decline estimations in Kansai

Based on the three parameters examined above and the benchmark household consumption expenditures, household consumption declines in the Kansai region's six prefectures during the two states of emergency were estimated (Table 2-1-4).

The household consumption decline in the Kansai region's six prefectures due to the first state of emergency was JPY 714 billion and the ratio relative to nominal GRP was 0.9%. The household consumption decline due to the second state of emergency is estimated to be JPY 350 billion and the ratio relative to nominal GRP 0.4%.

---

8) See Section 4 in this chapter for advanced estimations for the Kansai prefectures.

Table 2-1-4	Consumption decline due to the state of emergency

(Unit: JPY 100 million, %)

Period	Item	Osaka	Hyogo	Kyoto	Kansai (3 pref.)	Shiga	Nara	Wakayama	Kansai (6 pref.)
First SoE (20/4/7 ~5/21)	Consumption decline	3,193	1,877	888	5,959	455	450	276	7,140
	Composition ratio	44.7	26.3	12.4	83.5	6.4	6.3	3.9	100.0
	Relative to nominal GRP (FY2020)	0.8	0.9	0.9	0.9	0.7	1.2	0.8	0.9
Second SoE (21/1/14 ~2/28)	Consumption decline	1,565	920	435	2,921	223	221	135	3,500
	Composition ratio	44.7	26.3	12.4	83.5	6.4	6.3	3.9	100.0
	Relative to nominal GRP (FY2020)	0.4	0.4	0.4	0.4	0.4	0.6	0.4	0.4

Note: nominal GRP for FY2020-estimations by APIR
Source: based on Prefectural Economic Calculations (Cabinet Office) & KEIQNo.54(APIR)

5. The Go To Campaign and household consumption

In Japan, the number of new COVID-19 infections increased from March 2020, and the movement to refrain from going out spread, which reduced household consumption. In particular, the first state of emergency had the most serious impact on expenditure on recreational services, including accommodation and package tour fees. Therefore, the government implemented the Go To Campaign project in late July with the aim of supporting the travel, tourism, event, entertainment, restaurant, and other related industries, whose sales had dropped sharply due to the COVID-19 pandemic[9].

In this subsection, we will confirm expenditures for major expense items related to the Go To Travel Campaign that is part of the Go To Campaign project. Since the economic spillover effects of the Go To Travel Campaign are discussed in Chapter 4, Section 5, the main expense items from the Family Income and Expenditure Survey by the MIC are confirmed here.

Figure 2-1-9 shows the year-on-year changes in the total expenditure on goods and services, expenditure on recreational services[10], and travel expenditure consisting of accommodation and domestic package tour fees in the Family Income and Expenditure Survey.

This figure shows that the decreases in recreation services expenditure

---

9) The contents of the Go To Travel Campaign project are described in detail in Chapter 4, Section 1.
10) Recreational services expenditure includes accommodation and package tour fees, as well as admission fees to cultural establishments and amusement parks.

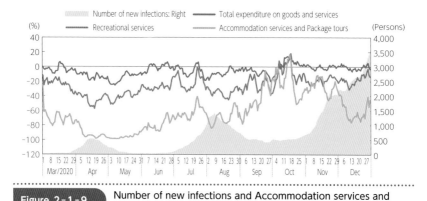

Figure 2-1-9   Number of new infections and Accommodation services and Package tours

Note: shows the seven-day moving average
Source: Open data by MHLW, the Family Income and Expenditure Survey by MIC

and travel expenditure were greater than that of total expenditure on goods and services, but that the rates of decrease gradually declined after the end of July when the Go To Travel Campaign started, and finally turned positive on a year-on-year basis in late October. In the background to this is the fact that from October 1, the Campaign started to cover trips to and from Tokyo and to issue regional common coupons that can be used at travel destinations. Since the Go To Travel Campaign offers a 35% discount on accommodation fees charged by accommodation facilities, a characteristic is that travel expenditure, consisting of accommodation and domestic package tour fees, showed a larger growth rate. After that, the Go To Travel Campaign was suspended due to the increase in the number of new infections. Although the Campaign partially supported service consumption, its effect seems to have been limited except for in the first half of October.

6. Future household consumption

When considering future household consumption trends, the following two points need to be taken into consideration: vaccination status and wage trends.

With regard to the vaccine rollout in Japan, advance vaccinations for medical professionals were started on February 17, 2021, and priority vaccinations for people aged 65 and older were started on April 12, 2021. After that, large-scale vaccination programs in urban areas and occupational vaccination programs accelerated the vaccination speed. As of the time of writing this report in November 17, 2021, Japan had surpassed Canada and reached the highest vaccination rate among the G7 countries of 78.7% for the first dose and 75.5%

for the second dose[11]. Vaccination is expected to increase the people's flow and promote consumption, leading to economic recovery. In particular, consumption expenditures mainly in the consumption of face-to-face services, such as recreation, dining out, accommodation services, and package tours, as well as semi-durable goods, such as clothes, that have been suppressed so far are expected to increase.

On the other hand, possible risk factors include the resurgence of infections (the sixth wave) of COVID-19, wage trends, and rising prices of daily necessities. The spread of infections has placed strong downward pressure on both wages and employment, especially for women working in face-to-face services or irregular jobs, leading to a severe household income environment. As described in Section 2 of this chapter, corporate performance is recovering mainly in the manufacturing industries, but it continues to deteriorate in the non-manufacturing industries. In the 2021 spring wage negotiations, many companies decided not to raise basic wages due to the deterioration of corporate performance in the previous year. Although companies with improved business performance are expected to raise basic wages, it may be difficult for companies and industries with poor business performance to do so. If the pace of wage increases slows, the pace of recovery of individual consumption will remain modest. In the current environment where prices of daily necessities such as gasoline keep on rising while wage increases are delayed, there is a concern that cost-push inflation will spread and adversely affect the purchasing power of households.

References

INADA, Yoshihisa; KINOSHITA, Yusuke; and NOMURA, Ryosuke (2021), Impact of the reissue of the state of emergency on the Kansai economy— Reflection and analysis using high-frequency and big data (Japanese title: *Kinkyu Jitai Sengen Saihatsurei no Kansai Keizai eno Eikyo – Kohindo Big Data o Mochiita Furikaeri to Bunseki*), APIRTrendWatch No. 72, January 26, 2021 (https://www.apir.or.jp/research/9215/).

KOMAKI, Yasuyuki (2021), Restraint on going out under the Covid-19 pandemic—people's voluntary restraint and business restriction requests for restaurants (Japanese title: *Covid-19 ni Okeru Gaishutsu Yokusei – Hitobito no Jihatsuteki na Yokusei to Inshokuten eno Eigyo Jishuku Yosei*), NLI Research Institute (Basic Research Report), June 10, 2021

Ministry of Health, Labour and Welfare's COVID-19 Advisory Board Data Analysis Team (2021), Quantitative evaluation of the effects of priority measures

---

11) Coronavirus (COVID-19) Vaccinations, by Our World in Data.

and declarations of emergency to prevent the expanding infection on the epidemic dynamics of COVID-19 (provisional version), National Institute of Infectious Diseases, June 14, 2021.

Section 2
THE COVID-19 PANDEMIC AND THE RESPONSES OF FIRMS: A DETERIORATING REVENUE ENVIRONMENT AND EMPLOYMENT ADJUSTMENT

KINOSHITA, Yusuke; KUO, Chiu-Wei

1. Impact of the COVID-19 Pandemic on Corporate Finance

With the spread of COVID-19, the revenue of firms has deteriorated significantly. As a result, firms have been forced to adjust their employment considerably. In this section, we will focus on the deterioration of firms' revenue environment during the COVID-19 pandemic and their employment adjustment.

First, we will look at the impact of the COVID-19 pandemic on the revenue of firms by analyzing the revenue index and financial index by industry. In particular, we will go over the financial data of the accommodations, food and beverage services industries to see how the revenue situation has deteriorated significantly among firms in the face-to-face services industry. In the second subsection, we will compare the economic shock and movements in the labor market with those of the 2008 global financial crisis. In the third subsection, we will discuss the characteristics of employment adjustment during the COVID-19 pandemic, and in the fourth subsection, about the Employment Adjustment Subsidy. The fifth subsection is the conclusion and outlook.

(1) Revenue and Financial Situation of the Face-to-Face Service Industry

A "K-shaped" economic recovery, where recovery is polarized depending on the industry of the firm, has been noted as one of the characteristics of the recent COVID-19 shock. Figure 2-2-1 shows the change in ordinary profits of all industries, manufacturing industries, and non-manufacturing industries nationwide.

Looking at the recovery process from 2020 Q2 when the economy hit bottom, manufacturing was supported by the recovery of the world economy and ordinary profits recovered to increase after 2020 Q4. Thanks to strong external demand, ordinary profits had increased for three consecutive quarters as of the most recent 2021 Q2. Meanwhile, non-manufacturing saw a decline in the decrease rate after hitting bottom in 2020 Q2, but the decrease in ordinary profits was continuing as of 2021 Q2, showing contrasting trends.

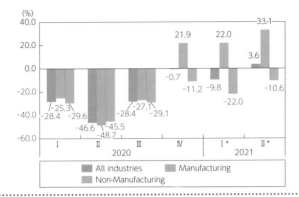

Figure 2-2-1   YoY change in ordinary profits by industry

Note: * change is relative to the same period of the pre-pandemic 2019.
Source: based on Survey of Corporate Business Statistics (Ministry of Finance)

Next, Figure 2-2-2 compares the ordinary profit to sales ratio, which shows the profitability of firms, by industry, for the 2020 Q2 period when the economy hit bottom. It shows that the ratios of decrease were large in the "Accommodations, eating and drinking services," "Living-related and personal services and amusement services," and "Transport and postal activities," in descending order, indicating that the revenue situations have been deteriorating in the face-to-

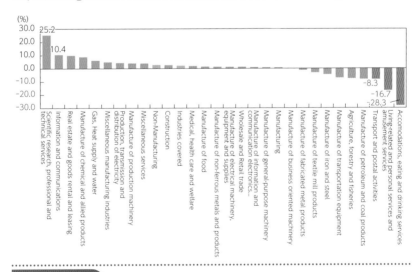

Figure 2-2-2   Ordinary profit to sales ratio by industry (all scales, 2020 Q2)

Source: based on Survey of Corporate Business Statistics (Ministry of Finance)

face service industries that have been hit hard by the decrease in flow of people due to the declarations of a state of emergency[1]. Below, we will analyze in detail the accommodation and eating and drinking services industries that have been among those particularly impacted among the face-to-face service industries.

(i) Trends in the Accommodation Industry

Table 2-2-1 summarizes the revenue of firms and the financial situation in the accommodation industry. In terms of revenue, items such as sales and ordinary profits have significantly decreased. Additionally, the decrease rate was somewhat smaller during the 2020 Q3 and Q4 periods, which is when the Go To Travel program was implemented. However, the decrease rate increased in 2021 Q1 after the program was suspended and when infections spread once again (the third wave), and also in Q2, which is when the third declaration of a state of emergency was issued.

The accommodation industry has many employees and has a higher ratio of fixed costs to sales (the fixed costs ratio) compared to the manufacturing industry[2], and many of its firms recorded losses due to significant decreases in sales due to the COVID-19 pandemic. With regards to employment adjustment, it is worth noting that labor costs decreased by double digits for five consecutive

| Table 2-2-1 | Earnings and financial trends in the accommodation industry |

Unit: %

		Total					
		20Q1	20Q2	20Q3	20Q4	21Q1*	21Q2*
Revenue	Sales	-25.1	-80.0	-59.0	-46.9	-61.7	-70.4
	Ordinary profits	-1,025.6	-624.0	-245.9	-116.4	-1,531.5	-371.0
	Labor costs	1.9	-42.6	-38.6	-40.3	-23.2	-46.2
	Fixed costs ratio**	40.6	92.7	54.3	41.0	77.1	59.5
Assets	Cash/deposits	-25.2	-2.3	6.0	15.7	-4.9	-2.5
	Tangible fixed assets	-0.5	-29.7	-10.2	-15.4	-9.6	-30.6
Liability /Net assets	Short-term debts	-10.8	-32.7	-2.7	-24.7	15.9	-27.8
	Corporate bonds	-35.4	-27.6	-31.4	-36.0	-47.9	-34.5
	Long-term debts	26.4	-23.6	2.0	4.7	24.0	-18.0
	Total net assets	-0.7	13.9	-12.5	-52.2	-54.8	-49.3
	Retained earnings	-39.7	-8.1	-46.0	-66.8	-110.4	-120.7

Note: *relative to the same period in 2019 **Raw figures
Source: based on Survey of Corporate Business Statistics (Ministry of Finance)

1) See Section 1 of this chapter regarding flow of people and trend in household consumption.
2) The fixed costs ratio for the manufacturing industry after 2020 Q2 was approximately 20% for all scales.

quarters from 2020 Q2. With the likelihood of an improvement to the decreases in sales looking uncertain due to the prolonged spread of infections, it appears that firms are keeping down labor costs by adjusting work hours and personnel to reduce fixed costs.

With regards to finance, the retained earnings is decreasing significantly. Additionally, due to concerns over worsening finances due to the decrease in sales, it appears that firms are securing their liquidity from hand as cash and deposits by financing through interest-bearing debt, mainly borrowing.

(ii) Trends in the Eating and Drinking Services Industry

Next, looking at the revenue-related index for the eating and drinking services industry in Table 2-2-2, we see the continued worsening of sales and ordinary profits, although not to the extent seen in the accommodation industry. In particular, due to requests for shorter business hours and for suspension of restaurants serving alcohol under the second and third declarations of a state of emergency, the decrease rate grew in 2021 Q1 and Q2. Additionally, similar to the accommodation industry, the eating and drinking services industry is also an industry with high fixed costs, such as labor costs and rent, and many firms are believed to have recorded a loss due to decreased sales. Even with support from the Employment Adjustment Subsidy, the pressure to adjust employment due to deteriorating revenue must have been high.

In terms of finance, the earned surplus has decreased significantly. Anoth-

| Table 2-2-2 | Earnings and financial trends in the eating and drinking services industry |

Unit: %

		Total					
		20Q1	20Q2	20Q3	20Q4	21Q1*	21Q2*
Revenue	Sales	-2.1	-29.6	-8.0	-6.1	-19.2	-24.5
	Ordinary profits	-182.6	-435.6	-237.6	-103.8	-300.1	-145.7
	Labor costs	7.3	-17.4	-7.6	-3.9	-5.0	-39.2
	Fixed costs ratio**	34.7	34.0	31.4	31.7	37.5	25.8
Assets	Cash/deposits	23.6	19.2	41.9	32.7	69.6	67.4
	Tangible fixed assets	12.6	-11.5	5.4	13.3	-4.5	0.2
Liability / Net assets	Short-term debts	-10.1	-28.8	-15.7	-13.0	-8.2	-7.5
	Corporate bonds	-22.7	-39.7	-44.9	-39.3	-24.0	-30.2
	Long-term debts	15.5	6.3	47.2	32.8	27.2	132.7
	Total net assets	30.8	-13.4	-7.0	-27.7	5.0	-18.2
	Retained earnings	53.9	-15.1	-54.7	-51.9	-45.1	-58.4

Note: *relative to the same period in 2019 **Raw figures
Source: Based on Survey of Corporate Business Statistics (Ministry of Finance)

er characteristic is an increase in financing through long-term debt. Government-affiliated financial institutions are increasing their financial support in response to the prolonging of the COVID-19 pandemic, and such policy factors may have also backed the financing of firms[3].

(2) Revenue and Financial Situation of Firms in Kansai

Next, we will discuss the revenue and financial situation of firms in Kansai, categorizing them into manufacturing and non-manufacturing industries and describing their characteristics compared to the nationwide situation.

First, in the manufacturing industry, sales and ordinary profits after 2020 Q2 not only declined less significantly compared to other companies nationwide, but they recovered to increase in Q4 and 2021 Q1 (Table 2-2-3). This may be because in Kansai, production among firms recovered thanks to increase in exports such as semiconductors.

In the non-manufacturing industry, the decrease rate was larger compared to nationwide for both sales and ordinary profits in 2020 Q2 and Q3 (Table 2-2-4). It then gradually contracted until the decrease rate grew again with the issuing of the third declaration of a state of emergency, and the difficult revenue environment is continuing. As seen in Table 2-2-3, since sales and ordinary

Table 2-2-3   Earnings and financial trends in the manufacturing industry

Unit: %

		Kansai						Japan					
		20Q1	20Q2	20Q3	20Q4	21Q1*	21Q2*	20Q1	20Q2	20Q3	20Q4	21Q1*	21Q2*
Revenue	Sales	-4.5	-11.3	-8.9	0.7	1.1	-0.2	-3.3	-19.1	-11.6	-2.6	4.3	-2.7
	Ordinary profits	-7.5	-5.7	-18.5	11.5	71.5	49.7	-22.6	-37.2	-26.8	21.9	29.5	38.3
	Fixed costs ratio	-4.2	-4.4	-3.4	-1.7	-1.8	-0.2	-0.2	-2.2	-2.9	-2.8	-3.3	-0.7
Assets	Cash/deposits	-9.1	18.2	12.0	13.7	15.2	29.4	1.4	25.6	26.1	22.6	20.0	19.3
Liability / Net assets	Short-term debts	11.4	27.0	20.5	-9.3	32.6	21.4	14.0	23.2	21.7	10.1	14.9	9.1
	Corporate bonds	22.4	12.8	31.1	34.4	64.2	44.5	23.4	15.9	28.0	23.9	51.5	41.8
	Long-term debts	11.7	17.3	5.6	-6.3	3.5	-6.9	10.1	18.8	18.7	8.0	9.4	9.0
	Total net assets	1.0	11.9	7.6	-1.4	6.4	10.1	-0.6	1.2	0.8	0.3	3.2	6.0
	Retained earnings	9.9	19.0	14.7	-0.1	16.3	13.0	2.7	3.1	2.1	0.7	7.2	7.5

Note: *relative to the same period of 2019
Source: Based on Survey of Corporate Business Statistics (Kinki Local Finance Bureau, Ministry of Finance)

3) As an example, unsecured, interest-free loans are available through both the COVID-19 Special Loan Program by Japan Finance Corporation and the Special Interest Subsidy Program. The deadline is expected to be extended from the end of December 2020 to March of next year.

Table 2-2-4   Earnings and financial trends in the non-manufacturing industry

Unit: %

		Kansai						Japan					
		20Q1	20Q2	20Q3	20Q4	21Q1*	21Q2*	20Q1	20Q2	20Q3	20Q4	21Q1*	21Q2*
Revenue	Sales	-5.8	-19.8	-12.2	-5.0	-2.5	-14.0	-8.6	-16.5	-11.8	-7.0	-8.0	-12.1
	Ordinary profits	-41.4	-48.2	-26.3	-62.0	-6.6	-20.2	-45.2	-26.7	-25.8	-35.7	-25.9	-3.0
	Fixed costs ratio	-1.3	-6.0	-1.1	-2.7	-0.0	-3.2	-3.2	-7.3	-4.4	-3.5	-7.7	-5.5
Assets	Cash/deposits	0.4	26.1	24.8	26.7	26.7	36.9	-0.8	28.5	19.4	24.4	18.5	18.5
Liability / Net assets	Short-term debts	10.1	19.7	10.7	10.3	33.1	42.0	7.0	29.7	29.3	25.8	24.8	24.8
	Corporate bonds	6.9	10.6	24.2	25.7	42.2	43.5	9.7	15.9	18.4	16.3	31.2	31.2
	Long-term debts	1.3	3.6	6.4	3.8	4.5	8.7	2.4	9.3	8.8	8.9	10.2	10.2
	Total net assets	4.6	2.8	1.8	0.1	6.3	4.6	1.5	3.5	1.4	0.0	3.2	3.2
	Retained earnings	7.0	5.3	2.8	0.3	6.7	7.2	-0.0	2.1	-0.3	-2.4	0.9	0.9

Note: *relative to the same period in 2019
Source: Survey of Corporate Business Statistics. (Kinki Local Finance Bureau, Ministry of Finance)

profits recovered to increase in the manufacturing industry, a "K-shaped" recovery has been observed in Kansai as well. Additionally, fixed costs continue to decrease both nationwide and in Kansai, indicating that employment adjustment has been implemented. Financially, cash and deposits grew more in the non-manufacturing industry in Kansai compared to nationwide, showing that they are carefully accumulating funds on hand.

2. Economic Shock and the Labor Market

(1) Spread of Infections and Characteristics of the Labor Market

With employment adjustments increasing in response to the worsening performance of firms, the local employment situation is also increasingly deteriorating. Here, we will outline the movement of the labor market in Kansai in FY 2020, when it was greatly impacted by the COVID-19 pandemic.

On average in FY 2020, the labor force in Kansai decreased by −30,000 compared to the previous year to 10.82 million people, while the non-labor force population increased by +10,000 for the same period to 7.18 million people. The number of employed persons decreased by −90,000 for the same period to 10.49 million people, while unemployed persons increased by +60,000 for the same period to 340,000 people. The unemployment rate was 3.1%, up +0.5%pt from the previous year (2.6%).

Particularly noteworthy is the number of employed persons not at work[4], which increased by +140,000 from the previous year (290,000 people) to 420,000 people on average in FY 2020. Such an increase in the number of employed persons not at work may have suppressed the rise in the unemployment rate to some extent. Consequently, the rate of employed persons not at work (no. of employed persons not at work / no. of employed persons) was 4.0%, up +1.3%pt from the previous year (2.7%). The nationwide average rate of employed persons not at work for FY 2020 was 3.9%, thus the rate was higher in Kansai.

Next, we will divide the period of analysis into three as we did in Section 1 of this chapter to look at the movements in the labor market in Kansai during the COVID-19 pandemic and describe the characteristics. The three periods are (i) The early phase of the spread of infections to the declaration of a state of emergency period (January to June 2020), (ii) The period of recovery from bottom (July to December 2020), and (iii) The period of infection resurgence (January to September 2021).

(i) Early Phase of the Spread of Infections to the Declaration of a State of Emergency Period: January to June 2020

Table 2-2-5 shows the movements in the labor market in Kansai based on quarterly data for the period being discussed.

Since 2020 Q1, the employment environment in Kansai, which had been favorable, changed for the worse. In particular, the number of employed persons that previously had continued to increase changed to a decrease and the unemployment rate, which was in the low 2% range, rose to 2.8%, beginning to show the impact of COVID-19.

The biggest change occurred in 2020 Q2. Due to an increase in new infections, people began refraining from job seeking activities to avoid being infected, leading to a significant +210,000 increase in the non-labor force population compared to in the previous period (out of the labor force). Additionally, with the issuing of the declaration of a state of emergency and restricted economic activities, demand for labor dropped rapidly and the number of employed persons decreased significantly, down −240,000 people for the same period. However, unemployed persons increased by only +20,000 for the same period (the unemployment rate was up +0.2%pt for the same period), which was a small increase

---

4) An employed person not at work refers to a person who did not work at all during the week of the survey despite having a job, who is (1) an employee who received or is expected to receive salary or wages (including leave allowance) or who is (2) a self-employed worker who has kept his/her business and for who 30 days have not passed since being absent from the job.

| Table 2-2-5 | Movements in the labor market in Kansai during the COVID-19 pandemic |

[Real Number]

(Unit: 10thousand people, %pt)

		Labour force	Not in la-bour force	Employed persons	Employed person not at work	Unem-ployed persons	Unemploy-ment rate
2019	III	1,087	715	1,062	28	26	2.4
	IV	1,091	711	1,063	32	27	2.5
2020	I	1,092	710	1,062	30	30	2.8
	II	1,071	731	1,038	72	32	3.0
	III	1,074	728	1,041	34	32	3.0
	IV	1,089	710	1,054	33	36	3.3
2021	I	1,096	703	1,062	30	35	3.2
	II	1,088	711	1,051	37	35	3.3
	III	1,081	714	1,049	35	32	3.0

[Difference]

(Unit: 10thousand people, %pt)

		Labour force	Not in la-bour force	Employed persons	Employed person not at work	Unem-ployed persons	Unemploy-ment rate
2019	III	15	-16	20	3	-3	-0.3
	IV	4	-4	2	4	1	0.1
2020	I	1	-1	-1	-1	3	0.3
	II	-21	21	-24	42	2	0.2
	III	3	-3	2	-38	0	0.0
	IV	15	-18	13	-0	3	0.3
2021	I	7	-6	8	-3	-1	-0.1
	II	-8	7	-10	7	0	0.1
	III	-7	3	-2	-1	-3	-0.3

Note: Seasonal Adjusted by APIR
Source: Labour Force Survey. (Statistics Bureau, MIC)

compared to the decrease rate in the number of employed persons. This was possibly due to the fact that in addition to labor supply side factors, such as an increase in the non-labor force population, the number of people losing their job remained within the number of employed persons not at work, which is included in the number of employed persons, due to the expansion of the Employment Adjustment Subsidy that is described later (the number of employed persons not at work increased by +420,000 for the same period).

(ii) Period of Recovery from Bottom: July to December 2020

In 2020 Q3, the decrease rate of the number of employed persons declined due to activities of firms resuming on the lifting of the declaration of a state of emergency. Additionally, the number of employed persons not at work, which had increased rapidly in Q2, decreased by –380,000 to 340,000 people. In the meantime, the labor force and unemployed persons increased slightly, indicating that some people had resumed job seeking activities and shifted to being unemployed persons.

In Q4, there was an increase in the number of employed persons. The reason for this was that demand for labor recovered in the service industries, such as food service and travel, as a result of consumer stimulus programs like Go To Travel (began on July 22) and Go To Eat (began on October 1).

(iii) Period of Infection Resurgence: January to September 2021

In 2021 Q1, the labor force recovered above the 2019 Q4 pre-COVID-19 level. Additionally, the number of employed persons increased by 210,000 in 2020 Q4 and 2021 Q1 thanks in part to the resumption of economic activities and the government's consumer stimulus programs. However, because the number of employed persons fell by –230,000 from 2020 Q1 to Q3 due to the COVID-19 shock, there is still about 20,000 people needed in order to recover from the decline.

After that, in 2021 Q2, which was affected by the fourth wave of infections and the third declaration of a state of emergency, the labor force and the number of employed persons both decreased down to levels below those in 2020 Q4. The number of employed persons not at work increased again to 370,000 people. In the most recent 2021 Q3, unemployed persons decreased while the number of employed persons also decreased at a similar level, which was by no means good. Behind this was the downward pressure on employment caused by economic activities being suppressed because of infection control measures taken in response to the surge in the number of new positive cases due to the spread of a COVID-19 variant[5]. The employment situation in Kansai continues to be harsh.

(2) Comparison with the Global Financial Crisis

Figure 2-2-3 compares how the key labor indicators recovered in Kansai from this COVID-19 shock and from the global financial crisis. In particular, we will focus on the range of declines after the shocks occurred and how long it took to recover to levels similar to the peaks before the crises occurred. The peak

---

5) Since the economic share in Kansai of the three prefectures (Kyoto, Osaka, and Hyogo) where infection control measures were implemented exceeds 80%, the impact on economic and social activities is believed to have been greater compared to the nationwide share of prefectures (60%) in which infection control measures were implemented.

Part I

Part II

Part III

Part IV

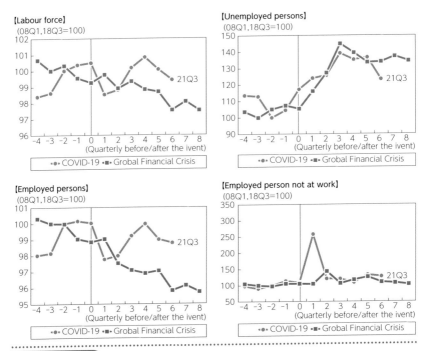

Figure 2-2-3   Changes in labor-related indicators after the economic shock

Note: Seasonal Adjusted by APIR
Source: Labour Force Survey. (Statistics Bureau, MIC)

corresponds to the adjusting of the Japanese economy after the shock[6].

Looking at these graphs, the difference between the two economic shocks is clear. In relation to the labor force, the decline immediately following the shock was greater with the COVID-19 shock than with the global financial crisis. However, looking at the time it took to recover, a gradual decrease continued for a long period with the global financial crisis, but with the COVID-19 shock, the pre-COVID-19 peak had been exceeded by four quarters after the shock occurred (2021 Q1). The number of employed persons shows a similar trend, more or less recovering to the pre-COVID-19 peak four quarters after the shock occurred. With the COVID-19 shock, a major evaporation of demand occurred within a short period, impacting the labor market as well. However, the recovery after the shock occurred much faster than after the global financial crisis. These results show that the COVID-19 shock has the characteristics of being a "supply

---

6) The peak prior to the crisis is 2008 Q1 for the global financial crisis and 2019 Q3 for the COVID-19 shock. See Section 3 of this chapter for the adjustment process of real GDP, etc.

shock" caused by suppressed economic activity due to the avoidance of personal contact to prevent infections.

However, despite such sudden pressure to adjust employment, the increase rate in unemployment persons with the COVID-19 shock has been more gradual than with the global financial crisis. Additionally, it is different in that the number of employed persons not at work has been increasing significantly. It appears that through support, such as the Employment Adjustment Subsidy, the number of employed persons not at work, which is a category in the breakdown of the number of employed persons, increased, preventing a sudden increase in the number of unemployed persons in Kansai as well.

3. Trends in Employment Adjustment during the COVID-19 Pandemic

In the first subsection, we saw from national financial data that the COVID-19 shock can be characterized by its significant impact on the non-manufacturing industry, particularly the face-to-face services industry, as a result of the suspension of economic activity. While an improvement of the sales-decrease situation seems uncertain, firms are adjusting employment to reduce fixed costs. In this subsection, we will analyze the characteristics of employment adjustment in Kansai during the COVID-19 pandemic.

(1) Characteristics by Industry: Impact Is Significant in Face-to-Face Services and among Women

First, we will look at the characteristics by industry in Kansai. Figure 2-2-4 shows the contribution by industry for the number of employed persons (YoY) in Kansai. Looking at the total for males and females, in Kansai, employment had been increasing in industries such as "Accommodations, eating and drinking services" and "Living-related and personal services and amusement services" supported by strong inbound demand. However, when inbound-related demand evaporated due to the COVID-19 shock, it changed to a decrease, down −0.5% YoY in 2020 Q2. In the order of contribution, they were "Accommodations, eating and drinking services" (−0.9%pt), "Education, learning support" (−0.7%pt), and "Wholesale and retail trade" (−0.4%pt), and they account for a large portion of the decrease in the overall number of employed persons, which was mainly in the face-to-face service industry.

Similarly, looking at the contribution by industry for females, in 2020 Q2, there was a −0.9% decrease YoY, which is a greater decrease compared to the male and female total. By industry, the contributions were greater in the order of

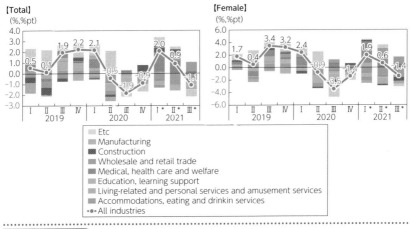

Figure 2-2-4   Contribution by industry for the number of employed persons in Kansai

Note: *relative to the same period of 2019
Source: Labour Force Survey. (Statistics Bureau, MIC)

"Accommodations, eating and drinking services" (–1.3%pt), "Education, learning support" (–1.3%pt), and "Wholesale and retail trade" (–0.6%pt). So, even by industry, females have been particularly impacted.

(2) Characteristics by Employment Type: Adjustment Pressure Is High for Part-Time Workers

Next, we will look at the characteristics by employment type. Figure 2-2-5 looks at the YoY changes in the overall number of regular employees, full-time employees, and part-time employees in the six Kansai prefectures.

The overall number of regular employees changed to a decrease YoY in April 2020 when the first declaration of a state of emergency was issued and subsequently remained negative. Looking at the breakdown, the number of full-time employees dropped below the previous year in Kansai in January 2020 and continued to decrease until recovering with the return of production activities. On the other hand, the number of part-time employees continue to remain below the number in the previous year since May 2020. Comparing nationwide and Kansai, the decrease rate in part-time employees was larger in Kansai. This suggest that employment adjustment pressure was higher in Kansai than nationwide mainly for part-time employees who are relatively easier to adjust compared to full-time employees.

In general, the face-to-face service industry has a high ratio of non-regular employees and part-time employees and is more likely to be impacted when the

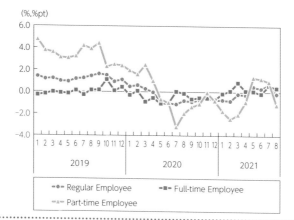

| Figure 2-2-5 | Employment indices in Kansai |

Note: Establishment with 5 or more employees, YoY % change
Source: Monthly Labour Survey. (Ministry of Health, Labour and Welfare)

revenues of firms deteriorate. Since the ratio of part-time employees is higher in Kansai than nationwide, the impact may have been significant. In Figure 2-2-4 shown previously, we mentioned that female employees in face-to-face service industries such as "Accommodations, eating and drinking services" decreased due to the COVID-19 pandemic. Looking at the decrease in female employees by age group (Figure 2-2-6), in 2020 Q2, the 35 to 44 years group decreased most significantly, but with the economy worsening, we can see that the decrease has spread to more age groups, such as the 25 to 34 years group. These age groups include many women who work part-time or as temporary or contracted workers on who the impact is believed to have been significant.

In summary, due to decrease in the sales of firms, the COVID-19 pandemic hit women in Kansai particularly hard, as they work as non-regular part-time employees in face-to-face service industries in which the fixed costs ratio is high.

4. Trends in Employment Adjustment Subsidy

The Employment Adjustment Subsidy (hereinafter referred to as "EAS") is a subsidy program to support firms that were forced to downsize their businesses due to reasons such as economic fluctuations but that strived to retain their employees. EAS subsidizes the costs of reduction in working time in the form of temporary leave, training, or secondment. The purpose of this subsidy is to avoid layoffs during temporary recessions to prevent social unrest caused by a rising unemployment rate.

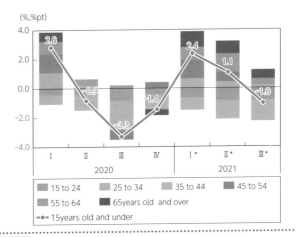

| Figure 2-2-6 | Contribution by age of employed women in Kansai |

Note: *relative to the same period of 2019
Source: Labour Force Survey. (Statistics Bureau, MIC)

Since its establishment in 1975, the EAS has been utilized as a means of retaining employment, and a temporary relaxation of its payment requirements and expansion of the subsidy have been implemented whenever a major economic shock hit[7]. Faced with the sudden deterioration of the employment situation due to the COVID-19 pandemic, the government implemented measures, such as simplifying the application process, in addition to extending eligibility to non-standard workers and easing the payment requirements. Other unprecedented expansions were implemented as well. The eligibility criterion which requires the decline in production or sales of an establishment in the last three months to reach a certain threshold is relaxed to one month. Moreover, the eligibility is extended to non-standard workers who are not enrolled in employment insurance, and the maximum amount of the subsidy received is significantly increased. These special measures were extended until March 2022.

As a result, the number and amount of EAS payments have been rising rapidly. Looking at the cumulative number of EAS payment decisions for the global financial crisis and the COVID-19 pandemic shown in Figure 2-2-7, the rapid increase in payments due to the COVID-19 pandemic is striking. In one year since

7) Expansions in the past include special measures for the global financial crisis in 2008, special measures for the Great East Japan Earthquake in 2011, relaxing of requirements in response to the appreciation of the yen in the same year, and special measures for typhoons No. 15 and 19 in 2019.

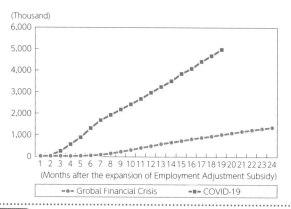

Figure 2-2-7 Cumulative number of EAS payment decisions due to the global financial crisis and the COVID-19 pandemic

Source: Based on open data. (Ministry of Health, Labour and Welfare)

May 2020, the cumulative number of payment decisions reached 3.23 million cases, far exceeding the 790,000 cases in FY 2009 when the impact of the global financial crisis was at its greatest. The cumulative number of payment decisions in Osaka Prefecture (EAS and Emergency Employment Stabilization Subsidy combined) increased from zero cases in the previous year to 270,000 cumulative cases in FY 2020[8].

On a macro basis, EAS is said to have suppressed the rise in the unemployment rate because the increase in the unemployment rate was small relative to the significant decrease in working hours and production during the COVID-19 pandemic, but these effect needs to be investigated further using statistical methods. Additionally, special measures, which are positioned as measures for a short-term recession, have been extended multiple times due to the prolonged COVID-19 pandemic and continued for over a year and a half. The exhaustion of financial resources for EAS and damage from its prolonged use are concerned. In the future, the focus must be shifted to policies that move surplus labor to growth sectors, such as support for firms that change their business, job placement and training for job seekers, etc.

5. Conclusion

In this section, we looked at the trends relating to the deteriorating revenue

---

8) Based on materials from Osaka Labour Bureau distributed in a regular press conference on March 29, 2021.

environment and employment adjustment in firms during the COVID-19 pandemic. COVID-19 significantly decreased the revenue of firms in the non-manufacturing industry. Among them, fixed costs are high in the face-to-face service industries such as the accommodation industry and eating and drinking services industry, and many firms have incurred large deficits. With an improvement to the decreasing sales situation looking unlikely due to the prolonged spread of infections, firms are cutting labor costs by reducing personnel, etc. Particularly in Kansai, employment had been increasing in industries such as the accommodation industry and eating and drinking services industry thanks to the strong inbound demand. However, with the COVID-19 shock, significant employment adjustment pressure has been imposed mainly on women working as non-regular part-time employees in these industries.

As of the time of writing this report on November 9, the fifth wave that became the biggest spread of infections due to a highly contagious variant has subsided and the infection situation has improved nationwide. However, the situation in face-to-face service industries continues to be harsh. In order for sales to increase in the face-to-face service industries, the number of new infections must continue to remain low while tourism demand recovers. Under these circumstances, the government announced on October 26 that the vaccination rate of the second dose of the COVID-19 vaccine has exceeded 70%. With the vaccination program making good progress, economic activities are expected to normalize and employment adjustment pressure to ease. Meanwhile, at the same time surplus labor that has stagnated due to EAS, which is meant to be a short-term measure for maintaining employment, must be shifted to growth sectors and industries with labor shortages.

Section 3
THE JAPANESE ECONOMY: RECENT DEVELOPMENTS AND SHORT-TERM FORECASTS

INADA,Yoshihisa; SHIMODA, Mitsuru

1. A Retrospective Overview of the Japanese Economy in FY2020

(1) Recovery in world trade in Q3 will be paused

According to the CPB World Trade Monitor, world trade (in volume terms: 2010=100) declined for the first time in two months in September 2021, by -0.8% MoM, resulting in a decline of -1.1% QoQ in 2021 Q3. Global trade, which had been expanding for four consecutive quarters since 2020 Q3, temporarily lost its upward momentum. In Q3, both advanced economies and emerging economies saw their trade levels decline, by -0.8% QoQ and -1.8% QoQ, respectively, for the first time in five quarters (Figure 2-3-1).

Looking at another export statistic, we can see that in Q3 Japan's machinery orders from overseas increased for the fifth consecutive quarter (+3.2%), although they slowed somewhat from Q2 (+3.6%). The outlook for Q4 is an in-

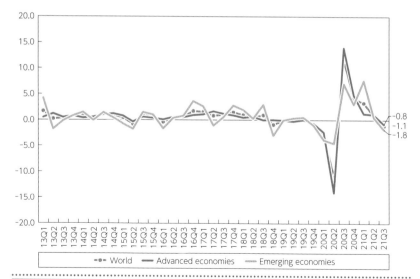

Figure 2-3-1   Dynamics of World Trade

Source: CPB World Trade Monitor, 25 September 2021

crease for the sixth consecutive quarter, by +18.7%. Japan's capital goods exports are expected to grow steadily. According to the Global Semiconductor Market Statistics, global semiconductor sales (3-month moving average) in September rose +27.6% YoY, the 20th consecutive month of growth. Although somewhat slowing down from the peak (+30.4% in June), sales are still growing at a high rate amid the global shortage of semiconductors.

(2) Current state of the economy

According to the second advance GDP estimate for 2021 Q3, released on December 8, the real GDP growth rate in Q3 was -0.9% QoQ, or -3.6% if annualized, a downward revision from the first advance estimate (-0.8% QoQ, or -3.0% if annualized) (Table 2-3-1). It should be noted that the second advance estimate shows that the historical peak of the GDP was in 2019 Q2, as opposed to the previous estimate, which placed the peak of the GDP in 2019 Q3, just before the consumption tax hike.

2021 Q3 featured the fourth declaration of a state of emergency, and supply constraints had a strong impact on automobile purchases. As a result, the eco-

Table 2-3-1   Real GDP and its components (demand-side): QoQ % changes

	Annualized GDP	GDP	Domestic demand	Private demand	Private final consumption expenditure	Private residential investment	Private non-residential investment	Private inventory changes	Public demand	Government final consumption expenditure	Public investment	Public inventory changes	Net exports	Exports	Imports	GDI
18Q2	1.3	0.3	0.2	0.2	0.1	-3.1	1.1	0.1	0.1	0.1	2.1	0.0	0.1	0.7	0.3	0.1
18Q3	-3.1	-0.8	-0.5	-0.5	-0.2	0.2	-2.7	0.1	-0.1	0.0	-1.3	0.0	-0.3	-1.8	-0.4	-1.1
18Q4	0.1	0.0	0.5	0.5	0.0	1.6	2.0	0.2	0.0	0.5	-1.8	0.0	-0.5	1.4	4.5	-0.2
19Q1	1.6	0.4	0.1	0.0	0.2	2.6	0.3	-0.3	0.2	0.4	2.0	0.0	0.3	-1.9	-3.4	1.0
19Q2	1.7	0.4	0.6	0.4	0.0	1.4	0.2	0.3	0.2	0.9	0.4	0.0	-0.2	0.1	1.1	0.2
19Q3	-0.5	-0.1	0.3	0.1	0.4	0.7	2.3	-0.6	0.2	0.7	1.4	0.0	-0.4	0.2	2.4	0.0
19Q4	-9.2	-2.4	-2.8	-2.9	-3.2	-1.8	-7.0	0.1	0.0	0.1	0.0	0.0	0.5	-0.2	-2.6	-2.4
20Q1	1.2	0.3	0.5	0.5	0.6	-4.9	2.7	0.0	0.0	0.1	-1.0	0.0	-0.2	-4.6	-3.5	0.5
20Q2	-28.5	-8.0	-5.3	-5.5	-8.7	-0.1	-7.0	0.4	0.3	0.4	4.3	0.0	-2.8	-18.1	-1.6	-7.0
20Q3	22.1	5.1	2.6	2.0	5.0	-4.8	-0.4	-0.5	0.6	2.1	1.6	0.0	2.5	8.7	-6.7	5.0
20Q4	9.6	2.3	1.4	1.2	2.3	0.0	1.2	-0.2	0.2	0.8	0.6	0.0	0.9	11.1	5.0	2.3
21Q1	-2.9	-0.7	-0.6	-0.4	-1.1	0.9	0.4	0.1	-0.2	-0.6	-1.5	0.0	-0.1	2.3	3.2	-1.3
21Q2	2.0	0.5	0.7	0.7	0.6	1.0	2.0	0.0	0.0	0.7	-2.6	0.0	-0.2	2.5	3.9	0.0
21Q3	-3.6	-0.9	-0.9	-1.0	-1.3	-1.6	-2.3	0.1	0.1	1.0	-2.0	0.0	0.0	-0.9	-1.0	-1.5

Note: Figures for domestic demand, private demand, private inventory changes, public demand, and net exports are contributions. Other figures are QoQ changes.

Source: "Second advance quarterly GDP estimate for Q3 2021" by the Cabinet Office.

nomic performance centering on private consumption was weak.

In terms of the contribution to real GDP growth, domestic demand suppressed growth for the first time in two quarters, by -0.9 %pt QoQ. Therein, public demand contributed by +0.1 %pt, supporting growth for the second consecutive quarter, while private demand contributed a negative -1.0 %pt, suppressing growth for the first time in two quarters. The headline indicators (private final consumption expenditure, private housing, and private business equipment) all fell sharply. External demand (net exports) made a positive contribution for the first time in three quarters, but it was almost negligible (0.0%pt). While the exports of goods and services declined, the imports of goods and services declined even more, reflecting weak domestic demand. This can be attributed to supply constraints, including the prolonged state of emergency as well as semiconductor shortages.

Looking at trends in demand components, private final consumption expenditure declined for the first time in two quarters, down -1.3% QoQ. By type, spending on real durable goods, such as passenger cars and household durable goods, fell for the first time in two quarters, down -16.3% QoQ. Spending on real semi-durable goods, such as clothing, fell for the first time in two quarters, down -3.7% QoQ. Real spending on services also fell for the first time in two quarters, down -0.2% QoQ. On the other hand, spending on non-durable goods, such as food, increased by +1.1% QoQ for the third consecutive quarter.

Within fixed capital formation, real private housing declined for the first time in four quarters, down -1.6% QoQ. Nominal private-sector housing increased by +1.4%, for the third consecutive quarter, but real private-sector housing growth was negative due to a large increase in the private-sector housing deflator (+3.1%) caused by the wood supply shock. Real private-sector investment in business equipment declined for the first time in four quarters, by -2.3% QoQ.

The contribution of real private-sector inventory change to real GDP growth was +0.1 %pt QoQ, the third consecutive quarter of positive contribution.

Within real public demand, real government final consumption expenditure rose for the second consecutive quarter, by +1.0% QoQ. Vaccination has boosted government consumption expenditure (due to increased medical expenditure). However, real public fixed capital formation declined for the third consecutive quarter, by -2.0% QoQ.

Real exports of goods and services fell for the first time in five quarters, -0.9% QoQ. Goods exports declined for the first time in five quarters, by -1.2% QoQ, while services exports increased for the fourth consecutive quarter, by + 0.6% QoQ. Meanwhile, the real imports of goods and services declined for the first time in four quarters, by -0.7% QoQ. Therein, goods imports of goods

Table 2-3-2	Adjustment to the COVID-19 pandemic: Real GDP and its components (demand side, peak=100)							
	GDP	Goods imports	Services imports	Private final consumption expenditure	Private invest-ment	Govern-ment spending	Goods exports	Services exports
19Q2	100.0	100.0	100.0	100.0	100.0	100.0	100.0	100.0
19Q3	99.9	101.5	105.5	100.4	99.3	100.8	100.6	98.8
19Q4	97.5	99.5	100.5	97.2	93.9	101.0	100.3	98.7
20Q1	97.8	95.2	99.9	97.8	94.8	100.9	98.1	85.8
20Q2	89.9	95.6	92.1	89.3	91.2	102.0	79.3	74.0
20Q3	94.5	88.3	88.6	93.8	88.0	104.0	89.0	70.5
20Q4	96.7	94.3	88.0	95.9	87.9	104.8	100.4	73.2
21Q1	96.0	97.5	90.3	94.9	88.9	104.0	102.6	75.1
21Q2	96.5	100.4	96.6	95.4	90.6	104.0	105.0	77.5
21Q3	95.6	99.7	94.7	94.2	89.1	104.4	103.7	78.0

Source: Authors' calculations based on "the second advance quarterly GDP estimate for Q3 2021" by the Cabinet Office.

declined by -0.7% QoQ, for the first time in four quarters. Services imports declined for the first time in three quarters, by -2.0% QoQ.

Looking at deflators, the domestic demand deflator rose +0.5% QoQ, for the third consecutive quarter. Therein, the private final consumption expenditure deflator rose +0.3%, for the first time in two quarters. In terms of external demand deflators, the export deflator for goods and services rose by +2.1% (for the fifth consecutive quarter), and the import deflator rose by +5.6% (for the fifth consecutive quarter). As the latter exceeded the former, the terms of trade deteriorated for the fifth consecutive quarter. As a result, the GDP deflator remained negative for the fourth consecutive quarter, -0.1%.

As the terms of trade deteriorated for the fifth consecutive quarter, the real Gross Domestic Income (GDI), which takes into account changes in gains from trade, declined by -1.5% QoQ, or -6.0% if annualized. Nominal GDP declined for the first time in two quarters to -1.0% QoQ, or -4.1% if annualized.

Assuming that the peak of the real GDP (557.3 trillion JPY in 2019 Q2) is 100, the pandemic caused a major bottom in Q2 2020, at 89.9 (501.1 trillion JPY). Although the GDP recovered for two consecutive quarters in Q3 and Q4 2020, the recovery temporarily stopped in Q1 2021. While it recovered somewhat in Q2 2021, it remained stagnant at 95.6 (538.2 trillion JPY) in Q3. With the prolonged declaration of the state of emergency, the current GDP level is still 4.4% (JPY 24.5 trillion) below the peak (Table 2-3-2).

Looking at the adjustment process by GDP component, only government spending (104.4) and goods exports (103.7) exceeded their peaks in 2021 Q3. On the other hand, the recovery in goods imports (99.7), services imports

(94.7), private final consumption expenditure (94.2), and private capital formation (89.1) has been sluggish. In particular, the recovery in services exports (78.0) is lagging by a large margin.

2. Forecasts for the Japanese Economy: FY2021-FY2023

(1) Assumption about exogenous variables

According to the Ministry of Land, Infrastructure, Transport and Tourism, public works in September decreased for the third consecutive month on a volume basis, down -6.9% YoY. The seasonally adjusted figure (APIR estimate) was -2.1% MoM, a decline for the third consecutive month. As a result, the Q3 change was -2.7% QoQ, the third consecutive quarter decline. Due in part to the effects of the pandemic, the shortage of labor in the construction industry may have become a supply constraint. It will take until 2022 for the FY2021 supplementary budget, including disaster recovery and land reinforcement projects, to take effect and for public works projects to start increasing. As a result, real public fixed capital formation is forecast to shrink by -3.3% in FY2021, before expanding by +2.4% in FY2022, and by +2.0% in FY2023.

The vaccination rate has accelerated since May. As a result, real government spending has increased for two consecutive quarters in Q2 and Q3. Assuming that the third round of vaccinations will begin in 2022 Q1, we have raised our forecast for real government spending in FY2021 to +2.7%, and are forecasting further growth of +1.8% in FY2022 and +0.9% in FY2023.

The most important factor in our assumptions for the overseas environment is the price of crude oil. Crude oil prices (average of WTI, Dubai, and North Sea Brent prices per barrel) plummeted to $21.96 in April 2020 due to the rapid slowdown of the global economy and evaporation of demand caused by COVID-19. Since then, due to economic recovery and sustained crude supply constraints, the price of crude oil has been on an upward trend, soaring to $82.15 in October 2021, the highest since October 2014 ($86.13). In our current forecast, crude oil prices are expected to continue to soar through 2021 Q4, but are expected to decline gradually from 2022 through 2024 Q1. For this reason, we have assumed a price of 71.9 dollars for FY2021, 73.7 dollars for FY2022, and 69.7 dollars for FY2023.

(2) Forecast for real GDP growth: +2.7% in FY2021, +2.6% in FY2022, and +1.7% in FY2023

We have revised our forecast for the Japanese economy for FY2021-2023, reflecting the second official advance GDP estimate for 2021 Q3, and incorporating

Table 2-3-3   Forecast summary

	Latest forecast(2021/12/20)			
	2020	2021	2022	2023
Real GDP (%)	▲ 4.5	2.7	2.6	1.7
Private demand (contribution)	▲ 4.7	1.7	1.8	1.0
Private final consumption expenditure (%)	▲ 5.5	2.5	2.3	0.8
Private residential investment (%)	▲ 7.8	▲ 0.6	▲ 0.8	1.2
Private non-residential investment (%)	▲ 7.5	1.7	3.4	3.8
Private inventory changes (contribution)	▲ 0.2	0.1	0.1	▲ 0.0
Public demand (contirbution)	0.8	0.2	0.5	0.3
Government final consumption expenditure (%)	2.5	2.3	1.5	0.9
Public investment expenditure (%)	5.1	▲ 5.7	2.9	1.9
Public inventory changes (contribution)	0.0	▲ 0.0	0.0	▲ 0.0
External demand (contribution)	▲ 0.7	0.9	0.4	0.4
Exports of goods and services (%)	▲ 10.5	11.6	4.6	5.5
Imports of goods and services (%)	▲ 6.6	6.3	2.6	3.5
Nominal GDP (%)	▲ 3.9	1.8	3.1	2.2
GDP deflator (%)	0.7	▲ 0.9	0.5	0.4
Domestic corporate price index (%)	▲ 1.4	6.5	2.1	0.7
Core consumer price index (%)	▲ 0.4	0.0	0.9	0.6
Industrial production index (%)	▲ 9.5	6.1	3.5	2.4
New housing starts (%)	▲ 8.1	6.7	▲ 3.2	0.3
Unemployment rate (%)	2.9	2.8	2.8	2.6
Current account balance (JPY trillion)	16.3	13.2	11.4	13.8
% of nominal GDP	3.0	2.4	2.0	2.4
Crude oil price (USD/barrel)	44.1	71.9	73.7	69.7
USD/JPY exchange rate	106.0	112.2	115.2	116.5
USA real GDP (%, calendar year)	▲ 3.4	5.6	4.3	2.6

Note: Percentages are YoY figures, others are annotated.

some new assumptions concerning exogenous variables (fiscal and monetary policies, and variables related to the global economy). We forecast real GDP growth rate of +2.7% in FY2021, +2.6% in FY2022, and +1.7% in FY2023 (Table 2-3-3). On a calendar year basis, the growth rates are +1.5% in 2021, +2.7% in 2022, and +2.0% in 2023.

Looking at the contribution to real GDP growth by major component, in FY2021, the contribution of private demand (+1.7 %pt) and net exports (+0.9 %pt) will both turn positive. And public demand will also continue to support the economy with +0.2%pt. In FY2022, the contribution of private demand is expect-

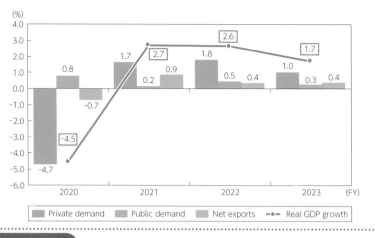

Figure 2-3-2   Real GDP growth rate and contribution by major component: %.

ed to be +1.8 %pt, that of public demand +0.5 %pt, and that of net exports +0.4%pt. In FY2023, the contribution of private demand, public demand and net exports will decline to +1.0%pt, +0.3%pt, and +0.4%pt, respectively. (Figure 2-3-2).

Looking at the content of private demand, in FY2021, real private-sector final consumption expenditure will contribute to growth by + 1.4 %pt, real private-sector housing by -0.0 %pt, real private non-residential investment by + 0.3 %pt, and real private-sector inventory changes by + 0.1 %pt. All components are expected to make positive contributions, with the exception of private housing investment. In FY2022, real private final consumption expenditure will contribute by +1.2 %pt, real private housing investment by -0.0 %pt, real private non-residential investment by +0.5 %pt, and real private inventory changes by +0.1 %pt. In FY2023, real private final consumption expenditure will contribute by +0.4 %pt, real private housing by +0.0 %pt, real private non-residential investment by +0.6 %pt, and real private inventory changes by -0.0 %pt. With the exception of private inventory changes, private demand components will contribute positively but modestly (Figure 2-3-3).

In terms of the quarterly real GDP growth forecast, 2021 Q3 saw the first negative growth in two quarters due to the reemergence of COVID-19 (the 5th wave) as well as the fourth declaration of an emergency state. In Q4, the easing of the COVID-19 pandemic is expected to lead to a rapid expansion of private final consumption expenditure, which will boost the growth rate. The pace of growth will continue to exceed the potential growth rate from 2022 onward, and the real GDP will exceed its pre-pandemic level (543.3 trillion JPY in 2019 Q4) in 2022 Q1, and its pre-pandemic peak (557.3 trillion JPY in 2019 Q2) in 2023 Q1.

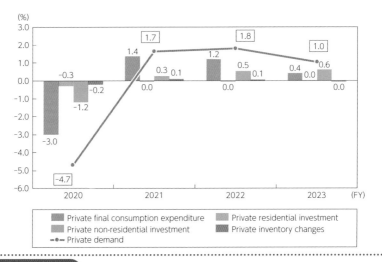

Figure 2-3-3   Contributions to growth by private-demand components: %.

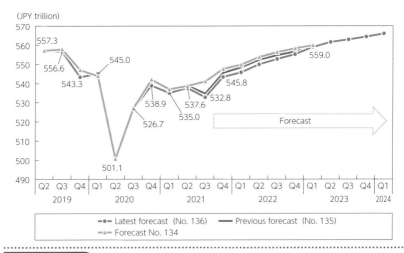

Figure 2-3-4   Quarterly GDP: Actual and Forecast (JPY trillion)

Note: Actual figures through Q3 2021, forecast figures thereafter.

Due to the negative growth in 2021 Q3, it will take one quarter longer than we had previously expected for the GDP to exceed the pre-pandemic peak (Figure 2-3-4).

(3) Household sector: forced savings and revenge consumption

According to the Ministry of Internal Affairs and Communications (MIC), the unemployment rate (seasonally adjusted) was 2.8% in September, remaining unchanged for two consecutive months. The number of working people (seasonally adjusted) declined by 280,000 to 66.48 million, shrinking for the second consecutive month. Therein, the number of employed people (seasonally adjusted) increased by 20,000 to 59.69 million, the first increase in two months, and the number of people on administrative leave (due to temporarily closed businesses), jumped to 5.97 million (9.0%, non-adjusted figure) in April 2020. It improved thereafter, but it remains relatively high at 2.08 million (3.1%) as of September 2021. The unemployment rate has not increased, but that is mostly due to the high number of people on administrative leave.

Although the labor market is gradually recovering due to the resumption of production and policy support, households' income environment is not improving. As a result, household consumption has been sluggish. According to MIC, the total consumption index (2020=100, seasonally adjusted), which estimates changes in total household consumption expenditures, rose +0.8% MoM in real terms in September, logging the first increase in three months. However, on a quarterly basis it fell -1.5% QoQ in Q3, marking the first decline in two quarters. Private consumption has stagnated due to the three emergency states declared throughout 2021.

As the latest state of emergency was lifted at the end of September, the flow of people has been recovering, and a sharp recovery in consumer sentiment is expected. As a result, we expect private final consumption expenditure to rebound in Q4 (see Box: Forced Saving and Revenge Consumption). As a result, we forecast that real private final consumption expenditure will increase by +2.5% YoY in FY2021, by +2.3% in FY2022, and by +0.8% in FY2023.

Part I

Part II

Part III

Part IV

Box) Forced saving and revenge consumption

Based on the quarterly preliminary report on household disposable income and household savings rate (Q2 2021) by the Cabinet Office, we describe the trends before the COVID-19 pandemic (Q1 1994 to Q4 2019) and thereafter (Q1 2020 to Q2 2021). First, Figure 2-3-5 (seasonally adjusted, annualized figures) shows that employment compensation hardly increased before the COVID-19 pandemic, and that household disposable income (after adjusting for changes in pension entitlements) increased only by about JPY 10 trillion before the COVID-19 pandemic.

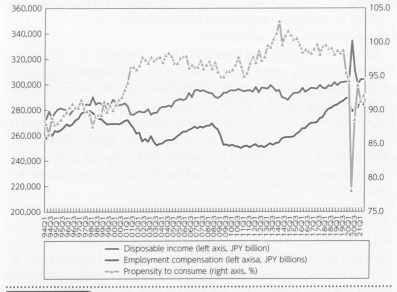

— Disposable income (left axis, JPY billion)
— Employment compensation (left axisa, JPY billions)
--▲-- Propensity to consume (right axis, %)

| Figure 2-3-5 | Employment compensation, disposable income, and propensity to consume (GDP basis) |

Source: Authors' calculations based on "preliminary figures of household disposable income and household savings rate", Cabinet Office.

Household final consumption expenditure rose from 262.0 trillion JPY in 1994 Q1 to a peak at the time of the consumption tax hike, but is currently only around 280 trillion JPY. Despite the lack of growth in disposable income, the average propensity to consume rose, from an average of 94.8% in 1994-2014 to an average of 99.0% in 2015-2019, while the savings rate fell from 5.2% to 1.0% during this period. In 2020 Q2, employee compensation decreased by about JPY 11 trillion QoQ (from JPY 289.8 trillion to JPY 278.9 trillion), but disposable income increased by about JPY 31 trillion QoQ (from JPY 309.2 trillion to JPY 340.1 trillion), partly due to the effect of the one-off stimulus payment (JPY 100 thousand per person) by the government. The disposable income re mained high at JPY 315.2 trillion in 2020 Q3, and then returned to the average level of the year 2019 in 2021 Q2 (JPY 306.0 trillion).

Since the COVID-19 pandemic caused households to miss out on consumption opportunities, they gave up consumption that they would have otherwise been able to realize and saved (forced saving). In fact, the propensity to consume fell by 16.2 %pt from 94.3% in 2020 Q1 to 78.1% in 2020 Q2. It then returned to 92.2% in 2021 Q2, but has yet to recover to the average propensity to consume in the 2015-2019 period (99.0%).

Assuming that the recent average propensity to consume (2015-2019) of 99.0% is maintained, we estimated disposable income in the absence of the impact of COVID-19 (adjusted for one-off stimulus payment by the government). We then deducted the actual household final consumption expenditure from the estimated disposable income in order to calculate the magnitude of forced savings. Our calculations show that forced savings for the five quarters from Q2 2020 to Q2 2021 amounted to about JPY 27.3 trillion. If the decline in the number of COVID-19 infections continues (i.e., if the pandemic comes to an end), we can expect an increase in consumption ("revenge consumption") of about JPY 30 trillion thanks to those forced savings (Figure 2-3-6).

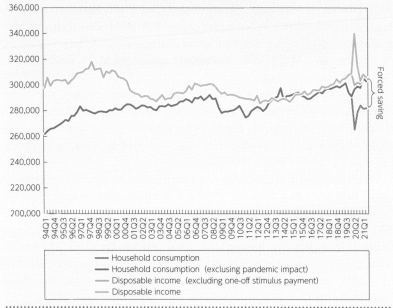

Figure 2-3-6   Infections and forced saving (JPY billion)

Source: Authors' calculations based "on preliminary figures of household disposable income and household savings rate", by the Cabinet Office.
Reference: Box 3 of "Outlook for Economic activity and prices," April 2021, Bank of Japan.

According to the Ministry of Land, Infrastructure, Transport and Tourism (MLIT), the number of new housing starts in September (seasonally adjusted) fell for the second consecutive month, down -1.2% MoM, marking the third consecutive quarter increase. By type, owner-occupied housing increased by +6.5% for the third consecutive quarter, while housing for rent and sale declined by -2.1% and -3.8%, respectively, for the first time in three quarters.

Planned construction expenditure (residential + 0.7× combined residential-industrial), a good indicator of GDP-based private housing investment, fell for the first time in three months in September (seasonally adjusted, APIR estimate), down -6.4% MoM. As a result, although Q3 saw the third consecutive quarter increase, it was a modest +0.7% QoQ.

Reflecting the current slowdown in planned construction, we forecast that private housing will decline by -0.6% YoY in FY 2021 and -0.8% YoY in FY 2022, before recovering by +1.2% YoY in FY 2023.

(4) Corporate sector: Downside risk is prolonged production stagnation due to supply constraints

According to the Ministry of Economy, Trade and Industry (METI), the Industrial Production Index (seasonally adjusted: 2015=100, official report) fell for the third consecutive month in September, down -5.4% MoM. On a quarterly basis, in Q3 the index fell for the first time in five quarters, by -3.7% QoQ (Figure 2-3-7). In September, METI left its assessment unchanged MoM, stating that the economy was at a standstill.

According to the Manufacturing Production Forecast Survey, manufacturing production in October is expected to increase by +6.4% MoM and by +5.7% in November. If the forecasts are correct, the October-November average will rise by +4.1% from the Q3 average, reaching 97.9. However, it will fail to reach its pre-pandemic level of 98.0 in 2020 Q1.

According to METI, the index of tertiary industrial activity (seasonaly adjusted: 2015 average = 100) rose for the first time in three months by +0.5% MoM (August: -1.1% MoM) (Figure 2-3-8). As a result, Q3 saw a decline (-0.8% YoY) for the third consecutive quarter. The level for the same period (96.0) is 5.2 points lower than the pre-pandemic level (101.2 in Q4 2019). Therein, the face-to-face services index for Q3 was 77.3, down -1.5% QoQ, marking the third consecutive quarter of decline. The index is 23.1 points lower than its pre-pandemic level (100.4).

The recovery in the production of goods (industrial production) and services (tertiary industry) seems to have come to a halt due to supply constraints and the prolonged state of emergency. Therefore, we forecast that the industrial

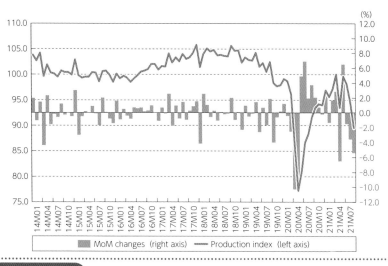

Figure 2-3-7   Index of Industrial Production

Source: Ministry of Economy, Trade and Industry, "Index of Industrial Production"

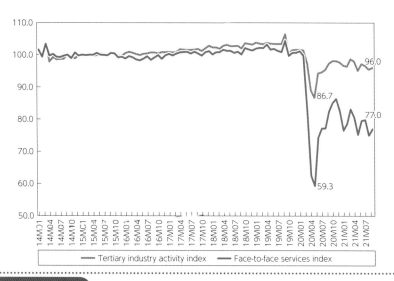

Figure 2-3-8   Face-to-face services vs. the tertiary industry

Source: "Tertiary Industry Activity Index" , Ministry of Economy, Trade and Industry.
Note: The face-to-face service industry index is the weighted average of the indexes for transportation, accommodation, restaurant, food services, entertainment and other lifestyle-related services (2015 average = 100).

production index will increase by +6.1% YoY in FY2021, by +3.5% YoY in FY2022 to be, and by +2.4% YoY in FY2023.

According to Financial Statements Statistics of Corporations 2021 Q3, profit for all industries (seasonally adjusted, excluding the financial and insurance sectors) declined for the first time in five quarters, down -7.4% YoY. Therein, the manufacturing sector declined for the first time in five quarters, down -8.2% YoY, and the non-manufacturing sector declined for the second consecutive quarters, down -6.8% YoY. In Q3, the profits of both the manufacturing and the non-manufacturing industries were low due to sluggish exports, deteriorating terms of trade, and the declaration of a fourth state of emergency.

Looking at investment-related indicators, the capital goods shipment index declined for the second consecutive month in September, down -5.7% MoM. As a result, the Q3 figure fell for the first time in four quarters, down -2.4% QoQ. Core machinery orders, a leading indicator of private-sector capital investment (private sector demand excluding ships and electric power), declined -0.0% MoM in September, the second consecutive monthly decline. As a result, the Cabinet Office left its assessment unchanged from the previous month, stating that the recovery trend has stalled. Q3 machinery orders increased slightly, up +0.7% QoQ, marking the second consecutive quarterly increase. The outlook for Q4 is for a further increase of +3.1%. Since the improvement in the corporate earnings environment is slow, our forecast for private non-residential investment in FY2021 is +1.7% YoY, the first increase in three years, but only a modest recovery, followed by a steady recovery of +3.4% YoY in FY2022 and +3.8% YoY in FY2023.

(5) External sector: Goods trade temporarily stagnant due to supply constraints

GDP statistics show that in Q3, goods exports declined for the first time in five quarters, and goods imports fell for the first time in four quarters, reflecting weak domestic demand. As a result, the expansion of trade in goods (exports plus imports) came to a temporary halt.

According to the Ministry of Finance the export volume index increased by +0.0% MoM in October, the first increase in three months. While, the import volume index decreased by -9.1% MoM, up for the second consecitve month. Comparing October with the Q3 average, the export volume index declined by -3.8%. The import volume index fell sharply by -8.2%. As a result, the growth contribution of net exports was positive in October (Figure 2-3-9).

In Q3, the exports of services increased for the fourth consecutive quarter QoQ. Service imports declined for the first time in three quarters. Service imports and exports remain at low levels, mainly due to the slump in inbound and

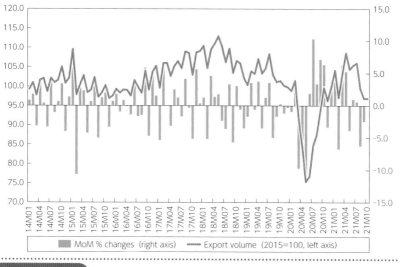

Figure 2-3-9   Export Volume Index

Source: Trade Statistics, Ministry of Finance

outbound tourism.

Taking these factors into account, we forecast that the real exports of goods and services will increase by +11.6% YoY in FY2021, by +4.6% YoY in FY2022, and by +5.5% YoY in FY2023. On the other hand, the real imports of goods and services are expected to increase by +6.3% in FY2021, by +2.6% in FY2022, and by +3.5% in FY2023. As the terms of trade are deteriorating, we expect that the trade balance will turn into a deficit in 2022 and 2023. The deficit in the services balance is likely to increase in FY2021 and FY2022, but then it is likely to start shrinking in FY2023.

On the other hand, since the primary income balance will likely remain high, the current account balance is projected to remain positive at 13.2 trillion JPY in FY2021, 11.4 trillion JPY in FY2022, and 13.8 trillion JPY in FY2023.

(6) Price trends: Energy prices rise, but consumer price trend not expected to increase

According to the Bank of Japan, the domestic corporate goods price index (2015 average=100) rose for the 11th consecutive month in October 2021, up +1.2% MoM. On a YoY basis, the index rose for the eighth consecutive month, by +8.0%. The increase is the largest since January 1981 (+8.1%), and the impact of the sharp rise in resource prices, especially crude oil, and the depreciation of the Japanese yen is conspicuous.

A breakdown shows that the prices of raw materials rose for the eighth consecutive month in October 2021, up +63.0% from a year earlier. Intermediate goods prices rose +14.3%, increasing for the eighth consecutive month. Prices of final goods rose +3.8%, increasing for the eighth consecutive month. From these figures it is clear that there has been no apparent pass-through to final goods prices.

In JPY terms, the Export Price Index in October 2021 rose for the ninth consecutive month, by +13.7% YoY. The Import Price Index rose for the eighth consecutive month, by +38.0% YoY. This is the highest increase since 1981 (the year comparable data became available). As a result, the terms of trade index (Export Price Index/Import Price Index*100) in October was at its lowest level since November 2014. The October index fell 19.2 points YoY, marking the eighth consecutive month of deterioration. It was also the sixth consecutive month of double-digit deterioration.

According to MIC, the National Consumer Price Index (2020 average=100) rose for the second consecutive month in October 2021, up +0.1% YoY. However, the core index (which excludes fresh food, whose prices fluctuate sharply) declined for the seventh consecutive month (-0.7% YoY).

A breakdown shows that energy prices (petroleum products, electricity, and city gas) rose +11.3% YoY, increasing for the sixth consecutive month. Their contribution to the overall index was a positive +0.79%pt. On the other hand, non-energy prices declined for the eighth consecutive month, falling -0.7% YoY. Their contribution to the overall index was a negative -0.70%pt. Therein, food prices (excluding fresh food) rose for the fourth consecutive month (+0.7% YoY, a contribution of +0.17%pt). Accommodation prices rose for the fifth consecutive month (+59.1% YoY, a contribution of +0.35%pt), reflecting a rebound from the large decline caused by the "Go To" campaign in October last year. Lastly, communication charges (cell phones) declined for the seventh consecutive month (-53.6% YoY, a contribution of -1.47%pt).

As the rate of increase in energy prices accelerated toward the end of 2021, the core CPI is expected to rise to the upper zero percent range. The core CPI will accelerate again as the impact of the sharp decline in telecom charges fades away in FY2022. For some time to come, accommodation and communication charges will keep disrupting the basic CPI trend, and should therefore be excluded when analyzing the underlying CPI trend. Although the supply-demand gap is expected to narrow in the future, downward pressure on prices will remain strong, and the upward pressure exerted by non-energy prices (excluding accommodation and communication) is likely to be weak considering the stagnation of wages. Therefore, we expect that the underlying CPI trend will remain weak.

In consideration of the above, our inflation forecast is as follows. The domestic corporate goods price index is projected to increase by +6.5% in FY2021, +2.1% in FY2022, and +0.7% in FY2023. The national CPI core index is forecast to be 0.0% in FY2021, +0.9% in FY2022, and +0.6% in FY2023. The GDP deflator is forecast to be -0.9% in FY2021, +0.5% in FY2022, and +0.4% in FY2023 (Figure 2-3-10).

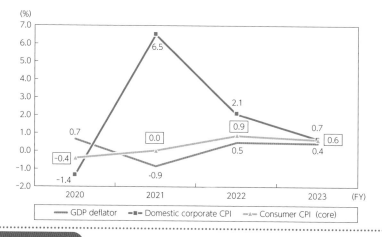

Figure 2-3-10   Inflation Dynamics (YoY % changes)

Section 4
KANSAI'S ECONOMY: RECENT DEVELOPMENTS AND SHORT-TERM FORECASTS

IRIE,Hiroaki; INADA,Yoshihisa

1. A Retrospective Overview of Kansai's Economy in FY2020

In FY2020, Kansai's economy deteriorated rapidly due to the spread of COVID-19. After the first state of emergency was lifted (May 2020), the economy has been recovering, but the pace of recovery has generally been sluggish. Many economic indicators have not yet returned to their pre-pandemic levels.

Looking at the economy by sector, the household sector reached its lowest point in May 2008 and has been recovering gradually since then, but has yet to reach a full-fledged recovery. In the corporate sector, the impact of COVID-19 differs by industry and firm size, with the pace of recovery being polarized (a so-called "K-shaped" recovery). In the external sector, the "two exports" that supported Kansai's economy before the pandemic have faced a transformation. While the exports of goods have picked up significantly as China's economy recovered, inbound tourism demand (i.e., the export of services), has been non-existent due to restrictions on the entry of people from overseas into Japan for tourism purposes.

Therefore, the COVID-19 disaster had a serious impact on the Kansai economy in FY2020. However, a look at the situation before the pandemic reveals that domestic demand and employment had already peaked out. One reason for that was the October 2019 consumption tax hike, as a result of which real incomes and household consumption declined. In addition, exports had been falling year on year since the second half of fiscal 2018 due to the slowdown of the Chinese economy caused by the intensifying trade conflict between the US and China. The Cabinet Office's Business Climate Index Study Group has tentatively determined that the Japan's economy entered a recession in October 2018. In addition to this, the unprecedented COVID-19 shock plunged Kansai's economy into a recession of historic proportions in FY2020.

One of the reasons for the slow pace of recovery is thought to be the fact that both emergency states and other measures to prevent the spread of the virus were enacted several times, in response to the rising number of infections. For example, in Osaka Prefecture, a state of emergency was imposed four times, in April 2020, January 2021, April 2021, and August 2021, and other measures to prevent the spread of the disease were enacted in April 2021 and July 2021. Specific measures included requests for restaurants to stop serving alcoholic beverages and shorten their business hours, for large commercial facilities to close or shorten business hours, and for events to be postponed or cancelled. These measures inevitably had a negative impact on consumer spending and businesses as most of the social and economic activities were restricted.

Figure 2-4-1 shows the economic share of the regions under a state of emergency both in the Japan as a whole and in Kansai from April 2020 onward. The percentages in this figure are calculated based on the nominal Gross Regional Product (GRP) of the prefectural accounts for FY2018.

For example, when Japan's first state of emergency was declared on April 7, 2020, the target areas were Saitama, Chiba, Tokyo, Kanagawa, Osaka, Hyogo, and Fukuoka prefectures. The share of these five prefectures is 47.4% of the national GDP. In the Kansai region, Osaka and Hyogo prefectures account for 71.3% of the total Kansai economy. Then, on April 16 of the same year, the target

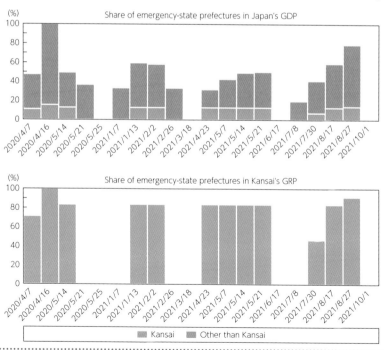

Figure 2-4-1   Economic share of regions under a state of emergency

Note: GRPs for each prefecture are nominal values for FY2018.
Source: Prepared by the authors based on "Prefectural Accounts" by the Cabinet Office.

regions were expanded to all 47 prefectures. At that time, the economic share of the targeted areas was 100%, both in Japan and in Kansai. Since states of emergency tend to be issued in urban areas, such as Osaka and Hyogo prefectures, the impact of the state of emergency is expected to be greater in Kansai than in other regions, at least from the perspective of economic share.

The following is a retrospective overview of the Kansai economy in fiscal 2020 and beyond, focusing on monthly economic indicators.

(1) Household sector: Moderate recovery, but noticeably weaker than the national economy

In FY2020, the household sector in Kansai cooled down sharply due to the spread of COVID-19 and the resulting state of emergency. Many economic indicators bottomed out in May 2020 and have been recovering since the beginning of FY2021. However, the pace of recovery has been slow. Sentiment is fluctuating in tandem with the spread of COVID-19. The income environment and employment have been weaker than in Japan as a whole.

Consumer sentiment worsened significantly (Figure 2-4-2), with the Consumer Confidence Index for the full FY2020 at 29.7, lower than the 30.2 level of FY2008, during the Global Financial Crisis. This was a 7.7 point drop from the previous year and the third consecutive year of deterioration. In particular, April 2020, when the state of emergency was declared, recorded the largest month-on-month decline (-10.6 points) and the lowest level on record (20.0). It recovered to its pre-pandemic level in June 2021, but has since leveled off.

Figure 2-4-2   Consumer Confidence Index

Note: Seasonally adjusted figures are APIR estimates.
Source: Survey of Consumer Sentiment, Cabinet Office

The income environment is picking up from the bottom, but the pace of recovery is slow (Figure 2-4-3). In FY2020, the average monthly wage (cash earnings) in Kansai (APIR estimate) was JPY 309,870, a decrease of 2.2% YoY, marking the second consecutive year of YoY decline. Although in FY2021 the figure rose compared to FY2020, this was simply due to a rebound, suggesting that the income environment remains severe.

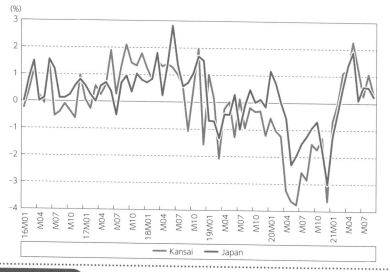

Figure 2-4-3   Total Cash Earnings (YoY changes, %)

Note: Calculated as a weighted average of total cash earnings in each prefecture, based on the number of permanent workers.
Source: Monthly Labor Statistics Survey , Ministry of Health, Labour and Welfare

The employment environment deteriorated rapidly in the first half of FY2020 (Figure 2-4-4). The effective job offers-to-applicants ratio in the Kansai region in FY2020 was 1.08, a sharp decline of 0.49 points from the previous year, marking the second consecutive year of deterioration in the employment environment.

In FY2020, the sales of large retailers in the Kansai region (the total sales of department stores and supermarkets) totaled JPY 3,436 billion, a decrease of 10.4% from the FY2019, marking the third consecutive year of decline.

A breakdown shows that department store sales totaled JPY 1,110.0 billion, down -25.5% from the previous year, marking the third consecutive year of decline (Figure 2-4-5). In April, when the first state of emergency was declared, sales plummeted to -74.9% YoY, the largest decline on record. Although there

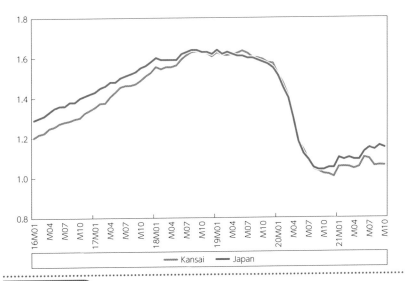

Figure 2-4-4   Effective job offers-to-applicants ratio (seasonally adjusted)

Source: "General Employment Placement Situation", Ministry of Health, Labour and Welfare.

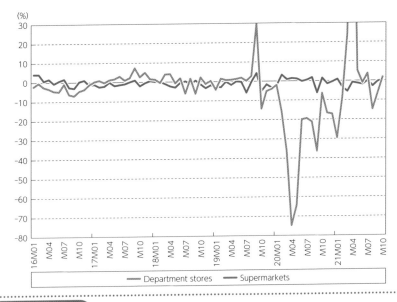

Figure 2-4-5   Department Store and Supermarket Sales (YoY changes, %)

Note: Based on all stores; 150.4% in April 2009.
Source: "Sales of Department Stores and Supermarkets", Kinki Bureau of Economy, Trade and Industry

has been a rebound from the previous year since the beginning of FY2021, it has not been a remarkable recovery due to the fact that a state of emergency was declared several times. Meanwhile, supermarket sales totaled JPY 2.326 trillion. This was the fifth consecutive year of decline, down -0.9% YoY. The decline was smaller than that in department store sales due to an increase in demand for food and beverage products for in-house consumption as people refrained from going out due to the state of emergency, and restaurants closed or shortened their hours.

(2) Corporate sector: recovering after the decline in the first half of FY2020, but the pace of recovery remains sluggish

The corporate sector in Kansai deteriorated rapidly in FY2020 due to the spread of COVID-19 and the declaration of a state of emergency. Although the corporate sector has since bottomed out and is now recovering, the pace of recovery has diverged among firms, depending on firm size, type of industry, and other factors – a phenomenon known as a "K-shaped recovery". In 2021, the recovery is generally moderate as the number of COVID-19 infections remains low, and economic activities normalize. However, the manufacturing sector is at a standstill due to the global shortage of semiconductors.

The business sentiment has been deteriorating since its peak in the December 2018 survey (Figure 2-4-6). In particular, the June 2020 survey was the first significant deterioration since the March 2009 survey during the Global Financial Crisis. In the December 2021 survey, the Diffusion Index (DI) for business conditions in Kansai (firms of all sizes in all industries) was +5, returning to positive territory for the first time in eight quarters. The recovery was particularly rapid for large manufacturing companies, whose DI had been in positive territory since the March 2021 survey, staying positive for four consecutive quarters. The non-manufacturing sector is also on a recovery trend in general, although there are still some difficulties in accommodation and food services, retail and other face-to-face services.

Industrial production has bottomed out after a sharp decline in the first half of 2020, but the pace of recovery is slow and growth is sluggish (Figure 2-4-7). The production index (2015=100) for FY2020 was 91.1, down -8.2% from the previous year, marking the third consecutive year of decline in production, as both domestic and foreign demand declined due to the spread of COVID-19. Although it had been gradually recovering thanks to the normalization of economic activities, the growth has been sluggish since the beginning of FY2021 due to the global shortage of semiconductors.

Capital investment was stagnant in FY2020 due to the impact of COVID-19,

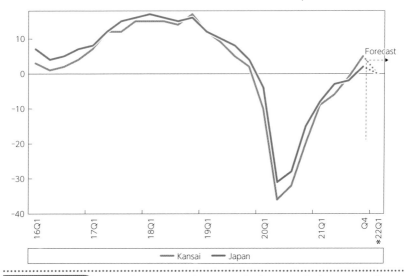

Figure 2-4-6   DI for business conditions (Bank of Japan's Tankan survey, firms of all sizes in all industries)

Note: * denotes outlook.
Source: "Short-term Economic Survey of Corporations", Bank of Japan, Osaka Branch

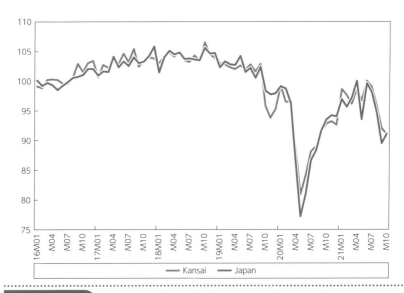

Figure 2-4-7   Index of industrial production (seasonally adjusted, 2015=100)

Source: "Kinki Region Industrial Production Trends", Kinki Bureau of Economy, Trade and Industry

but is expected to increase significantly in FY2021. According to the Bank of Japan's Tankan survey conducted in December 2021, Kansai firms' planned capital investment in FY2021 (firms of all sizes in all industries) are expected to increase by +9.2% YoY (Table 2-4-1). By industry, it is expected to increase by +11.3% in the manufacturing sector, and by +7.9% in the non-manufacturing sector. The actual figure for FY 2020 was -0.2%, the first time in five years that planned capital investment in Kansai declined YoY. However, compared to the -8.5% decline in Japan as a whole, Kansai's economy fared better.

| Table 2-4-1 | Planned Capital Investment (Bank of Japan Tankan Survey) |

	Kansai			Japan		
	All indus-tries	Manufac-turing	Non-manu-facturing	All indus-tries	Manufac-turing	Non-manu-facturing
FY 2020	-0.2	-1.3	0.6	-8.5	-10.0	-7.5
FY 2021	9.2	11.3	7.9	7.9	11.6	5.7

Source: "Nationwide Survey of Enterprises and the Short-Term Economic Outlook for the Kansai Region", Bank of Japan, Osaka Branch.)

(3) External sector: Exports and imports of goods are recovering after deteriorating in FY2020, but inbound tourism demand remains non-existent

In FY2020, the external sector of the Kansai region showed a weak trend. Both the exports and imports of goods contracted. However, the decline was moderate compared to the rest of Japan due to the strong performance of exports to China. Since the beginning of FY2021, economic activity in Europe and the United States has normalized, so trade is recovering. On the other hand, the exports of services (i.e., inbound tourism demand), remains non-existent.

Looking at the status of Kansai's international trade in FY2020, both exports and imports shrank (Figure 2-4-8). Exports totaled JPY 15,711.3 billion, down -2.7% from the previous year, marking the third consecutive year of decline. Although the exports of electronic components, such as semiconductors increased, the decline in the exports of mineral fuels and steel had a significant negative impact. Imports totaled JPY 13,249.7 billion, down -8.0% from the previous year, marking the second consecutive year of decline. The import of crude oil, natural gas and manufactured gas decreased. Pharmaceutical products increased due to the import of vaccines. The trade balance, i.e. exports minus imports, was JPY +2,489.8 billion, logging a surplus for the seventh year in a row. Compared to Japan as a whole (exports down -8.4%, imports down -10.0%), the decline in Kansai was moderate. This is because China is normalizing its

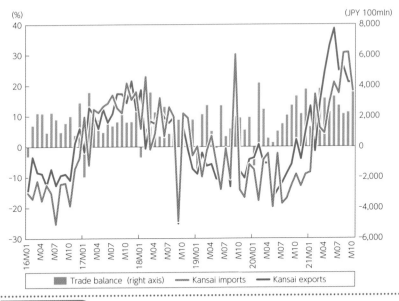

Figure 2-4-8   Exports, Imports and Trade Balance

Source: "Trade in the Kansai Region", Osaka Customs

economic activities ahead of Europe and the U.S., and Kansai's share of trade with China is larger than that of Japan as a whole.

In this regard, we take a closer look at exports by region. Exports to the U.S. fell by -11.7% YoY and those to the EU by -6.5%, both declining for the second year in a row, while those to Asia rose for the first time in three years, by +1.9% YoY (Figure 2-4-9). In particular, exports to China grew at a high rate of +9.9%. China-bound exports began to recover ahead of those to Europe and the U.S., surpassing the previous year's level in June 2020 and growing since then (as of November 2021).

Next, we a look at service exports. Inbound tourism demand has almost disappeared. According to the Ministry of Justice's "Immigration Statistics," the number of foreign visitors to Japan in FY2020 was 324,000. Of this number, 53,000 entered Japan through Kansai International Airport (Figure 2-4-10). As of December 2021, the global COVID-19 scourge has not been halted, and new variants (Omicron) are spreading. Therefore, there is no prospect of resumption of travel for tourism purposes within FY 2021.

Similar to the number of foreign visitors to Japan, duty-free sales also faced a difficult situation in FY2020 (Figure 2-4-11). According to the Osaka Branch of the Bank of Japan, duty-free sales in department stores in Kansai in FY2020 decreased by -87.3% YoY, marking the second consecutive year of decline. The level is extremely low, and there are still no prospects for recovery.

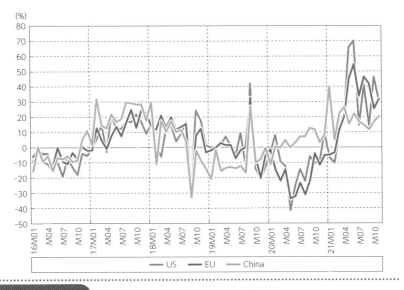

| Figure 2-4-9 | Exports by region (year-on-year change) |

Source: Osaka Customs

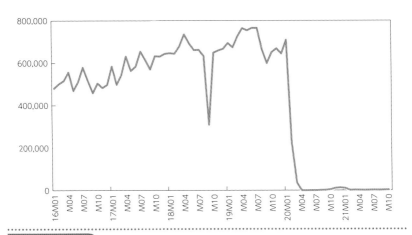

| Figure 2-4-10 | Number of international visitors to Japan (persons) |

Source: "Immigration Statistics," Ministry of Justice

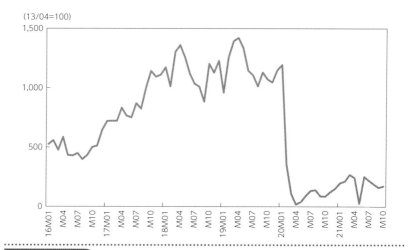

Figure 2-4-11   Department Store Duty Free Sales (April 2013=100)

Source: "Department Store Duty Free Sales (Kansai Region)," Bank of Japan, Osaka Branch

(4) Public sector: Public works steady in FY2020, decline in FY2021

The value of public works contracts remained stable in FY2020 (Figure 2-4-12). The contract amount for public works was JPY 1,713.1 billion, an increase of +6.2% YoY, marking the second consecutive year of growth.

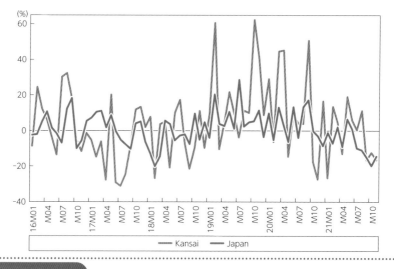

Figure 2-4-12   Contract amount of public works (YoY)

Source: Statistics on Public Works Advance Payment Guarantees, East Japan Construction Guarantee Co.

2. Forecasts for Kansai's Economy: FY 2021-2023

Here, we present our economic forecast for the Kansai region for FY2020 through FY2023 (Table 2-4-2 and Figure 2-4-13). This forecast is based on the latest economic indicators in and outside the Kansai region, including the second advance GDP estimate for 2021 Q3, and our forecast for the Japanese economy presented in Section 3.

Table 2-4-2   APIR's Forecast for Kansai's Economy

FY	Kansai					Japan				
	2019	2020	2021	2022	2023	2019	2020	2021	2022	2023
Private final consumption expenditure	▲ 1.0	▲ 5.9	2.0	2.2	1.1	▲ 1.0	▲ 5.5	2.5	2.3	0.8
Private residential investment	▲ 0.9	▲ 1.8	0.2	0.5	1.3	2.6	▲ 7.8	▲ 0.6	▲ 0.8	1.2
private non-residential investment	0.5	▲ 5.0	1.1	3.2	2.3	▲ 0.6	▲ 7.5	1.7	3.4	3.8
Government final consumption expenditure	1.6	3.0	2.8	1.8	0.9	2.1	2.5	2.3	1.5	0.9
Public investment	1.2	4.7	1.0	2.8	2.5	1.6	5.1	▲ 5.7	2.9	1.9
Exports	0.6	▲ 2.9	7.9	5.7	4.9	▲ 2.2	▲ 10.5	11.6	4.6	5.5
Imports	0.3	▲ 1.7	4.9	4.8	4.3	0.2	▲ 6.6	6.3	2.6	3.5
Real GRP/GDP	▲ 0.2	▲ 3.9	2.8	2.8	1.8	▲ 0.7	▲ 4.5	2.7	2.6	1.7
Private demand (contribution)	▲ 0.7	▲ 4.4	1.2	1.7	1.1	▲ 0.7	▲ 4.7	1.7	1.8	1.0
Public demand (contribution)	0.4	0.7	0.6	0.5	0.3	0.5	0.8	0.2	0.5	0.3
Net exports (contribution)	0.1	▲ 0.3	1.1	0.6	0.4	▲ 0.4	▲ 0.7	0.9	0.4	0.4
Nominal GRP/GDP	0.8	▲ 3.2	2.1	3.3	2.4	0.2	▲ 3.9	1.8	3.1	2.2
GRP/GDP deflator	1.0	0.7	▲ 0.7	0.5	0.6	0.8	0.7	▲ 0.9	0.5	0.4
Consumer price index	0.6	▲ 0.2	0.0	0.8	0.7	0.6	▲ 0.4	0.0	0.9	0.6
Indices of Industrial Production	▲ 4.5	▲ 8.2	6.3	3.5	3.0	▲ 3.8	▲ 9.5	6.1	3.5	2.4
Unemployment rate	2.6	3.1	3.1	3.1	3.0	2.3	2.9	2.8	2.8	2.6

Note: Unit= %. Figures for all components except 'Total unemployment rate' are growth rates.
Source: Compiled by the authors.

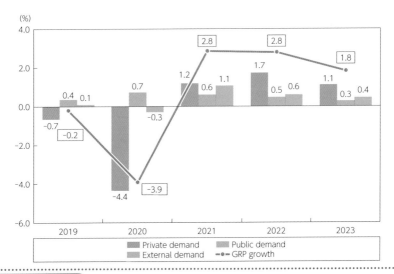

Figure 2-4-13   GRP forecast and contributions to growth

Note: FY2019-2020 are actual forecasts; FY2021-2023 are forecasts.

(1) Real GRP growth forecast: +2.8% in FY2021, +2.8% in FY2022, +1.8% in FY2023

After two consecutive years of contraction in FY2019 and FY2020, Kansai's economy will begin to recover in FY2021. However, the recovery will be modest compared to the large decline in FY2020, due to the sluggish growth in consumption caused by the prolonged state of emergency. The pre-pandemic level will not be achieved until FY2022.

Look at the contributions to the GRP growth rate (Figure 2-4-13). In FY2021, private demand will contribute to growth for the first time in four years, by +1.2%pt, while public demand and external demand will support growth by +0.6%pt and +1.1%pt, respectively. Similarly, in FY2022, all three components will contribute to growth, private demand by +1.7%pt, public demand by +0.5%pt, and external demand by +0.6%pt. In FY2023, the contributions of all three components will remain positive, but they will be smaller: +1.1%pt by private demand, +0.3%pt by public demand, and +0.4%pt by external demand.

Comparing the forecasts for Kansai and Japan (Figure 2-4-14), Kansai's economy is expected to outperform the nation as a whole from FY2021 onward. In FY2021, the contribution of private demand will be smaller than that of Japan, as the economic share of the regions under a state of emergency in Kansai was higher than the nationwide share. On the other hand, the contribution of public

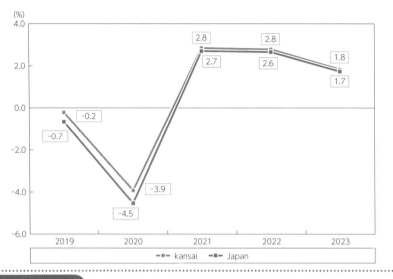

Figure 2-4-14   Economic Growth Rates in Kansai and in Japan

Source: Compiled by the authors

demand and external demand will be somewhat larger in Kansai. The contribution of external demand in FY2022 and that of private demand in FY2023 is expected to be larger in Kansai than in Japan as a whole.

(2) Key points by sector
(2-1) Private sector: First positive contribution to growth in four years in FY2021

The contribution of private demand to GRP growth will be 1.2%pt in FY2021, 1.7%pt in FY2022, and 1.1%pt in FY2023, marking the first positive contribution in four years in FY2021, followed by three consecutive years of growth.

Therein, the household sector consists of real private final consumption expenditure and real private residential investment. Growth in real private final consumption expenditure is forecast to be +2.0% in FY2021, +2.2% in FY22, and +1.1% in FY2023. Private consumption has declined for three consecutive years since FY2018, but in FY2021 it will exceed the previous year's level for the first time in four years. However, this is a rather low growth rate for a recovery, considering the large decline in the previous year. Real private residential investment growth is forecast to be +0.2% in FY2021, +0.5% in FY2022, and +1.3% in FY2023.

Concerning the corporate sector, we forecast that real private non-residential investment will grow by +1.1% in FY2021, +3.2% in FY2022, and +2.3% in FY2023.

(2-2) Public sector: contribution to growth through expenditures related to COVID-19 measures.

The contribution of public demand to real GRP growth will be +0.6%pt in FY2021, +0.5%pt in FY2022, and +0.3%pt in FY2023. The public sector will provide solid support to growth.

Real government final consumption expenditure growth is expected to increase by +2.8% in FY2021, +1.8% in FY2022, and +0.9% in FY2023. It will be boosted by spending related to COVID-19 measures. Real public investment is expected to grow by +1.0% in FY2021, +2.8% in FY2022, and +2.5% in FY2023. In our forecast of the Japanese economy, public investment is expected to slow down to -5.7% in FY2021. However, in consideration of the current trends, our forecast for Kansai assumes a slight increase.

(2-3) External sector: both exports and imports expected to grow steadily, with net exports contributing to growth.

The external sector consists of international trade (exports minus imports) and the extra-regional trade (economic transactions with other regions in Japan). The contribution of external demand to real GRP growth will be +1.1%pt in FY2021, +0.6%pt in FY2022, and +0.4%pt in FY2023.

In terms of international transactions, we forecast that real exports will grow by +7.9% in FY2021, +5.7% in FY2022, and +4.9% in FY2023. In FY2021, exports will increase for the first time in two years. Real import growth is forecast to be +4.9% in FY2021, +4.8% in FY2022, and +4.3% in FY2023. As a result, the contribution of net international exports to Kansai's real GRP growth will be +1.0%pt in FY2021, +0.5%pt in FY2022, and +0.4%pt in FY2023. On the other hand, the contribution of real net domestic exports, which are transactions with other regions in Japan, is forecast to be +0.1%pt in FY2021, +0.1%pt in FY2022, and +0.1%pt in FY2023.

(2-4) Employment environment: unemployment will hover around 3%, higher than the pre-pandemic level

The employment environment is expected to remain severe for some time due to the rapid deterioration of the economy and restrictions on social and economic activities caused by the state of emergency. The unemployment rate, which had remained in the 2% range until FY2019, worsened to 3.1% in FY2020. It is forecasted to remain 3.1% in FY2021 and FY2022, before improving slightly to

3.0% in FY2023.

3. Estimates of Kansai prefectures' GRPs: FY2019-2020

The release of the GRP figures ("Prefectural Accounts") for each prefecture is usually delayed by about two years compared to the release of the national GDP. In consideration of that, APIR has been making its own early estimates of the actual GRPs for the six Kansai prefectures for the fiscal years for which data is not yet available. In this section, we present our estimations up to FY2020.

Table 2-4-3 summarizes our estimates. The total real GRP of the six Kansai prefectures is estimated at JPY 83.51 trillion in FY2019 and JPY 80.23 trillion in FY2020. The real GRP growth rate is respectively -0.2% in FY2019 and -3.9% in FY2020. FY2019 was the first negative growth in five years, as was the case with Japan as a whole (-0.7%), and FY2020 was be the second consecutive year of negative growth, although the decline rate was somewhat smaller than that of the Japanese economy as a whole (-4.5%).

Table 2-4-3   Summary of Advance Estimates and Very Short-Term Forecasts

	Osaka	Hyogo	Kyoto	Shiga	Nara	Wakayama	Kansai	Japan
Goodness of fit								
Adjusted R-square	0.93	0.95	0.80	0.67	0.75	0.77	-	-
GRP level MAPE(%)	0.39	0.36	1.08	1.84	0.77	0.88	-	-
GRP growth MAPE(%)	0.71	0.68	1.72	2.06	1.13	1.49	-	-
Durbin-Watson statistic	2.47	3.07	2.41	1.52	1.93	2.80	-	-
Real GRP(JPY trillion)								
FY2018 (actual value)	38.98	20.61	10.36	6.61	3.64	2.44	83.64	554.35
FY2019 (estimate)	39.24	20.56	10.17	6.59	3.60	3.35	83.51	551.47
FY2020 (estimate)	37.73	19.67	9.85	6.28	3.54	3.16	80.23	525.85
Real GRP growth rate (%)								
FY2018 (actual value)	0.1	-0.4	-0.6	1.2	1.6	3.5	0.2	0.2
FY2019 (estimate)	0.7	-0.3	-1.8	-0.4	-1.1	-2.6	-0.2	-0.7
FY2020 (estimate)	-3.9	-4.3	-3.2	-4.6	-1.7	-5.6	-3.9	-4.5
Contribution to real GRP growth(%)								
FY2018 (actual value)	0.1	-0.1	-0.1	0.1	0.1	0.1	0.2	-
FY2019 (estimate)	0.3	-0.1	-0.2	0.0	0.0	-0.1	-0.2	-
FY2020 (estimate)	-1.8	-1.1	-0.4	-0.4	-0.1	-0.2	-3.9	-

Note: MAPE stands for Mean Absolute Percentage Error.
Source: Compiled by the author

Part I

Part II

Part III

Part IV

The growth rate of Kansai's economy (calculated by summing up the real GRPs of its prefecture) in FY2008 and FY2009, the period of recession caused by the Global Financial Crisis, was -3.1% and -4.2% respectively. On a single-year basis, the impact of COVID-19 in FY2020 is comparable to that of the Global Financial Crisis.

A look at the contribution of each prefecture to Kansai's economy as a whole (Figure 2-4-15) shows that while the real GDP growth rate of the Japanese economy slowed to -0.7% in FY2019, Osaka Prefecture was the only prefecture in Kansai to maintain positive growth. However, Kansai prefectures other than Osaka likely posted negative growth. Hyogo and Kyoto prefectures experienced negative growth for three consecutive years starting in FY2018.

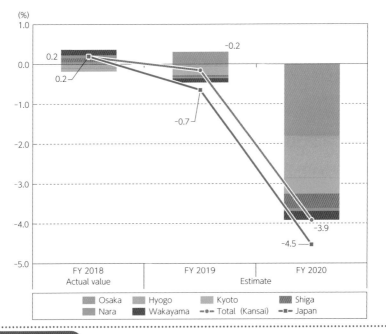

Figure 2-4-15   Contributions by Prefectures to Kansai's real GDP growth

Source: Compiled by the author

Chapter 3

STRUCTURAL CHANGES IN KANSAI'S ECONOMY DUE TO THE COVID-19 PANDEMIC

Section 1
MIGRATION DYNAMICS IN OSAKA PREFECTURE DURING THE COVID-19 PANDEMIC

NOMURA, Ryosuke; KINOSHITA, Yusuke

1. Introduction

According to the National (Population and Housing) Census (preliminary figures) published in June 2021 by the Ministry of Internal Affairs and Communications (MIC), the total population of Japan as of October 1, 2020, decreased 0.7% from 2015 to 126.2 million people, but the rate of decrease (2015/10: –0.8%) was slightly smaller than that of the previous Census. This was due to an increase in the number of foreigners living in Japan and an increase in the number of Japanese who returned to Japan from abroad due to the spread of COVID-19 infection, although the natural decrease in the number of deaths exceeding the number of births increased[1]. By prefecture, the population of Tokyo increased 4.1% from the previous Census, exceeding 14 million people for the first time and accounting for approximately 11% of the nationwide population. On the other hand, Kansai was down 0.8% from last time to 20.5 million. Within Kansai, the population increase rate declined in Shiga prefecture while Osaka changed from a decrease to an increase, and the remaining prefectures increased their decrease rates (Table 3-1-1).

While the population continues to decrease in Japan, a state of emergency declaration was issued four times due to COVID-19, forcing people to significantly modify their behavior. The flow of people was suppressed in an effort to control the spread of infections, which had a great impact on migration dynamics. In particular, while net migration to Tokyo where population is concentrated

---

1) See The Yomiuri Shimbun (2021).

Table 3-1-1	Population increase/decrease in the six prefectures of Kansai, Tokyo, and nationwide		

Prefecture	Total : thousands people	Increase-decrease rates (2020/15) : %	Increase-decrease rates (2015/10) : %
Shiga	1,414	0.09	0.15
Kyoto	2,580	-1.17	-0.98
Osaka	8,843	0.03	-0.29
Hyogo	5,469	-1.19	-0.95
Nara	1,325	-2.85	-2.60
Wakayama	923	-4.21	-3.85
Kansai	20,554	-0.83	-0.85
Tokyo	14,065	4.07	2.70
Nationwide	126,227	-0.68	-0.75

Source: Created by the author based on the Statistics Bureau, the Ministry of Internal Affairs and Communications' (MIC) 2020 National (Population and Housing) Census and 2015 National (Population and Housing) Census.

shrank, net migration to Osaka increased, showing different dynamics. Looking at the migration dynamics of 2021 by month, we see changes in the migration dynamics due to the COVID-19 pandemic, such as the trend of a net loss continuing in Tokyo, with the population decreasing for four consecutive months to 14,037,872 as of September 1[2].

Thus in this section, we will focus mainly on Osaka and provide an outline and analysis of how the trend in migration dynamics over the last few years has changed due to the impact of the COVID-19 pandemic. We will also look at how the four state of emergency declarations impacted migration dynamics on a monthly basis.

2. Change in Migration Dynamics in Osaka Prefecture

(1) Change in Migration Dynamics in 2020: Tokyo vs. Osaka

Before looking at the migration dynamics in Osaka Prefecture, let's look at the situation in Tokyo. According to MIC's Report on Internal Migration in Japan Derived from the Basic Resident Registration, in 2020, in-migrants to Tokyo were 432,930 and out-migrants were 401,805. As a result, net migration was 31,125, down 51,857 from 2019. This was the lowest since 2014 when they began including foreign nationals in their records, showing a shift away from the social structure of so-called "overconcentration in Tokyo" up until that time (Figure 3-1-1). Possible factors include people not being able to move to advance into higher education or to start a new job due to the state of emergency declaration,

---

2) See Nikkei (2021-b).

etc., and an increase in people moving out of Tokyo due to the spread of tele-working.

Next, looking at the situation in Osaka Prefecture, in-migrants were 172,563 and out-migrants were 159,207. As a result, net migration was 13,356, up 5,292 from 2019. Looking at the trend, since shifting to net migration in 2015, net migration has continued for six consecutive years (Figure 3-1-2). In Kansai, inbound tourism demand has increased mainly centered on Osaka since 2014,

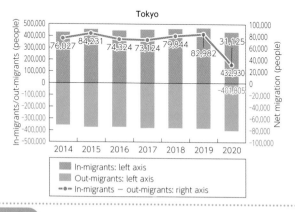

Figure 3-1-1   Shifts in in-migrants and out-migrants in Tokyo: 2014–2020

Note: Includes foreign migrants.
Source: Created by the author based on the Ministry of Internal Affairs and Communications' (MIC) Report on Internal Migration in Japan Derived from the Basic Resident Registration.

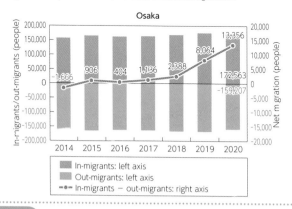

Figure 3-1-2   Shifts in in-migrants and out-migrants in Osaka: 2014–2020

Note: Includes foreign migrants.
Source: Created by the author based on the Ministry of Internal Affairs and Communications' (MIC) Report on Internal Migration in Japan Derived from the Basic Resident Registration.

which may have led to people working in services such as restaurants and accommodation[3]. However, in 2020, due to the impact of the COVID-19 pandemic, both in-migrants and out-migrants decreased for the first time in four years. The decrease in out-migrants was greater than that of in-migrants, resulting in net migration.

(2) Migration Dynamics in Osaka Prefecture: Characteristics by Region and Age Group: 2018 to 2020

First, let's look at the characteristics of migration dynamics in Osaka Prefecture by region. Figure 3-1-3 shows net migration in Osaka by region[4].

As shown in the figure, net migration from Kansai was the largest, increasing from 6,293 in 2018 to 8,385 in 2019. In 2020, even though the flow of people was suppressed due to COVID-19, net migration was 10,665, increasing further from 2019.

The migration dynamics within Southern Kanto show a continuing net loss trend although contracting somewhat, from 12,116 in 2018 to 11,852 in 2019. In 2020, it contracted even more to 8,567. The fact that relocations for higher education or to start a new job were restricted due to the state of emergency declarations, etc., may have played a role.

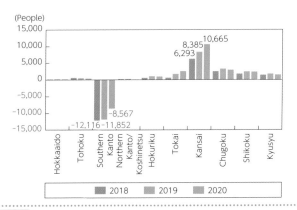

Figure 3-1-3   Comparison of net migration in Osaka by region: 2018–2020

Note: Includes foreign migrants. For Kansai, migration within Osaka Prefecture is excluded.
Source: Created by the author based on the Ministry of Internal Affairs and Communications' (MIC) Report on Internal Migration in Japan Derived from the Basic Resident Registration.

3) The high employment capacity of these industries is described in detail in Chapter 4 Section 4 of this book.
4) The regional classifications are in accordance with the definitions by MIC. Kinki has been changed to Kansai. (https://www.soumu.go.jp/main_content/000611949.pdf)

In other regions, net migration increased in Chugoku, Shikoku, and Kyusyu from 2018 to 2019, but it somewhat decreased in 2020. It is possible that migrants from far away were also influenced by the above-mentioned factors, such as the issuing of the state of emergency declarations.

Next, let's look at the change in net migration over time by age group (Table 3-1-2).

The age group with the most net migration in 2018 was the 20 to 24 group, with 4,472 in Kansai, 1,710 in Chugoku, 1,364 in Kyusyu, and 1,299 in Shikoku.

Furthermore, in 2019, net migration in the 20 to 24 age group in the four regions above all increased compared to in 2018. Additionally, net migration in the 25 to 29 age group also increased, with Kyusyu shifting from a net loss in 2018 to net migration.

However, looking at the net migration for the 20 to 24 age group in 2020,

Table 3-1-2	Net migration and net loss by age group and region: 2018–2020: Osaka Prefecture

(Unit : people)

2018										
Age	Nationwide	Hokkaido	Tohoku	Southern Kanto	Northern Kanto / Koshinetsu	Hokuriku	Tokai	Kansai	Chugoku	Shikoku	Kyusyu
Total	2,388	189	642	-12,116	218	606	636	6,293	2,569	1,845	1,506
15-19	2,034	8	52	-902	31	123	199	336	597	545	1,045
20-24	5,778	96	182	-3,904	2	449	108	4,472	1,710	1,299	1,364
25-29	548	103	128	-2,897	46	135	-190	2,704	268	299	-48
2019										
Age	Nationwide	Hokkaido	Tohoku	Southern Kanto	Northern-Kanto/ Koshinetsu	Hokuriku	Tokai	Kansai	Chugoku	Shikoku	Kyusyu
Total	8,064	253	553	-11,852	278	1,064	1,739	8,385	3,321	2,504	1,819
15-19	2,344	46	46	-708	-22	126	260	362	640	605	989
20-24	6,783	65	154	-4,332	82	557	360	4,710	2,007	1,648	1,532
25-29	2,327	149	136	-2,748	46	187	284	3,382	434	263	194
2020										
Age	Nationwide	Hokkaido	Tohoku	Southern Kanto	Northern-Kanto/ Koshinetsu	Hokuriku	Tokai	Kansai	Chugoku	Shikoku	Kyusyu
Total	13,356	199	420	-8,567	82	986	2,585	10,665	3,002	2,448	1,536
15-19	2,846	24	53	-516	25	114	352	633	591	669	901
20-24	8,768	121	181	-4,018	68	652	634	6,392	1,901	1,549	1,288
25-29	3,737	65	67	-2,143	50	143	466	4,160	402	307	220

Note: Includes foreign migrants. For Kansai, migration within Osaka Prefecture is excluded.
Source: Created by the author based on the Ministry of Internal Affairs and Communications' (MIC) Report on Internal Migration in Japan Derived from the Basic Resident Registration.

Part I

Part II

Part III

Part IV

Kansai saw an increase while Chugoku, Shikoku, and Kyusyu saw decreases.

Meanwhile, looking at the situation for southern Kanto, there was an out-flow of the younger age group, with net loss increasing from 2018 to 2019 for the 20 to 24 age group. However, due to the effect of the COVID-19 pandemic suppressing the flow of people, the net loss to Southern Kanto in the above age group decreased in 2020.

From the above, we can see the net migration to Osaka is mainly from west-ern Japan and that many of the migrants are from a generation that move for work. This is possibly due to Osaka having been supported by strong inbound tourism demand, which increased the number of people working in the ser-vice industry. However, due to the flow of people being limited as a measure to prevent the spread of COVID-19, in-migrants, particularly those in the younger generation, decreased.

(2) Migration Dynamics within Osaka Prefecture

Having discussed the characteristics of the migration dynamics by region and by age group, we will now look at them by municipality in Osaka Prefecture. During the three years from 2018 to 2020, 16 municipalities experienced net migration while 27 municipalities experienced a net loss in Osaka Prefecture. Among them, net migration to Osaka City expanded from 12,081 in 2018 to 13,762 in 2019 and 16,802 in 2020. Migration dynamics vary depending on the area within Osaka Prefecture. Many of the municipalities with net migration are in the northern part of Osaka Prefecture, with more areas having an increase in net migration. Meanwhile, many of the municipalities with a net loss are in the southern part of Osaka Prefecture, with a continuing trend of a net loss.

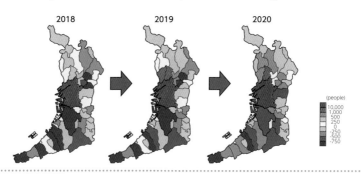

| Figure 3-1-4 | Comparison of net migration by municipality: 2018–2020 |

Note: Includes foreign migrants.
Source: Created by the author based on the Ministry of Internal Affairs and Communications' (MIC) Report on Internal Migration in Japan Derived from the Basic Resident Registration

Thus, Osaka Prefecture as a whole may show net migration, but by municipality, net migration figures vary between the Osaka City area, and the northern and southern areas (Figure 3-1-4).

3. Impact of the Declaration of State of Emergency on Migration Dynamics

In the previous section, we looked at the migration dynamics during the COVID-19 pandemic by region and age group on an annual basis. In this section, we will look at the impact of the state of emergency declarations, which were issued four times, on the migration dynamics of Osaka Prefecture on a monthly

Table 3-1-3 Comparison of in-migration/out-migration situation by gender during the state of emergency declaration in Osaka Prefecture

(Unit: people)

Men	In-migrants	Out-migrants	Net migration (loss)	In-migrants: Difference from same period (month) in previous year	Out-migrants: Difference from same period (month) in previous year	In-migrants: Difference from same period (month) in 2019	Out-migrants: Difference from same period (month) in 2019
1st (Apr to May 2020)	20,548	19,462	1,086	-1,758	-2,963		
2nd (Jan to Feb 2021)	11,541	11,572	-31	81	528	429	138
3rd (2021 Q2)	25,959	26,172	-213	-1,213	556	-2,522	-2,136
4th (Aug to Sep 2021)	11,562	11,528	34	-916	-3	-1,076	-828

Women	In-migrants	Out-migrants	Net migration (loss)	In-migrants: Difference from same period (month) in previous year	Out-migrants: Difference from same period (month) in previous year	In-migrants: Difference from same period (month) in 2019	Out-migrants: Difference from same period (month) in 2019
1st (Apr to May 2020)	15,893	14,285	1,608	-2,738	-3,203		
2nd (Jan to Feb 2021)	9,715	9,625	90	-524	207	-257	104
3rd (2021 Q2)	21,115	20,034	1,081	131	1,076	-2,505	-2,223
4th (Aug to Sep 2021)	9,695	9,743	-48	-479	240	-1,030	-706

Note: Includes foreign migrants.
Source: Created by the author based on the Ministry of Internal Affairs and Communications' (MIC) Report on Internal Migration in Japan Derived from the Basic Resident Registration.

basis (Table 3-1-3).

Looking at April to May of 2020, the period when the first state of emergency declaration was issued for Osaka Prefecture (April 7 to May 21, 2020), there were 20,548 men and 15,893 women in-migrants. April is when in-migrants tend to increase to advance into higher education or to start a new job, but compared to in the same period in the previous year (April to May of 2019), there was a 1,758 decrease in men and 2,738 decrease in women. Similarly, looking at out-migrants, there were 19,462 men (–2,963 YoY) and 14,285 women (–3,203 YoY), both decreasing. In-migrants and out-migrants both decreased significantly, and the impact of restrictions on movement across prefectures due to the issuing of the state of emergency declarations was more apparent among women.

In 2021, state of emergency declarations were issued three times. Looking at the period when it was issued for the second time (January 14 to February 28, 2021), in-migrants for the January to February 2021 period were 11,541 men (+81 YoY) and 9,715 women (–524 YoY), with a bigger decrease among women than men compared to in the previous year. On the other hand, looking at out-migrants for the same period, 11,572 were men (+528 YoY) and 9,625 were women (+207 YoY).

Looking at the in-migrants for 2021 Q2, the period in which the third state of emergency declaration (April 25 to June 20, 2021) was issued, partly due to it being a time to advance into higher education or to start a new job, there were 25,959 men and 21,115 women. However, compared to the same period in the year before the previous year (2019 Q2), when the COVID-19 pandemic had no impact, both men and women decreased significantly, –2,522 and –2,505 respectively. Looking at the out-migrants for the same period, there were 26,172 men (–2,136 YoY) and 20,034 women (–2,223 YoY). Consequently, both men and women saw significant decreases in both in-migrants and out-migrants, but because women finished with net migration (1,081), the overall result remained net migration (868).

During the fourth period (August 2 to September 30, 2021), in-migrants in the August to September period decreased for both men and women, of 11,562 (–1,076 compared to the same period of the year before the previous year) and 9,695 (–1,030 of the same period) respectively. Additionally, out-migrants were 11,528 (–828 of the same period) for men and 9,743 (–706 of the same period) for women, with the decrease in in-migrants greater than that of out-migrants, resulting in a shift to a net loss.

Thus, the state of emergency declarations issued four times have influenced migration dynamics. The impact has varied depending on gender, and in general, it has been greater for women in-migrants.

4. Conclusion

As discussed above, migration dynamics are changing due to the impact of the COVID-19 pandemic. In Tokyo, population is flowing out of Tokyo due to the spread of teleworking, etc. and net migration is shrinking. In Osaka Prefecture, there has been a continuing trend of net migration due to people moving there to work in inbound tourism-related industries that have been strong thus far. However, with inbound tourism demand having vanished today due to the COVID-19 pandemic, service industries such as restaurant and accommodation have been hit hard. The impact can be particularly seen among people in their 20s who move to Osaka Prefecture from western Japan to work in these related industries. Additionally, looking at the municipalities in Osaka Prefecture, an increase in net migration in Osaka City is continuing and in the northern part of Osaka Prefecture, areas that previously had a net loss are shifting to net migration. Meanwhile, in the southern part of Osaka Prefecture, net losses are continuing in many areas and migration dynamics vary between areas.

Moreover, two years has passed since the COVID-19 pandemic began, and the state of emergency declarations issued four times for Osaka Prefecture have had a major impact on migration dynamics.

Despite being affected by the COVID-19 pandemic, the net migration trend of Osaka Prefecture continues. As mentioned earlier, this is largely due to the inflow of population not only into Osaka City, but also into the northern part of Osaka. One of the factors behind the expansion of net migration into the northern area is that it is located in the middle of a key transportation hub facing the east and west to the central part of Osaka Prefecture, neighboring Kyoto Prefecture, etc., and it has convenient transportation and redevelopments of residential areas creating a comfortable living environment for local residents[5].

With many events planned for Osaka Prefecture in the future, including the EXPO Osaka, Kansai, Japan, its migration dynamics will draw more attention. Access to the southern area that has had a net loss until now is expected to improve with the development of a transportation infrastructure network toward the hosting of the EXPO Osaka, Kansai, Japan. With the EXPO Osaka, Kansai, Japan approaching in three and a half years' time, if we can stimulate innovation such as ICT and create new industries and employment to revitalize not only the movement of people between Osaka Prefecture and other prefectures, but also between the north and south within Osaka Prefecture, some impact should be

---

5) Nikkei (2021-a) also refers to the convenient transportation and comfortable living in the northern area of Osaka Prefecture.

visible in the migration dynamics of Osaka Prefecture in the future.

References

Nikkei (2021-a), "Kansai's Population Further Concentrating in City Centers: Marked Increase in Commuter Towns" (Japanese title: *Kansai no Jinko, Toshin Shuchu Ichidan to—Bedtown no Zouka Kencho*), July 16, (https://www.nikkei.com/article/DGXZQOUF2942W0Z20C21A6000000/, last viewed: October 6)

Nikkei (2021-b), "Population in Tokyo in September, Decreased Four Consecutive Months" (Japanese title: *Tokyo no 9 gatsu no Jinko, 4 kagetsu Renzoku de Gensho*), September 30, (https://www.nikkei.com/article/DGXZQOC-C305K00Q1A930C2000000/, last viewed: October 3)

The Yomiuri Shimbun (2021), "Japan's Population 126.22 Million: 2020 National (Population and Housing) Census, Down Twice in a Row" (Japanese title: *Nihon no Jinko 1 oku 2,622 man nin: 20 nen Kokusei Chosa 2 kai Renzoku no Gensho*), June 25, evening edition

Section 2
THE COVID-19 PANDEMIC AND PROBLEMS IN THE MEDICAL CARE PROVISION SYSTEM

FUJIWARA, Yukinori

1. Introduction

In 2020, the world was hit by an unprecedented pandemic. On January 28, 2020, the Japanese government enacted a Cabinet Order for COVID-19 to categorize it as a designated infectious disease under the Act on the Prevention of Infectious Diseases and Medical Care for Patients with Infectious Diseases and took measures to hospitalize infected patients. In the subsequent spread of the infection, there was a concern about the shortage of hospital beds depending on the region, so the national and local governments dealt with the situation by securing hospital beds for critically ill patients and reducing the hospitalization period or by promoting accommodation- and home-based recuperation for patients with no or mild symptoms. Thus, triage measures were undertaken to classify patients according to their medical conditions because hospital beds would be insufficient, which could lead to a medical collapse if patients with no or mild symptoms were hospitalized.

In the background to the issuance of a declaration of a state of emergency four times in Japan, there was a concern about a significant shortage of hospital beds coupled with the shortage and fatigue of health care workers, which could lead to a crisis in which the lives of critically ill patients could not be saved. If this situation continued, there was the risk that the medical care provision system could not be maintained, leading to a collapse of the health care system itself (there was a view that the collapse of the health care system actually occurred). Should the health care system collapse, the death toll from COVID-19 would increase and sufficient treatment of diseases other than COVID-19 infections could be interrupted. This situation had to be absolutely avoided.

This report discusses issues for Japan's medical care provision system that have been revealed in the wake of the COVID-19 pandemic based on data. I believe that this will contribute to a drastic restructuring of the post-COVID-19 medical care provision system in Kansai, as well as in Japan as a whole.

2. Characteristics of the Medical Care Provision System in Japan

(1) Comparison with Other Major Developed Countries

Table 3-2-1 compares the medical care provision systems of Japan and of other major developed countries in Europe and the US based on the statistics of the Organization for Economic Co-operation and Development (OECD).

Japan has the largest number of hospital beds per 1,000 population among the major developed countries. The total number of hospital beds per 1,000 population is 13.0 beds per 1,000 population, which is 4.5 to 5.2 times that of the US and the UK. Hospital beds are unevenly distributed across Japan, and the number is large in rural areas but insufficient in metropolitan areas.

There is no major difference in the number of health care workers (doctors and nurses) on a population basis among developed countries. However, the number of health care workers per 100 hospital beds in Japan is very small compared to other developed countries. The number of doctors per 100 hospital beds in Japan is 2.8 to 6.7 times smaller and the number of nurses per 100 hospital beds in Japan is 1.8 to 4.6 times smaller than that in other developed countries. The small number of health care workers per hospital beds is attributable to the large number of hospital beds in Japan.

Unlike general hospital beds and long-term care hospital beds, infectious disease hospital beds require many health care workers, as well as additional equipment, including mechanical ventilation equipment, blocking equipment, and disinfection facilities for infection prevention. The small number of health care workers per hospital beds hinders the conversion of other beds to and the

| Table 3-2-1 | Comparison of medical care provision systems in major developed countries |

	Total number of hospital beds (per 1,000 population)	Number of doctors (per 1,000 population)	Number of nurses (per 1,000 population)	Number of doctors (per 100 hospital beds)	Number of nurses (per 100 hospital beds)
Japan	13.0	2.5	11.8	19.2	90.6
US	2.9[*1]	2.6	11.9[*3]	91.5	417.0[*3]
Germany	8.0[*1]	4.3	13.2	54.0	165.7
France	5.9	3.2	10.8[*3]	53.7	182.6[*3]
UK	2.5[*2]	3.0[*2]	7.8	120.1[*2]	315.5
Italy	3.1	4.0[*2]	5.6[*2]	127.8[*2]	179.3[*2]

Note 1: *1 shows data for 2017. *2 shows data for 2019.
Note 2: *3 includes nurses who directly care for patients as well as nursing staff engaging in administration, management, research, etc. who do not directly care for patients.
Source: Created based on OECD Health Data 2020 (based on 2018 data).

increase in the number of infectious disease hospital beds. It can be said that since before the COVID-19 pandemic, there have been problems in Japan's medical care provision system to deal with infectious diseases.

(2) Infectious Disease Measures that Have Not Been Deemed Important

The problems in the medical care provision system to deal with infectious diseases existing since before the COVID-19 pandemic are also reflected in the decrease in the number of infectious disease hospital beds and the contraction of the public health center system.

Figure 3-2-1 shows changes in the number of infectious disease hospital beds and the number of infectious disease patients in Japan. Before the COVID-19 pandemic, major nationwide outbreaks of infectious diseases had not occurred in Japan for a long time and the number of infectious disease patients had decreased, so the number of infectious disease hospital beds was significantly reduced in the early 2000s and has remained at a low level since then due to small needs and higher maintenance costs compared to general hospital beds.

The total number of infectious disease hospital beds is small nationwide

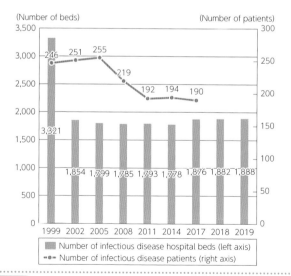

| Figure 3-2-1 | Changes in the number of infectious disease hospital beds and the number of infectious disease patients |

Note 1: The number of infectious disease patients includes parasitic infections.
Note 2: The number of infectious disease patients represents the total number of inpatients and outpatients.
Source: Created based on the results of a survey by the Ministry of Health, Labour and Welfare.

Part I

Part II

Part III

Part IV

and they are unevenly distributed across regions. Figure 3-2-2 shows the number of infectious disease hospital beds per 100,000 population in 19 prefectures where the state of emergency has been declared.

In the prefectures with metropolitan areas, such as Tokyo, Kanagawa, Aichi, Osaka, and Hyogo that had large numbers of COVID-19 infections, the number of infectious disease hospital beds per 100,000 population is at an extremely low level of 1.0 or less.

Public health centers are at the forefront of Japan's response to infectious diseases. With the spread of COVID-19, public health centers are in charge of arranging consultations with medical institutions, taking specimens, performing PCR tests, reporting test results, coordinating hospitalization and accommodation- and home-based recuperation, conducting active epidemiological investigations, and providing follow-up health services (for home recuperators, etc.). In particular, active epidemiological investigations to identify behavioral histories of infected patients are extremely important. However, it has been pointed out that the workload of public health centers has become extremely heavy alongside the spread of the infection.

Both the number of public health centers and their staff in charge of extremely important, heavy workload operations have decreased since the latter half of the 1990s, and the public health center system had become vulnerable

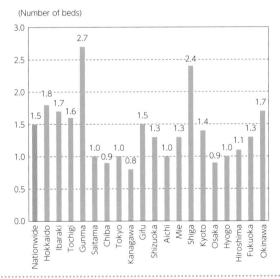

Figure 3-2-2 Number of infectious disease hospital beds per 100,000 population (2019)

Source: Created based on the results of a survey by the Ministry of Health, Labour and Welfare.

since before the COVID-19 pandemic.

There were 850 public health centers nationwide in 1990, which decreased to 469 in 2020 due to consolidation. The number of staff nationwide decreased from 34,571 in 1990 to 27,902 in 2017. Figure 3-2-3 shows the changes in the number of public health centers and the number of staff.

In short, the reason for the decrease in the number of infectious disease hospital beds and the weakened public health center system is because infectious disease measures have not been deemed important due to the small number of infected patients. The background to this is that non-communicable diseases such as cancer have become the main causes of death among Japanese people since the 1960s and infectious diseases are no longer a major concern in terms of medical policy. It can also be added that public interest has shifted to health promotion, disease prevention, rehabilitation, etc., for aging populations.

Experts have pointed out that the reduction of the threat of infectious diseases such as tuberculosis and the decrease in the weight of public health in medical policy, along with the progress of administrative and financial reforms and decentralization reforms from the 1990s, has led to a decrease in the number of infectious disease hospital beds and the weakened public health center

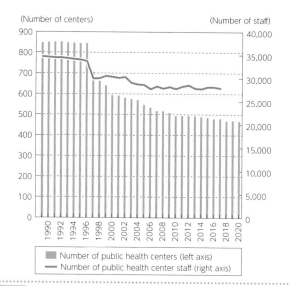

| Figure 3-2-3 | Changes in the number of public health centers and the number of public health center staff |

Note: The source materials do not include data on the number of staff for 2018 and subsequent years.
Source: Created based on the database from the National Institute of Population and Social Security Research and materials from the Ministry of Health, Labour and Welfare.

system[1].

In 2009, the threat of infectious diseases surfaced due to the outbreak of the novel influenza pandemic that affected Japan, and the Report of the Review Meeting on Measures against Pandemic Influenza (A/H1N1) compiled by specialists and experts in June 2010 after the end of the pandemic recommended the strengthening of the medical care provision system by enhancing the public health center system and securing medical staff and equipment for specialized medical institutions that accommodate high-risk patients to address future emerging and re-emerging infectious diseases. However, this recommendation was not fully utilized and overlooked without serious discussion.

3. Problems in the Medical Care Provision System in Japan

(1) Shortage of Health Care Workers per Hospital Beds

The medical care provision system in Japan has had five waves of the rapid spread of COVID-19 infections without sufficient countermeasures in place against infectious diseases, including COVID-19.

As a result, despite the number of infected people per capita being only one tenth that of the US and the UK, Japan encountered a problem of a strained medical care provision system.

The government took steps to support medical institutions to ensure hospital beds for COVID-19 patients and suspected patients. In addition, under the amended Act on the Prevention of Infectious Diseases and Medical Care for Patients with Infectious Diseases enacted in February 2021, prefectural governors were allowed to request medical institutions to secure hospital beds for COVID-19 patients. As this is a legal request, the names of the hospitals would be disclosed if they did not comply with the request. Under the amended Act, Nara Prefecture made the nation's first request to medical institutions in April 2021, followed by Osaka Prefecture and Tokyo. On September 30, 2021, Osaka Prefecture opened the Osaka COVID-19 Large-Scale Medical Care and Recuperation Center for mildly ill patients as a temporary medical facility.

However, it did not provide a sufficient number of hospital beds to accommodate the sharply increased number of COVID-19 patients. In particular, Japan is lagging behind in terms of securing hospital beds, such as ICU beds for critically ill patients on the verge of death who need a ventilator or ECMO (Extracorporeal Membrane Oxygenation) or treatment in the Intensive Care Unit

---

1) Mihara, Takashi (2020)

(ICU) or High Care Unit (HCU)[2]. The number of hospital beds including those in ICUs per 100,000 population is 34.7 in the US, 29.2 in Germany, and 13.5 in Japan which is less than half that of Germany[3]. Therefore, as the number of critically ill patients increases, hospital beds will soon run out.

The essence of the problem identified is not the shortage of hospital beds. As shown in Table 3-2-1, the number of hospital beds in Japan is very large, so inherently the number of health care workers per hospital beds is small. The essence of the problem is the significant shortage of workers in medical institutions identified as accommodating COVID-19 patients who need 24-hour care by a large number of health care workers. It can be said that this is a serious structural problem of the Japanese medical system.

Converting other beds to infectious disease hospital beds is not easy because they require mechanical ventilation, blocking for infection prevention, and other equipment. Even if there are hospital beds, they cannot be utilized without properly trained health care workers, which is also a major problem.

Critically ill patients with COVID-19 take a long time to recover after being admitted to hospitals. They also require advanced medical equipment and devices, as well as careful deployment of health care workers and their careful treatment. Medical institutions that accommodate critically ill COVID-19 patients also need to provide emergency medical care and treatment and surgeries for patients with other serious illnesses. Therefore, it is not surprising that labor shortages become serious.

(2) Dispersion of Special Health Care Workers

In order to save life-threatened, critically ill patients with COVID-19, the involvement of intensive care physicians is essential, in addition to intensive care unit facilities.

The problem of the dispersion of intensive care physicians has already been pointed out by health economics researchers[4]. According to an analysis of hospital bed usage in 341 hospitals that accommodated 5,018 COVID-19 patients in the period from February to June 2020, 62% of the hospitals that accommodated COVID-19 patients had ICUs, and 73% had ECMO, but only 48% had intensive care physicians, and the analysis pointed out that the shortage of human re-

---

2) An intensive care unit is a special unit in a hospital used to provide intensive treatment for critically ill patients who are difficult to treat in a general ward. The high care unit is a unit where patients with a slightly less severe condition than ICU patients are accommodated.
3) Based on the results of the survey conducted by the Ministry of Health, Labour and Welfare (May 2020).
4) Watanabe, Sachiko and Aki, Yoshikawa (2021)

| Table 3-2-2 | Hospitals with intensive care physicians (Kansai) |

Number of intensive care physicians	Number of hospitals					
	Shiga	Kyoto	Osaka	Hyogo	Nara	Wakayama
15–21	0	0	2	0	0	0
10–14	1	2	1	2	0	0
5–9	0	3	8	3	2	0
2–4	3	2	16	10	1	2
1	4	11	22	12	3	1

Source: Created based on the materials published on the website of the Japanese Society of Intensive Care Medicine.

sources was the bottleneck rather than the hardware.

Next, let's look at the deployment status of intensive care physicians belonging to medical institutions in six prefectures in Kansai based on the registration list published on the website of the Japanese Society of Intensive Care Medicine (Table 3-2-2).

As shown in Table 3-2-2, intensive care physicians are dispersed in Osaka, Hyogo, and Kyoto Prefectures with a large number of infected people. Of particular concern is that many medical institutions, of 22 hospitals in Osaka, 12 in Hyogo Prefecture, and 11 in Kyoto Prefecture, have only 1 intensive care physician per hospital.

When critically ill COVID-19 patients who require ECMO are admitted, they need specialists and 24-hour continuous care, and it is very difficult for a single doctor to deal with this. At least two specialists need to be assigned to respond to unexpected circumstances as well. In addition, in order to ensure the quality of advanced medical care and to increase the number of lives that can be saved, it is better to concentrate in one place a limited number of specialists for treatment.

The Osaka Covid-19 Critical Care Center that began operations on December 15, 2020, has been highly evaluated in that it concentrates in one place specialists and nurses with experience in intensive care for patients on ventilators. Going forward, it will be an important issue to promote the concentration of specialists over a wide area across prefectures in the Kansai region.

4. Establishing a Medical Care Provision System, Taking into Account Emergency Situations

Through its response to COVID-19, we learned how vulnerable Japan's medical care provision system is to infectious diseases that could cause pandemics. The issues revealed include inherent structural problems coupled with insufficient responses to COVID-19.

As with other large-scale disasters, it is necessary to position the spread of an infectious disease as an emergency (situation) in which medical demand greatly exceeds the medical supply capacity and to develop a medical care provision system accordingly in the future, including what should be prepared during normal times and how to respond to an emergency situation quickly and flexibly.

In the medium to long term, population decline and aging are projected to continue. Taking into account changes in the structure of diseases, we need to promote differentiation and coordination of hospital bed functions to maintain a high-quality and efficient medical care provision system to meet future medical demand. In that sense, Community Health Care Visions[5] need to be steadily promoted by prefectures during normal times.

On the other hand, based on the lessons from COVID-19, responses to emerging infectious diseases must be clearly defined in prefectural Medical Care Plans[6]. It is also necessary to develop specialized human resources and secure advanced medical facilities, while cooperating with local hospital associations and medical associations, and formulate measures to convert other beds to infectious disease care beds and to concentrate and coordinate specialized health care workers across medical institutions during normal times to prepare for emergency situations[7]. It is important to build a mechanism to flexibly switch to emergency medical care while maintaining a balance with general medical care.

Similar to the idea of redundancy in disaster countermeasures, there may be an idea that it is necessary to maintain empty hospital beds as a buffer for infectious disease measures. But since there is a positive correlation between the number of hospital beds and medical expenses per person, this idea must be carefully examined to avoid imposing a heavy financial burden on the public during normal times.

In FY 2023, the 8th Medical Care Plan (FY 2024–FY 2029) is scheduled

---

5) Community Health Care Visions are the visions of the medical care provision system that should be aimed at based on the demand for health care in 2025 and that had been formulated by all prefectures by the end of FY 2016. General beds and long-term care beds are covered by the Visions, but not infectious disease hospital beds.

6) Medical Care Plans are formulated by each prefecture to ensure the medical care provision system in each prefecture. The Plans intend to manage the medical care provision in terms of quantity (the number of hospital beds) and evaluate quality (medical coordination, medical safety).

7) In the revised Medical Care Act enacted on May 21, 2021, it was decided to clearly define matters related to ensuring the medical care provision system in the event of the spread of emerging and other infectious diseases in the Medical Care Plans.

to be formulated in each prefecture, so we expect the medical care provision system to be reviewed and examined with emergency situations in mind. The government should provide the necessary support along with strengthening the system of public health centers.

Now that socio-economic activities are once again becoming widespread, infectious disease measures may not be sufficient on a prefectural basis alone. Kansai is one of the advanced areas in terms of wide-area medical cooperation across prefectures that is currently required. On March 15, 2020, the Union of Kansai Governments decided to promote wide-area supply coordination of pharmaceuticals, medical equipment, and medical professionals; wide-area cooperation for medical testing; and wide-area patient acceptance system.

In addition, since ICT networking has been delayed in Japanese medical care, it is also important to build a network that connects individual hospitals so that the government and medical care and emergency-related organizations can identify the availability of hospital beds, including ICU beds, in individual hospitals online at any time.

Finally, Figure 3-2-4 is a diagram that explains the medical care provision system during normal times and during an emergency. In an emergency situation when an infectious disease spreads, it is expected that the treatment effect will be improved by setting up separate wards and dedicated hospitals

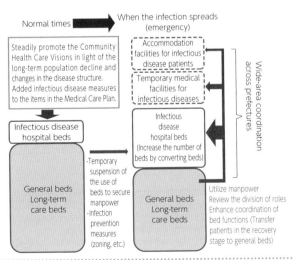

Figure 3-2-4   Medical care provision systems at normal times and in emergencies (Image diagram)

Source: Created based on the materials (dated December 25, 2020) of the Healthcare Subcommittee, Social Security Council, Ministry of Health, Labour and Welfare.

and concentrating[8] specialized health care workers and critically ill patients in them. At the same time, patients who have entered a recovery stage need to be transferred to general beds in other hospitals. In order to achieve that, wide-area coordination of hospital beds across prefectures may be required[9].

By concentrating medical resources and promoting the division of roles and cooperation across medical institutions, medical resources such as hospital beds and health care workers can be effectively utilized. Since saving as many lives as possible improves people's sense of security, information should be provided to the public at any time it is necessary and the mechanism for switching between normal and emergency medical care provision systems should be visualized.

References

Mihara, Takashi (2020), Why have infectious disease measures been overlooked?, a report issued by the NLI Research Institute, September 2020

Ministry of Health, Labour and Welfare (2010), Report of the Review Meeting on Measures against Pandemic Influenza (A/H1N1), June 2010

Ministry of Health, Labour and Welfare, the Committee for the Revision of the Medical Care Plan (2020), Ideas for building the future medical care provision system based on measures against the novel coronavirus infection, December 2020

Neil A. Halpern & Kay See Tan (2020), "United States Resource Availability for COVID-19," Society of Critical Care Medicine, 5/12/2020

Watanabe, Sachiko and Yoshikawa, Aki (2021), The truth of the collapse of medical care (Japanese title: *Iryo Hokai no Shinjitsu*), MdN Corporation, January 2021

---

8) It is the same idea as that of the Society of Critical Care Medicine (SCCM) that recommends implementing a "tiered staffing model" with intensive care staff at the top during a pandemic (Neil A. Halpern & Kay See Tan (2020)).

9) Fundamentally, the government should consider a system that allows it to give direct and strong instructions to medical institutions and local governments regarding hospital bed coordination.

Section 3
THE UTILIZATION OF DX IN KANSAI:
OPPORTUNITIES AND RISKS FOR FIRMS

OSHIMA, Hisanori

1. Introduction

DX is the abbreviation of "digital transformation" and broadly means business model reforms with ICT. According to the Ministry of Economy, Trade and Industry (METI), the definition[1] of DX is that a firm handles drastic changes in its business environment and reforms its products, services and business model using data and digital technologies based on customer and social needs, and that the firm reforms its operations, organization, processes, corporate culture and nature to establish competitive advantages. This paper will describe environmental changes, new opportunities and risks in Japan and the Kansai Area, assuming DX mainly for firms.

2. The Significance of DX in Japan and the Promotion Status

(1) The Significance of DX in Japan

In 2018, the METI pointed out the delay in DX in Japan and has prepared DX facilitation measures for firms since then. We will now look at the significance of advancing DX and its current status.

In Japan, commercial systems such as ERP are used with made-to-order software or customized general-use software in many cases. This may have been because the personnel system of long-term employment and career development was consistent with the long-held system operations that were improved when needed. However, it has been pointed out that operational expertise is lost due to staff replacements, which obscures the system. This becomes a hindrance that results in DX not being carried out. If an update of an operation system is delayed, "A user firm cannot fully utilize explosively increasing data and realize DX, which may lead to the firm losing digital competitiveness. The

---

[1] The word "digital transformation" was first used in Stolterman and Fors (2004) as the meaning of "changes that the digital technology causes or influences in aspects of human life." (p.689) Since then, the word has been used, emphasizing changes particularly in business.

absence of IT operation and maintenance staff also results in a great technical debt and difficulties in maintaining and inheriting the business foundation." These issues may surface as a massive economic loss. The METI estimates that an economic loss of JPY 12 trillion per year will incur after 2025.

(2) DX Promotion Status

The Japan Electronics and Information Technology Industries Association (JEITA) and IDC Japan surveyed Japanese and American firms with 300 employees or over. The survey shows that 37.5% of Japanese firms answered that they do not implement DX yet (the total responses of "Collecting DX information," "Do not implement DX," and "Do not know of DX"). This greatly exceeds the 17% of American firms (Figure 3-3-1). Another survey conducted by the In-formation-Technology Promotion Agency, Japan also concludes that many large and medium-sized firms are making little progress on DX practices.

Further, the Japan Users Association of Information Systems surveyed the firms that are listed on the first section of the Tokyo Stock Exchange or considered equivalent on the issues that they want to solve with ICT investment. The survey shows that an interest in "reforming the business model" increased for three consecutive years, but that other issues aiming to ascertain business performance and efficiency still ranked higher (Figure 3-3-2).

As seen, acceleration of DX is prompted in Japan. This paper will discuss opportunities and risks when advancing DX, based also on the environmental

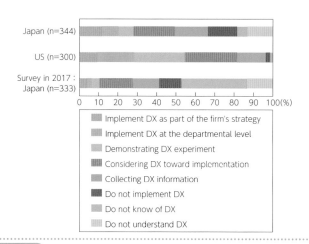

| Figure 3-3-1 | Comparison of the status of DX efforts in Japan and the US |

Source: JEITA (2021), p. 4, extracted from "*3 The Status of DX Efforts"

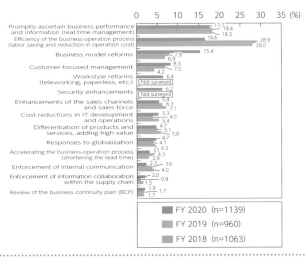

Figure 3-3-2
Changes in medium and long-term management issues that firms want to solve with IT investment over the years (from FY 2018 to FY 2020)

Source: Japan Users Association of Information Systems (2021), p.73, Figure 2-2-3

changes due to the COVID-19 pandemic.

3. Changes in the DX Environment Due to the COVID-19 Pandemic

The COVID-19 epidemic that occurred at the end of 2019 has changed the world a great deal. We will now look at the social changes from three aspects: cities, firms and startups. When doing so, we will refer to trends observed at CES (former name: Consumer Electronics Show), a consumer technology exhibition held online in January 2021, and at South by Southwest (SXSW) conferences held online in March of the same year.

(1) Responsive Cities

One of the changes that has occurred due to the COVID-19 pandemic is that cities have demonstrated a "pivot" ability, which means changing flexibly and swiftly in line with environmental changes. Various activities in cities have avoided crowds and moved to rural areas from city centers. People's flow also changed its sphere from wide areas like traveling to narrow areas like daily life. In response to demand generated by these changes, new services have been created. Cities are evolving as "responsive cities," providing new services with the pivot ability or demonstrating resilience[2].

A typical example of services that have grown with the pivot ability is Uber Eats. It has popularized a service that meets stay-at-home demand by using bicycles as the infrastructure and connecting the last one mile between restaurants and customers by creating a structure where the needs of restaurants, customers and delivery partners are matched.

There are also many kinds of support that can be provided with aging-population-specific services going forward. At the SXSW, a case where a supermarket's delivery network supports resilience was introduced[3]. In the healthcare field, Amazon Care started operations throughout the US in 2021 to provide medical services, and this is exactly what a delivery network is. It is a service that completes the whole process: remote diagnosis, delivery of medication, and dispatch of nurses. In the background to this is a matching technology for doctors and nurses' visits. Although Osaka Prefecture and Osaka City also have a healthcare concept in their smart city strategies, it is limited to remote diagnoses.

Note, however, that the pivot ability may change even the operations of tangible aspects in cities. The City of Austin, known as the venue of SXSW in Texas, has implemented an administrative measure for rapidly popularizing rental E-scooters, such as establishing ridable zones based on riding histories[4].

(2) Firms' Missions

The COVID-19 pandemic has also changed firms' viewpoints. Particularly notable points are that they highlight "social missions" more than ever before and that they have global viewpoints.

Along with the keynote speeches and press conferences at the CES, many firms conducted conferences and exhibitions focusing on changes in lifestyles and workstyles, such as stay-at-home and teleworking, and on sustainability, such as energy saving and climate change (for the keynote speeches, refer to Table 3-3-1). This did not seem unrelated to policy changes due to the US presidential election immediately before the CES, and the viewpoints already seen in the past CES exhibitions were apparently more emphasized. Japanese firms exhibiting there were also asked to show a deep understanding of diversity, the environment, and the seriousness of their initiatives.

---

2) For example, from the panel discussion of the CES 2021 "Smart Cities: Traditional City-Living Makes Way"
3) From the panel session "Adaptable Cities: Tech & the Urban Evolution"
4) Refer to http://austintexas.gov/sharedmobility.

| Table 3-3-1 | Outline of each firm's keynote speech at CES 2021 |

Firm	Outline
AMD	Value creation for such sectors as education, jobs and entertainment by using new high-speed processors
Best Buy	Responses to the COVID-19 pandemic prioritizing consumers' safety, and initiatives concerning innovation creation and diversification
General Motors	Electric vehicles aiming for zero CO_2 emissions, and smart vehicles aiming for zero accidents and no traffic jams
Microsoft	Appealing to the importance of using technologies with a conscience, using security risks and the appropriate use of AI as examples
Verizon	Value creation in sports broadcasting, education, transportation and entertainment, etc. using 5G
Walmart	Measures to maintain supply chains in the COVID-19 pandemic, and initiatives concerning climate change and inclusion, including development of human resources

Source: Prepared by the author based on each firm's keynote speech

At SXSW as well, sessions were titled including the words "diversity" and "inclusion" along with global viewpoints, indicating an awareness that firms are a public organ of society. Japanese firms used to have some of these viewpoints. In fact, we may find answers to the latest issues around us and this might be an opportunity to study the old to understand the new.

I believe that advancing DX will require reliable ideas for businesses as well as a sense of crisis. Firms are realizing significant changes in the business background, but they also need to reform their awareness that values to be provided are becoming social factors. If they do not respond to this, they may be unable to maintain their businesses.

(3) Innovation Creation

In the COVID-19 pandemic, new services for meeting stay-at-home demand grew, such as home fitness, online games, and photo-sharing service. On the other hand, startup development aiming to solve medium and long-term social issues has been continuing regardless of the environmental changes.

In 2019, the EU established a fund for EIC (Europe Innovation Council) to support firms in implementing new technologies[5]. In addition, global smart cities in each country have shown developments aiming for innovation creation. One example is the City of Oslo, Norway, known as one of the most advanced smart cities in the world. The City introduced the large-scale event Oslo In-

---

5) Refer to the website of the European Innovation Council (https://ec.europa.eu/commission/presscorner/detail/en/IP_19_1694)

novation Week as one of the sponsors at the SXSW[6]. Among municipalities in Japan, Aichi Prefecture sponsors an SXSW event as a startup support initiative[7]. Municipalities also recognize startups as something to bring forth and develop.

Many of such startups regard solving social issues as their primary reason for existing and aim to establish sustainable businesses. Further, startups form teams which attract various human resources with strong feelings. Global-scale competition to hire excellent human resources has begun among startups, and we need to create an environment where the competitiveness of Japan does not fall behind the world.

4. DX Status and New Opportunities in Kansai

(1) DX Status in Kansai

In addition to the environmental changes stated earlier, Kansai has unique environmental conditions concerning DX.

According to the Teikoku Databank's survey, the number of head offices moving out of the Osaka area (Osaka, Kyoto, Hyogo, and Nara Prefectures) exceeded the number of those moving into the area for 29 consecutive years up to 2019. Considering that highly successful DX initiatives are promoted by relatively senior staff like CEOs and officers (Figure 3-3-3), it may be becoming difficult to advance DX based on Kansai's business environment due to its loss of head office functions. I believe that reforming business models associated with DX requires obtaining broad and global information even from Kansai and to foster a sense of crisis and the necessity of DX. We need to consider more how an organization should be in the sense of preventing it from receiving biased information.

In terms of firms' assertiveness toward business model reforms in Kansai, notable movements have been observed in small and medium-sized firms and communities other than metropolitan areas. For instance, Miserubayao in Yao City is an example of a base facility that is jointly operated by small or medium-sized firms in the community for handing down manufacturing and cooperating for creating new value.

In terms of solving regional issues, some municipalities have recognized the need to take measures to address the severely decline population and to

---

6) Appeared in the panel discussion of the SXSW "Scandinavia: Re-Thinking Mobility, Munch & Green Biz"
7) Startup Division of Aichi Pref. hosted the online session "Regional Startup Ecosystems by Academic Incubators" at the SXSW 2021 as part of supporting startups that aim for overseas business development. Five Japanese startups made a short presentation there.

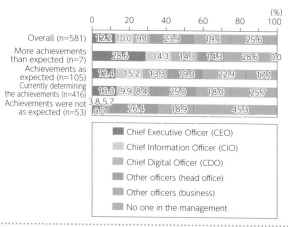

Figure 3-3-3 Digital promotion leader by achievement for digitalizing products and services

Source: Japan Users Association of Information Systems (2021), p. 138, Figure 4-5-3

promote industry, such as Aizuwakamatsu City, Takamatsu City and Kakogawa City. These cities are clearly DX-oriented as one of their future strategies, having a stronger sense of crisis about their survival than large cities. Compared to them, there is little broad collaboration among prefectures in Kansai and local collaboration sharing a sense of crisis.

It is notable that advanced cases with regards to a sense of crisis, speed of change and collaboration are occurring in small and medium-sized firms and provincial cities, or in slightly different places than conventionally.

(2) Trends in New Town Development

1. Large-Scale Projects in Osaka

As is widely known, new opportunities emerge in Kansai. In April 2021, aiming to be designated as the Cabinet Office's Super City-type National Strategic Special Zones, Osaka Prefecture and Osaka City applied for designation with three projects—the Yumeshima Construction, the Osaka-Kansai World Expo, and the Umekita 2nd Project—at two greenfield areas[8] (Yumeshima and the Umekita 2nd Project). In this application, state-of-the-art future social services are planned.

Meanwhile, there is a brownfield development plan for the district to the east of Osaka Castle. This area includes the Morinomiya district where the Osa-

---

8) Greenfield refers to new development in undeveloped areas and brownfield refers to redevelopment in existing urban areas.

ka Metropolitan University's campus will be built, and innovation creation is planned with a central focus on the university.

All of these plans are raised in Osaka Prefecture and Osaka City's smart city strategies as area development cases, and they are expected to provide new business opportunities and to collect and utilize data as one of the measures to improve quality of life.

2. Participation of Civic Tech

The participation of civil engineering technology or "civic tech" in solving towns' issues has greatly increased, like the Tokyo Metropolitan Government's COVID-19 measures website, for example. At the same time, the regional administrations have also become generous and positive toward citizen participation. In Osaka's case, the Code for Osaka, a civic tech NPO, constructed Osaka Prefecture's COVID-19 measures website. It then concluded a business cooperation agreement with Osaka Prefecture and has engaged in activities related to towns' issues, such as holding a great many hackathons and other events.

In civic tech, the administration, citizens and engineers discuss, learn, identify issues and consider solutions together as a group. Looking at such an approach, the group formed should be suitable for these initiatives, find it easy to make decisions speedily and be the right size. I believe that it is essential particularly for large cities to go through the following process: 1) a measure is conducted experimentally in a small unit, 2) a sense of ownership is fostered through dialogue with citizens, and then 3) the measure is moved to a large-scale implementation. One example is the "super block" initiative in Barcelona, Spain, which puts small city blocks together into a large block and prohibits cars from driving into that block[9].

On considering the objective for solving issues in line with a community, it is important to have the value of "it is for the community." We need to consider how to enhance communication with the relevant people, starting first from a scale that is easy to function.

(3) Ecosystems for Business Creation

1. Place Creation by Firms and Universities

Innovation creation is impossible by a company alone and has increasingly been conducted through inter-firm and industry-academia collaborations as a matter

---

9) The concept of super block was planned by the Urban Ecology Agency of Barcelona, which ensured the explanations and information disclosure to residents using the civil participation website "decidim" (https://www.decidim.barcelona/). As a result, the super block was first tried in a small district, and then gradually implemented in wider areas in the city.

of course. Places are created for jointly considering new businesses.

Examples include LINKSPARK founded by NTT West to provide customers with DX support, Xport jointly founded by the Osaka Chamber of Commerce and Industry (OCCI) and the Osaka Institute of Technology as a cross-industry exchange base, and the Common Ground Living Lab founded by the OCCI specializing in cyber-physical technology. Monetizing the proof of new concepts will be an issue in the future for each project, but they will create ecosystems that will bring forth innovation from various aspects.

Universities have also expanded their role and increasingly provide places for industry-academia collaborations. For instance, the Osaka Institute of Technology founded and opened the Robotics & Design Center as a robotics base for industry-academia collaboration. The Osaka Metropolitan University mentioned earlier is also expected to play a role as the "innovation core" in the Morinomiya district.

2. Place Creation by the Administrations

Meanwhile, each administration also conducts startup creation initiatives in various forms.

In Osaka City, Osaka Innovation Hub (OIH) created over 350 projects since its establishment in 2013. Similarly, the municipalities provide support places like the ANCHOR KOBE in Kobe City and the Kyoto Open Innovation Network (KOIN) in Kyoto City. Places created by municipalities for raising startups, as stated earlier, have also expanded in Kansai (Table 3-3-2).

Table 3-3-2   Examples of open innovation places in Kansai

Name of Base	Location (city)	Founder
LINKSPARK	Osaka, Nagoya and Fukuoka	NTT West
Xport	Osaka	Osaka Chamber of Commerce and Industry Osaka Institute of Technology
Common Ground Living Lab	Osaka	Osaka Chamber of Commerce and Industry
Osaka Innovation Hub	Osaka	Osaka City
KOIN (Kyoto Open Innovation Network)	Kyoto	Kyoto City
ANCHOR KOBE	Kobe	Kobe City

Note: Osaka Prefecture's "Osaka Co-creation Business Program" is currently discontinued due to the COVID-19 measures
Source: Prepared by the author

5. DX Risks Requiring Special Attention

DX is part of the pivot ability to respond to environmental changes, and it can also be investment accompanied by significant shifts in businesses and operations. In order for the investment to be sustainable, the direction that an organization itself aims at should be reasonable. In addition, the organization needs to respond to various external risks, such as relating to security, the environment, and laws and regulations. Next, we will consider two aspects, security and ELSI (discussed later), and discuss the ideas that are required for handling them.

(1) Security

When DX is advanced, a large amount of data is placed on an IT system and the data itself generates a profit. For this reason, investment in security means protecting a profit source, and the significance of this has largely increased. In complex supply chains, it should also be noted that, if a firm allows an intrusion into the system from somewhere vulnerable, the damage will expand beyond the firm and organization to the upstream and downstream areas.

Further, new risks have emerged from the changes in workstyles due to the COVID-19 pandemic. The Information-technology Promotion Agency, Japan (IPA) selects 10 Major Security Threats every year based on information security cases in the previous year. According to the 2021 version, attacks on tele-working that has rapidly spread due to the COVID-19 pandemic appeared for the first time and ranked third, meaning that the issue was evaluated to be serious (Table 3-3-3).

Table 3-3-3	The 10 major security threats based on the security cases that occurred in 2020	

Ranking	Threat	Last-year Ranking
1	Damage caused by ransomware	5
2	Theft of confidential information by a targeted attack	1
3	Attack on new normal workstyles, such as teleworking	NEW
4	Attack by exploiting weaknesses in the supply chain	4
5	Financial damage caused by fraud business e-mail	3
6	An information leak caused by internal fraud	2
7	Business suspension due to the unexpected failure of the IT infrastructure	6
8	Fraudulent access to an online service	16
9	Damage such as an information leak caused by carelessness	7
10	Increase in the misuse of published information on vulnerability measures	14

Source: IPA website

Part I

Part II

Part III

Part IV

Against such a backdrop, the METI has put great efforts into security-related measures in recent years. In addition to developing guidelines for proprietors, the METI creates a support system for small and medium-sized firms and compiles ideas about ensuring security with a "digital twin," in which manufacturing is conducted in cyberspace based on real data. Further, it supports the formation of a security-related community in each region.

We should be prepared, being aware that security is important as much as it is indispensable for DX. The conventional method of applying patches to a legacy system complicates the system more than necessary and causes vulnerability. We should be aware that, taking the opportunity provided by DX, we can greatly contribute to security improvements by simplifying systems and adapting to the latest technologies.

(2) ELSI

ELSI is the abbreviation of "Ethical, Legal, and Social Issues," and indicates the perspectives to note when implementing new technologies in a society. In addition to the laws and regulations stipulated, we need to pay attention to society's reactions, even though they are not legalized yet, which arise from a sense of ethics and emerge as public opinions in many cases. Detecting people's flows with street cameras and handling personal data are applicable to the new technologies. In DX, some risk reduction measures should be taken in advance for activities for which public opinions are unreadable, such as trying the activity on a small scale first and informing people about it as well.

Taking Uber Eats as an example of legal issues, deliverers or riders' behaviors and legal positions on the road have drawn much attention as an issue alongside the popularization of the service, because the main infrastructure is the bicycle. In addition, many delivery partners undertaking the actual delivery work do it in their spare time. Overseas judiciaries are recognizing such so-called "gig-workers" as employees[10], which may impact on discussions in Japan down the road.

From an ethical viewpoint, raising the satisfaction levels of all relevant people including employees also contributes to the sustainability of a business. Uber Eats improves business operations every day by introducing AI technology to match demand and supply among restaurants, customers and delivery partners

---

10) The respective Supreme Court successively ruled that Uber Eats delivery partners were to be recognized as employees in France and the UK in March 2020 and February 2021, respectively. Note that the referendum conducted in November 2020 in California, the US, resulted delivery partners being treated as independent contractors. At the moment, there are different perspectives in Europe and the US.

in a well-balanced manner.

ELSI is a concept that should be positioned higher than mere technology management due to its broad coverage. In particular, the idea of ELSI in DX does not seem to have been sufficiently recognized yet. From a viewpoint of solving social issues, we can enlarge the scope of identifying issues when expanding the users of new services realized by DX. For example, issues will extend to what reactions are expected from an expanded range of users to children and elderly people, and what impacts are expected on future children and the Earth's resources. Civil participation discussed earlier can be a structure that complements this enlarged scope in terms of incorporating various viewpoints

6. Conclusion

Assuming a situation in which COVID-19 continues for a while, firms need to perceive changes in the social environment and to adapt to these changes with business and operational reforms.

This paper provided an overview of the status of DX in Japan and Kansai and future opportunities using the pivot ability, and it discussed the need for global viewpoints and sustainable perspectives to make DX investment more effective. Japanese firms may originally have a sustainability perspective, as was said by Konosuke Matsushita, as part of their DNA. This paper also discussed that DX sustainability will be improved by two factors: securing security and considering ELSI accompanied by introductions of new technologies.

Toward the post-COVID-19 period, a new scene is expected to appear in which firms in Japan and Kansai will solve social issues and respond to needs by starting to prepare for environmental changes in society with measures, including for DX, from now. Conversely, firms should consider that a delay in responding to such changes may result in them having to discontinue conventional business activities.

References

Information-technology Promotion Agency, Japan Website, "10 Major Security Threats 2021" (Japanese title: *Joho Sekyuriti 10-dai Kyoi 2021*) https://www.ipa.go.jp/security/vuln/10threats2021.html (last access date: November 10, 2021)

Japan Electronics and Information Technology Industries Association, (2021), "Survey on Japan and American Firms concerning DX 2020" (Japanese title: *2020 Nen Nichibei Kigyo no DX ni Kansuru Chosa*) https://www.jeita.or.jp/japanese/topics/2021/0112.pdf (last access date:

November 10, 2021)

Japan Users Association of Information Systems, (2021), "Survey Report on IT Trend of Firms 2021" (Japanese title: *Kigyo IT Doko Chosa Hokokusho 2021*) https://juas.or.jp/cms/media/2021/04/JUAS_IT2021.pdf (last access date, November 10, 2021)

Stolterman E., Fors A.C., (2004), "Information Technology and the Good Life," Information Systems Research, pp. 687–692. https://link.springer.com/content/pdf/10.1007%2F1-4020-8095-6_45.pdf (last access date: November 10, 2021)

Chapter 4

INBOUND TOURISM IN KANSAI: A FY 2020 RETROSPECTIVE AND OUTLOOK

The COVID-19 pandemic had an unprecedented impact on both the economy and people's flow, its effects on Japan being even more profound than those of the 2008 Global Financial Crisis or the 2011 Great East Japan Earthquake. Countries around the world imposed strict border enforcement measures to limit the spread of the virus, which also led to severe restrictions on people's flow. Despite experiencing steady growth prior to the COVID-19 outbreak, inbound tourism demand in Japan in general and Kansai in particular has virtually evaporated due to the disruptions in both international and domestic travel, and prospects for recovery are not yet in sight.

In last year's *Economic Outlook* (Chapter 4, Section 1) we argued that "although the current COVID-19 pandemic has caused a crisis in inbound tourism, it also provides an opportunity to review past strategies and reshape the tourism industry into a more sustainable one." In other words, inbound tourism must transition from its volume-driven mindset to a more sustainable one. With that in mind, this year's *Economic Outlook* will shed light on the realities that underpin the inbound tourism industry and its strategies.

This chapter is structured as follows. In Section 1, we take a look at key statistics in order to analyze how the absence of inbound tourism demand has affected the economy. In Section 2, we discuss the findings of a survey targeting the tourism departments of the Kansai prefectures. Thus, we identify the main issues that DMOs (Destination Management/Marketing Organizations) are facing in terms of inbound tourism strategy, and shed light on their role in regional tourism. In Section 3 we focus on DMOs in the Kansai prefectures, summarizing their activities and policies, and examining their characteristics from multiple perspectives. Section 4 provides a quantitative overview of the tourism industry in Japan based on the travel and tourism satellite accounts. In addition, we conduct an original analysis of the tourism industry using the extended 2017 Input-Output table. We clarify the position of the tourism industry in the national economy in terms of the employment and income it generates, and of its impact on other industries.

Lastly, in Section 5, we conduct an inter-industry relationship analysis of the pandemic impacts on the tourism industry in 2020. We estimate the decrease in consumption by foreign visitors as well as the decline in domestic travel, including the ripple effect of the "Go To" travel campaign.

Section 1
A FY 2020 Retrospective: The COVID-19 Pandemic and Its Impact on Each Prefecture

INADA, Yoshihisa; NOMURA, Ryosuke; OSHIMA, Hisanori

1. Introduction

In this section we will first review the state of the tourism industry, therein including inbound tourism, which was severely hit by the COVID-19 pandemic. Subsection 2 examines inbound tourism-related trends for 2020 and 2021, while Subsection 3 examines domestic tourism trends. In addition, we discuss the economic effects of anti-COVID-19 measures. Lastly, in Subsection 4 we review the analytical perspectives required by future inbound tourism strategies as a preparatory step toward the analysis in the next section.

2. Trends in inbound tourism

In this subsection we provide a timeline of the border enforcement measures imposed by the Japanese government starting with 2020, which affected mainly foreign travelers. Then, we analyze the impact of these measures on the number of foreign visitors (including the number of foreign arrivals at Kansai International Airport, hereinafter referred to as KIX), and on travel consumption.

(1) Border enforcement measures in Japan

Table 4-1-1 shows the chronology of Japan's border enforcement measures targeting foreigners since 2020. Hubei (China) was the first province to be added to Japan's entry ban list on February 1, 2020, after the first reports of COVID-19 infections had emerged. It was soon followed by other regions in Asia, and then Europe. By August 30, 2020 the entry ban list covered 159 regions and countries. This led to an almost complete disappearance of foreign visitors and inbound tourism demand.

While strict border control is still the norm, starting with the second half

| Table 4-1-1 | Border enforcement measures |

Implementation date	Border enforcement measure
Feb 1, 2020	An entry ban is imposed on travelers from Hubei Province, China.
Jul 29	The Residence Track framework is implemented in collaboration with Thailand and Vietnam.
Aug 30	Japan expands the entry ban list from 146 to 159 countries.
Sep 1	Resident card holders are allowed re-entry.
Sep 8	Cambodia, Taiwan, Malaysia, Myanmar, and Laos are added to the Residence Track framework.
Sep 18	The Business Track framework is implemented in collaboration with Singapore.
Sep 30	Singapore is added to the Residence Track framework.
Oct 1	New entry permits can be issued for medium and long-term residents such as employees and foreign students, provided that their respective companies/institutions can guarantee they respect the quarantine measures.
Nov 1	Japan removes the following territories/countries from the entry ban list: Australia, South Korea, Singapore, Thailand, Taiwan, China (including Hong Kong and Macau), New Zealand, Brunei, and Vietnam. Vietnam is added to the Business Track framework.
Dec 28	Japan decides to temporarily ban new entry for all foreign nationals.
Jan 14, 2021	The Business Track and Residence Track frameworks are suspended.

Source: Prepared based on press releases by the Ministry of Justice, and the Ministry of Foreign Affairs.

of 2020 some measures were relaxed, mainly for exchange students and business travelers. On July 29, 2020 the government announced the implementation of a "Residence Track" framework[1] targeting long-term residents from Thailand and Vietnam, where the epidemiological situation had stabilized. Starting on September 1, 2020, resident card holders were allowed re-entry. In addition, during the same month, Singapore was added to the aforementioned Residence Track scheme, while a "Business Track" framework[2] was introduced for short-term residents. Since October 1, 2020, it has been possible to issue new entry permits for employees of companies and organizations that can guarantee quarantine measures, such as 14 days of self-isolation, and on November 1, 2020 entry restrictions for business travelers from Singapore, Thailand, and South Korea were lifted under certain conditions. Despite some requirements such as self-isolating and refraining from using public transportation for 14 days after

---

1) The Residence Track framework, despite allowing entry for citizens from certain partner countries, does not exclude them from the two week-long self-isolation period. This system is mainly for long-term residents such as expatriate staff.
2) The Business Track entrants are allowed to conduct business activities within a limited scope during the 14-day self-isolation period under certain conditions such as submitting a "Schedule of Activities in Japan." This system is mainly for short-term business travelers.

entering Japan, quarantine measures at arrival or departure have been relaxed.

Despite gradually lifting the border restrictions, starting with December 29, 2020 the government decided to suspend new entries for all foreign nationals due to the worsening epidemiological situation around the world. Moreover, as the virus continued to spread, a new state of emergency was imposed starting with January 8, 2021, and the Business Track and Residence Track frameworks were halted starting with January 14, 2021.

(2) Trends in the number of foreign visitors and their expenditure

As already mentioned, in 2020 the lack of foreign visitors due to strict border restrictions led to an almost non-existent inbound tourism expenditure. Next, we will analyze the data regarding the number of foreign visitors and their expenditure while comparing it to the pre-pandemic figures.

Figure 4-1-1 shows the annual evolution of the number of foreign visitors since 2010. Until the pandemic outbreak, the number of foreign visitors was on a steady upward trend despite the 2011 Great East Japan Earthquake and the natural disasters that hit Japan in 2018. However, in 2020 it reached only 4,115,828 (-87.1% YoY, provisional figure), as the COVID-19 pandemic brought severe restrictions on international mobility. The number of East Asian visitors, who comprise approximately 70% of the total of foreign visitors, also saw a sharp decline (Table 4-1-2).

While foreign visitor numbers saw an overall sharp decline, there are certain differences depending on the category. Figure 4-1-2 shows the monthly evolution of foreign visitor numbers by purpose of travel (tourism, business,

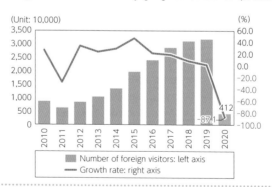

| Figure 4-1-1 | Evolution of foreign visitor numbers and annual growth rate: 2010-20 |

Source: Prepared based on *Foreign Visitors Statistics*, published by the Japan National Tourism Organization (JNTO)

| Table 4-1-2 | | Foreign visitor numbers by nationality: 2019-2020 comparison | | | | |

Country/ Region	2019			2020		
	Number of visitors	Change (%, YoY)	Share (%)	Number of visitors	Change (%, YoY)	Share (%)
Total	31,882,049	2.2	100.0	4,115,828	-87.1	100.0
South Korea	5,584,597	-25.9	17.5	487,939	-91.3	11.9
China	9,594,394	14.5	30.1	1,069,256	-88.9	26.0
Taiwan	4,890,602	2.8	15.3	694,476	-85.8	16.9
Hong Kong	2,290,792	3.8	7.2	346,020	-84.9	8.4
Thailand	1,318,977	16.5	4.1	219,830	-83.3	5.3
Singapore	492,252	12.6	1.5	55,273	-88.8	1.3
Malaysia	501,592	7.1	1.6	76,573	-84.7	1.9
Indonesia	412,779	4.0	1.3	77,724	-81.2	1.9
Philippines	613,114	21.7	1.9	109,110	-82.2	2.7
Vietnam	495,051	27.3	1.6	152,559	-69.2	3.7
India	175,896	14.2	0.6	26,931	-84.7	0.7
UK	424,279	27.0	1.3	51,024	-88.0	1.2
France	336,333	10.3	1.1	43,102	-87.2	1.0
Germany	236,544	9.8	0.7	29,785	-87.4	0.7
Italy	162,769	8.5	0.5	13,691	-91.6	0.3
Russia	120,043	26.6	0.4	22,260	-81.5	0.5
Spain	130,243	9.5	0.4	11,741	-91.0	0.3
USA	1,723,861	12.9	5.4	219,307	-87.3	5.3
Canada	375,262	13.5	1.2	53,365	-85.8	1.3
Mexico	71,745	4.8	0.2	9,528	-86.7	0.2
Australia	621,771	12.5	2.0	143,508	-76.9	3.5

Source: Prepared based on *Foreign Visitors Statistics*, published by the Japan National Tourism Organization (JNTO)

and other purposes).[3] Between February 2020, and February 2021, the number of foreign tourists and business travelers saw a consistent YoY decline which exceeded -90%. On the other hand, the drop rate of the number of visitors in the "other purposes" category fluctuated substantially, after bottoming out in May 2020 (-99.1% YoY). These fluctuations are partly the result of border relaxation measures implemented since July 2020 such as "Residence Track," which allowed entry for mid- to long-term residents such as foreign students and technical trainees. Due to the gradual easing of entry requirements, the rate of decline

---

3) According to JNTO, the number of tourists is obtained by deducting the number of business travelers from the total number of short-term visitors and it also includes those who are visiting relatives of friends. "Other purposes" refers to purposes other than tourism and business, including studying and training, as well as diplomatic and official ones.

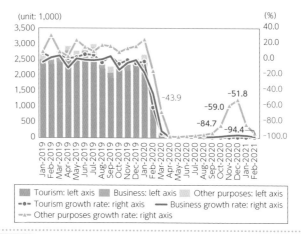

Figure 4-1-2   Foreign visitor numbers by travel purpose

Source: Prepared based on *Foreign Visitors Statistics*, published by the Japan National Tourism Organization (JNTO)

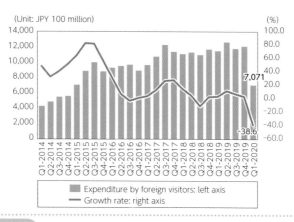

Figure 4-1-3   Evolution of expenditure by foreign visitors: 2014-2020

Note: Due to methodological changes applied in 2018, there may be some inconsistencies in comparisons with data from 2017 and earlier.
Source: Prepared based on *Consumption Trends of International Visitors to Japan Survey*, published by the Japan Tourism Agency (JTA).

shrank to -51.8% YoY in December 2020. However, after Japan decided to suspend the Business Track and Residence Track schemes on January 14, 2021, the decline deepened once again to over -90%.

Figure 4-1-3 shows expenditure by foreign visitors and its evolution. Between 2014 and 2015, Japan experienced an inbound tourism demand boom, and as a result of so-called "shopping sprees" (*bakugai*) expenditure saw quarterly increases of over 80%. Subsequently, despite the impact of exchange rate fluctuations[4] and natural disasters, inbound tourism expenditure recorded a record high of JPY 4.8135 trillion in 2019 (see Figure 4-1-4 in the Annex). However, in 2020 Q1 expenditure was only JPY 707.1 billion (-38.6% QoQ) due to the pandemic-induced border closures. We anticipate that it will take time for expenditure by foreign visitors to return to its pre-pandemic levels.

(3) Number of foreign arrivals at Kansai International Airport: 2019-20

Like the rest of Japan, Kansai was not spared from the lack of foreign visitors. Table 4-1-3 shows a 2019-2020 comparison in terms of the number of foreign arrivals by nationality at Kansai International Airport (hereinafter referred to as KIX). In 2019 the total number of foreign arrivals was 8,378,039, the highest number on record since the airport opened. Considering the geographic proximity, the share of arrivals from East Asia is higher than on a national level. Particularly, the share of Chinese arrivals was as high as 39.4% in 2019, surpassing the national average of 30.1% by 9.3% pt. However, in 2020 the total number dropped substantially to 1,011,186 (-87.9% YoY) as a result of border closures. By nationality, the largest number of arrivals was from China (370,923, -88.8% YoY), decreasing to a mere tenth of the 2019 level.

Part I

Part II

Part III

Part IV

---

4) As we pointed out in the 2019 Japanese-language edition of APIR's *Economic Outlook* (Chapter 5, Section 1), in 2015 the exchange rate was 1 USD=120 JPY, but in 2016 the yen strengthened against the dollar, reaching 1 USD=110 JPY. In general, as the yen appreciates, goods and services in Japan become more expensive; therefore expenditure is expected to decrease.

| Table 4-1-3 | Foreign arrivals numbers at KIX: 2019-2020 comparison |

Country/ Region	2019			2020		
	Number of arrivals at KIX	Change (%, YoY)	Share (%)	Number of arrivals at KIX	Change (%, YoY)	Share (%)
Total	8,378,039	9.6	100.0	1,011,186	-87.9	100.0
South Korea	1,510,776	-30.2	18.0	134,522	-91.1	13.3
China	3,302,710	43.6	39.4	370,923	-88.8	36.7
Taiwan	1,098,555	4.2	13.1	152,469	-86.1	15.1
Hong Kong	604,787	-1.9	7.2	76,090	-87.4	7.5
Thailand	310,615	18.6	3.7	42,645	-86.3	4.2
Singapore	114,459	25.7	1.4	11,024	-90.4	1.1
Malaysia	150,760	-1.5	1.8	19,919	-86.8	2.0
Indonesia	85,643	12.5	1.0	18,396	-78.5	1.8
Philippines	198,265	50.4	2.4	41,318	-79.2	4.1
Vietnam	148,247	55.9	1.8	37,263	-74.9	3.7
India	21,599	17.7	0.3	2,470	-88.6	0.2
UK	59,632	34.5	0.7	6,849	-88.5	0.7
France	61,340	18.7	0.7	6,532	-89.4	0.6
Germany	35,255	15.3	0.4	4,093	-88.4	0.4
Italy	24,571	22.1	0.3	1,830	-92.6	0.2
Russia	9,496	81.5	0.1	1,640	-82.7	0.2
Spain	28,072	10.8	0.3	1,625	-94.2	0.2
USA	220,341	24.6	2.6	21,903	-90.1	2.2
Canada	55,437	15.7	0.7	5,567	-90.0	0.6
Mexico	4,574	18.8	0.1	467	-89.8	0.0
Australia	94,752	17.9	1.1	18,068	-80.9	1.8

Source: Prepared based on *Immigration Control Statistics* (Ministry of Justice).

3. Domestic tourism trends in 2020-21: COVID-19 response

As already mentioned in the previous subsection, both inbound tourism demand, which until the COVID-19 pandemic had experienced steady growth, and Japan's outbound tourism demand have virtually disappeared and their recovery is not yet in sight. Under these circumstances, encouraging domestic tourism becomes all the more important. Figure 4-1-4 compares Japan's total travel expenditure in 2019 with 2020. In both years, Japan's domestic tourism generated the largest share of the total. In 2020, the restrictions imposed on people's flow during the states of emergency led to a significant drop in domestic tourism expenditure, which was approximately JPY 9.9 trillion (-54.5% YoY). In order to stimulate demand for domestic travel, the Japanese government decided to start the "Go To Travel" subsidy program in the second half of 2020. In the following, we will look at the dynamics of domestic travel during the COVID-19 crisis and the "Go To Travel" program as a measure to stimulate demand.

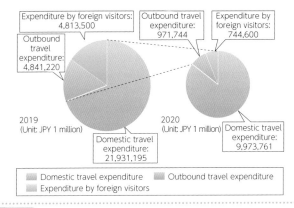

| Expenditure by foreign visitors: 4,813,500 | Outbound travel expenditure: 971,744 | Expenditure by foreign visitors: 744,600 |

Outbound travel expenditure: 4,841,220

2019 (Unit: JPY 1 million)

2020 (Unit: JPY 1 million)

Domestic travel expenditure: 21,931,195

Domestic travel expenditure: 9,973,761

■ Domestic travel expenditure   ■ Outbound travel expenditure
■ Expenditure by foreign visitors

Figure 4-1-4   Travel expenditure: 2019-2020 comparison

Note: Outbound travel by Japanese nationals is counted as services imports and it includes overseas travel-related payments. Moreover, due to the COVID-19 pandemic, collecting data for Q2, Q3, and Q4 of 2020 was suspended. For this reason, the expenditure generated by foreign visitors in 2020 is an estimate calculated using the travel expenditure per capita in Q1 2020.
Source: Prepared based on *Travel and Tourism Consumption Trend Survey* and *Consumption Trends of International Visitors to Japan Survey*, published by the Japan Tourism Agency (JTA).

(1) Trends in the total number of Japanese overnight guests

We will begin our analysis of domestic tourism during the COVID-19 pandemic by looking at the trends in the total number of Japanese overnight guests. Figure 4-1-5 shows the total number of Japanese guests nationwide and in the Greater Kansai area[5] as reflected in the *Overnight Travel Statistics Survey*, published by the Japan Tourism Agency (JTA). The number of guests has bottomed out both nationwide (-81.6% YoY) and in Kansai (-84.6% YoY) in May 2020, during the state of emergency (April 7-May 25).

After the state of emergency was lifted and economic activities resumed, the rate of decline started to shrink. Partly due to the "Go To Travel" campaign, which was launched in July 2020, by November the situation further improved (nationwide: -16.1% YoY, Kansai: -14.8% YoY). However, in December, when the campaign was temporarily suspended due to the virus resurgence, the rate of decline expanded once again. By February 2021, the effect of the "Go To Trav-

---

5) Greater Kansai include the following 10 prefectures: Fukui, Mie, Shiga, Kyoto, Osaka, Hyogo, Nara, Wakayama, Tottori, and Tokushima.

el" campaign wore off, and the rate of decline returned to a level similar to July 2020, when the campaign first started (nationwide: -46.5% YoY, Kansai: -48.0% YoY). In addition, Figure 4-1-6 shows the total number of overnight guests by residence. In April and May 2020, the ratio of guests from other prefectures decreased, while the ratio of guests from the same prefecture increased both nationwide and in Kansai, due to restrictions imposed on inter-prefectural travel during the state of emergency. Since June 2020, the ratio of guests from other prefectures returned to an upward trend due to restrictions on inter-prefectural travel being relaxed and the "Go To Travel" campaign. However, the ratio of guests from the same prefecture still increased as a result of the fact that an increasing number of tourists preferred to avoid regions where the virus was spreading, choosing instead to travel closer to home.[6]

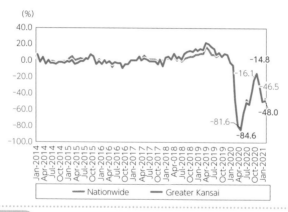

| Figure 4-1-5 | Growth rate of total number of Japanese overnight guests: Jan 2014-Feb 2021 |

Note: the figures are final for the period up until 2019, and preliminary for 2020-21.
Source: Prepared based on *Overnight Travel Statistics Survey*, published by the Japan Tourism Agency (JTA).

---

[6] Campaigns ran by each prefecture to stimulate intra-prefectural travel also played an important role. For more details, see the 2021 Japanese-language edition of APIR's *Economic Outlook* (Chapter 5, Section 1).

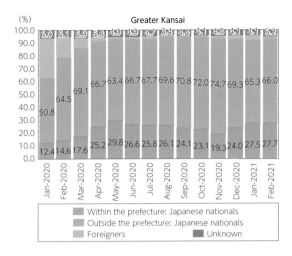

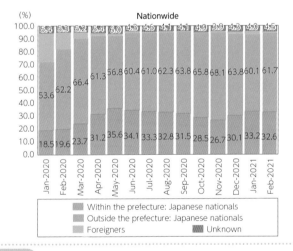

Figure 4-1-6   Ratio of overnight guests by residence: Jan 2020-Feb 2021

Note: The figures for 2020-21 are preliminary.
Source: Prepared based on *Overnight Travel Statistics Survey*, published by the Japan Tourism Agency (JTA).

(2) Trends in domestic travel spending

Next, we review the trends in domestic travel expenditure. Due to the measures taken to contain the spread of the virus, both the number of domestic travelers and travel expenditure decreased sharply. Figure 4-1-7 shows the expansion rate of domestic travel expenditure in Japan in general and Kansai in particular. Both across the country and in Kansai, the effects of pandemic started to be felt in Q1 2020. As a state of emergency was imposed in Q2, the growth rate slumped to -83.2% YoY nationwide, and to -87.2% YoY in Kansai, both surpassing the -80% threshold. In Q3, due to the reopening of economic activities and the start of the "Go To Travel" campaign, the rates of decline began to shrink, reaching -56.6% YoY nationwide, and -52.4% YoY in Kansai after bottoming out in Q2. The recovery trend continued in Q4, when the rate of decline reached -45.0% YoY nationwide, and -42.7% YoY in Kansai. However, the "Go To Travel" campaign was suspended in December, and a new state of emergency was declared in January 2021, which prompted a downward trend in Q1 2021. As a result, the nationwide rate of decline was 50.1% YoY, while in Kansai it was -54.6% YoY, also due to the fact that the state of emergency covered Kyoto, Osaka, and Hyogo prefectures.

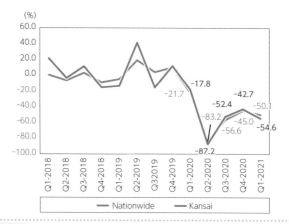

Figure 4-1-7   Domestic travel expenditure growth rate: Q1 2018-Q1 2021

Note: The figures for Q1 2021 are preliminary.
Source: Prepared based on *Travel and Tourism Consumption Trend Survey*, published by the Japan Tourism Agency (JTA).

(3) "Go To Travel" campaign

In order to stimulate the depressed travel demand, the government initiated the "Go To Travel" campaign. In this subsection, we review the effects of the campaign, while looking at its development and performance.[7] The campaign, which initially excluded Tokyo, started on July 22, 2020, and by the end of the

---

7) In Chapter 2, Section 1, Subsection 5 of this issue, the economic effects of the "Go To Travel" campaign are analyzed by using the *Family Income and Expenditure Survey*. In addition, in Chapter 4, Section 5 we analyze the pandemic-induced decrease in tourism expenditure and the economic effect of the "Go To Travel" campaign by using the input-output table.

month it had generated approximately 2,140,000 overnight stays. After Tokyo was included on October 1, the number grew to 51,860,000 at the end of October, an increase of 22,050,000 from the end of September. On December 14, the campaign was temporarily suspended, but counting guests who checked out on December 28 brings the total number of overnight stays to at least 87,810,000 (Figure 4-1-8).[8]

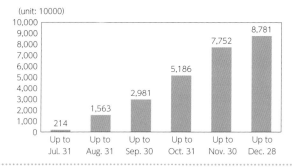

(unit: 10000)

	Up to Jul. 31	Up to Aug. 31	Up to Sep. 30	Up to Oct. 31	Up to Nov. 30	Up to Dec. 28
	214	1,563	2,981	5,186	7,752	8,781

Figure 4-1-8   Number of overnight stays by "Go To Travel" campaign participants

Note: The figures include estimative preliminary numbers and are not definitive.
Source: Prepared based on *Performance of the Go To Travel Campaign* by the Japan Tourism Agency

Next, we look at the discounts offered by the "Go To Travel" campaign. By September 15, 2020 the campaign had offered JPY 73.5 billion in discounts, and after Tokyo was included, the sum rose to JPY 188.6 billion by October 31. Until the campaign's temporary suspension, the amount of discounts provided came to a total of JPY 408.2 billion. In addition to discounts, regional coupons also became available, which increases the total amount of subsidies to JPY 539.9 billion (Figures 4-1-9 and 4-1-10).

---

8) According to the Japan Tourism Agency, the number of "Go To Travel" campaign participants who tested positive for COVID-19 was 411 (as of the end of May 2021). In addition, there are no report of the virus spreading to hotel or tourist facility employees. In November 2020, the Novel Coronavirus Infectious Disease Control Subcommittee declared that "As of now, there is no evidence that the *Go To Travel* campaign is a major factor in the spreading of the virus."

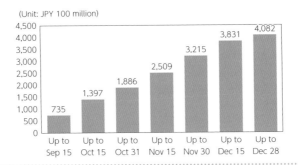

Figure 4-1-9   Amount of discounts offered by the "Go To Travel" campaign

Note: The figures include estimative preliminary numbers and are not definitive.
Source: Prepared based on *Performance of the Go To Travel Campaign* by the Japan Tourism Agency.

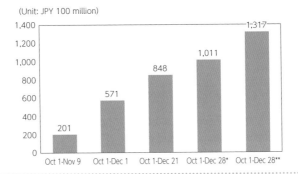

Figure 4-1-10   Amount of regional coupons used

Note: The figures include estimative preliminary numbers and are not definitive. * counts the redemption requests received by the Go To Travel Office by January 4, while ** counts the redemption requests received by February 1.
Source: Prepared based on *Performances of the Go To Travel Campaign* by the Japan Tourism Agency.

The "Go To Travel" campaign also had an impact on prices. Figure 4-1-11 shows the YoY change of accommodation fees as reflected by the Ministry of Internal Affairs and Communications' Consumer Price Index. While in July 2020, at the beginning of the campaign, the change was -4.5% YoY, in October the decline deepened to -37.1% YoY. The campaign offers discounts of up to 35% of the accommodation fee, so since Tokyo was included, the increasing travel demand drove the fees down. However, since then the campaign was suspended and the effect of discounts wore off, so in April 2021 the rate of decline shrank back to -5.7% YoY.

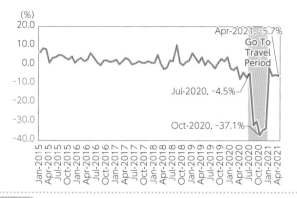

Figure 4-1-11	Consumer Price Index: accommodation fees (YoY): Jan 2015-Apr 2021

Note: 2020 average=100.
Source: Prepared based on *Consumer Price Index* by the Ministry of Internal Affairs and Communications.

4. The future of inbound tourism

As already stated, inbound tourism demand is expected to require more time to recover. While the government's measures to stimulate demand were effective to a certain extent, their positive effect faded once the "Go To Travel" campaign was suspended due to the resurgence of COVID-19. The progress of vaccination is important when considering the prospects for recovery of inbound tourism demand.[9] In July 2021 the EU, where the vaccination rate is relatively high, has adopted a "Digital COVID Certificate," which facilitates travel for vaccinated individuals. On the other hand, despite its higher vaccination rate, Japan still maintains strict border enforcement measures, and the outlook for border relaxation remains uncertain. The absence of foreign visitors provides a good opportunity to review past strategies and identify their issues. Considering that, in last year's Economic Outlook we provided new analytical perspectives for future inbound tourism strategies (see the Venn diagram A below). This year we further examined these analytical perspectives, and interviewed each prefecture's tourism authority, while having in mind the concept of "tourism regionalization." The next section compares and examines each prefecture's tourism strategy based on those survey results.

---

9) For details about the vaccination rollout situation, see Section 5 of "COVID-19 Chronology."

Box1) An analytical perspective for future inbound tourism strategies

In the 2020-21 edition of *Kansai and the Asia Pacific Economic Outlook*, Chapter 4, Section 5, we examined inbound tourism strategies in anticipation of the post-pandemic era. As illustrated in Figure 4-1-12, we pointed out that an inbound tourism demand analysis must take into consideration safety, security and comfort as fundamental factors, in addition to brand power, innovation, and tourism regionalization. We defined safety as "a physical condition in which there is no imminent danger to the visitor and his or her property," security as "a condition in which there is no cause for concern for the visitor in case something unforeseen happens," and comfort as "being able to enjoy a relaxed and stress-free travel experience." We further argued that "when all these conditions are met, it can be assumed that tourists will feel satisfied with their travel experience" (p. 220).

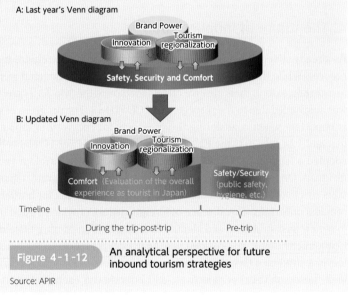

Figure 4-1-12   An analytical perspective for future inbound tourism strategies

Source: APIR

From a foreign visitor's perspective, safety and security are factors which influence decision-making before the trip, while comfort is what the visitors should feel during and after the trip. Based on the "before, during and after" time-frame, we can change the base layer of the Venn diagram as illustrated in version B. To be specific, visitors expect to feel safe and secure before they decide to choose Japan as their destination. After arrival, the feeling of comfort can be earned through first-hand tourism experience. By considering these three elements, it is possible to enhance the tourism experience before and during the trip, and solve concerns that might appear while traveling. We must go further than offer a superficially enjoyable experience, and gain the visitors' confidence by meeting their expectations and even surpassing them. Thus, if we can instill the feeling of comfort even before the trip, it may be possible to raise foreign visitors' expectations.

References

Asia Pacific Institute of Research (2020) "Kansai and the Asia Pacific Economic Outlook 2019-20."

Asia Pacific Institute of Research (2021) "Kansai and the Asia Pacific Economic Outlook: 2020-21."

Japan Tourism Agency (2021) "White Paper on Tourism 2021" (Japanese title: Reiwa 3-nen-ban Kankō Hakusho).

Section 2
KANSAI'S TOURISM STRATEGY: CURRENT SITUATION AND ISSUES BASED ON SURVEYS

INADA, Yoshihisa; OSHIMA, Hisanori; NOMURA, Ryosuke

1. Introduction

In Section 1, we argued that an analysis of inbound tourism must examine the roles of brand power, tourism regionalization, and innovation, in addition to "safety, security and comfort" which is a concept advocated by APIR (see Figure B in Chapter 4 and Box 1 in Section 1). In particular, tourism regionalization plays a significant role when trying to encourage a more even distribution of tourists within a larger territory, beyond the crowded tourist attractions.

In order to shed light on the nature of tourism organizations in each prefecture, as well as their policies and issues, we have conducted a series of surveys. Based on the survey findings, we have identified the main policy issues and used these as a starting point for our discussion regarding post-pandemic inbound tourism strategies (for details, see Table 4-2-1 at the end of this section).[1]

2. Summary of survey findings by prefecture

(1) Survey structure

This subsection introduces an analysis of data regarding foreign overnight guests, then summarizes the main findings of the interviews with the authorities of each prefecture.

In order to better understand the behavior of foreign visitors in Kansai's six prefectures, we examined data regarding the total number of foreign overnight guests by municipality for 2012, the year before the surge in shopping sprees by Chinese tourists known as "bakugai" or "explosive buying," and for 2019, the year before the outbreak of the COVID-19 pandemic.[2]

The main findings of the interviews are summarized based on the following key themes:
- Organizations in charge of inbound tourism promotion

---

1) For details regarding the tourism strategy of each prefecture, please consult the bibliography at the end of this section.
2) The present study is the result of a joint-research project with the Kinki District Transport Bureau. We take this opportunity to extend our gratitude.

- Prefectural approaches to the concept of "brand" and its implementation
- Measures to increase tourism expenditure and the number of foreign visitors
- The main challenges of tourism regionalization
- Cooperation with other local governments and DMOs (Destination Management Organization)

(2) Survey findings

According to the Japan Tourism Agency (JTA), in 2019 the total number of foreign overnight guests in the greater Kansai area was 33,740,000. Of which, 17,930,000 guests chose Osaka Prefecture, while 12,030,000 guests chose Kyoto Prefecture. These figures correspond to 53.1% and 35.6% of the total and prove that overnight guests tend to concentrate in these two areas (Figure 4-2-1).

As for the rest of Kansai, the situation is as follows: Hyōgo, 1,370,000 guests (4.1%), Wakayama, 660,000 guests (2.0%), Nara, 540,000 (1.6%), and Shiga, 420,000 (1.3%). It is clear that the numbers paint a very different picture according to the prefecture.

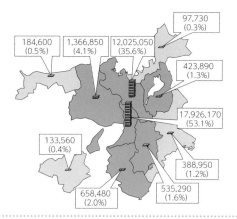

Figure 4-2-1   The total number of overnight guests in the greater Kansai region (2019)

Source: *Overnight Travel Statistics Survey* (JTA)

1) Shiga Prefecture
【Data regarding foreign overnight guests】

A comparison of data for 2012 with 2019[3] shows that the total number of foreign overnight guests grew by a factor of approximately 3 in the case of Ōtsu City, and 9 in the southern part of the prefecture (Moriyama and Yasu cities). In the northern part, in Takashima City, the number grew by a factor of approximately 8. Overall, there is an upward trend, especially in the southern part (Figure 4-2-2).[4]

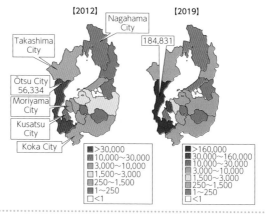

Figure 4-2-2   The total number of foreign overnight guests by municipality in Shiga Prefecture

Source: Prepared based on individual data from *Overnight Travel Statistics Survey* (JTA)

【Organization in charge of inbound tourism promotion】

In Shiga Prefecture the Tourism Promotion Bureau (20 employees), part of the Commerce, Industry, Tourism and Labor Department, is in charge of tourism policies, including inbound tourism. Its main tasks are planning, domestic tours, attracting the film industry, and promoting "Biwaichi" (cycling around Lake Biwa). One person is in charge of promoting inbound tourism.

---

3) For a detailed account of nationality-based data for each municipality, see APIR (2021). This applies for all prefectures covered below.

4) On the other hand, the day time/night time visitor ratio in Shiga Prefecture peaked in 2015 and has been following a downward trend since 2016. This suggests a tendency to visit the prefecture during the day time and spend the night outside of it. Considering that the day time/night time visitor ratio in neighboring Kyoto Prefecture is on an upward trend, we can infer that foreign visitors are inclined to visit Shiga during the day and spend the night in Kyoto.

【Prefectural approaches to the concept of "brand" 】

Considering that Lake Biwa is located within the prefecture, water and nature are an important part of the local identity. Looking forward to the post-pandemic era, the prefecture is taking advantage of its proximity to major urban areas and the fact that it is relatively sparsely populated to create new types of tourism, such as work vacations, and to promote itself as a "workation" destination.

【Measures to increase tourism expenditure and the number of foreign visitors】

Attracting visitors, especially from Kyoto City, was cited as a priority issue. For this reason, Kyoto Tower has been used to provide tourist information on Shiga Prefecture (Soko Shiga). In addition, promotion campaigns in the sister states/regions of Michigan (USA) and Hunan (China) advertised the history and the products of the prefecture, such as ninjas and Japanese sake. Since 2015, a PR campaign for cycling around Lake Biwa ("Biwaichi") was developed in association with the Taiwanese bicycle manufacturer GIANT.

【The main challenges of tourism regionalization】

Intermodal transportation to tourist attractions is a current issue. There are also ongoing efforts to translate information boards into foreign languages, starting with national heritage sites.

【Cooperation with other local governments and DMOs】

Tourism product development is secured through close collaboration with Regional DMOs (Biwako Visitors Bureau). It is also working with the Union of Kansai Governments, the Central Japan Tourism Organization, and the Fukui-Shiga-Kyoto Tourism Promotion Council to encourage tourism in a coordinated manner.

2) Kyoto Prefecture
【Data regarding foreign overnight guests】

A comparison of data for 2012 with 2019 shows that the total number of foreign overnight guests grew by a factor of approximately 4 in Kyoto City, 3.8 in Miyazu City (northern part of the prefecture), and 8.9 in Kameoka City (central part). The share of Kyoto City was 98.4% in 2012, and 98.5% in 2019, reflecting the unbalanced distribution of guests across the prefecture (Figure 4-2-3).

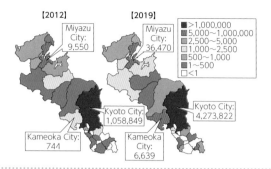

Figure 4-2-3   The total number of foreign overnight guests by municipality in Kyoto Prefecture

Source: Prepared based on individual data from *Overnight Travel Statistics Survey* (JTA)

【Organization in charge of inbound tourism promotion】

In Kyoto Prefecture, the Commerce, Industry, Labor and Tourism Department (23 employees) is in charge of tourism policies. Its main tasks are planning and coordination of tourism policies, development of accommodation facilities, promotion of tourism and information dissemination about each region of the prefecture, international tourism, tourism regionalization and attraction of MICE tourism.

【Prefectural approaches to the concept of "brand"】

The entire prefecture except Kyoto City is divided into four areas collectively branded as "Another Kyoto:" "Kyoto by the Sea" (northern part of the prefecture), "Woodland Kyoto" (central part), "Kyoto Tea Country" (southern part), and "Kyoto Otokuni Bamboo Grove" (Mukō and Nagaokakyō cities, and Ōyamazaki town).[5]

【Measures to increase tourism expenditure and the number of foreign visitors】

The Tourism Office conducts PR campaigns through online business meetings and videos promoting Kyoto in places such Hong Kong and Taiwan, which have a high ratio of repeat tourists. The campaigns also target markets with high potential such as Thailand. Since 2014, the prefecture has also established a "tour-

---

5) The DMOs established in these areas are registered with JTA as follows: Kyoto by the Sea, Woodland Kyoto, and Kyoto Tea Country. In the case of Kyoto Otokuni Bamboo Grove area, neither a registered DMO nor a candidate DMO has yet been established.

ism representative"[6] who has the role of liaising with local officials, gathering market data, and disseminating information in key markets such as Taiwan and Hong Kong.

Markets with high tourism expenditure, such as Europe, the USA, and Australia, are also targeted. Nevertheless, the emphasis is on the Australian market, which is easier to travel to and has fewer major cities, making it less complicated to narrow down PR campaign targets. Promotion campaigns and online business meetings are organized in Melbourne.

Each DMO also conducts independent PR activities. For example, the Kyoto by the Sea DMO focuses on Australia, where the idea of "seaside" is popular, while the Woodland Kyoto DMO focuses on the USA. There is no overseas PR campaign yet in the case of the Kyoto Tea Country DMO.

[The main challenges of tourism regionalization]

The main challenge is to encourage visitors, the majority of which concentrate in Kyoto City, to also visit other parts of the prefecture in order to increase the economic ripple effect of tourism.

[Cooperation with other local governments and DMOs]

There is a significant number of collaborations with other prefectures.

- The establishment of the "Japan Luxury Travel Alliance" (Ishikawa Prefecture, Kyoto City, Sapporo City, Takayama City, Nara City, Wakayama Prefecture) in order to attract wealthy Western tourists.
- Promotion of San'in Coast Geopark (with Hyōgo and Tottori prefectures).
- Overseas PR campaign implemented through cooperation between Japan Railways and the 12 prefectures along the Hokuriku Shinkansen line.
- Cooperation based on the national heritage (with Fukui and Shiga prefectures).
- Educational travel promotion campaign in Taiwan (with Osaka, Nara, Hyōgo, Wakayama prefectures).

All of the DMOs in the prefecture have the vice-governor of Kyoto Prefecture as their vice-president, and Kyoto Prefecture officials among their staff. In addition, Kyoto Prefecture is in charge of the secretariat of the Tourism Sector Bureau (Union of Kansai Governments), and is also working on promoting the entire Kansai region overseas in cooperation with the Kansai Tourism Bureau.

---

6) In addition to gathering information regarding the local travel trends, the tourism representative also offers information about the sightseeing areas in Kyoto Prefecture to the local companies and media, and conducts promotional campaigns to attract foreign visitors.

In most cases, cooperation with the municipalities within the prefecture is done indirectly through the respective local DMOs.

3) Osaka Prefecture
【Data regarding foreign overnight guests】

A comparison of data for 2012 with 2019 shows that the total number of foreign overnight guests grew by a factor of approximately 4.7 in Osaka City, 4.8 in Sakai City, and 2.2 in Izumisano City where Kansai International Airport (KIX) is located. While the number of foreign guests has been increasing steadily in both the north and south of the prefecture, the overwhelming majority continue to choose Osaka City for their stay (Figure 4-2-4).

Osaka City's share within Osaka Prefecture expanded from 79.1% in 2012 to 86.0% in 2019, while during the same interval Izumisano City's share shrank from 14.4% to 7.7%. It appears that Osaka City's increasing number of lodging facilities improved its capacity to accommodate guests arriving at KIX.

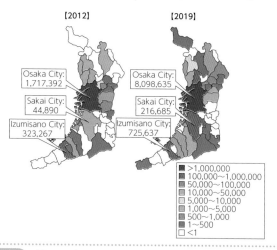

Figure 4-2-4   The total number of foreign overnight guests by municipality in Osaka Prefecture

Source: Prepared based on individual data from *Overnight Travel Statistics Survey* (JTA)

【Organization in charge of inbound tourism promotion】

Osaka Prefecture's organizations in charge of tourism are the Planning and Tourism Division (27 employees) and the Urban Development Promotion Division (23 employees), both are part of the Urban Development Bureau. The planning and implementation of measures such as tourism promotion are entrusted to the Osaka Convention & Tourism Bureau (DMO for regional cooperation).

[Prefectural approaches to the concept of "brand"]

Osaka Prefecture tries to appeal to tourists by promoting itself as a place of diversity[7] in terms of cuisine, culture, history, entertainment, etc.

[Measures to increase tourism expenditure and the number of foreign visitors]

Considering that 75% of foreign visitors are from East Asia, one of the main post-pandemic goals is to encourage their return. Europe, the USA, and Australia are also seen as potential target markets due to their high tourism expenditure. Nevertheless, considering the current restrictions on international travel, for now the primary objective is to stimulate domestic tourism.

While the Osaka Convention & Tourism Bureau is in charge of promotion, the aforementioned Urban Development Bureau divisions are in charge of developing new tourist routes across the prefecture, as well as urban zoning and uncovering potential tourist attractions in Osaka City.

[The main challenges of tourism regionalization]

One of the main goals is to attract visitors from Western markets and encourage them to stay longer and spend more by integrating the north, east and south of the prefecture with Osaka City. This is believed to expand the positive economic effects of tourism across the prefecture. The main measures to achieve that goal are:

- PR campaigns promoting history (tumuli, Osaka Castle, etc.), culture, and cuisine.
- the implementation of a regulatory system for special private lodging areas in order to cope with the increasing number of foreign visitors.
- testing the feasibility of a sightseeing bus linking Osaka and Sakai cities.

[Cooperation with other local governments and DMOs]

The Urban Development Bureau divisions in charge of tourism share their strategy with Osaka City, while also offering support to other municipalities for their respective initiatives.

In terms of cooperation with DMOs, the Osaka Convention & Tourism Bu-

---

7) This idea is also reflected by the "Osaka City Urban Development Strategy – 2025," one of the goals of which is to project the image of a "diverse tourist city."

reau enjoys a high degree of freedom in developing policies, in addition to its role in marketing, promotion and information dissemination.

4) Hyōgo Prefecture
【Data regarding foreign overnight guests】

Comparing the data for 2012 and 2019 shows that the total number of foreign overnight guests grew by a factor of approximately 3 in Kobe City, but just 2 in Harima and Tamba provinces. On the other hand, in Tajima province (Toyo'oka City, Kami and Shin'onsen towns) the number of guests expanded ten-fold. However, the large majority of guests are concentrated in Kobe, Toyo'oka and Himeji cities. Fixing this uneven distribution represents a major challenge (Figure 4-2-5).

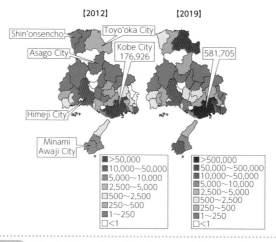

Figure 4-2-5　The total number of foreign overnight guests by municipality in Hyōgo Prefecture

Source: Prepared based on individual data from *Overnight Travel Statistics Survey* (JTA)

【Organization in charge of inbound tourism promotion】

In Hyōgo Prefecture, the Tourism Bureau (14 employees), part of the Industry and Labor Department, is in charge of tourism policies. It is further divided into the Planning and Promotion divisions which are handling both domestic and foreign affairs. In addition, the bureau is sharing the same location with the Hyōgo Tourism Head Office (27 employees), the prefecture-level DMO, thus encouraging a close relationship between the two.

【Prefectural approaches to the concept of "brand"】

Given the distinct nature of each of the five regions forming it and although each region has abundant tourist resources, there is not a single unified brand of "Hyōgo Prefecture." The PR campaigns revolve around promoting the prefecture as a place of different elements with tourist potential such as Himeji Castle, Kobe beef, and so on.

【Measures to increase tourism expenditure and the number of foreign visitors】

The bureau has established an overseas office for PR purposes and it is also planning to attract more visitors via regional airports in neighboring Chugoku and Shikoku. As in Nara Prefecture, described below, Hyōgo also uses former school principals to assist with welcoming school trips from abroad.

The bureau is also involved in numerous overseas travel expos in collaboration with the major cities in the prefecture. It has also adopted a proactive stance in developing a certain amount of tourist products in association with prefectural DMOs.

【The main challenges of tourism regionalization】

In terms of regional PR, the bureau is struggling to find a balance between focusing on the core strengths of the prefecture and fairness toward all of its five provinces. As the five regions are dispersed, the development of tourist routes and intermodal transportation are a current issue.

【Cooperation with other local governments and DMOs】

The Hyōgo Tourism Head Office is also playing a part in inbound tourism-related activities, while the prefecture is the one initiating the action plans.

5) Nara Prefecture
【Data regarding foreign overnight guests】

Comparing the data for 2012 and 2019 shows that the total number of foreign overnight guests grew by a factor of approximately 10 in Nara City, while in Ikoma City it grew by an impressive factor of 34 (both are located in the northern part of the prefecture). In the western part, in Heguri Town, where Mount Shigi is located, the number grew by a factor of approximately 10. Meanwhile in the eastern part, it grew approximately ten fold in Tenri City, and by 3 in Kashihara City. In the southern part, it grew by a factor of approximately 26 in Gojō City, 9 in Yoshino Town, 13 in Tenkawa Village, and 8 in Totsukawa Village (Figure 4-2-6).

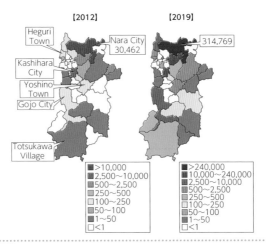

【2012】

Heguri Town
Nara City 30,462
Kashihara City
Yoshino Town
Gojo City
Totsukawa Village

■>10,000
■2,500~10,000
■500~2,500
■250~500
□100~250
■50~100
■1~50
□<1

【2019】

314,769

■>240,000
■10,000~240,000
■2,500~10,000
■500~2,500
■250~500
□100~250
■50~100
■1~50
□<1

Figure 4-2-6 The total number of foreign overnight guests by municipality in Nara Prefecture

Source: Prepared based on individual data from *Overnight Travel Statistics Survey* (JTA)

While the increase rate is significant overall, considering that overnight guests tend to concentrate in the northern part, attracting them to entire prefecture remains an issue.

【Organization in charge of inbound tourism promotion】

In Nara Prefecture, the Tourism Bureau (approximately 50 employees), part of the Industry, Tourism and Employment Promotion Department, is in charge of tourism policies, which includes inbound tourism. Its main tasks cover improving tourism infrastructure, accommodations, attracting tourists, disseminating information, and attracting MICE tourism.

【Prefectural approaches to the concept of "brand" 】

The core of Nara Prefecture's brand is represented by its rich "nature, history and cultural assets." In order to attract new tourists, it is necessary to capitalize on Nara's rich heritage, and to make its charm more widely known.

【Measures to increase tourism expenditure and the number of foreign visitors】

One coordinator is appointed to promote Nara Prefecture to the Chinese-speaking world. Similarly, a former school principal is appointed to use their connections and experience in order to attract school trips from overseas. One of the current challenges is to increase Nara's popularity among Europeans, so the bureau is focusing on activities such as travel exhibitions.

Policies to increase expenditure by foreign tourists aim to develop nature-based experiences and to improve the attractiveness of the city. The prefecture is focusing on improving the overall accommodation capacity of traditional Japanese inns (*ryokan*) and hotels, while making efforts to promote a more even distribution of accommodation facilities, considering that most are located in Nara City.

〔The main challenges of tourism regionalization〕

One of the main challenges when trying to attract tourists to the prefecture is the transport infrastructure.

In order to tackle this issue, the prefecture is making efforts to ensure that public transportation is smooth, comfortable, and easy to use for foreigners. It is also promoting the use of major highways, such as the Keinawa Expressway (connecting Kyoto, Nara and Wakayama), and cycling routes which can contribute to the encouragement of tourism.

〔Cooperation with other local governments and DMOs〕

Municipalities, tourism associations, and DMOs have been cooperating with each other through city planning agreements and meetings at various levels. However, it is necessary to clarify the roles and responsibilities of each entity and to further strengthen cooperation so that they can work on tourism promotion in a coordinated and proactive manner.

6) Wakayama Prefecture
〔Data regarding foreign overnight guests〕

Comparing the data for 2012 and 2019 shows that the total number of foreign overnight guests grew by a factor of approximately 4.1, the upward trend being the most prominent in the south of the prefecture. By main municipality, the number of guests grew by a factor of approximately 9 in Wakayama City, 4 in Shirahama Town, 5 in Kōya Town, and 17 in Tanabe City (Figure 4-2-7).

Part I

Part II

Part III

Part IV

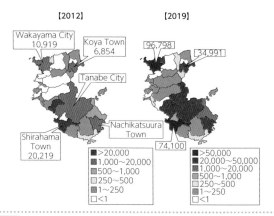

Figure 4-2-7 The total number of foreign overnight guests by municipality in Wakayama Prefecture

Source: Prepared based on individual data from *Overnight Travel Statistics Survey* (JTA)

【Organization in charge of inbound tourism promotion】

In Wakayama Prefecture, the Tourism Bureau, part of the Department of Commerce, Industry, Tourism and Labor, is in charge of tourism policies, which includes inbound tourism. Its main tasks are divided between domestic and foreign operations. Including members of the Wakayama Tourism Federation, which has its office within the Tourism Bureau, the total number of employees is approximately 50.

【Prefectural approaches to the concept of "brand"】

Wakayama prefecture is blessed with a wide variety of tourist attractions such as the Kumano Kodo Pilgrimage Routes, Mount Kōya, and the Shirahama hot springs, which it can use to attract foreign visitors.[8] Its PR campaigns aim to make use of historical and cultural assets, including World Heritage sites, in a sustainable way.

【Measures to increase tourism expenditure and the number of foreign visitors】

Even before Japan's foreign tourism boom, businesses in the prefecture were proactively building relationships with major travel agencies in Hong Kong, Taiwan, and South Korea, and were adapting their tourist products to the needs of the respective markets. As a result, a large number of overnight guests in destinations such as Shi-

---

8) Since before the COVID-19 pandemic, the prefecture is targeting domestic customers in the Tokyo area by running a marketing campaign promoting itself as a "workation" destination. The campaign takes advantage of the short travel time between Tokyo and Wakayama due to direct flights from Haneda Airport to Nanki Shirahama Airport.

rahama were from East Asia. In addition, numerous promotion campaigns launched in collaboration with international news websites such as BBC or CNN, and travel websites such as Lonely Planet, led to a high ratio of visitors from Western countries.

[The main challenges of tourism regionalization]
Most accommodation facilities in the prefecture are tailored for group tours, so their main challenge is to adapt to the needs of individual tourists and increase expenditure per capita.

Another issue is developing tourist routes that enhance regional interconnectivity between different attractions of the Kii Peninsula area.

[Cooperation with other local governments and DMOs]
Considering the developmental stage of private DMOs and other players in the prefecture, Wakayama is taking the lead in inbound tourism policies.

3. The current situation and the main challenges in the six prefectures of Kansai

Our analysis showed that policies and approaches toward tourism differ greatly from one prefecture to another, according to their geographical conditions and maturity as tourist destinations. We can summarize our analysis through the following main ideas.[9]

(1) Shiga Prefecture is taking advantage of its rich natural assets, including Lake Biwa, to develop a unique appeal mindful of the post-pandemic travel trends. It takes advantage of these assets as a PR tool and tries promoting them through PR campaigns such as "Soko Shiga."

(2) Kyoto Prefecture is trying to overcome the problem posed by the unbalanced tourist distribution in favor of Kyoto City by promoting less known destinations within the prefecture.

(3) Osaka Prefecture is focusing on diversity as the main distinguishing factor to increase its appeal, mainly through the Osaka Convention & Tourism Bureau.

(4) Hyōgo Prefecture is bringing to the forefront of its PR campaign the distinct characteristics of its five regions.

(5) Nara Prefecture is trying to encourage forms of tourism which imply overnight accommodation within the prefecture and a higher level of expenditure per capita.

(6) Wakayama Prefecture, under the leadership of the local government, is

9) For details regarding the tourism strategy of each prefecture, see the reference literature.

running PR campaigns for its numerous tourist attractions and encourages cooperation among stakeholders.

Each prefecture has its own unique system to stimulate the development of inbound tourism, leading to differences in terms of scale, policies, and division of responsibilities. This reflects the differences in each prefecture's stance toward inbound tourism and the importance it gives to this sector.

While the specifics of each prefecture's situation may vary, all of them are working on tourism regionalization. In this context, detailed measures are required to compensate for the lack of infrastructure and encourage coordination with local communities. Regional development cannot be carried out by the government alone, and the role of DMOs will become even more important, considering their ability to lead the way in public-private sector synergy, and work closely with local communities while enjoying a certain degree of freedom of action.

References

Asia Pacific Institute of Research (2021) "Kansai as an Advanced Inbound Tourism Destination: Towards a Sustainable Tourism Strategy - Research Report (2020)."

Hyōgo Prefecture (2020) "Hyōgo Tourism Strategy" (Japanese title: *Hyōgo tsūrizumu senryaku*), retrieved from: https://www.hyōgo-tourism.jp/files/pdf/ strategy/ doc05_05 (last verified on July 6, 2021).

Kyoto Prefecture (2019) "A Comprehensive Tourism Strategy for Kyoto Prefecture" (Japanese title: *Kyōto-fu Kankō Sōgō Senryaku*), retrieved from: https://www.pref.kyoto.jp/kanko/news/2018/documents/kankousougousenryaku.pdf (last verified on July 6, 2021).

Nara Prefecture (2021) "A Comprehensive Tourism Strategy for Nara Prefecture" (Japanese title: *Nara-ken Kankō Sōgō Senryaku*), retrieved from: http://www.pref. nara.jp/item/250854.htm (last verified on July 21, 2021).

Osaka Prefecture (2021) "Osaka City Urban Development Strategy – 2020" (Japanese title: *Ōsaka Toshi Miryoku Sōzō Senryaku 2025*), retrieved from: https://www.pref.osaka.lg.jp/attach/18716/00000000/strategy2025.pdf (last verified on July 6, 2021).

Shiga Prefecture (2021) "Healthy Shiga: Tourism Vision 2022" (Japanese title: *"Kenkōshiga" tsūrizumu bijon 2022*), retrieved from: https://www.pref.shiga.lg.jp/file/attachment/ 5107670.pdf (last verified on July 6, 2021).

Wakayama Prefecture (2021) "Wakayama Prefecture Tourism Promotion Action Plan (Tourism Promotion Action Program 2021)" (Japanese title: *Wakayama ken kankō shinkō jisshi kōdō keikaku (kankō shinkō akushon puroguramu 2021)*), retrieved from: https://www.pref.wakayama.lg.jp/prefg/062400/ actionprogram2016_d/fil/00AP.pdf (last verified on July 6, 2021).

Part I

Part II

Part III

Part IV

Table 4-2-1   Survey items and content

	Shiga Pref.	Kyoto Pref.	Osaka Pref.
Organization	Tourism Bureau (approx. 20 employees in total, 1 employee in charge of inbound tourism)	Commerce, Industry, Labor and Tourism Department (23 employees)	Planning and Tourism Division (27 employees), part of the Urban Developmen Bureau
Measures to increase the number of foreign visitors	· PR campaign in Taiwan in association with the bicycle manufacturer GIANT. · Participation to travel expos in 2018-19. · Promotion campaigns in Michigan (USA) and Hunan (China), in addition to France and the UK.	· Promoting less-known areas of the prefecture in places such as Hong Kong and Taiwan, which have a high ratio of repeat tourists. An increase in the number of visitors from Thailand is also expected.	· Attracting both Asian and non-Asian tourists.
Measures to increase consumption	· Online advertising of nature, water sports, ceramics, etc. Planning a PR campaign centered around cycling in France and the UK.	· PR campaigns in markets with high tourism expenditure, such as Europe, the USA, and Australia.	· Future PR campaigns in Western countries focusing on history, culture and cuisine. · Increase the accommodation capaci of hotels and private lodging. · Develop new tourist routes across th prefecture and uncover Osaka's hidc tourist potential.
Views toward the "brand" concept	· Lake Biwa and nature are an important part of the local identity. Tries to promote itself as a "workation" destination.	· The entire prefecture except Kyoto City is divided into three categories collectively branded as "Another Kyoto," which is made up of "Kyoto by the Sea," "Woodland Kyoto," "Kyoto Tea Country," and "Kyoto Otokuni Bamboo Grove."	· Promote Osaka Prefecture as a place of diversity in terms of cuisine, cultur history, entertainment, etc., not bour by stereotypes.
Tourism regionalization	· Trying to attract foreign visitors from Kyoto. · Ongoing efforts to improve intermodal transportation and to translate information boards into foreign languages.	· Encourage visitors concentrated in Kyoto City to also visit other parts of the prefecture. · Subsidize bus companies to offer bus passes for the aforementioned regions: "Kyoto by the Sea," "Woodland Kyoto," and "Kyoto Tea Country."	· Attract tourists from Osaka City to north, east and south of the prefectu. · Test the feasibility of a sightseeing bus linking Osaka and Sakai cities, and publish tourist maps of the area surrounding the tumuli, etc.
Cooperation with other local governments	· Collaboration with Fukui Prefecture for a PR campaign in Europe promoting World Heritage sites. Advertisements in overseas magazines, invitations to domestic tour operators, etc.	· Promotion of the San'in Coast (with Hyōgo and Tottori), national heritage (with Fukui and Shiga), Miketsukuni Food Country (with Mie, Fukui, Hyōgo), etc. In addition, an Overseas PR campaign implemented through cooperation between Japan Railways and the 12 prefectures along the Hokuriku Shinkansen line.	· It is cooperating with the Union of Kansai Governments (Tourism Divisic for promotion campaigns such as the creation and distribution of pamphle The theme is decided by the Union c Kansai Governments.
Cooperation with municipalities within the prefecture	· PR campaigns are almost always done through local DMOs. In some cases, direct communication with municipalities is also used.	· In most cases, cooperation with the municipalities within the prefecture is done indirectly through the respective local DMOs.	· It offers support to local municipaliti for their PR initiatives. · Shares the same tourism strategy wi Osaka City."
Cooperation with DMOs & Division of responsibilities	· In PR campaigns, it collaborates with the Kansai Tourism Bureau, while tourist product development is secured through close collaboration with local DMOs.	· Constant cooperation for inbound tourism. · Collaboration with the Kyoto Tourism Federation and three regional DMOs, including personnel.	· The Osaka Convention & Tourism Bureau enjoys a high degree of freedom in developing policies in terms promotion and marketing.
DMOs & Tourism associations within the prefecture	· Biwako Visitors Bureau (30 employees) (according to the "Japanese DMO Formation and Establishment Plan")	· Collaborating with the Kyoto Tourism Federation and the three regional DMOs, including sharing personnel.	· The Osaka Convention & Tourism Bureau is responsible for promotion campaigns.
Form of cooperation with the Kansai Tourism Bureau	· Strong relationship. Consensus must be reached for every action.	· All the DMOs in the prefecture have the vice-governor of Kyoto Prefecture as their vice-president, and Kyoto Prefecture officials as their staff. · The prefecture entrusts some of its PR campaigns to the Bureau, and it is also participating in familiarization trips organized by the Bureau as part of its mass media campaigns.	· Collaboration for promotion campaigns (creation and distribution of pamphlets). · While the theme is decided by the Union of Kansai Governments, the pr fecture is in charge of tourist product development.
Cooperation with DMOs from other regions	Central Japan Tourism Organization	–	–

Source: based on the surveys conducted by APIR at tourist organizations in each prefecture.

Hyōgo Pref.	Nara Pref.	Wakayama Pref.
Bureau (14 employees) (& Hyōgo Head Office (27 employees))	Tourism Bureau (approx. 50 employees)	Tourism Bureau & Wakayama Tourism Federation (approx. 50 employees in total, 13 or 14 employees in charge of inbound tourism)
refecture's overseas offices and t information counters conduct PR aigns. er school principals are in charge of ational exchanges between schools.	· It focuses on PR campaigns in Europe (especially France). · One coordinator is appointed to promote the prefecture to Chinese visitors. · Former school principals are in charge of international exchanges between schools.	· Even before Japan's foreign tourism boom, businesses in the prefecture were developing tourist products in cooperation with travel agencies in Hong Kong, Taiwan, and South Korea, while strengthening their relationships. · Numerous promotion campaigns run in collaboration with international news and travel websites.
ntly, two producers of the Hyōgo sm Head Office are in charge of oping new tourist products.	· Development of accommodation facilities on prefectural land. · Tourist product development in order to attract more visitors to the southern part of the prefecture. · Development of activities that can be done in the morning.	· Accommodation facilities tailored to groups are making investments in order to become able to accommodate the needs of individual tourists, and increase consumption per capita.
mpaigns focus on each individual st location, such Kobe or Himeji, r than trying to promote a unified e of the prefecture.	· The promotion campaign focuses on the historical and cultural heritage. In addition, tourist products centered around nature and tumuli ("Walking Nara") are also being refined.	· Its PR campaigns promote sustainable tourism based on nature and historical heritage such as Kumano Kodo, Mount Kōya and the Shirahama hot springs.
to attract tourists from Osaka and to the prefecture's five provinces. also planning to attract more visitors egional airports located in Western n.	· Encourage visitors concentrated in the north to also visit other parts of the prefecture. · Currently, it is investing in major highways, such as the Keinawa Expressway (connecting Kyoto, Nara and Wakayama), and cycling routes.	· The limited accommodation capacity of tourist attractions during certain seasons represents a current issue (for example, Shirahama during the summer season, and Mount Koya the during autumn season). · It aims to involve Mie Prefecture in the development of tourist routes that cover all of Kii Peninsula.
ocusing on promotion through the ai Tourism Bureau and the Union of ai Governments.	· Cooperation with Wakayama Prefecture to jointly promote tourist attractions such as Mount Kōya and Kumano Hongū Shrine.	· Developing tourist routes in cooperation with the southern part of Nara Prefecture. · Developing the "Pilgrim and Mount Kōya" route in cooperation with Tokushima and Kagawa prefectures.
ers consultancy for each proposal.	· It offers consultancy for each proposal.	· Conducting a promotion campaign in association with Wakayama City. In addition, the prerogatives of the city and those of the prefecture are clearly delineated.
prefecture is in charge of planning, e DMOs are in charge of tourist duct development and promotion paigns.	· The prefecture is in charge of planning and promotion campaigns, while DMOs are in charge of tourist product development.	The prefectural government is collaborating with city halls, chambers of commerce and industry, etc., by focusing on social networking.
ares the same office space with Hyōgo Tourism Head Office (27 loyees).	· Nara Prefecture Visitors Bureau (approx. 20 employees)	· The Wakayama Tourism Federation and the prefectural Tourism Bureau have a total of 13 or 14 employees in charge of inbound tourism.
cepts or rejects the initiatives (exhibi- s, familiarization trips, etc.) created by Bureau on a case-by-case basis.	· It accepts or rejects the initiatives (exhibitions, familiarization trips, etc.) created by the Bureau on a case-by-case basis.	· Field trips, etc.
chi Tourism DMO	–	–

Section 3
FUTURE ROLES AND CHALLENGES FOR DMOS: EXAMPLES FROM KANSAI CASE STUDIES

INADA, Yoshihisa; OSHIMA, Hisanori; KOYAMA, Kenta;

ICHIMIYA, Masato; NOMURA, Ryosuke

1. DMOs in Japan

As mentioned in Section 2, in addition to local governments, the role of DMOs will become increasingly important for future inbound tourism strategies. Therefore, we would like to begin by describing the background and outlining the establishment of DMOs in Japan.

The first time DMOs were mentioned in official documents was in the "Comprehensive Strategy for Overcoming Population Decline and Vitalizing Local Economy in Japan" approved by the Japanese Cabinet on December 27, 2014. Following this decision, the Japan Tourism Agency began accepting candidates for DMO status in December 2015, and in November 2017, 41 applications were officially registered.[1]

Since then, the number of registered DMOs has increased, and as of November 2021, a total of 213 DMOs have been registered for wide-area, regional, and local cooperation. Additionally, there is a total of 90 candidates registering for regional and local DMO status (Table 4-3-1).[2]

Table 4-3-1   Types of DMOs and number of registered DMOs

	Wide-area	Regional	Local	Total
Registered DMO	10	95	108	213
Candidate DMO		24	66	90

Source: Prepared by the author based on the "Registration List" published on the Japan Tourism Agency's website.

---

1) For a detailed description of the establishment of DMOs, see Takahashi (2017). Note that the terminology was changed from "Japanese DMO" to "Registered DMO" on April 15, 2020, due to the revision of the registration guidelines, which led to stricter criteria in alignment with international standards.
2) Each type of DMO is described below.
   Wide-area DMO: an organization that focuses on a unified marketing and management approach for the tourist destination development of a wider area than regional DMOs.
   Regional DMO: an organization that focuses on a unified marketing and management approach for the tourist destination development of an area covering several municipalities.
   Local DMO: an organization that focuses on a unified marketing and management approach for the tourist destination development on a municipality level.

In order to be registered in Japan, a DMO must fulfill a number of basic roles and functions, and meet the five requirements shown in Table 4-3-2. The guidelines of the Japan Tourism Agency also acknowledge the category of "candidate DMOs," which refers to DMOs that have not yet met all the requirements to be considered "registered DMOs."

Table 4-3-2	Role of DMOs

Basic roles of DMOs
(1) Build consensus on regional tourism development among various stakeholders
(2) Constantly collect and analyze various data, formulate strategies (branding) based on a clear concept and data, set KPIs and establish a PDCA cycle
(3) Promote local initiatives for destination development, such as improving tourist attractions which increase the region's overall attractiveness; transportation access, including intra-regional inter-connectivity; and the tourism infrastructure, including multilingual signage.
(4) Coordinate, develop, and promote consistent strategies for tourism-related projects implemented by related parties
Requirements for registered DMOs
(1) Play a central role in building consensus on regional tourism development among various stakeholders
(2) Collect data constantly, formulate strategies, set KPIs, establish a PDCA cycle
(3) Coordinate, develop, and promote consistent strategies for tourism-related projects implemented by related parties
(4) Acquire legal personality, clarify the responsible parties, ensure that data collection and analysis is done by experts.
(5) Ensure stable operating funds

Source: Prepared by the author based on "What is a Destination Management Organization (DMO)?" published on the Japan Tourism Agency's website.

2. Tourism policies of DMOs in Kansai

In the previous subsection, we looked at the background and outline of the establishment of DMOs in Japan. In this section, we focus on DMOs in the six prefectures of Kansai.

First, we look at the number and geographic distribution of DMOs in each prefecture. Next, we analyze their activities from several perspectives, which are summarized below based on the basic roles of DMOs shown in Table 4-3-2.

- Marketing based on objective data and indicators
- Coordination of intra-regional public-private partnerships and wide-area co-operation
- Increasing the attractiveness of tourist destinations
- Discovering new tourist attractions and advertising
- Analyzing regional issues and using available data

- Increasing brand power
- Innovation
- Human resources development

After describing the situation in each prefecture, we provide one or two examples of noteworthy DMOs. Based on the results, at the end of this section, we discuss the role and future challenges of DMOs in Kansai.

Table 4-3-3 shows the main DMOs in Kansai's six prefectures. The number and types of DMOs located in each prefecture are different. Kyoto Prefecture is unique in that it does not have a DMO that manages the entire prefecture. In addition, there are DMOs that collaborate with other prefectures in the case of common themes such as historical and cultural heritage, and cuisine.

Table 4-3-3   List of DMOs in Kansai

| Prefecture | Registered DMO | | Candidate DMO | | Existence of DMOs covering the whole prefecture |
	Regional	Local	Regional	Local	
Shiga	2	1			O
Kyoto	3	2			×
Osaka	2	2	1		O
Hyogo	3(+1)	2		1	O
Nara	1	2			O
Wakayama	1	6	2	1	O

Note: The numbers in this table are as of November 4, 2021. For DMOs that cover multiple prefectures, the count is based on the prefecture where the headquarters are located. The "+1" note in the case of Hyogo Prefecture refers to the "Kirin-no-machi Tourism Bureau" which is located in Tottori Prefecture.
Source: Prepared by the author based on "List of Organizations for Destination Development" published on the Japan Tourism Agency's website.

Next, Figure 4-3-1 shows the geographic distribution of DMOs in each of the Kansai prefectures. The DMOs in each prefecture can be summarized as follows.

The regional DMOs in Shiga Prefecture are the Biwako Visitors Bureau, which covers the entire prefecture, and the Omi Tourism Board. Also, the Omi Hachiman Tourism and Products Association is a local DMO.

The regional DMOs in Kyoto Prefecture are the Northern Kyoto Company for Regional Cooperation and Urban Development, the Woodland Kyoto Regional Promotion Company, and the Kyoto Yamashiro Regional Promotion Company. In addition, the Kyoto City Tourism Association and the Nantan City Miyama Tourism Town Development Association[3] can be given as of local DMOs.

---

3) The Nantan City Miyama Tourism Town Development Association, which covers the town of Miyama in Nantan City, is also a member of the regional DMO "Woodland Kyoto."

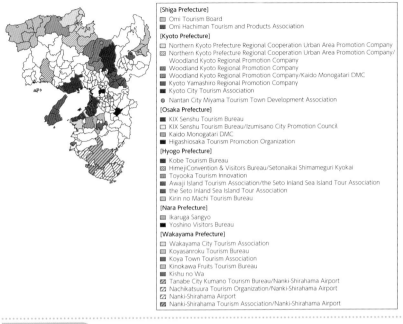

[Shiga Prefecture]
▨ Omi Tourism Board
■ Omi Hachiman Tourism and Products Association
[Kyoto Prefecture]
▢ Northern Kyoto Prefecture Regional Cooperation Urban Area Promotion Company
▨ Northern Kyoto Prefecture Regional Cooperation Urban Area Promotion Company/
   Woodland Kyoto Regional Promotion Company
▨ Woodland Kyoto Regional Promotion Company
▨ Woodland Kyoto Regional Promotion Company/Kaido Monogatari DMC
▨ Kyoto Yamashiro Regional Promotion Company
■ Kyoto City Tourism Association
◉ Nantan City Miyama Tourism Town Development Association
[Osaka Prefecture]
■ KIX Senshu Tourism Bureau
▢ KIX Senshu Tourism Bureau/Izumisano City Promotion Council
▨ Kaido Monogatari DMC
■ Higashiosaka Tourism Promotion Organization
[Hyogo Prefecture]
■ Kobe Tourism Bureau
▨ HimejiConvention & Visitors Bureau/Setonaikai Shimameguri Kyokai
▨ Toyooka Tourism Innovation
■ Awaji Island Tourism Association/the Seto Inland Sea Island Tour Association
■ the Seto Inland Sea Island Tour Association
▨ Kirin no Machi Tourism Bureau
[Nara Prefecture]
▨ Ikaruga Sangyo
■ Yoshino Visitors Bureau
[Wakayama Prefecture]
▢ Wakayama City Tourism Association
▨ Koyasanroku Tourism Bureau
■ Koya Town Tourism Association
▨ Kinokawa Fruits Tourism Bureau
■ Kishu no Wa
▨ Tanabe City Kumano Tourism Bureau/Nanki-Shirahama Airport
▨ Nachikatsuura Tourism Organization/Nanki-Shirahama Airport
▨ Nanki-Shirahama Airport
▨ Nanki-Shirahama Tourism Association/Nanki-Shirahama Airport

Figure 4-3-1   **Geographical distribution of Kansai DMOs**

Note: In addition to the DMOs listed above, there are regional DMOs that manage the entire prefecture: Biwako
     Visitors Bureau in Shiga Prefecture, Osaka Convention & Visitors Bureau in Osaka Prefecture, Hyogo Tour-
     ism Headquarters in Hyogo Prefecture, Nara Visitors Bureau in Nara Prefecture, and Wakayama Tourism
     Federation in Wakayama Prefecture.
Source: Prepared by the author based on "List of Organizations for Destination Development" published on
     the Japan Tourism Agency's website.

The regional DMOs in Osaka Prefecture are the Osaka Convention & Visitors Bureau, which covers the entire prefecture, and the KIX Senshu Tourism Bureau. Local DMOs include the Higashiosaka Tourism Promotion Organization, the Izumisano City Promotion Council, and the Kaido Monogatari DMC.

The regional DMOs in Hyogo Prefecture are the Hyogo Tourism Head Office, which covers the entire prefecture, Toyooka Tourism Innovation, the Kirin no Machi Tourism Bureau, and Awaji Island Tourism Association. The local DMOs are the Kobe Tourism Bureau, the Seto Inland Sea Island Tour Association and the Himeji Convention & Visitors Bureau.

In Nara Prefecture, the Nara Prefecture Visitors Bureau is the regional DMO which covers the entire prefecture. The local DMOs are Ikaruga Sangyo and Yoshino Visitors Bureau.

The regional DMOs in Wakayama Prefecture are the Wakayama Tourism Federation, which covers the entire prefecture, Koyasanroku Tourism Bureau, and the Nanki-Shirahama Airport. Local DMOs include the Wakayama City Tourism Association, Tanabe City Kumano Tourism Bureau, Kinokawa Fruits Tourism Bureau, Koya Town Tourism Association, Nanki-Shirahama Tourism Association, Kishu no Wa, and Nachikatsuura Tourism Organization.

In the following, we will take a detailed look at the status of DMOs, their regional characteristics, and tourism policies in each prefecture.[4]

(1) Shiga Prefecture
Main Activities

Based on its mid-term plan titled "Healthy Shiga Tourism Vision 2022—Tourism as a Bridge to a Connected and Enduring Shiga," Biwako Visitors Bureau is reviewing tourism resources by capitalizing on Shiga's uniqueness and building a system for sustainable tourism and product promotion. The Omi Tourism Board is developing tours that allow visitors to experience history and nature through a sustainable form of tourism which respects "nature, culture, tradition and humanity." The Omi Hachiman Tourism and Products Association works with citizens' groups and various companies to improve local attractiveness based on the concept of "a town you want to visit, revisit and live in."

Examples of tourism product development, promotion, etc.

The Omi Tourism Board is investigating the potential of local products through its "Omi—Gastronomic City" project.

Measures to increase brand power

The Omi Tourism Board is developing nature tours based on activities such as cycling and trekking, targeting wealthy tourists in the US and Australia. For affluent people in the UK and France, the Omi Tourism Board is developing premium cultural experience tours which include tea ceremony, traditional meals, and accommodation at temples and shrines. For affluent people in Asian countries such as Singapore, Thailand, and Malaysia, it is also creating tours centered on scenery and food, such as enjoying cherry blossoms or autumn foliage in the precincts of temples and shrines, and outdoor dining.

Regional synergy: public-private partnerships within the region and wide-area cooperation initiatives

The Biwako Visitors Bureau promotes tourism in close cooperation with the

---

4) This section deals with DMOs registered with the Japan Tourism Agency as of November 4, 2021. The same applies henceforth.

prefectural authorities, municipalities and local DMOs. In addition, the "Formation and Development Plan for Local Tourism Service Providers" of the Biwako Visitors Bureau is based on the principle of "Tourism During the Coronavirus Pandemic," and will strengthen cooperation with municipalities and tourism related businesses in the prefecture.

Innovation

The websites are available in multiple languages, and the Biwako Free Wi-Fi access points are being expanded and upgraded to support cashless payment.

Human Resource Development

The Biwako Visitors Bureau has been fostering human resources to lead the development of tourism under the three-year "Tourism Human Resource Development and Regional Support Program" since FY 2019.

The path to self-sustainability

The Biwako Visitors Bureau and the Omi Tourism Board are considering acquiring travel agency licenses and monetizing them. In addition, the Omi Tourism Board is working to generate revenue through the rental of food trucks that use local produce and the development of inbound tourism products.

Marketing and management initiatives using objective data and indicators

Key Performance Indicators (KPIs) have been established based on website traffic data obtained through Google Analytics, and surveys of visitors to Shiga Prefecture. Target groups specific to each region have also been determined.

Examples of DMOs

We will focus on the Omi Tourism Board as a notable DMO in Shiga Prefecture. The Omi Tourism Board aims to provide sustainable tourism products that respect the local environment, culture, and people. In order to do so, it takes advantage of the geographical features of the region, its relaxed atmosphere and generous space, and the spirit of the local merchants.

In addition, the organization's efforts to become self-sustaining include obtaining income from the rental of food trucks using local produce, and royalty income from the development of specialty products (local brand products).

(2) Kyoto Prefecture
Main Activities
In 2021, the Kyoto City Tourism Association promoted the Kyoto Tourism Code of Conduct, which aims to "harmonize the lives of citizens and tourism." On the other hand, the three regional DMOs will continue to act as the main drivers of tourism development, create regional brands, and stimulate tourism consumption in order to increase the region's revenue.

Examples of tourism product development, promotion, etc.
The area covered by the Kyoto by the Sea DMO has prospered since ancient times as a place for cultural exchange with the Asian mainland, and has a deep connection with the imperial family, making it a place imbued with ancient history and myths. On the other hand, the area covered by the Kyoto Tea Country DMO is a region representative of Japanese tea, and has been well-known for the production of different types of teas such as matcha, sencha, and gyokuro, ever since tea culture was introduced to Japan from China. In addition, the region is also known for its leading role in the development of Japanese tea culture.

Measures to increase brand power
As part of its efforts to enhance the Kyoto brand, the Kyoto City Tourism Association is working to decentralize tourist by visualizing the degree of congestion at tourist sites in addition to raising awareness of good manners. On the other hand, the three regional DMOs are working on the creation of regional tourism areas through Agritourism.

Regional synergy: public-private partnerships within region and wide-area regional cooperation initiatives
The three regional DMOs have assigned specialists to transform traditional buildings such as old private houses into facilities that can provide a genuine local experience through accommodations and food.

Innovation
In areas covered by the Kyoto by the Sea and Woodland Kyoto DMOs, e-bikes are deployed in areas where intermodal passenger transport is insufficient for touring the region.

Human Resource Development
The Kyoto City Tourism Association is working to train Kyoto City-certified interpreter guides. The Kyoto by the Sea DMO is holding regular training courses

for local guides in anticipation of a recovery in inbound tourism.

The path to self-sustainability

The three regional DMOs are registered as travel agencies and earn revenue by selling their own travel products.

However, there is still a high degree of dependence on contributions and subsidies from the national and local governments.

Marketing and management initiatives using objective data and indicators

The Kyoto City Tourism Association and the three regional DMOs will provide information and benefits according to the individual needs of tourists based on the data obtained through the reservation system. This is expected to encourage tourists to revisit and extend their stays.

Examples of DMOs

The three regional DMOs promote the "Alternative Kyoto" both in Japan and abroad by updating their multilingual websites and conducting campaigns that target the residents of neighboring prefectures.

(3) Osaka Prefecture
Main Activities

The Osaka Tourism Bureau is promoting tourism in cooperation with 43 municipalities in the prefecture. Kaido Monogatari DMC is trying to attract visitors to the Nose Road region, while the Higashiosaka Tourism Promotion Organization is doing the same for Higashiosaka city, by promoting experience-based tourism. KIX Senshu Tourism Bureau tries to attract visitors by promoting its numerous attractions such as hot springs, and Izumisano City Promotion Council focuses on culinary tourism.

Examples of tourism product development, promotion, etc.

In order to build the Osaka brand, the Osaka Convention & Visitors Bureau focuses on the Semba area, which is the birthplace of Osaka's culture and is expected to become an important transportation node once the Naniwasuji rail line is finished.

Regional synergy: public-private partnerships within the region and wide-area regional cooperation initiatives

The Osaka Convention & Visitors Bureau is working to rediscover and refine

Part I

Part II

Part III

Part IV

the tourism sites of the 43 municipalities within Osaka Prefecture. It is also pro-actively promoting micro tourism and lodging campaigns for prefectural residents.

Innovation

The Osaka Convention and Visitors Bureau launched a new QR-code travel pass in January 2021. The bureau will also work to promote the implementation of cashless payment systems.

Human Resource Development

The Osaka Convention & Visitors Bureau works to train interpreter guides and to establish a platform (Osaka Global Student Support Association) to support and train international students. Its aim is to help them to gain a deeper understanding of Osaka Prefecture and Japan.

The path to self-sustainability

About 60–70% of the budget of the Osaka Convention & Visitors Bureau is covered by subsidies from the Osaka prefectural and municipal governments, while its own financial resources include sponsorship from about 600 organizations and commission fees from the Osaka Loop Pass. However, considering that the number of tickets sold for the Osaka Loop Pass has fallen sharply along with the number of foreign visitors due to the COVID-19 pandemic, the lack of business expenses has become an issue.

Marketing and management initiatives using objective data and indicators

The Osaka Convention & Visitors Bureau is constructing a data management platform (DMP) to integrate its data on tourism facilities, data on approximately 60 million tourists from Taiwan, Hong Kong, China and other Asian countries, and third-party data. The DMP will enable the bureau to visualize the current situation for each KPI by implementing the PDCA method from the stage of tourism policy planning to the development of tourism products. The DMP also facilitates the development of tourism policies for each municipality by revealing the profile of potential visitors.

Examples of DMOs

We will focus on the KIX Senshu Tourism Bureau as a notable DMO in Osaka Prefecture.

The bureau is developing its business based on the strategic pillars of "food," "activities," and "industrial tourism," and is promoting the construction of cycle routes. In addition to the Senshu Cycling Route, the Kumano Kaido Road leading to the World Heritage site Kumano Sanzan (Wakayama Prefecture), and places where visitors can fully experience nature such as marine sports are being developed. The bureau is also working to improve the appeal of industrial tourism to inbound and individual tourists, by advertising traditional industries and night views of factories, and by establishing tourist centers that can offer information in multiple languages.

(4) Hyogo Prefecture
Main Activities
The Hyogo Tourism Head Office has set up the "Hyogo Tourism Strategy (FY2020–2022)" to attract more tourists and encourage them to travel around the prefecture by focusing on improving the attractiveness of tourist spots and their capacity to welcome tourists. The Kobe Tourism Bureau promotes tourism in Kobe City and its neighboring municipalities. Himeji Convention & Visitors Bureau is working to build up the Himeji City brand centered around Himeji Castle. Toyooka Tourism Innovation is working to improve the attractiveness of the region by focusing on Kinosaki hot springs. The Awaji Island Tourist Association is promoting the island by advertising the myth according to which it was the first island among the Japanese archipelago to be created by the gods. The Kirin no Machi Tourism Bureau is conducting efforts to raise the profile of the traditional Kirin Lion Dance specific to adjacent areas in Tottori and Hyogo prefectures. Finally, the Seto Inland Sea Island Tour Association plans to develop a maritime passenger transportation business centered on Awaji Island.

Examples of tourism product development, promotion, etc.
In order to attract tourists from around the world, the Awaji Island Tourist Association is promoting the unique character of Awaji Island among European and American tourists who are particularly interested in history and culture. In doing so, the association is emphasizing the island as the "birthplace of Japan," as already mentioned.

Measures to increase brand power
While Himeji Castle is a well-known World Heritage site, other tourist attractions in Himeji City do not enjoy the same level of public recognition. For this reason, the Himeji Convention & Visitors Bureau is working to build the "Himeji brand" through its "Himeji Plus One" strategy, in order to encourage visitors to stay longer in the area.

Regional synergy: public-private partnerships within the region and wide-area regional cooperation initiatives

Half of the visitors to Kobe City are day-trippers. Therefore, the Kobe Tourism Bureau, along with neighboring municipalities and tourist associations that share common tourist attractions with Kobe City, is working to encourage tourists to prolong their stay in the area.

Innovation

The Hyogo Tourism Head Office is working to develop story-based tour routes for existing experience-type and tour-stay-type contents. In addition, it is working to establish a system for selling these products through OTAs (online travel agencies).

On the other hand, Toyooka Tourism Innovation is developing a reservation website in English and French to promote the region world-wide and to expand its business opportunities.

Human Resource Development

In cooperation with the College of Arts, Culture and Tourism (Toyooka City), which opened in April 2021, the Hyogo Tourism Head Office will hold seminars for businesses and young people who aim to work in the tourism industry.

The path to self-sustainability

Several DMOs are registered as travel agencies and earn revenue through lodging fees and selling travel products, but they are still highly dependent on subsidies from the national and local governments.

Marketing and management initiatives using objective data and indicators

Toyooka Tourism Innovation has been developing its marketing strategy based on visitor data collected from an early stage and attract visitors to its tourist sites.

Examples of DMOs

We will focus on the Toyooka Tourism Innovation DMO, which is attracting foreign visitors mainly to the Kinosaki hot springs.

Toyooka Tourism Innovation collects and analyzes data through "Visit Kinosaki," a multilingual website for foreign visitors that not only provides information about the region's attractions, but also provides a number of integrated services for booking activities and accommodation.

A constant percentage of the foreign visitors who use the above website booked accommodation in Toyooka City after arriving in Japan.[5] The reason for this is that they learned about Toyooka while traveling in Kyoto, Osaka, etc. and decided to extend their trip. In March 2020, the company distributed an advertising video (Air Travel) on Facebook and other social media networks. The reactions to the video were particularly positive in traditional Chinese, and the number of Facebook followers increased by about 17,000 from the previous year. As a result, according to a survey of the number of hashtags used by Instagram users conducted by the UK-based company Parkdean Resorts in 2020, Kinosaki hot springs were ranked eighth in the world and first in Japan among the top 25 most Instagrammable hot springs in the world.

(5) Nara Prefecture

Main Activities

The Nara Visitors Bureau promotes the famous tourist attractions in the prefecture, such as Nara Park, and creates and sells custom-made tours for foreign visitors, promoting the prefecture as "The Birthplace of Japan." Ikaruga Sangyo aims to become the "tourist's gateway to Nara" by creating tourism products centered on historical and cultural heritage such as the Horyuji Temple, the world's oldest wooden structure. Finally, the Yoshino Visitors Bureau is developing activities centered around history and nature, aiming to "transform Yoshino into a year-round tourist destination that people want to visit again and again."

Examples of tourism product development, promotion, etc.

All three DMOs are working to discover, refine and promote tourism attractions in their respective areas under the themes of history, culture, and nature. The Nara Visitors Bureau operates and manages the Nara Prefecture Tourism official website, which collects and disseminates information on tourism throughout the prefecture from municipalities and tourism businesses.

Measures to increase brand power

As already mentioned, the Nara Prefecture Visitors Bureau has been working with local businesses to discover and refine tourism attractions in the prefecture. After creating the tourism products, the bureau advertises and sells them on its website.

---

5) For more details, see "Smart Resort Handbook," published by the Ministry of Economy, Trade and Industry in March 2020: https://www.meti.go.jp/policy/mono_info_service/mono/creative/downloadfiles/fy31/handbook2.pdf

Regional synergy: public-private partnerships within the region and wide-area regional cooperation initiatives

Among its staff, the Nara Prefecture Visitors Bureau has representatives from a wide range of related fields, such as government, commerce and industry, working as directors and councilors. In addition, Ikaruga Sangyo is working to enhance collaboration with local tourism businesses, universities, and many other industries.

Innovation

The Nara Prefecture Visitors Bureau has been developing multilingual mobile applications for cultural properties such as Kasuga Taisha Shrine and the Garden of the former Daijo-in Temple as part of a project to improve the accessibility to information regarding cultural properties. It has also installed multilingual signboards and digital signage at Horyuji Temple, a World Heritage site.

The path to self-sustainability

All three DMOs have acquired travel agency licenses and are aiming to become self-sustaining by developing and selling tourism products. Ikaruga Sangyo is also working with its own departments to utilize idle assets such as vacant houses, land, and tenant shops owned by local residents. The Yoshino Visitors Bureau sells local products at tourist information centers and on its website.

Marketing and management initiatives using objective data and indicators

All three DMOs have established KPIs based on the traffic data on their websites and statistical surveys conducted by tourist information centers, and are working to understand the weaknesses of each region.

Examples of DMOs

We will focus on the Ikaruga Sangyo as a notable DMO in Nara prefecture. Taking advantage of its role as a private-sector company, Ikaruga Sangyo is promoting its business in close cooperation with industry, academia, the government and the finance. It has also established the West Nara Regional Tourism Promotion Council to promote wide-area cooperation with neighboring municipalities.

In December 2020 and January 2021, it conducted a "workation" demonstration experiment in cooperation with the Nara prefectural government, and it is working to uncover new markets and to build a new strategy fit for times of pandemic. As a regional DMO, it is focusing on creating and refining tourism products in cooperation with neighboring municipalities.

(6) Wakayama Prefecture
Main Activities
Each DMO in the prefecture has its own characteristics and its activities are strongly connected to the local background.

The Wakayama City Tourism Association, a DMO closely linked to the tourism associations of local governments, is headed by the mayor of Wakayama City and aims to promote the tourist attractions of the city. Similarly, the Nanki-Shirahama Tourism Association and the Nachikatsuura Tourism Organization, represented by the deputy mayor of Shirahama Town and the mayor of Nachikatsuura Town, respectively, aim to become a year-round destination by utilizing the numerous accommodation facilities in the area.

The Kinokawa Fruits Tourism Bureau, Kishu no Wa, represented by people from local agricultural and fishing cooperatives and Koyasanroku Tourism Bureau, represented by people from commerce and industry associations, are DMOs with strong ties to local industries. The Tanabe City Kumano Tourism Bureau is headed by business owners and focuses on the promotion of the Kumano Kodo Pilgrimage Routes, which cover a large portion of the area. The same is true for the Koya Town Tourism Association, which is represented by people from the Koya Town Chamber of Commerce and Industry and pilgrim accommodation facilities.

The Nanki-Shirahama Airport DMO is a joint-stock company established for the privatization of Nanki-Shirahama Airport. In addition to its activities as a DMO, it is working to increase the number of operated flights, including international ones, and to improve airport facilities.

As mentioned above, Wakayama Tourism Federation was registered as a candidate DMO in November 2021.

Examples of tourism product development, promotion, etc.
The Nachikatsuura Tourism Organization organized an online tour, "Tour to Enjoy Nachikatsuura's Tuna to the Fullest," to promote the town's specialties, "fresh tuna," "soy sauce," and "salt," which was well received.

Measures to increase brand power
DMOs with well-known tourist attractions such as Mount Kōya, the Shirahama hot springs, and Kumano Kodo Pilgrimage Routes, are cooperating with each other for promotion.

Part I

Part II

Part III

Part IV

Regional synergy: public-private partnerships within the region and wide-area regional cooperation initiatives

There are numerous examples of mutual cooperation, which is also the result of the fact that many of the tourist attractions span across the jurisdiction of several DMOs. For example, the Koyasanroku Tourism Bureau has collaborated with the Tanabe City Kumano Tourism Bureau, the Kinokawa Fruits Tourism Bureau, the Wakayama City Tourism Association, the Higashiosaka Tourism Promotion Organization (Osaka Prefecture), and the Izumisano City Promotion Council (Osaka Prefecture).

Initiatives to increase the attractiveness of the area as a tourist destination

Each DMO is working to deepen the local residents' understanding of inbound tourism by holding roundtable discussions, opinion exchange meetings, and workshops. The Wakayama City Tourism Association and the Koya Town Tourism Association have set KPIs to measure the level of satisfaction of local residents and the ripple effect of tourism on the local economy, respectively.

Innovation

The initiatives organized by the Nanki-Shirahama Airport DMO are noteworthy. In 2020, it conducted a demonstration experiment with Japan Airlines and NEC Corporation to measure the wait time for baggage claim using face recognition technology. It envisions the creation of a cashless payment system based on face recognition, which would cover airport procedures upon arrival, hotel check-in, and accommodation fee payments.

Human Resource Development

The Tanabe City Kumano Tourism Bureau is an example of recognizing the importance of a foreigner's perspective, as proved by its decision to hire foreign employees. On the other hand, the Nanki-Shirahama Airport DMO is also committed to offer job opportunities to the local community. Specifically, it is hiring in cooperation with local companies and offering internships to local university students. In order to promote regional revitalization through industry-academia collaboration, including in the field of local human resources development, it also concluded a comprehensive cooperation agreement with Wakayama University in 2018.

The path to self-sustainability

Although, like each DMO, it relies on commission fees and subsidies from the local government, the Tanabe City Kumano Tourism Bureau is particularly unique in terms of financial independence. This DMO, which covers Tanabe City, is registered as a Type 2 travel agency, is in charge of tour planning in its jurisdiction, and acts as a local tour operator for its overseas business partners. Before the COVID-19 pandemic, travel business income accounted for 80% of the organization's total income, and it has become a model for other DMOs aiming for similar growth.

Marketing and management initiatives using objective data and indicators

In cooperation with Wakayama Prefecture, the Wakayama City Tourism Association conducts surveys to determine the level of travel consumption and the rate of repeat visitors. In addition, Nanki-Shirahama Tourism Association and Tanabe City Kumano Tourism Bureau use Google Analytics to analyze their websites' traffic data. The Tanabe City Kumano Tourism Bureau analyzes visitor data, and effectively uses a CRM (customer relationship management) system by sending automatic e-mails to request post-trip feedback.

Examples of DMOs

The Tanabe City Kumano Tourism Bureau mentioned above is a notable success story of self-sustainability in the travel industry. The Nanki-Shirahama Airport DMO, which covers the southern half of Wakayama Prefecture, has created a new business model in which it generates its own travel demand by acquiring a travel agency license, and by playing an active role in local revitalization, while managing the regional airport as its main business.

3. Conclusion

In this section, we examined the activities of DMOs in each of the Kansai's six prefectures, and clarified their differences.

(1) In Shiga Prefecture, DMOs play a leading role in developing the entire region's tourism potential while focusing on Lake Biwa, and in creating a new direction while having the post-pandemic trends in mind.

(2) Kyoto Prefecture has established three regional DMOs along its main north-south axis and is promoting nature, tradition, and local products.

(3) In Osaka Prefecture, under the leadership of the Osaka Convention & Visitors Bureau, which covers the entire prefecture, and the regional DMOs in the southern, eastern, and northern parts of the prefecture work to further promote the attractions of each region.

(4) In Hyogo Prefecture, while the prefectural DMO is responsible for over-all PR campaigns and encourage tourist to travel around the prefecture, the cities of Kobe and Himeji, as well as regions where popular tourist attractions are located, have their own DMOs.

(5) In Nara Prefecture, prefectural DMOs are developing content for north-south tour of the prefecture, while local DMOs specializing in each region are also active.

(6) In Wakayama Prefecture, while the government takes a leading role on a prefectural level, DMOs are active in each region in accordance with the local circumstances.

As we have seen, DMOs have a multilayered scope of activities that differs from the three categories of wide-area cooperation, regional cooperation, and local. In addition, DMOs are active in regional units that share a common background, and in some cases, the scope of their activities exceeds that of the prefecture, and their boundaries are not necessarily consistent with administrative divisions. This characteristic of DMOs is related to the fact that the "value" of tourist attractions is in large part given by "invisible" factors such as history and culture. The DMOs of the post-pandemic era will have to create "stories" that are based on the regional culture and history and to develop their marketing strategies around them. This is a topic we would like to explore in depth in the future.

In the first half of Chapter 4, we have examined the state of tourism in Kansai while focusing on inbound tourism. Let us briefly review each section.

In Section 1, we examined the impact of the COVID-19 pandemic on tourism and inbound tourism demand.

In Section 2, we focused on each of Kansai's six prefectures to assess the situation of inbound tourism, the structure of public institutions in charge of tourism and their policies. We also emphasized the importance of the role of DMOs as a complementary entity to ensure a better understanding of local circumstances.

The contents of Section 3 are outlined above.

Two years have passed since the COVID-19 outbreak, and vaccination campaigns are now underway worldwide. Although it will take some time for inbound tourism to fully recover, and for border controls to be relaxed, APIR has stressed the importance of using this opportunity to discuss sustainable inbound tourism strategies. As a result of our discussions, it became clear how important the role of DMOs is in developing solutions for local problems.

The resumption of inbound travel largely depends on the progress of vaccination. Needless to say, ensuring the safety and security of visitors is of utmost importance, but as shown in Chapter 4, Section 1, offering a sense of comfort will play a vital role in future inbound tourism strategies. The DMOs listed here are expected to play an even more active role when the government promptly promotes inbound promotion measures again.

References

Japan Tourism Agency (2021) "Plan for the Formation and Establishment of 'Registered Destination Marketing Organizations'" (Japanese title: *Tōroku Kankōchi-zukuri Hōnin "Tōroku DMO" no Keisei/Kakuritsu Keikaku*), retrieved from: https://www.mlit.go.jp/kankocho/page04_000078.html (last verified on November 8, 2021).

Japan Tourism Agency (2021) "Plan for the Formation and Establishment of Candidate Destination Marketing Organizations" (Japanese title: *Kōho Kankōchi-zukuri Hōnin "Kōho DMO" no Keisei/Kakuritsu Keikaku*), retrieved from: https://www.mlit.go.jp/kankocho/page04_000055.html (last verified on November 8, 2021).

Kyoto City Tourism Association (2020), "Kyoto Tourism Code of Conduct" (Japanese title: *Kyōto Kankō Kōdō Kijun*), retrieved from: https://www.kyokanko.or.jp/kyoto_tourism_kodokijun/ (last verified on July 6, 2021).

Takahashi, K. (2017) "DMO—Innovation in Tourist Destination Management" (Japanese title: *DMO Kankōchi Keiei no Inobēshon*), Gakugei Publishing Co.

Part I

Part II

Part III

Part IV

Section 4
ANALYSIS OF THE TOURISM INDUSTRY USING THE TOURISM SATELLITE ACCOUNT AND INPUT-OUTPUT TABLES

SHIMODA, Mitsuru; INADA, Yoshihisa; SHIMOYAMA, Akira;
and TAKABAYASHI, Kikuo

1. Objective and Positioning of this Section

In this section, we will shed light on an analysis of the influence of tourism industry in the Japanese economy and the Kansai economy using input-output analysis methods. A feature of the input-output table is that it allows the influence of the industry in question and that of other industries to be compared. We will take advantage of this feature to conduct a comparative analysis of the positioning and influence of the tourism industry in the national economy.

In the second subsection, we will outline the tourism industry in Japan based on the Tourism Satellite Account. We will also process the 2017 Extended Input-Output Tables for the purpose of analyzing the tourism industry to demonstrate the positioning of the tourism industry in the national economy in terms of employment, income, and influence on other industries.

Tourism is an important industry for Kansai, not only in the current situation in which it has been hit hard by the COVID-19 pandemic, but also for the future. Thus, in the third subsection, we used the input-output tables for the 10 Kansai prefectures to compare the characteristics of the tourism industry in each Kansai prefecture. Specifically, we focused on the five main industries that constitute the tourism industry and analyzed the characteristics of each prefecture.

In addition to the analysis of sustainable strategies for the tourism industry in Kansai up to the previous section, the input-output analysis described in this section and the following section should help to deepen the understanding of the tourism industry even more.

2. Overview of the TSA and Outline of the Tourism Industry

Tourism is a broad industry, but there is no sector named "tourism" in the Japan Standard Industrial Classification. The Tourism Satellite Account (TSA) is an estimate used as a framework for quantitatively capturing tourism through a unified method. The TSA is one of the satellite accounts of the System of National Accounts (SNA), and the World Tourism Organization (UNWTO) described the international standard in the TSA Recommended Methodological Framework 2008 (TSA: RMF08). In this subsection, we will outline the tourism industry in Japan and conduct a unique tourism industry analysis by processing the Ministry of Economy, Trade and Industry's 2017 Extended Input-Output Tables (hereinafter referred to as the "Extended Tables") based on the TSA.

(1) Overview of the TSA

In Japan, the latest version of TSA available as of June 2021 was for 2018. We will outline the trends in the tourism industry based on the figures listed there.

(1.3) at the top of Table 4-4-1 is domestic tourism expenditure by foreigners visiting Japan, (2.9) is domestic tourism expenditure by Japanese citizens, (4.2) is imputed rent from vacation homes, and (4.3) is the total of the three left columns, which the TSA refers to as internal tourism consumption. (6.15) is domestic supply under the SNA and the percentages of internal tourism consumption in this are listed as the tourism ratios in (6.16).

Next, looking at the table, "A. Consumption products" is divided into "A.1. Tourism characteristic products" and "A.2. Other consumption products." "Tourism characteristic products" are major products (mainly services) used for an international comparison of tourism expenditure. "Other consumption products" consist of "tourism connected products" and "non-tourism related consumption products." "Tourism connected products" consist mainly of goods such as souvenirs and the few services that exist are exhibition/convention participation fees, hot spring/hot bath facilities, etc. "Non-tourism related consumption products" are entirely services and consist of cleaning, hairdressing/beauty industry, etc. Internal tourism consumption in 2018 was JPY 27,431 billion, of which, consumption by foreigners visiting Japan was JPY 5 trillion, accounting for 18% and consumption by Japanese citizens was JPY 21,985 billion, accounting for 80%.

Looking first at consumption by foreigners visiting Japan (inbound tourism expenditure), "Tourism characteristic products" were JPY 3,388 billion, while "Other consumption products" were JPY 1,585 billion. The former accounted for 67.8% and the latter 31.7% of the total inbound tourism expenditure.

"Tourism characteristic products" consist mainly of service expenditures, with expenditure high in "Accommodation services for visitors" and "Food- and beverage-serving services," accounting for JPY 1,391 billion and JPY 1,025 billion respectively. The next highest expenditure was in "Air passenger transport services" at JPY 368 billion and "Railway passenger transport services" at JPY 349 billion, followed by "Road passenger transport services" at JPY 72 billion, "Sports and recreational services" at JPY 61 billion, "Transport equipment rent-

Table 4-4-1   Internal tourism consumption by products and tourism ratios

(Billion ¥)

Products	Inbound tourism expenditure (1.3)	Domestic tourism expenditure (2.9)	Other components of tourism consumption (4.2)	Internal tourism consumption (4.3)	Domestic supply (at purchasers prices) (6.15)	Tourism ratios (%) (6.16) =(4.3) / (6.15) x 100
A. Consumption products	4,973	21,985	446	27,404	1,061,119	2.6
A.1. Tourism characteristic products	3,388	13,387	446	17,220	60,384	28.5
1. Accommodation services for visitors	1,391	3,748	446	5,585	6,147	90.9
1.a. Accommodation services for visitors other than 1.b	1,391	3,748	X	5,139	5,701	90.1
1.b. Vacation home ownership (imputed)	X	X	446	446	446	100.0
2. Food- and beverage-serving services	1,025	2,694	X	3,720	26,758	13.9
3. Railway passenger transport services	349	2,448	X	2,796	5,460	51.2
4. Road passenger transport services	72	611	X	683	3,363	20.3
5. Water passenger transport services	3	109	X	112	131	85.6
6. Air passenger transport services	368	2,159	X	2,527	3,304	76.5
7. Transport equipment rental services	56	306	X	363	1,956	18.5
8. Travel agencies and other reservation services	23	349	X	372	2,309	16.1
9. Cultural services	40	336	X	376	6,057	6.2
10. Sports and recreational services	61	625	X	686	4,900	14.0
A.2. Other consumption products	1,585	8,599	X	10,184	1,000,735	1.0
1. tourism connected products	1,554	7,777	X	9,331	275,079	3.4
1.a. goods	1,530	6,362	X	7,892	197,587	4.0
1.b. services	24	1,415	X	1,439	77,492	1.9
2. non-tourism related consumption products	31	821	X	853	725,655	0.1
2.a. goods	X	X	X	X	270,883	0.0
2.b. service	31	821	X	853	454,772	0.2
B. Non-consumption products	27	X	X	27	1,570	1.7
B.1. Valuable	27	X	X	27	1,570	1.7
Total	5,000	21,985	446	27,431	1,062,689	2.6

Source: the Japan Tourism Agency (2020)

al services" at JPY 56 billion, and "Cultural services" at JPY 40 billion.

In "Other consumption products," "tourism connected products," which are mainly souvenirs, was JPY 1,554 billion. Next, for consumption by Japanese citizens (Domestic tourism expenditure), "Tourism characteristic products" was JPY 13,387 billion while "Other consumption products" was JPY 8,599 billion. The former accounted for 60.9% and the latter 39.1% of the total domestic tourism expenditure.

The breakdown of "Tourism characteristic products" shows "Accommodation services for visitors" was high at JPY 3,748 billion, and then "Food- and beverage-serving services" at JPY 2,694 billion, "Railway passenger transport services" at JPY 2,448 billion, and "Air passenger transport services" at JPY 2,159 billion more or less the same. Among "Other consumption products," "tourism connected products" was JPY 7,777 billion, of which, "goods" had a large share at JPY 6,362 billion. Looking at the "Tourism ratios," it was 2.6% for the total for "Consumption products," 28.5% for "Tourism characteristic products," and 4.0% for "goods" in "tourism connected products." While the tourism ratio was 90.1% for "Accommodation services for visitors" where the weight of "Internal tourism consumption" is high, it remained at 13.9% in "Food- and beverage-serving services" where the weight is also high. "Water passenger transport services" and "Air passenger transport services" were high at 85.6% and 76.5% respectively, while "Railway passenger transport services" was 51.2%.

Additionally, changes in tourism GDP based on the TSA are shown in Table 4-4-2. Tourism GDP is defined as "the gross value added of goods and services (tourism supply) provided to tourists." It trended in the range of JPY 11 trillion in the late 2010s, accounting for around 2% of GDP.

Table 4-4-2   Tourism GDP and Tourism GDP/ GDP

(Billion ¥)

	2014	2016	2018
Tourism GDP	8,631	10,585	10,712
Tourism GDP/ GDP	1.7%	2.0%	2.0%

Source: the Japan Tourism Agency (2020)

(2) Outline of the Tourism Industry

The Japan Tourism Agency (2018) estimated the economic ripple effect of tourism based on the 2015 Input-Output Tables[1]. However, in this analysis, the relative size of the economic ripple effect of tourism as a single industry was not identified. Thus, in this subsection, we separate the goods and services related to tourism (tourism sector) and those not related to tourism (non-tourism sector) from the 2017 Extended Tables to identify the characteristics of the economic ripple effect of the tourism industry[2].

1) Inducement Coefficient for Production, etc., Caused by Tourism Goods and Services

To compare the tourism industry with other industries, we separated tourism goods and services from the 2017 Extended Tables and compiled them as major aggregated classifications (37 sectors). However, three types of compilations were made for tourism goods and services, as shown in Table 4-4-3. Compilation type 1 has 10 sectors in the tourism sector and consists of a total of 47 sectors together with the non-tourism sectors. Compilation type 2 has 3 tourism sectors and has a total of 40 sectors, while compilation type 3 consists of 38 sectors.

Below, we will obtain the Production inducement coefficients, gross value

| Table 4-4-3 | Pattern of tourism goods and services |

Type 1	Type 2	Type 3
Tourism: Beverages and Foods	Tourism: Goods	Tourism
Tourism: Non-Beverages and Foods		
Tourism: Transport (passengers)	Tourism: Service	
Tourism: Accommodation		
Tourism: Restaurant		
Tourism: Sports Facilities		
Tourism: Information Service		
Tourism: Car rental		
Tourism: Trade margins	Tourism: Fare and margins	
Tourism: Fare		

Source: Compiled by the author.

---

1) It is estimated that the internal tourism consumption of JPY 27.4 trillion in 2018 led to an induced production value of JPY 36.9 trillion, gross value added of JPY 18.7 trillion, and employment of 3.145 million people. All are the total of the direct effect and the primary indirect effect.
2) Refer to Shimoda, Inada, and Takabayashi (2021) for the specific method of dividing the tourism sectors from the non-tourism sectors.

added, and employment by compilation type. In this subsection, the inducement coefficient caused by an industry is defined as the inducement of production, gross value added, and employment in the overall economy when final demand for the relevant industry increases by one unit[3]. Table 4-4-4 shows the inducement coefficients calculated based on compilation type 1 (47 sectors) with the tourism sector being shaded. Those high in production inducement (left column) are the manufacturing industries, such as Transportation equipment (2.45), Iron and steel (2.43), and Pulp, paper and wooden products (1.98). Conversely, the production inducement of tourism sectors is not that high. The highest is Restaurant (1.91) ranked in 8th place, followed by Beverages and Foods (1.82) in 15th, Non-Beverages and Foods (1.77) in 19th, Accommodation (1.73) in 23rd, and Information Service (1.70) in 24th. Other tourism sectors, such as Transport (passengers) and Trade margins, ranked 30th or lower.

Meanwhile, in terms of gross value added inducement (center column), the ranks change completely, with tourism sectors that ranked low in production inducement moving to the higher ranks. For example, Car rental, which was highest in value added inducement, ranked 41st in production inducement but ranked 2nd in gross value added inducement (41st to 2nd, same hereinafter). Other tourism sectors that moved up the ranks include Sports Facilities (43rd to 4th), Trade margins (38th to 7th), Fare (42nd to 8th), Information Service (24th to 15th), Transport (passengers) (30th to 18th), and Accommodation (23rd to 20th). Conversely, Restaurant, which was relatively high in production inducement, lowered its rank (8th to 23rd). In general, since the service industry has a high value added ratio, its value added inducement tends to be relatively high compared to production inducement.

The inducement of employment (right column) by the tourism sector shows a trend similar to the inducement of value added, ranking relatively higher than the inducement of production. However, there are individual differences. First, Restaurant, which was 23rd in value added inducement, rose to 2nd in employment inducement. The same applies to Accommodation, which was 20th in value added inducement and 7th in employment inducement.

Next, below are the inducement coefficients based on compilation type 2.

---

3) "Production inducement coefficient" commonly used in input-output analysis refers to the multiplying factor of the production value induced by a final demand item and represents the size of production induced by one unit of demand for the final demand item. Conversely, the "inducement coefficient for production" in this subsection is defined as the column sum of the Leontief inverse matrix. Note that this represents the size of production induced by one unit of demand for goods and services in the column, which is a different definition from that of "production inducement coefficient."

Table 4-4-4		Production Inducement coefficients, gross value added, and employment based on compilation type 1 (47 sectors)				

#	Industry	Production	Industry	GVA	Industry	Employment
1	Transportation equipment	2.45	Real estate	0.98	Agriculture, forestry and fishery	0.38
2	Iron and steel	2.43	Tourism: Car rental	0.97	Tourism: Restaurant	0.25
3	Pulp, paper and wooden products	1.98	Finance and insurance	0.96	Personal services	0.21
4	Beverages and Foods	1.95	Tourism: Sports Facilities	0.95	Textile products	0.17
5	Metal products	1.95	Commerce	0.95	Membership-based associations, n.e.c.	0.17
6	Plastic products and rubber products	1.93	Education and research	0.95	Tourism: Sports Facilities	0.16
7	General-purpose machinery	1.92	Tourism: Trade margins	0.95	Tourism: Accommodation	0.15
8	Tourism: Restaurant	1.91	Tourism: Fare	0.94	Beverages and Foods	0.15
9	Chemical products	1.91	Information and communications	0.93	Tourism: Beverages and Foods	0.15
10	Electrical machinery	1.90	Business services	0.93	Medical, health care and welfare	0.15
11	Information and communication electronics equipment	1.87	Waste management service	0.93	Tourism: Trade margins	0.14
12	Production machinery	1.85	Transport and postal services	0.92	Commerce	0.14
13	Electronic components	1.85	Public administration	0.92	Tourism: Fare	0.14
14	Water supply	1.82	Membership-based associations, n.e.c.	0.92	Business services	0.14
15	Tourism: Beverages and Foods	1.82	Tourism: Information Service	0.91	Construction	0.13
16	Business oriented machinery	1.80	Water supply	0.91	Miscellaneous manufacturing products	0.13
17	Construction	1.79	Medical, health care and welfare	0.91	Waste management service	0.13
18	Miscellaneous manufacturing products	1.77	Tourism: Transport (passengers)	0.91	Pulp, paper and wooden products	0.11
19	Tourism: Non-Beverages and Foods	1.77	Personal services	0.90	Metal products	0.11
20	Information and communications	1.76	Tourism: Accommodation	0.90	Education and research	0.11
21	Agriculture, forestry and fishery	1.75	Construction	0.88	Tourism: Transport (passengers)	0.10
22	Non-ferrous metals	1.74	Mining	0.87	Tourism: Information Service	0.10
23	Tourism: Accommodation	1.73	Tourism: Restaurant	0.87	Plastic products and rubber products	0.10
24	Tourism: Information Service	1.70	Miscellaneous manufacturing products	0.87	Tourism: Non-Beverages and Foods	0.10
25	Personal services	1.69	Tourism: Beverages and Foods	0.87	Public administration	0.09
26	Mining	1.67	Agriculture, forestry and fishery	0.86	Transport and postal services	0.09
27	Public administration	1.66	Production machinery	0.86	Ceramic, stone and clay products	0.09
28	Ceramic, stone and clay products	1.65	Metal products	0.85	Production machinery	0.09
29	Textile products	1.64	General-purpose machinery	0.84	Information and communications	0.08
30	Tourism: Transport (passengers)	1.59	Beverages and Foods	0.84	Finance and insurance	0.08
31	Business services	1.58	Ceramic, stone and clay products	0.82	Mining	0.08
32	Membership-based associations, n.e.c.	1.56	Pulp, paper and wooden products	0.82	General-purpose machinery	0.08
33	Medical, health care and welfare	1.53	Plastic products and rubber products	0.81	Business oriented machinery	0.08
34	Transport and postal services	1.52	Tourism: Non-Beverages and Foods	0.80	Electronic components	0.08
35	Electricity, gas and heat supply	1.51	Business oriented machinery	0.80	Electrical machinery	0.08
36	Waste management service	1.50	Electrical machinery	0.77	Information and communication electronics equipment	0.07
37	Finance and insurance	1.49	Transportation equipment	0.77	Transportation equipment	0.07
38	Tourism: Trade margins	1.47	Electronic components	0.76	Water supply	0.07
39	Education and research	1.45	Iron and steel	0.75	Tourism: Car rental	0.07
40	Commerce	1.44	Chemical products	0.75	Chemical products	0.05
41	Tourism: Car rental	1.37	Textile products	0.74	Non-ferrous metals	0.05
42	Tourism: Fare	1.37	Information and communication electronics equipment	0.74	Iron and steel	0.04
43	Tourism: Sports Facilities	1.36	Electricity, gas and heat supply	0.64	Electricity, gas and heat supply	0.04
44	Real estate	1.23	Non-ferrous metals	0.55	Real estate	0.02
45	Petroleum and coal products	1.17	Petroleum and coal products	0.42	Petroleum and coal products	0.01

Source: Estimated by the author.

The table has been omitted. In production inducement, the rankings were low for the tourism sector, with Goods (15th), Service (21st), and Fare and margins (34th) ranking in that order. The order was reversed for value added inducement, with Fare and margins (5th), Service (15th), and Goods (24th). Service ranked at the top in employment inducement, with Services (6th), Fare and margins (7th), and Goods (15th).

2) Comparison with Other Industries

Next, we will outline the results for compilation type 3, which consolidates the tourism sector into one (Table 4-4-5). For comparison, we will show the results for Iron and steel, Electrical machinery, and Transportation equipment as well.

For production inducement, the ripple effect was greatest in the order of Transportation equipment, Iron and steel, Electrical machinery, and Tourism, but this order was reversed for value added inducement to Tourism, Electrical machinery, Transportation equipment, and Iron and steel. Looking at the relative sizes, in production inducement, Transportation equipment at the top is about 1.5 times the size of Tourism at the bottom. Conversely, the difference was nearly seven-fold for employment inducement. The inducement effect for employment varied greatly depending on the sector, and we can see that the impact on employment was particularly strong in the tourism industry.

3) The Impact on Employment

Table 4-4-5	Abstract of inducement coefficients based on compilation type 3 (38 sectors)	
Production	**Gross Value Added**	**Employment**
1st Transportation equipment (2.45)	14th Tourism (0.90)	7th Tourism (0.14)
2nd Iron and steel (2.43)	27th Electrical machinery (0.77)	25th Electrical machinery (0.08)
9th Electrical machinery (1.9)	28th Transportation equipment (0.77)	29th Transportation equipment (0.07)
21st Tourism (1.68)	28th Iron and steel (0.75)	33rd Iron and steel (0.02)

Source: Estimated by the author.

In Table 4-4-5, we saw that tourism's impact on employment is relatively great. Next, we will sort employment into the employment types of "Self-employed worker and Family worker," "Regular employee," and "Non-regular employee" and calculate the inducement for each. Here, non-regular employee is defined as the sum of "Non-regular employees/staff" and "Temporary employees" among the full-time employees in the employment table. Figure 4-4-1 shows the employment ripple effect by employment type, with the average of manufacturing added in addition to the industries in Table 4-4-5[4]. What is notable for Tourism is that inducement for non-regular employees accounts for 36%, which is higher than the 22% as the average of manufacturing. In Japan, regular employ-

---

4) The average of manufacturing is the simple average of 18 manufacturing sectors.

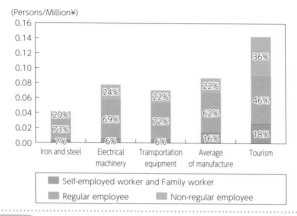

Figure 4 - 4 - 1   Ripple effect on employment by employment type

Source: Estimated by the author.

ees increased by 330,000 while non-regular employees decreased by 970,000 on average in FY 2020. We can see from here also that the decreased demand for tourism due to the COVID-19 pandemic had a direct impact on non-regular employees.

(3) Summary: Characteristics of the Tourism Industry

Thus far, we have outlined the characteristics of the tourism industry nationwide based on TSA. According to the most recent TSA available, tourism consumption in 2018 was JPY 27,431 billion, of which, approximately 20% was consumption by foreigners visiting Japan and 80% by Japanese citizens. Expenditure on goods was around 30% for both, and the rest was service expenditure, with expenditure particularly high in the accommodation services and food- and beverage-serving services. However, the percentage of tourism consumption in domestic supply (tourism ratio) differed, with approximately 90% for accommodation services and 14% for food- and beverage-serving services. Tourism GDP remained around 2% of the total in the late 2010s.

We also combined the 2017 Extended Tables and the TSA to create an input-output table separating out the tourism sector and measured the relative size of the economic ripple effect of the tourism industry. The production inducement coefficients of the tourism industry was 21st, ranking low among the 36 sectors (excluding activities not elsewhere classified and office supplies), but it ranked higher in the inducement coefficient for value added (14th) and the inducement for employment (7th). The tourism industry falls short of manufacturing in terms of the production ripple effect, but it exceeds manufacturing for the ripple effect on value added and employment, particularly employment. Additionally, in terms of employment, we saw that the impact on non-regular employment was particularly great, relatively. This suggests that the impact of COVID-19 pandemic on non-regular employment has been more serious.

3. The Tourism Industry in Kansai: Analysis Based on the 2015 Table for Each Prefecture

When considering what's on the horizon for Kansai, the tourism industry is very important for it, with the Expo 2025 Osaka, Kansai, Japan to be held in 2025, among other things. In the previous subsection, we discussed the importance of the tourism industry based on the input-output tables for Japan. In this subsection, we will use the input-output tables for each prefecture to examine the characteristics of the tourism industry in Kansai's economy.

The main analysis method is as follows. First, we will look at the characteristics in terms of the scale of the tourism industry within Kansai's economy. Then, we will look at the economic ripple effect of the tourism industry based on the production/employment inducement coefficients and the diversity of industries that are affected by the economic ripple effect.

(1) Characteristics of the Tourism Industry in Each Prefecture

In this subsection we will examine the tourism industry in 10 prefectures in Kansai, but since the consumption trend of domestic tourists is not clearly indicated by prefecture in the statistics publications, it is difficult to separate sectors associated with tourism in the input-output tables to analyze the tourism industry, as we did nationally. In general, when analyzing the tourism industry in prefectures using input-output tables, the economic ripple effect is often examined by associating existing industry sectors with tourism sectors. The input-output table, due to its structure, assumes that if there is no difference in quality and that the input structure is the same, so the accommodation industry is considered to conduct similar production regardless of whether its purpose is tourism or non-tourism. Thus, in this section we will follow the methods of earlier studies and associate the TSA tourism industry sectors with the industry sectors in the input-output tables of the 10 prefectures.

First, Table 4-4-6 shows the association between the industrial classification by the TSA, the common industrial classification, and the input-output table of each prefecture.

The industrial classification by the TSA consists of Accommodation services for visitors, Vacation home ownership (imputed), Food- and beverage-serving,

Table 4-4-6	Tourism industry in TSA and industries in the input-output table		

	Industrial Classification by TSA	Industrial Classification by SNA	Industrial Classification (Input-Output Table, Osaka)
Tourism Industry	Accommodation services for visitors	Accommodations	Hotels
	Vacation home ownership (imputed)	Real estate lessors	–
	Food- and beverage-serving services	Eating and drinking services	Eating and drinking services
	Railway passenger transport services	Railway passenger transport	Railway transport
	Road passenger transport services	Road passenger transport	Road freight transport (except self-transport)
	Water passenger transport services	Water transport	Water transport
	Air passenger transport services	Air transport	Air transport
	Services relating to transport	Other transport	Services relating to transport
	Sports and recreational services	Services for amusement and hobbies	Amusement and recreational services
	Other services	Services, N.E.C	–

Source: Created by the author.

Railway passenger transport services, Road passenger transport services, Water passenger transport, Air passenger transport services, Services relating to transport, Sports and recreational services, and Other services. These industries are mostly classified as those that produce tourism-specific products and that cannot exist without tourists or the consumption level drops significantly without them, and they are believed to play a central role in the tourism industry[5]. Associations of these industries with the common industrial classifications by the SNA are listed in the center column, and the right column shows the associations with the industrial classifications by the input-output table[6]. Of these industrial classifications, we targeted the five sectors with relatively high domestic tourism expenditure in Table 4-4-1; namely Hotels, Eating and drinking services, Amusement and recreational services, Railway transport, and Road freight transport (except self-transport) (described according to classification in input-output table, hereinafter referred to as the "Five tourism industry

---

5) To ascertain the situation in the tourism industry in accordance with international standards, standards for tourism-specific products were presented in the World Tourism Organization's (UNWTO) International Recommendations for Tourism Statistics 2008.
6) For the industrial classifications for Osaka, the medium aggregated classification (107 sectors) from the most recent FY 2015 input-output tables for Osaka were used.

sectors.")[7].

To compare with nationwide, Table 4-4-7 looks at the specialization coefficients based on the production values of the five tourism industry sectors in the national input-output table[8]. Industries and prefectures with a specialization coefficient value of 1.05 or higher are shaded. Looking at the characteristics by prefecture, even in Kyoto, the specialization coefficient is higher than 1 in four sectors except for Amusement and recreational services, and it is particularly high in Hotels and Eating and drinking services. In Hyogo, all five sectors have specialization coefficients higher than 1 but lower than Kyoto in Hotels and Eating and drinking services. By industry, Railway transport and Eating and drinking services were high mainly in Osaka and Kyoto. Road freight transport (except self-transport) is higher in areas where automobiles are used more than railway (rural areas). Hotels were high in Kyoto and Tottori, followed by Wakayama and Fukui[9]. Amusement and recreational services was below the national average in all prefectures except in Hyogo and Tokushima. Thus, we can see that in the tourism industry in the Kansai economy, the weights of Hotels and Eating and drinking services are higher than nationwide.

Table 4-4-7	Specialization coefficients by prefecture for the five tourism industry sectors									
Nationwide=1										
	Fukui	Mie	Shiga	Kyoto	Osaka	Hyogo	Nara	Wakayama	Tottori	Tokushima
Railway transport	0.16	0.60	0.59	1.65	1.51	1.05	1.18	0.31	0.28	0.12
Road freight transport (except self-transport)	1.18	0.85	0.77	1.07	1.06	1.41	0.86	0.92	1.14	1.29
Hotels	1.32	1.00	0.72	1.91	0.91	1.19	0.66	1.36	1.94	1.09
Eating and drinking services	1.15	0.74	0.59	1.37	1.22	1.16	1.12	0.76	1.02	0.44
Amusement and recreational services	0.65	0.75	0.66	0.94	0.98	1.09	0.95	0.67	0.84	2.56
GRP (Billion¥)	5,959	19,269	12,381	18,002	67,148	38,959	6,194	7,356	3,252	5,076

Source: Estimated by the author.

7) Since Air transport is normally a means to travel to a destination and is generally expected to be excluded from consumption by tourists visiting Kansai, it is not analyzed.
8) Specialization coefficient describes how specialized an industry of a prefecture is and compares the ratio of the production value of an industry of a prefecture with the national ratio. Thus, if it exceeds 1, it indicates that the production value is great in that industry sector compared to nationally.
9) In many of these prefectures, the impact of hot springs resorts as tourism accommodation is believed to be significant.

(2) Size of Employment Inducement and Impact on a Wide Range of Industries

Next, we will examine the characteristics of the economic ripple effect of the tourism industry from the perspective of production and employment inducement coefficients and which industries are affected by the economic ripple effect.

1) Inducement Coefficient for Production/Employment

As in the previous subsection, we will calculate the inducement coefficients for production and employment for the five tourism industries by prefecture. The production inducement coefficient caused by an industry is defined as the inducement on production in the overall economy when final demand for the relevant industry increases by one unit. The results are shown in Table 4-4-8. The production inducement coefficient and the ranking in the prefecture by industry, and the employment inducement coefficient and the ranking in the prefecture by industry, are listed by industry and by prefecture. Since the medium aggregated classifications are used in the input-output table of the prefectures, the total number of sectors is between 103 sectors (Fukui) and 108 sectors (Nara, Tottori, Tokushima), and the rankings show the relative sizes of the economic ripple effect in the region. Additionally, the shaded area in the box indicating the rankings indicates a case that exceeds the rankings of the production-induced coefficient and the employment-induced coefficient.

First, looking at the characteristics of the production inducement coefficient by industry, the rankings of the prefectures for Hotels and Eating and drinking services were between 9th (Shiga) and 23rd (Tokushima), and 15th (Kyoto) and 48th (Mie) respectively, indicating that they are industries with a high production inducement. The coefficient values were also 1.3 or higher in Hotels and Eating and drinking services and approximately 0.1 point higher than Railway transport, Road freight transport (except self-transport), and Amusement and recreational services. On the other hand, Road freight transport (except self-transport) was quite low, between 92nd (Fukui) and 100th (Tokushima)[10]. Looking at the characteristics by prefecture, Railway transport's production inducement was relatively high in Fukui, Shiga, Kyoto, and Hyogo, while it was around the middle in Mie, Osaka, and Tottori. Additionally, for Eating and drinking services, Mie was 48th, ranking low compared to other prefectures, while for

---

10) Since the medium classifications are used for Road freight transport (except self-transport) for both the production inducement effect and employment effect, it may have been more impacted by "road freight" than "road passenger."

| Table 4-4-8 | | Production inducement coefficients, employment inducement coefficient and ranking | | | | | |

	Railway transport				Road freight transport (except self-transport)			
	Production	(Rank)	Employment	(Rank)	Production	(Rank)	Employment	(Rank)
Fukui	1.313	(32)	0.183	(11)	1.179	(92)	0.113	(32)
Mie	1.213	(68)	0.053	(56)	1.125	(93)	0.124	(18)
Shiga	1.291	(23)	0.046	(62)	1.141	(97)	0.160	(15)
Kyoto	1.305	(23)	0.042	(82)	1.145	(97)	0.163	(19)
Osaka	1.248	(65)	0.042	(76)	1.179	(96)	0.150	(9)
Hyogo	1.282	(39)	0.038	(79)	1.154	(96)	0.123	(17)
Nara	1.220	(54)	0.064	(60)	1.130	(94)	0.155	(20)
Wakayama	1.264	(52)	0.111	(28)	1.182	(83)	0.141	(16)
Tottori	1.272	(65)	0.080	(62)	1.158	(96)	0.139	(28)
Tokushima	1.229	(57)	0.122	(31)	1.108	(100)	0.105	(45)

	Hotels				Eating and drinking services			
	Production	(Rank)	Employment	(Rank)	Production	(Rank)	Employment	(Rank)
Fukui	1.493	(11)	0.190	(8)	1.349	(24)	0.169	(14)
Mie	1.335	(22)	0.110	(20)	1.262	(48)	0.169	(9)
Shiga	1.389	(9)	0.159	(16)	1.320	(17)	0.181	(11)
Kyoto	1.403	(11)	0.140	(27)	1.370	(15)	0.405	(4)
Osaka	1.387	(21)	0.111	(24)	1.367	(23)	0.164	(7)
Hyogo	1.362	(16)	0.110	(22)	1.336	(24)	0.192	(4)
Nara	1.320	(13)	0.300	(4)	1.258	(30)	0.248	(5)
Wakayama	1.428	(19)	0.168	(7)	1.348	(26)	0.228	(5)
Tottori	1.413	(20)	0.206	(10)	1.376	(25)	0.228	(8)
Tokushima	1.314	(23)	0.161	(18)	1.286	(29)	0.270	(4)

	Amusement and recreational services			
	Production	(Rank)	Employment	(Rank)
Fukui	1.303	(36)	0.128	(25)
Mie	1.144	(88)	0.123	(19)
Shiga	1.210	(62)	0.128	(21)
Kyoto	1.239	(51)	0.126	(31)
Osaka	1.229	(73)	0.105	(26)
Hyogo	1.201	(86)	0.092	(30)
Nara	1.203	(66)	0.156	(19)
Wakayama	1.229	(66)	0.126	(20)
Tottori	1.274	(64)	0.125	(34)
Tokushima	1.211	(71)	0.106	(43)

Source: Estimated by the author.

Amusement and recreational services, Fukui ranked high at 36th.

Next, in terms of the employment inducement coefficient, Kyoto, Hyogo, and Tokushima were 4th for Eating and drinking services and the lowest rank was Fukui's at 14th, which indicates that it is an industry with a relatively high employment effect. Additionally, Hotels was between 4th (Nara) and 27th (Kyoto), with results similar to Eating and drinking services. Amusement and recreational services was slightly lower than Eating and drinking services and Hotels, but it was generally around the 20th to 40th range, indicating that the employment effect is relatively high. Meanwhile, the employment effect varied in Railway transport and Road freight transport (except self-transport). The former ranked quite high at 11th in Fukui, but Osaka (76th), Hyogo (79th), and Kyoto (82nd) show that the regional gap is large. The latter was generally high except for Fukui (32nd) and Tokushima (45th).

Lastly, we look at the differences in rankings between the production inducement coefficient and the employment inducement coefficient. In Hotels, which ranked relatively high for the production inducement coefficient to start with, the rankings for the employment inducement coefficient were slightly lower in Shiga, Kyoto, and Hyogo but were more or less the same, showing that both its production inducement effect and employment coefficient are high. Similarly, in Eating and drinking services where the production inducement coefficient was high, employment inducement coefficient rankings were even higher in all prefectures, with results similar to the analysis in the previous section. From these results, we can see that in Hotels and Eating and drinking services in particular, there is the strong tendency for not only production inducement, but also employment inducement to be high.

2) Which Industries are Affected by the Economic Ripple Effect?

Lastly, we will look at which industries are affected by the economic ripple effect. A greater economic ripple effect is more desirable, but even if the economic ripple effect is great, if it only affects certain industries, the effect on the overall region will be localized. Conversely, if it affects various industries, the effect on the overall region will be broad. Thus, of the five tourism industries, we will focus on Hotels, which had a high influence coefficient in the previous subsection, and examine its impact on other industries. In so doing, we will compare it with electrical machinery, which is one of the main industries in Kansai. The values excluding the production ripple effects to the industry concerned and summarized into nine sectors are represented in Figure 4-4-2.

Hotels was highest in Fukui at 0.493 and lowest in Tokushima at 0.282. The impact on other industries was relatively great in the three sectors of Electricity, gas and heat supply, Transport and postal service, and Service, but Agriculture,

[Hotels]

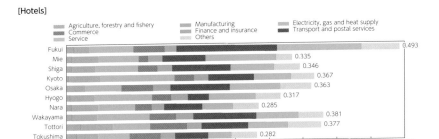

[Electrical machinery]

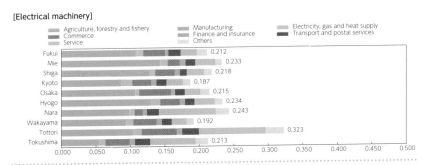

Figure 4-4-2   Production inducement destination of Hotels (excluding inducement to own industry)

Source: Estimated by the author.

forestry and fishery, Commerce, and Finance and insurance were also somewhat impacted. On the other hand, in Electrical machinery, which is a key industry in Kansai, the impact on other industries excluding the value for the industry concerned was small among the prefectures compared to Hotels, with Tottori's being the highest at 0.323 and Kyoto's the lowest at 0.187. Looking at the impact on other industries, it was mostly in the manufacturing industry and the impact on other industries was around half.

(4) Summary: Characteristics of the Tourism Industry in the 10 Kansai Prefectures

In this subsection, we looked at the characteristics of the tourism industry in the Kansai economy using the latest input-output tables for the 10 Kansai prefectures. As a result, we saw that 1) in the tourism industry in the Kansai economy, the importance of Hotels and Eating and drinking services is high compared to nationwide, 2) it strongly impacts other industries, mainly Hotels, in the region and can generate earnings from other regions, and therefore is a very important industry for each region, and 3) the economic ripple effect does not only affect certain industries but also affects various industries, and its impact on the overall region is broad. Thus, the importance of the tourism industry in the Kansai economy has been clarified.

References

Doi, E., Asari, I., and Nakano, C. (2019), "Regional Input-Output Analysis for Beginners: Basics—From Introduction to Practice in Excel (Revised Edition)" (Japanese title: *Hajimeyo Chiiki Sangyo Renkan Bunseki: Kisohen—Excel de Shoho kara Jissen made [Kaiteiban]*), Nippon Hyoron sha, p. 69

Japan Tourism Agency (2020), Research study on economic impacts of tourism in Japan, Japanese Tourism Satellite Account, 2018, (https://www.mlit.go.jp/common/001354466.pdf, last viewed: November 19, 2021)

Shimoda, M., Inada, Y., and Takabayashi, K. (2021), "Chapter 6 Section 1 Quantitative Assessment Using the Tourism Satellite Account and the National Input-Output Tables" (Japanese title: *Dai 6 Sho 1 Setsu Ryoko/Kanko Satellite Kanjo to Zenkoku Sangyo Renkan Hyo niyoru Teiryoteki Hyoka*), APIR Kansai and the Asia Pacific, Economic Outlook: 2020-21, Nikkei Printing Inc.

Section 5
IMPACT OF THE COVID-19 PANDEMIC ON TOURISM INDUSTRY AND THE EFFECT OF POLICIES TO GENERATE DEMAND

INADA, Yoshihisa; SHIMODA, Mitsuru; SHIMOYAMA, Akira;
NOMURA, Ryosuke; KINOSHITA, Yusuke

1. Impact of the COVID-19 Pandemic on Tourism Consumption

In this section, we will conduct an input-output analysis of the COVID-19 pandemic, which impacted the tourism industry significantly in 2020. In particular, we will analyze not only the negative impact on consumption by foreigners visiting Japan and domestic tourism consumption, but also the effect of the Go To Campaign as an economic policy.

Total tourism consumption mainly consists of three items (a) Japanese domestic travel consumption, (b) Japanese international travel consumption (domestic consumption), and (c) travel consumption by foreigners visiting Japan. Table 4-5-1 outlines the impact of the COVID-19 pandemic on tourism consumption assumed in this section.

Table 4-5-1   Impact of travel consumption by COVID-19

(JPY trillion)

	2019	2020	19-20
(a) Japanese Domestic travel	21.9	10.0	-11.9
(b) Japanese International travel(domestic consumption)	1.2	0.3	-0.9
(c) Consumption expenditure of foreigners	4.8	0.7	-4.1
(d) Driving consumer demand by "Go to Travel Campaign"		1.1	1.1
The impact of declining by COVID-19=(a-d)+b+c			-18.0

Source: Travel and Tourism Consumption Trend Survey and Survey on the consumption trends of foreign visitors by Japan Tourism Agency

In 2020, with the flow of people suppressed due to the declaration of a state of emergency, (a) Japanese domestic travel consumption (overnight/one-day total) was approximately JPY 10.0 trillion, a significant decrease of JPY 11.9 trillion compared to the previous year when the COVID-19 pandemic had no impact. Next, (b) Japanese international travel consumption (domestic consumption) was JPY 0.3 trillion in 2020, dropping JPY 0.9 trillion from JPY 1.2 trillion in the previous year due to countries imposing entry restrictions. (c) Travel consumption by foreigners visiting Japan was JPY 0.7 trillion in 2020, decreasing JPY

4.1 trillion from JPY 4.8 trillion in the previous year due to entry restrictions imposed by the Japanese government.

The government was by no means being a bystander under these circumstances. It implemented the Go To Campaign project in late July as a demand stimulus plan to recover the lost domestic travel demand and local tourism-related consumption, while thoroughly implementing measures to prevent the spread of infection[1]. According to the Japan Tourism Agency's "White Paper on Tourism in Japan, 2021," the Go To Travel project applies between July 22 and December 28 (checkout by this date), and the discount on accommodation and travel costs was estimated at approximately JPY 408.2 billion. Since the Go To Travel project gives a 35% discount on accommodation costs at accommodation facilities, by calculating back from the discount (JPY 408.2 billion), we can assume that the demand generated was around JPY 1.1 trillion (see Table 4-5-1).

However, the (a) Japanese domestic travel consumption for 2020 includes the effect of the Go To Travel project. The impact of the COVID-19 pandemic on tourism consumption without the policy is, (a) Japanese domestic travel consumption minus (d) demand stimulated by Go To Travel project plus (b) Japanese international travel consumption (domestic consumption) and (c) travel consumption by foreigners visiting Japan, or (a − d) + b + c. In this section, we will analyze the economic ripple effect of the COVID-19 pandemic on the tourism industry, focusing on three key items (a), (c), and (d) as the impact of COVID-19, using input-output tables (2017 Extended Input-Output Tables and 2015 Regional Input-Output Table).

2. Estimation of Tourism Consumption Final Demand

In this subsection, we will estimate the tourism consumption by expense item (final demand) before performing an input-output analysis of (a) Japanese domestic travel consumption, (c) travel consumption by foreigners visiting Japan, and (d) demand stimulated by Go To Travel project impacted by the COVID-19 pandemic.

Table 4-5-2 prorates domestic travel consumption nationwide and in three Kansai prefectures by expense item based on the national tourism consumption by expense item in the 2020 Travel and Tourism Consumption Trend Survey by Japan Tourism Agency.

For the nationwide travel consumption by foreigners visiting Japan in 2020, the total was allocated based on expenditure pattern by expense item in 2019.

---

1) See Chapter 4 Section 1 of this book for details on the Go To Travel project.

| Table 4-5-2 | Impact of the COVID-19 pandemic on tourism consumption |

[Declining of domestic tourism expenditure]

(JPY 100million)

	Tourism expenditure	Spending						
		Package tour	Accommo-dation	Restaurant, fast food, café etc.	Transport	Service costs, including entertainment	Shopping	Other
Nationwide	-107,911	-7,908	-22,767	-17,136	-34,358	-7,210	-17,746	-787
Kyoto	-6,693	-947	-1,255	-1,470	-1,315	-381	-1,262	-63
Osaka	-8,187	-559	-1,546	-1,697	-1,466	-1,054	-1,822	-42
Hyogo	-7,286	-439	-1,653	-1,425	-1,527	-702	-1,505	-34

[Declining of Inbound tourism expenditure]

(JPY 100million)

	Tourism expenditure	Spending						
		Package tour	Accommo-dation	Restaurant, fast food, café etc.	Transport	Service costs, including entertainment	Shopping	Other
Nationwide	-40,689	-	-11,946	-8,789	-4,215	-1,613	-14,108	-19

[Go to Travel Campaign]

(JPY 100million)

	Tourism expenditure	Spending						
		Package tour	Accommo-dation	Restaurant, fast food, café etc.	Transport	Service costs, including entertainment	Shopping	Other
Nationwide	11,663	855	2,461	1,852	3,713	779	1,918	85
Kyoto	723	102	136	159	142	41	136	7
Osaka	885	60	167	183	158	114	197	5
Hyogo	787	47	179	154	165	76	163	4

Note: "Domestic travel consumption" includes income at the destination which is included in group/package tour fares. "Travel consumption" by prefecture does not include inter-prefectural transportation costs.
Source: Travel and Tourism Consumption Trend Survey and Survey on the consumption trends of foreign visitors by Japan Tourism Agency

Additionally, we excluded the three Kansai prefectures, since regional information for 2020 is not available.

3. COVID-19 Pandemic and the Effect of Measures to Generate Demand

In this subsection, we estimate the economic ripple effect nationwide (Table 4-5-3) and in the three Kansai prefectures (Table 4-5-4) based on the tourism consumption final demand presented in the previous subsection. Since it is difficult to grasp the tourism consumption pattern of foreigners visiting Japan in each region, we limit the analysis to declining of Japanese domestic travel con-

Table 4-5-3   The economic ripple effect of spending by tourists (Nationwide)

【Declining of domestic tourism expenditure】

(JPY 100million, persons)

	Direct effect	Total	Primary ripple effect	Secondary ripple effect
Production	-104,690	-217,517	-180,866	-36,652
Value added	-52,998	-114,697	-92,877	-21,820
Employment	-1,066,231	-1,872,447	-1,609,327	-263,120

【Declining of Inbound tourism expenditure】

(JPY 100million, persons)

	Direct effect	Total	Primary ripple effect	Secondary ripple effect
Production	-40,689	-88,411	-73,699	-14,712
Value added	-18,788	-44,200	-35,442	-8,758
Employment	-491,877	-843,937	-738,321	-105,615

【Go to Travel Campaign】

(JPY 100million, persons)

	Direct effect	Total	Primary ripple effect	Secondary ripple effect
Production	11,315	23,509	19,548	3,961
Value added	5,728	12,396	10,038	2,358
Employment	115,236	202,371	173,933	28,438

Source: Estimations by the author

Table 4-5-4   The economic ripple effect of spending by tourists (Kyoto, Osaka, Hyogo)

■ Kyoto ■

【Declining of domestic tourism expenditure】

(JPY 100million, persons)

	Direct effect	Total	Primary ripple effect	Secondary ripple effect
Production	-4,976	-7,893	-6,600	-1,293
Value added	-2,614	-4,281	-3,413	-869
Employment	-79,585	-100,635	-90,719	-9,916

【Go to Travel Campaign】

(JPY 100million, persons)

	Direct effect	Total	Primary ripple effect	Secondary ripple effect
Production	538	853	713	140
Value added	283	463	369	94
Employment	8,601	10,876	9,805	1,072

■ Osaka ■
[Declining of domestic tourism expenditure]

(JPY 100million, persons)

	Direct effect	Total	Primary ripple effect	Secondary ripple effect
Production	-6,328	-9,666	-8,292	-1,374
Value added	-3,581	-5,598	-4,690	-908
Employment	-67,078	-87,934	-78,768	-9,166

[Go to Travel Campaign]

(JPY 100million, persons)

	Direct effect	Total	Primary ripple effect	Secondary ripple effect
Production	684	1,045	896	149
Value added	387	605	507	98
Employment	7,250	9,504	8,513	991

■ Hyogo ■
[Declining of domestic tourism expenditure]

(JPY 100million, persons)

	Direct effect	Total	Primary ripple effect	Secondary ripple effect
Production	-5,351	-8,502	-6,903	-1,599
Value added	-2,919	-4,735	-3,740	-995
Employment	-52,366	-72,722	-61,716	-11,005

[Go to Travel Campaign]

(JPY 100million, persons)

	Direct effect	Total	Primary ripple effect	Secondary ripple effect
Production	578	919	746	173
Value added	315	512	404	108
Employment	5,660	7,860	6,670	1,189

Source: Estimations by the author

sumption and the effect of the Go To Travel project. Additionally, for the three Kansai prefectures, we look at the impact of the declining of Japanese domestic travel consumption (Table 4-5-5) and effect analysis of the Go To Travel project (Table 4-5-6) by industry.

| Table 4-5-5 | The economic ripple effect by Declining of domestic tourism expenditure (by sector) |

【Declining of domestic tourism expenditure】

(JPY 100 million, persons)

Industries	[Kyoto]			[Osaka]			[Hyogo]		
	Production	Value added	Employment	Production	Value added	Employment	Production	Value added	Employment
Agriculture, forestry and fisheries	-50	-24	-347	-21	-13	-635	-89	-48	-435
Mining	-0	-0	0	-0	-0	-0	0	0	0
Manufacturing	-609	-255	-3,411	-404	-169	-1,967	-662	-228	-2,787
Construction	-33	-15	-327	-40	-18	-266	-23	-10	-154
Electricity, gas, heat supply and water	-472	-166	-534	-277	-113	-314	-338	-117	-289
Commerce	-542	-378	-7,838	-1,144	-804	-11,827	-437	-299	-6,406
Finance and insurance	-179	-124	-1,205	-237	-163	-1,418	-174	-117	-760
Real estate	-378	-331	-1,135	-429	-355	-638	-423	-358	-575
Transport and postal activities	-1,262	-840	-10,120	-1,467	-1,001	-11,843	-1,389	-1,002	-11,324
Information and communications	-134	-68	-284	-186	-96	-514	-104	-54	-300
Government, except elsewhere classified	-13	-10	-99	-18	-12	-85	-12	-8	-63
Services	-4,186	-2,056	-75,328	-5,403	-2,841	-58,419	-4,822	-2,479	-49,622
Industries unable to classify	-35	-15	-7	-39	-15	-8	-30	-13	-7
Total	-7,893	-4,281	-100,635	-9,666	-5,598	-87,934	-8,502	-4,735	-72,722

Source: Estimations by the author

| Table 4-5-6 | The economic ripple effect by "Go to Travel Campaign" (by sector) |

【Go to Travel Campaign】

(JPY 100 million, persons)

Industries	[Kyoto]			[Osaka]			[Hyogo]		
	Production	Value added	Employment	Production	Value added	Employment	Production	Value added	Employment
Agriculture, forestry and fisheries	5	3	38	2	1	69	10	5	47
Mining	0	0	0	0	0	0	-0	-0	0
Manufacturing	66	28	369	44	18	213	72	25	301
Construction	4	2	35	4	2	29	3	1	17
Electricity, gas, heat supply and water	51	18	58	30	12	34	37	13	31
Commerce	59	41	847	124	87	1,278	47	32	692
Finance and insurance	19	13	130	26	18	153	19	13	82
Real estate	41	36	123	46	38	69	46	39	62
Transport and postal activities	136	91	1,094	159	108	1,280	150	108	1,224
Information and communications	14	7	31	20	10	56	11	6	32
Government, except elsewhere classified	1	1	11	2	1	9	1	1	7
Services	452	222	8,141	584	307	6,314	521	268	5,363
Industries unable to classify	4	2	1	4	2	1	3	1	1
Total	853	463	10,876	1,045	605	9,504	919	512	7,860

Source: Estimations by the author

(1) Impact Nationwide

Using the national input-output tables, we examine the impact of the three cases by sorting them into direct effect and ripple effect.

The direct effect of the declining of Japanese domestic travel consumption was JPY -10.469 trillion in induced production value, JPY -5.2998 trillion in induced value added, and -1,066,231 in employment inducement. Looking at the ripple effect (total of primary and secondary ripple effects), induced production value was JPY -21.7517 trillion, induced value added was JPY -11.4697 trillion, and employment inducement was -1,872,447 persons.

The direct impact of the declining of travel consumption by foreigners visiting Japan was JPY -4.0689 trillion in induced production value, JPY -1.8788 trillion in induced value added, and -491,877 persons in employment inducement. Looking at the ripple effect, induced production value was JPY -8.8411 trillion, induced value added was JPY -4.42 trillion, and employment inducement was -843,937 persons.

Meanwhile, the direct impact of the Go To Travel project was JPY 1.1315 trillion in induced production value, JPY 572.8 billion in induced value added, and 115,236 persons in employment inducement. Looking at the ripple effect, induced production value was JPY 2.3509 trillion, induced value added was JPY 1.2396 trillion, and employment inducement was 202,371 persons.

We looked at how much of the negative impact of the declining of Japanese domestic travel consumption and travel consumption by foreigners visiting Japan was mitigated by the economic policy (Go To Travel project). In terms of the total ripple effect, induced production value was 7.7%, induced value added was 7.8%, and employment inducement was 7.5%. The policy effect was a little under 8%.

(2) Impact in Kansai

Next, we estimate the impact of the declining of Japanese domestic travel consumption and the Go To Travel project using the input-output tables (2015 tables) for Kyoto, Osaka, and Hyogo.

In Kyoto, the direct effect of the declining of Japanese domestic travel consumption was JPY -497.6 billion in induced production value, JPY -261.4 billion in induced value added, and -79,585 in employment inducement. Looking at the ripple effect (total of primary and secondary ripple effects), induced production value was JPY -789.3 billion, induced value added was JPY -428.1 billion, and employment inducement was -100,635 persons. The direct impact of the Go To Travel project was JPY 53.8 billion in induced production value, JPY 28.3 billion in induced value added, and 8,601 in employment inducement. Looking at the ripple effect, induced production value was JPY 85.3 billion, induced value added was JPY 46.3 billion, and employment inducement was 10,876 persons.

In Osaka, the direct effect of the declining of Japanese domestic travel consumption was JPY -632.8 billion in induced production value, JPY -358.1 billion in induced value added, and -67,078 in employment inducement. Looking at the ripple effect (total of primary and secondary ripple effects), induced production value was JPY -966.6 billion, induced value added was JPY -559.8 billion, and employment inducement was -87,934 persons. The direct impact of the Go To Travel project was JPY 68.4 billion in induced production value, JPY 38.7 billion in induced value added, and 7,250 in employment inducement. Looking at the ripple effect, induced production value was JPY 104.5 billion, induced value added was JPY 60.5 billion, and employment inducement was 9,504 persons.

In Hyogo, the direct effect of the declining of Japanese domestic travel consumption was JPY -535.1 billion in induced production value, JPY -291.9 billion in induced value added, and -52,366 persons in employment inducement. Looking at the ripple effect (total of primary and secondary ripple effects), induced production value was JPY -850.2 billion, induced value added was JPY -473.5 billion, and employment inducement was -72,722 persons. The direct impact of the Go To Travel project was JPY 57.8 billion in induced production value, JPY 31.5 billion in induced value added, and 5,660 persons in employment inducement. Looking at the ripple effect, induced production value was JPY 91.9 billion, induced value added was JPY 51.2 billion, and employment inducement was 7,860 persons.

Looking at how much of the negative impact of the declining of Japanese domestic travel consumption was mitigated by the economic policy (Go To Travel project), in terms of the total ripple effect, all prefectures were around 10.8% for induced production value, induced value added, as well as employment inducement[2].

Next, Table 4-5-5 and Table 4-5-6 look at the industrial ripple effect of the declining of Japanese domestic travel consumption and the Go To Travel project in three key Kansai prefectures. We narrowed down to three industries with the highest impact in employment inducement in each prefecture and focused on the decrease and share (value in parentheses below).

By prefecture, in Kyoto, in the case of the declining of Japanese domestic

---

2) As shown earlier, the degree of mitigation of the declining of Japanese domestic travel consumption and travel consumption by foreigners visiting Japan by the economic policy (Go To Travel project) nationwide was a little under 8%. The degree of mitigation of the declining of Japanese domestic travel consumption by the Go To Travel project was similar to that of the three key Kansai prefectures using the regional input-output table.

travel consumption, Services was -75,328 (74.9%), Transport and postal activities was -10,120 (10.1%), followed by -7,838 (7.8%) in Commerce. In Osaka, in the case of the declining of Japanese domestic travel consumption, Services was -58,419 (66.4%), Transport and postal activities was -11,843 (13.5%), followed by -11,827 (13.5%) in Commerce. In Hyogo, in the case of the declining of Japanese domestic travel consumption, Services was 49,622 (68.2%), Transport and postal activities was -11,324 (15.6%), followed by -6,406 (8.8%) in Commerce.

Impact on employment reflects the industrial structure of each prefecture. In Kyoto, Services, in Osaka, Commerce, and in Hyogo, Transport and postal activities was impacted more significantly compared to other prefectures. The impact of the Go To Travel project on industries followed a similar pattern and thus, an explanation is omitted.

4. Conclusion

In this section, we analyzed the ripple effect of the declining of tourism consumption and measures to generate demand using the national input-output tables (2017 Extended Tables) and regional input-output tables (2015 tables).

Looking at how much of the total of the decrease in Japanese domestic travel consumption and decrease in travel consumption by foreigners visiting Japan was mitigated by the economic policy (Go To Travel project), in terms of the total ripple effect, induced production value was 7.7%, induced value added was 7.8%, and employment inducement was 7.5%. We can say that the negative impact was mitigated by the government economic policy by a little under 8%.

Next, looking at the impact of the decrease in Japanese domestic travel consumption using the regional input-output tables for Kyoto, Osaka, and Hyogo, by industry, the negative impact was great in the order of Services, Transport and postal activities, and Commerce. In particular, in Kyoto, Services, in Osaka, Commerce, and in Hyogo, Transport and postal activities was impacted more significantly compared to other prefectures. These reflected the industrial structure of each prefecture.

Part
III   COVID-19 Chronology

Table of Contents

1. COVID-19 situation around the world 281

2. COVID-19 situation in Japan 283

3. COVID-19 situation in Kansai 285

4. Anti-COVID-19 measures in Japan 288

    (1) Border restrictions 288

    (2) States of emergency timeline 289

5. COVID-19 vaccinations 293

    (1) Situation around the world 293

    (2) Situation in Japan and Kansai 295

6. Japan's fiscal policy 297

7. Japan's monetary policy 301

8. US fiscal and monetary policies 302

9. EU fiscal and monetary policies 303

Editing of the "COVID-19 Chronology"

• The "COVID-19 Chronology" has been authored by APIR's Chronology team.

• In this report, the number of infections reflects the number of positive PCR test results.

• We have used the COVID-19 epidemiological dataset provided by the "Our World in Data" website, which has been compiled based on official reports from various governments, the World Health Organization (WHO), and Johns Hopkins University (JHU).

• Unless otherwise indicated, Japan-related data has been obtained mainly from the "Visualizing the data: information on COVID-19 infections" (Ministry of Health, Labor and Welfare), and from the "Novel Coronavirus Vaccines" (Prime Minister of Japan and His Cabinet) webpages. Our data may differ from that published on the websites of Japanese prefectures and media organizations.

• Japan population data was obtained from the "Basic resident registration by age group and municipality (2021)."

• Unless otherwise indicated, the data provided below was last updated on November 30, 2021.

1. COVID-19 situation around the world

○ As of November 30, 2021, the total number of COVID-19 infections had exceeded 262 million worldwide, while the total number of deaths was more than 5.2 million.

○ The International Monetary Fund (IMF) continued to revise downward its forecast for the world economy in 2021, from 5.8% in April 2020 to 5.4% in June 2020, and 5.2% in October 2020. However, the forecast was revised upward to 6.0% in April 2021, partly due to improved vaccination prospects. In October 2021, IMF lowered its forecast again to 5.9% due to concerns about the resurgence in the number of new COVID-19 infections.

○ The weekly average of the number of new COVID-19 infections in the USA surged starting with the end of October 2020 and peaked at the beginning of January 2021. In India, the virus spread rapidly starting with April 2021. Despite a temporary slowdown, the USA experienced a new COVID-19 surge caused by the new Delta variant starting with August (Figure 1).

○ On the other hand, judging by the number of confirmed COVID-19 cases per million people, the situation was more severe in European countries such as the UK and France, and Asian countries such as Singapore or Israel than in the USA or India (Figure 2).

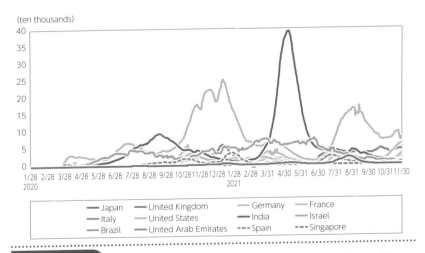

Figure 1   The number of new infections in countries around the world

Note: weekly moving average
Source: Compiled by APIR based on data from Our World in Data.

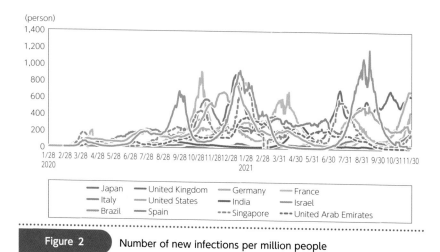

Figure 2   Number of new infections per million people

Note: Weekly moving average.
Source: Compiled by APIR based on data from Our World in Data.

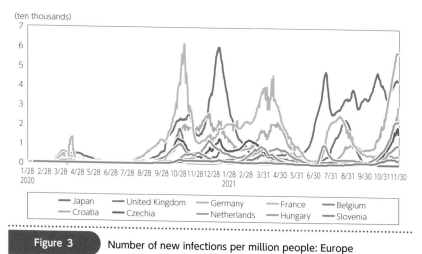

Figure 3   Number of new infections per million people: Europe

Note: Weekly moving average.
Source: Compiled by APIR based on data from Our World in Data.

○ In Europe, starting with November 2021 the virus spread rapidly, particularly in Germany. On November 25 Slovakia imposed a two-week lockdown, while Czechia declared a 30-day state of emergency (Figure 3).

○ In April 2020, the number of COVID-19-related deaths in Europe amounted to approximately 70% of the worldwide total, but in June the number of deaths started to increase in both North and South America. In November 2020 the number started to surge in Europe and North America, and April 2021 in South America and Asia. As already mentioned, since November 2021, the number of deaths is on an upward trend in Europe. Although vaccination has started worldwide and is expected to limit the number of deaths, the world-wide total is still around 7,000 per day (Figure 4).

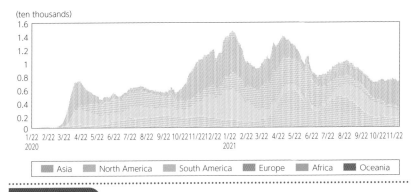

Figure 4   Number of new deaths worldwide by region

Source: Compiled by APIR based on data from Our World in Data.

2. COVID-19 situation in Japan

○ In April 2021, the number of new COVID-19 cases in Kansai expanded rapidly (the fourth wave). On the 25th of the same month, the third state of emergency was imposed, and as a result the number of infected topped out in late June. However, in July, the virus resurged in Kanto (the fifth wave). On July 12, the government imposed the state of emergency for the fourth time, and on August 13, the daily number of infected people exceeded 20,000. In September, the number of infections began to decrease, and the state of emergency was lifted nationwide on September 30 (Figure 5) (for details regarding the states of emergency, see Section 4-2 below).

○ The number of severe cases was larger during the fourth state of emergency than during the third one (Figure 6). On the other hand, the number of deaths during the fourth state of emergency increased at a slower pace than during the second and third states of emergency.

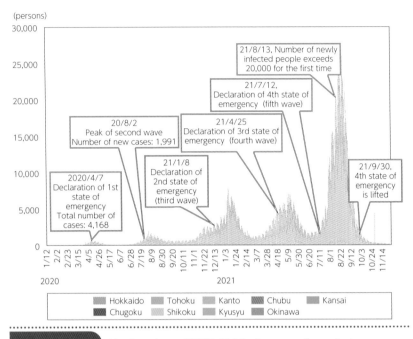

21/8/13, Number of newly infected people exceeds 20,000 for the first time

21/7/12, Declaration of 4th state of emergency (fifth wave)

20/8/2 Peak of second wave Number of new cases: 1,991

21/4/25 Declaration of 3rd state of emergency (fourth wave)

21/1/8 Declaration of 2nd state of emergency (third wave)

2020/4/7 Declaration of 1st state of emergency Total number of cases: 4,168

21/9/30, 4th state of emergency is lifted

2020   2021

Hokkaido   Tohoku   Kanto   Chubu   Kansai
Chugoku   Shikoku   Kyusyu   Okinawa

Figure 5   Number of new COVID-19 infection cases (by region)

Note: The increase in Kanto on Oct 29 was due to a correction in the number of infected people in Tokyo.
Source: Based on data published by the Ministry of Health, Labor and Welfare.

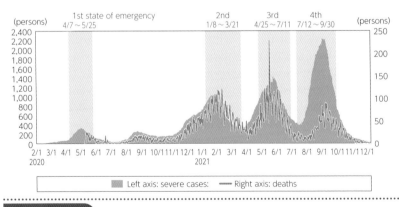

1st state of emergency 4/7～5/25   2nd 1/8～3/21   3rd 4/25～7/11   4th 7/12～9/30

Left axis: severe cases: Right axis: deaths

Figure 6   Number of new severe cases and new deaths in Japan

Note: The shadowed part covers the state of emergency periods.
Source: Based on data published by the Ministry of Health, Labor and Welfare

3. COVID-19 situation in Kansai

○ Since the second COVID-19 wave, Osaka Prefecture reported an overall higher number of infections per 100,000 people than the rest of the country. During the fifth wave, Shiga Prefecture faced a surge in the number of cases, which prompted the authorities to declare the fourth state of emergency (Figure 7).

○ In Kansai, the "reproduction number" of COVID-19, which represents the number of cases, on average, an infected person will cause during their infectious period, peaked at 1.81 on April 1, 2021. After that, it dropped to 0.67 on May 29 as a result of the semi-state of emergency and the third state of emergency. However, it rebounded to 1.00 on June 29, and then surged to 1.82 on August 1. After the fourth state of emergency was imposed, the reproduction number dropped again to 0.66 on September 17 (Figure 8).

○ During the third state of emergency, the occupancy rate of hospital beds for severe COVID-19 cases rose to 103.0% in Osaka Prefecture, 83.0% in Hyogo, and 91.0% in Nara. After a downward tendency since the middle of June, the number of new infections resurged in July. During the fourth state of emergency, the hospital bed occupancy rate in Kyoto Prefecture peaked at 75.9%, straining the healthcare system (Figure 9).

○ As shown in Figure 9, during the fourth state of emergency, the hospital bed occupancy rate was not as high as the during the previous state of emergency in the case of patients with severe symptoms. However, on August 30 it increased to 90.0% in the case of patients with mild to moderate symptoms, maintaining the pressure on the healthcare system (Figure 10).

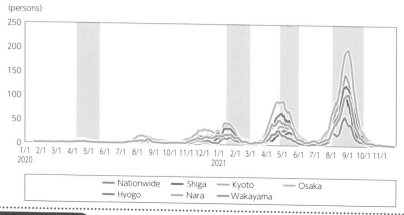

Figure 7 — Number of new infections per 100,000 people in Kansai

Note: Weekly moving average. The shadowed part covers the state of emergency periods.
Source: Based on data published by the Ministry of Health, Labor and Welfare, and local authorities.

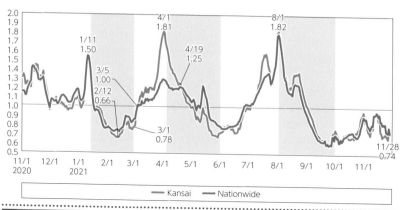

Figure 8 — Evolution of effective reproduction number: Nationwide vs. Kansai

Note: The red-shaded area shows the state of emergency periods, while yellow shows the period of quasi-state of emergency. The effective reproductive number (R) is the average number of secondary cases per infectious case in a population made up of both susceptible and non-susceptible hosts. In this case, it is the number of new infections in the past seven days divided by the number of new infections in the week before that, raised to the power of 5/7 (5 days is average incubation period, 7 days is the average infectious period).
Source: Ministry of Health, Labor and Welfare.

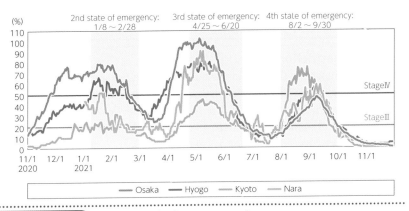

Figure 9   Critical care beds occupancy rates:
Kyoto, Osaka, Hyogo, and Nara prefectures

Note: The critical care beds occupancy rate is based on the standards set by each prefecture. Each stage is a
standard set by a government subcommittee until November 8, 2021.
Source: Data published by local authorities.

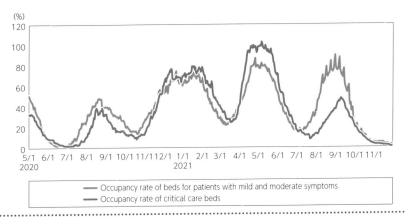

Figure 10   The occupancy rate of beds for patients with mild and moderate symptoms and the critical care beds occupancy rate: Osaka Prefecture

Note: Based on the standards set by Osaka Prefecture.
Source: Data published by Osaka Prefecture.

4. Anti-COVID-19 measures in Japan

(1) Border restrictions

○ Table 1 shows the timeline of the border restrictions imposed by Japan. In order to limit the spread of the virus, starting with February 1, 2020 Japan imposed restrictions on arrivals from China's Hubei Province. Initially, these measures were limited to some parts of China and South Korea, but by August 30, they covered 159 countries and territories.

○ On the other hand, on July 29, 2020 the Japanese government announced the implementation of the "Residence Track" framework targeting long-term residents from Thailand and Vietnam. In September, resident card holders were allowed re-entry, and the "Business Track" framework agreement was signed

Table 1 Timeline of border restrictions in Japan

Implementation date	Border enforcement measure
2020/2/1	An entry ban is imposed on travelers from Hubei Province, China.
2020/7/29	The "Residence Track" framework is implemented in collaboration with Thailand and Vietnam.
2020/8/30	Japan expands the entry ban list from 146 to 159 countries.
2020/9/1	Resident card holders are allowed re-entry.
2020/9/8	Cambodia, Taiwan, Malaysia, Myanmar, and Laos are added to the "Residence Track" framework.
2020/9/18	The "Business Track" framework is implemented in collaboration with Singapore.
2020/9/30	Singapore is added to the "Residence Track" framework.
2020/10/1	New entry permits can be issued for medium and long-term residents such as employees and foreign students, provided that their respective companies/institutions can guarantee they respect the quarantine measures.
2020/10/8	Began accepting business and residency track applications with Korea.
2020/11/1	Landing denials have been lifted in 9 countries, but Myanmar and Jordan have been added to the list, bringing the total number of countries covered to 152.
2020/11/1	Japan removes the following territories/countries from the entry ban list: Australia, South Korea, Singapore, Thailand, Taiwan, China (including Hong Kong and Macau), New Zealand, Brunei, and Vietnam. Vietnam is added to the "Business Track" framework.
2020/11/30	Acceptance of Business and Residence Tracks with China Begins
2020/12/28	Japan decides to temporarily ban new entry for all foreign nationals.
2021/1/14	The "Business Track" and "Residence Track" frameworks are suspended.
2021/7/9	Re-entry restrictions expanded from 41 to 60 countries and territories.
2021/11/8	Vaccination certificate holders are allowed to enter the country with shorter quarantine period.
2021/11/30	Temporary suspension of new entry for foreigners until Dec. 31

Source: Compiled from data published by the Ministry of Justice and the Ministry of Health, Labor and Welfare.

with Singapore targeting short-term residents. In October, new entry permits were allowed under certain conditions, while more countries were included into the Business Track and Residence Track frameworks.[1]

○ However, due to the COVID-19 resurgence around the world, on December 28, 2020 the government decided yet again to suspend new entries for all foreign nationals. Following this, on January 14, 2021 the "Business Track" and "Residence Track" frameworks were halted. Starting with May 14 re-entry was banned for arrivals from India, Nepal, and Pakistan, due to the new COVID-19 variants. By July 9, the measure was expanded to 60 countries.[2]

○ As vaccination is moving forward, the government decided to shorten the self-isolation period and allow new entries for vaccination certificate holders starting with November 8. These measures were expected to increase the number of international students and technical intern trainees. However, the government decided to temporarily bar all new foreign visitors starting with November 30 as fears over the new Omicron variant grow.

(2) States of emergency timeline

○ Table 2 shows the timeline of Japan's states of emergency. On April 7, 2020 the government imposed a state of emergency over COVID-19 for the first time in seven prefectures. However, on April 16 the state of emergency was expanded to the whole country.

○ On January 8, 2021 the second state of emergency was imposed, initially covering four prefectures. A week later it was expanded to seven more.

○ On April 25 the third state of emergency was imposed in four prefectures, and by May 28 it was expanded to a total of ten prefectures, while its period was extended until June 20.

○ On July 8 the fourth state of emergency was declared, and starting with July 12, it was imposed in Tokyo, in addition to Okinawa. On July 30, four more prefectures were added, while the period was extended until August 31. On August 17 another seven prefectures were added and the state of emergency period was extended once again until September 12. On August 25, the state of emergency was expanded to eight more prefectures. While in Miyagi and Okayama prefectures, the state of emergency was lifted on September 9, the period was extended until September 30 for the rest of 19 prefectures.

---

1) For more details regarding these two frameworks, see Section 1, Chapter 4.
2) Here, the new COVID-19 variants include the Beta, Gamma, and Delta variants.

Table 2	State of emergency timeline

Date	Content	Number of prefectures under SoE	GDP share (%)
2020/4/7	State of emergency is declared in Saitama, Chiba, Tokyo, Kanagawa, Osaka, Hyogo, and Fukuoka prefectures.	7	47.4
2020/4/16	The state of emergency is expanded nationwide.	47	100.0
2020/5/14	The state of emergency is lifted in 39 prefectures except for Hokkaido, Saitama, Chiba, Tokyo, Kanagawa, Kyoto, Osaka, and Hyogo.	8	49.3
2020/5/21	The state of emergency is lifted in Osaka, Kyoto and Hyogo prefectures.	5	36.6
2020/5/25	The state of emergency is fully lifted.	0	0.0
2021/1/7	The state of emergency is re-imposed in Saitama, Chiba, Tokyo, and Kanagawa prefectures (period: Jan 8~Feb 7)	4	33.1
2021/1/13	The state of emergency is re-imposed in Tochigi, Gifu, Aichi, Kyoto, Osaka, Hyogo, and Fukuoka prefectures (period: Jan 14~Feb 7)	11	59.6
2021/2/2	The state of emergency is lifted in Tochigi, but is extended until Mar 7 in the rest of the prefectures (period: Feb 8~Mar 7). Prefectures: Saitama, Chiba, Tokyo, Kanagawa, Gifu, Aichi, Kyoto, Osaka, Hyogo, Fukuoka.	10	58.0
2021/2/26	The government announces that on Mar 1 the state of emergency will be lifted in Gifu, Aichi, Kyoto, Osaka, and Hyogo prefectures. In Saitama, Chiba, Tokyo, and Kanagawa prefectures, the state of emergency will stay in place (until Mar 7).	4	33.1
2021/3/18	The government announces that on Mar 21 the state of emergency will be lifted in Saitama, Chiba, Tokyo, and Kanagawa prefectures.	0	0.0
2021/4/23	The government announces that the state of emergency will be imposed for the third time in Tokyo, Kyoto, Osaka, and Hyogo prefectures between Apr 25 and May 11.	4	31.7
2021/5/7	The government announces that starting with May 12 the state of emergency will be expanded to Aichi and Fukuoka prefectures, and that the period will be extended until May 31.	6	42.4
2021/5/14	The state of emergency is expanded to Hokkaido, Okayama, and Hiroshima prefectures (period: May 16~May 31).	9	49.3
2021/5/21	The state of emergency is expanded to Okinawa Prefecture (period: May 23~Jun 20).	10	50.1
2021/6/17	The state of emergency is lifted in Hokkaido, Tokyo, Aichi, Kyoto, Osaka, Hyogo, Okayama, Hiroshima, and Fukuoka prefectures, but the period is extended until Jul 11 in Okinawa Prefecture.	1	0.8
2021/7/8	A fourth state of emergency is declared in Tokyo between Jul 12 and Aug 22. In Okinawa, the state of emergency is extended until Aug 22.	2	19.7
2021/7/30	The state of emergency is expanded to Saitama, Chiba, Kanagawa, and Osaka prefectures (period: Aug 2~Aug 31). In Tokyo and Okinawa, the state of emergency is extended until Aug 31.	6	41.0
2021/8/17	The state of emergency is expanded to Ibaraki, Tochigi, Gunma, Shizuoka, Kyoto, Hyogo, and Fukuoka prefectures (period: Aug 20~Sep 12). The state of emergency is extended until Sep 12 in Saitama, Chiba, Tokyo, Kanagawa, Osaka, and Okinawa prefectures.	13	58.9
2021/8/25	The state of emergency is expanded to Hokkaido, Miyagi, Gifu, Aichi, Mie, Shiga, Okayama, and Hiroshima prefectures (period: Aug 27~Sep 12).	21	78.9
2021/9/9	The state of emergency is lifted in Miyagi and Okayama prefectures. The state of emergency in extended until Sep 30 in Hokkaido, Ibaraki, Tochigi, Gunma, Saitama, Chiba, Tokyo, Kanagawa, Gifu, Shizuoka, Aichi, Mie, Shiga, Kyoto, Osaka, Hyogo, Hiroshima, Fukuoka, and Okinawa prefectures.	19	75.8
2021/9/28	The government announces that the state of emergency will be lifted on Sep 30 in all prefectures.	0	0.0

Note: GRP data for each prefecture is based on nominal figures for FY2018.
Source: Prepared based on "Prefectural Accounts" (Cabinet Office)

○ The GDP share of the areas covered by the abovementioned states of emergency is as follows: the first state of emergency covered the entire country, so the maximum share was 100%; during the second one, the maximum share was 59.6%; during the third one, 50.1%; and during the fourth one, 78.9%. This shows that they had a significant impact on the Japanese economy (Figure 11).

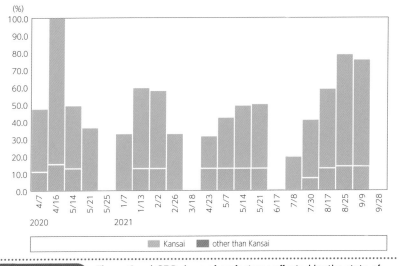

| Figure 11 | The national GDP share of prefectures affected by the state of emergency |

Note: GRP data for each prefecture is based on nominal figures for FY2018.
Source: Prepared based on "Prefectural Accounts" (Cabinet Office)

○ In Kansai, the economic share of the areas subject to the state of emergency exceeded 80% during all periods, and 90% during the fourth state of emergency, which included Shiga Prefecture. This indicates that Kansai was more affected than the rest of Japan in terms of economic activities (Figure 12).

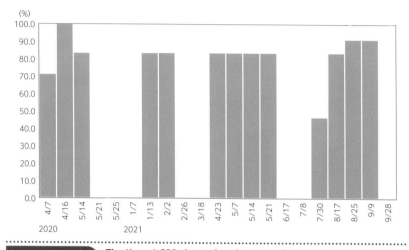

| Figure 12 | The Kansai GRP share of prefectures affected by the state of emergency |

Note: GRP data for each prefecture is based on nominal figures for FY2018.
Source: Prepared based on "Prefectural Accounts" (Cabinet Office)

5. COVID-19 vaccinations

(1) Situation around the world

○ As of November 30, 2021 more than 7.94 billion vaccine doses were administered worldwide.

○ Forty percent vaccination rate is widely believed to be the threshold at which the number of new infections should start to decrease. In terms of share of the population vaccinated with at least one dose, Israel is the first country to reach 40% (on Feb 7, 2021), followed by the UK (Mar 20), and the USA (Apr 21, see Figure 13).

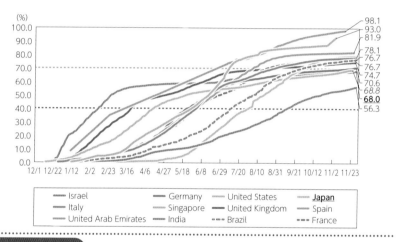

Figure 13 ▸ First dose vaccination rates evolution

Source: Compiled by APIR based on data from *Our World in Data*

○ In terms of fully-vaccinated population share, Israel reached 60% at the beginning of April, but the vaccination campaign slowed down since then. More recently, among the countries with a vaccination rate above 80% we can count: Singapore (91.9%), the UAE (88.4%), and Spain (80.4%). Despite a sluggish start, Japan has also managed to vaccinate more than 70% of its population (Figure 14).

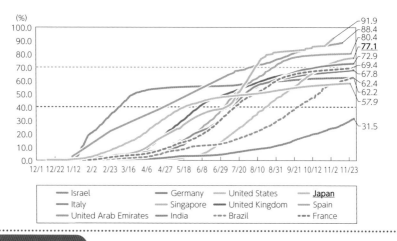

Source: Compiled by APIR based on data from *Our World in Data*

Figure 14   Second dose vaccination rates evolution

○ Israel and the UK have started to administer the third vaccine dose to the eligible population. In Israel and the UK, the booster vaccination campaign has pushed up the cumulative vaccination rates (the sum of the population percentages vaccinated with the first, second and third dose, respectively) (Figure 15).

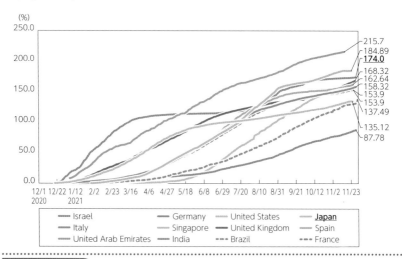

Figure 15   Cumulative vaccination rates around the world

Source: Compiled by APIR based on data from *Our World in Data*

○ The booster vaccination campaigns have already started in several countries around the world. The booster vaccination rate is 43.9% in Israel, 39.5% in Uruguay, and 25.8% in the UK (Figure 16). In Japan, booster shots started to be administered in December 2021, mainly among medical personnel.

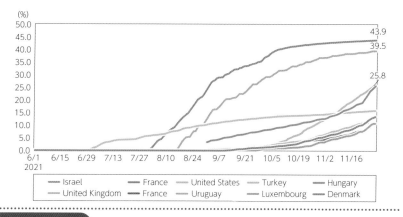

Figure 16 Booster dose vaccination rates evolution

Source: Compiled by APIR based on data from *Our World in Data*

(2) Situation in Japan and Kansai

○ The total number of vaccine doses administered in Japan was 196,915,615 as of November 29, 2021. The number increased with the start of workplace vaccination on June 21. In addition, medical personnel vaccination campaign was completed at the end of July.

○ In April 2021, when the vaccination of the elderly population began, the vaccination rollout was initially slow, but the situation started to improve in May, when large-scale vaccination campaigns were initiated by the Self-Defense Forces in Tokyo and Osaka. As of November 29, the first and second dose vaccination rates were 78.7% and 76.7%, respectively, relatively high compared to other major nations (Figure 17). In the Kansai region, the number of first dose vaccinations was 15,758,846, while the second dose vaccinations totaled 15,373,690. Meanwhile, the vaccination rate was 76.5% for the first dose and 74.6% for the second dose.

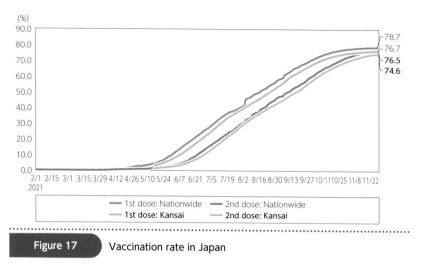

Figure 17   Vaccination rate in Japan

Source: Compiled by APIR based on data from the Prime Minister of Japan's Cabinet official home page.

○ As of August 30, Wakayama Prefecture had the highest vaccination rate in Japan at 52.7%, but as of November 29, it was replaced by Nara Prefecture with a vaccination rate of 77.4% (Figure 18).

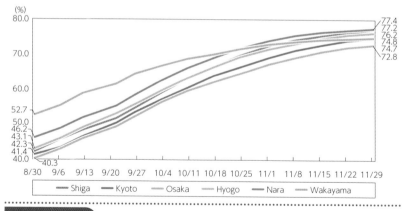

Figure 18   Trends in second dose vaccination rate in Kansai

Source: compiled by APIR based on data the Prime Minister of Japan's Cabinet official home page.

○ As of August 30, after the workplace vaccination campaign had started, the second dose vaccination rate was highest Yamaguchi Prefecture (55.8%), while it was lowest in Okinawa Prefecture (35.9%). However, as of November 29, Akita Prefecture (81.8%) had the highest rate (Figure 19).

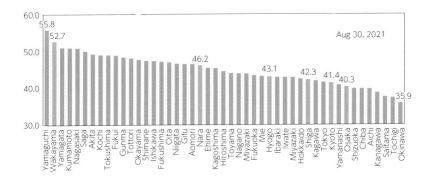

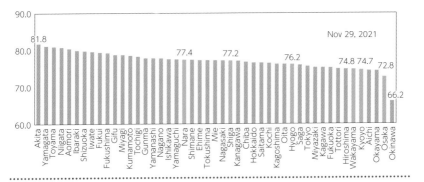

Figure 19 | Second dose vaccination rate by prefecture: Aug 30, 2021 vs. Nov 29, 2021 comparison

Source: Compiled by APIR based on data from the Prime Minister of Japan's Cabinet official home page.

6. Japan's fiscal policy

○ Table 3 summarizes Japan's budget for COVID-19-related measures. The first and second supplementary budgets provide support for the development of medical systems and businesses, while the third supplementary budget provides support for post-pandemic measures and to strengthen the vaccination system. In the FY 2020 budget, the sum of JPY 5 trillion has been set aside as a reserve fund to reinforce anti-COVID-19 measures, while the first supplementary budget provides support for the resumption of socioeconomic activities and preparation for the next crisis.

| Table 3 | | Japan's budget overview and timeline | |

Day	Content	Summary	Total budget
Apr 30, 2020	The Supplementary Budget for FY2020	Expenses related to Emergency Economic Package against the COVID-19: JPY 25,565.5 billion (1) Develop preventive measures against the spread of infection and medical treatment structures, as well as pharmaceuticals: JPY 1,809.7 billion (2) Protect employment and sustain business continuity: JPY 19,490.5 billion (3) Recover economic activities through public-private efforts, as the next phase: JPY 1,848.2 billion (4) Develop a resilient economic structure: JPY 917.2 billion (5) Prepare for the future: JPY 1,500.0 billion	JPY 117.1 trillion
Jun 12	The second Supplementary Budget for FY2020	Expenses related to cope with the COVID-19: JPY 31,817.1 billion (1) Enhancing the Employment Adjustment Subsidy: JPY 451.9 billion (2) Enhancing financial support: JPY 11,639.0 billion (3) Establishing a rent support grant for SMEs: JPY 2,024.2 billion (4) Supporting medical treatment providers: JPY 2,989.2 billion (5) Other supports: JPY 4,712.7 billion (6) Contingency funds for the COVID-19: JPY 10,000.0 billion	JPY 117.1 trillion
Jan 28, 2021	The third Supplementary Budget for FY 2020	1. Containment measures for the COVID-19: JPY 4,358.1 billion (1) Securing the medical treatment system & Supporting medical institutions: JPY 1,644.7 billion (2) Enhancing the testing system & Developing vaccine distribution system: JPY 820.4 billion (3) Containment measures based on data and technology: JPY 1,748.7 billion (4) International cooperation for containing the COVID-19: JPY 144.4 billion 2. . Promoting structural change & positive economic cycles for Post-Corona era: JPY 11,676.6 billion (1) Realizing digitalization and green society: JPY 2,825.6 billion (2) Enhancing productivity through structural changes and innovation: JPY 2,395.9 billion (3) Realizing positive economic cycles in regions & employment led by private demand: JPY 6,455.1 billion	JPY 19.2 trillion
Mar 26	The FY2021 Budget	Contingency fund for the COVID-19: JPY 5 trillion · In order to prepare for unexpected changes in the situation, JPY 5 trillion are secured for the contingency fund for the COVID-19 in the FY 2020 budget, and another JPY 5 trillion of the fund will be set aside in the FY 2021 budget. · In the 3rd supplementary budget, measures will be taken to secure hospital beds and accommodations, and to develop the COVID-19 vaccination system and inoculations. In addition, more measures will be taken to prevent the spread of the infection.	JPY 106.6 trillion

Day	Content	Summary	Total budget
Jul 30	General Account Settlement for FY2020	According to the general account settlement for FY 2020, the amount of money carried over to FY 2021 that was not spent within the fiscal year was JPY 30,780.4 billion, the largest amount ever. · Expenses that support corporate cash flow: JPY 6,414.0 billion · Business restructuring subsidies: JPY 1,148.5 billion · Expenses to be paid for cooperation in requesting shortening business: JPY 3,311.5 billion · Suspension of the "Go To Travel Campaign": JPY 1,335.3 billion	
Nov 26	The First Supplementary Budget for FY2021	Containment measures for the COVID-19: JPY 18,605.9 billion 1. Securing the medical treatment system, etc. · Emergency comprehensive support grant for the COVID-19 (securing beds, etc.) · Development of new coronavirus vaccine inoculation system and implementation of inoculation · Securing therapeutic drugs 2. Support for business, daily life, and livelihood (1) Support for businesses · Support for reviving business/ Funding support · Support for restaurants etc. cooperating on shortening business hours, etc. (Local Revitalization Grant) (2) Support for daily life and livelihood · Benefit for households exempt from resident tax/ Special lending for emergency small loans, etc. · COVID-19 payment for self-reliance support for those in need/ Emergency benefits for supporting students · Housing security benefit/Special measures for Employment Adjustment Subsidies, etc./ Financial stability of employment insurance (3) Measures against soaring energy prices · Reduction in burden of transportation fuel, etc Resumption of socioeconomic activities in the "Live-with-Corona" environment and preparation for the next crisis: JPY 1,768.7 billion 1. Resumption of socioeconomic activities with ensured safety and relief · "New Go To Travel campaign" · Expansion of free inspection without reservation(Local Revitalization Grant) 2. Fundamentally strengthening contingency plans for infectious diseases · Establishment of R&D and production systems for vaccines and therapeutic drugs	JPY 36 trillion

Note: Only the part related to anti-COVID-19 measures is excerpted.
Source: Compiled from data provided by various ministries.

Part I

Part II

Part III

Part IV

○ Table 4 outlines the travel subsidy programs for residents of the prefectures in the Kansai region.

| Table 4 | Travel subsidy campaigns in Kansai |

	Campaign name	Campaign period (accommodation fee discounts)	Target demographic
Fukui	Special Deal Fukui Campaign (Japanese: Fukui de Otoku Kyanpēn)	Oct 1, 2021~Dec 31, 2021※	Residents within the prefecture
Mie	Mie Discount Travel Coupon (Japanese: Mie Toku Toraberu Kūpon)	Part 2: Oct 15, 2021~Nov 30, 2021 Part 3: Dec 1, 2021~Dec 31, 2021	Residents within the prefecture
Shiga	Let's travel in Shiga now! (Japanese: Ima koso Shiga wo tabi shiyō)	Part 4: Jul 9, 2021~Dec 31, 2021	Residents within the prefecture
Kyoto	Rediscover the Charm of Kyoto Project (Japanese: Kyōto Miryoku Sai-hakken Tabi Purojekuto)	Oct 22, 2021~Decv 31, 2021	Residents within the prefecture
Osaka	Welcome to Osaka Campaign 2021 (Japanese: Ōsaka Irasshai Kyanpēn 2021)	Nov 24, 2021~Decv 31, 2021	Residents within the prefecture
Hyogo	Support your hometown! Let's travel in Hyogo Campaign (Japanese: Furusato Ōen! Hyōgo wo Tabi Shiyō Kyanpēn)	Advance sale for accommodation and travel tickets: Oct 14, 2021 ~ Dec 31, 2021 OTA reservations are eligible for discounts: Phase 1: Nov 12, 2021~Dec 2, Phase 2: Dec 3, 2021~Dec 31, 2021	Residents within the prefecture
Nara	Now is the time for Nara - Campaign 2021 (Japanese: Ima Nara Kyanpēn 2021)	Dec 1, 2021~Feb 28, 2022	Residents within the prefecture
Wakayama	Wakayama Refresh 3rd Plan (Japanese: Wakayama Rifuresshu Puran 3rd)	~ Dec 31, 2021	Residents within the prefecture
Tottori & Shimane	#WeLove San'in Campaign	~ Dec 31, 2021	Residents of Shimane and Tottori prefectures
Tokushima	Let's all support Tokushima" Discounts (Japanese: Minna de! Tokushima Ōen Wari)	Oct 1, 2021 (discount campaign restarted)~Dec 31, 2021	Residents within the prefecture

※Increased the maximum discount amount.
Source: Compiled from data released by each prefecture.

7. Japan's monetary policy

Table 5 outlines the Bank of Japan's monetary policy based on the official Monetary Policy Meetings (MPM) minutes. On December 18, 2020, the Bank decided to extend the duration of additional purchases of CP and corporate bonds until the end of September 2021 in response to COVID-19. However, due to the prolonged pandemic, on June 18, 2021, the deadline was again extended until the end of March 2022, in order to continue to support corporate financing.

Table 5   Monetary policy to counter the impact of COVID-19

Jan 21, 2021	· The Bank of Japan left its current short- and long-term interest rates policy unchanged. · It also decided to maintain its guidelines for asset purchases.
Mar 19	①With a view to enabling the Bank to cut short- and long-term interest rates nimbly while considering the impact on the functioning of financial intermediation, the Bank will establish the Interest Scheme to Promote Lending. ②In order to conduct yield curve control flexibly during normal times, the Bank will make clear that the range of 10-year Japanese government bond (JGB) yield fluctuations would be between around plus and minus 0.25 percent from the target level. At the same time, it will introduce "fixed-rate purchase operations for consecutive days" as a powerful tool to set an upper limit on interest rates when necessary. ③The Bank will purchase exchange-traded funds (ETFs) and Japan real estate investment trusts (J-REITs) as necessary with upper limits of about JPY 12 trillion and about JPY 180 billion, respectively, on annual paces of increase in their amounts outstanding. While these upper limits were originally set as a temporary measure in response to the impact of the novel coronavirus (COVID-19), the Bank will maintain them even after COVID-19 subsides. · Short-term and long-term interest rates policy: no change. · Guidelines for asset purchases: to be maintained.
Apr 27	· Short-term and long-term interest rates policy: no change. · Asset purchases policy: to be maintained.
Jun 18 Jul 16	· Short-term and long-term interest rates policy: no change. · Guidelines for asset purchases: to be maintained. · The Bank decided to purchase CP and corporate bonds until the end of March 2022, extending the period by six months.

Source: Prepared by the author based on statements by the Policy Board of the Bank of Japan.

8. US fiscal and monetary policies

| Table 6 | | US financial and monetary policies | |

Date	Institution	Policy	Outline
Dec 27, 2020	US government	Additional support measures	· The US adopted a USD 900 billion COVID-relief package including USD 600 direct individual payments, unemployment benefits, and support for small businesses.
Jan 20, 2021	Joe Biden becomes the 46th president of the USA.		
Jan 27	FOMC	No change in interest rates	· The Federal Reserve will continue to increase its holdings of Treasury securities by at least USD 80 billion per month and of agency mortgage-backed securities by at least USD 40 billion per month.
Mar 11	US government	American Rescue Plan	· The American Rescue Plan aims to deliver direct COVID-relief to the American people. The plan has a total budget of USD 1.9 trillion and includes measures such as giving working families a USD 1,400 per-person check.
Mar 17	FOMC	No change in interest rates	· The Committee decided to keep the target range for the federal funds rate unchanged.
Mar 31	US government	The American Jobs Plan	· President Joe Biden announced The American Jobs Plan, with a total budget of more than USD 2 trillion.
Apr 28	FOMC	No change in interest rates	· The Committee decided to keep the target range for the federal funds rate unchanged.
Apr 28	US government	The American Families Plan	· President Joe Biden announced his USD 1.8 trillion American Families Plan that seeks to invest in education and provide direct support to children and families. The plan is intended to complement The American Jobs Plan as part of a larger economic growth strategy.
Jun 16	FOMC	No change in interest rate	· The Committee decided to keep the target range for the federal funds rate unchanged.
Jun 24	US government	Infrastructure investment plan	· The White House announced its support for a bipartisan agreement on a infrastructure investment plan (Bipartisan Infrastructure Framework). The framework involves new spending of approximately USD 579 billion.
Jul 13	US government	Investment plan	Senate Democrats and the White House agreed on a USD 3.5 trillion investment plan. Adding this to the almost USD 600 billion Bipartisan Infrastructure Framework results in a total of approximately USD 4.1 trillion, which suggests that President Biden's American Jobs Plan and American Families Plan will receive the necessary funding.
Jul 28	FOMC	No change in interest rates	· The Committee decided to keep the target range for the federal funds rate unchanged.

Date	Institution	Policy	Outline
Sep 22	FOMC	No change in interest rates	· The Committee decided to keep the target range for the federal funds rate unchanged.
Oct 28	US government	Investment plan	President Biden unveils a scaled-down version of the earlier USD 3.5 trillion investment plan, known as the "Build Back Better Plan."
Nov 3	FOMC	No change in interest rates	· The Committee decided to keep the target range for the federal funds rate unchanged.
Nov 15	US government	Infrastructure investment plan	President Biden signs the infrastructure bill into law. The USD 1 trillion bill will enable states and local governments to upgrade roads and bridges, improve the communications and power networks, and build a national network of electric vehicle (EV) chargers.
Nov 19	US government	Investment plan	House of Representatives Democrats pass the "Build Back Better Plan." The total budget is approximately USD 2 trillion.

Source: Prepared by the author based on documents issued by the Federal Open Market Committee (FOMC), Japan External Trade Organization (JETRO), and various media reports.

9. EU fiscal and monetary policies

Table 7   EU financial and monetary policies

Date	Institution	Policy	Outline
Jan 21, 2021 Mar 11 Apr 22 Jun 10	European Central Bank (ECB)	No change in interest rates	· The Governing Council of the ECB decided that the key interest rates will remain unchanged.
Jun 15	European Commission	Recovery fund	· The EU issued a EUR 20 billion 10-year bond in order to finance its Recovery Fund. The EU also plans to raise EUR 750 billion through joint bond issuance by the end of 2026. Therein, approximately EUR 100 billion bonds, including EUR 80 billion of long-term bonds, are expected to be issued by the end of 2021.
Jul 22 Sep 9 Oct 28	European Central Bank (ECB)	No change in interest rates	· The Governing Council of the ECB decided that the key interest rates will remain unchanged.

Source: Prepared by the author based on documents issued by the European Central Bank (ECB), Japan External Trade Organization (JETRO), and various media reports.

Part I
Part II
Part III
Part IV

STATISTICAL ANNEX

The definitions of the geographical regions used in the annex are as follows unless otherwise noted.

Region	Prefecture
Kansai	Type A: Shiga, Kyoto, Osaka, Hyogo, Nara, Wakayama
	Type B: Shiga, Kyoto, Osaka, Hyogo, Nara, Wakayama, Fukui
	Type C: Shiga, Kyoto, Osaka, Hyogo, Nara, Wakayama, Fukui, Mie, Tottori, Tokushima
Kanto	Ibaraki, Tochigi, Gunma, Saitama, Chiba, Tokyo, Kanagawa, Yamanashi
Chubu	Nagano, Gifu, Shizuoka, Aichi, Mie
Japan	All prefectures including the Kansai, Kanto and Chubu regions

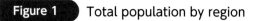

Figure 1   Total population by region

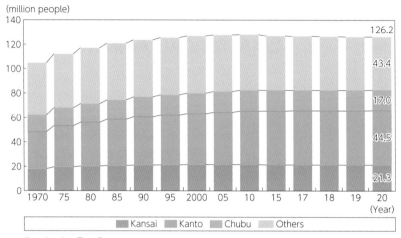

Kansai region: Type B
Note: Level as of October 1 for each year. The figures for 2020 are based on preliminary data from
    the 2020 national census.
Sources: Statistics Bureau, Ministry of Internal Affairs and Communications, *"Population Census"* and *"*
    Population Estimates"

Figure 2   Kansai population by age group

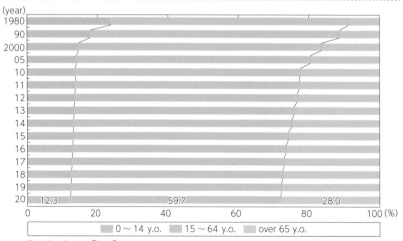

Kansai region: Type B
Note: Does not include persons with unspecified ages.
Sources: Statistics Bureau, Ministry of Internal Affairs and Communications,
    "Population Census", *"Population Estimates"* and *"Internal Migration in Japan Derived*
    from the Basic Resident Registration (for 2010-20 data)"

Figure 3 Population aging rates

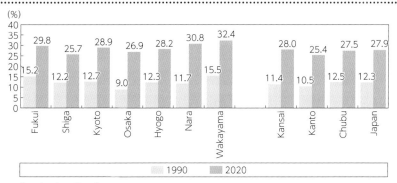

Kansai region : Type B

Note: Population aging rate (%) = Population aged 65 and above/total population x 100. Level as of
October 1 for 1990 and as of January 1 for 2020.

Sources: Health and Welfare Bureau for the Elderly, Ministry of Health, Labour and Welfare, *"Table of
Figures for Health and Welfare Services Map for the Elderly (1990)"*
Statistics Bureau, Ministry of Internal Affairs and Communications, *"Population Estimates"* and
"Internal Migration in Japan Derived from the Basic Resident Registers (for 2020 data)"

Figure 4 Gross regional product (GRP) trends

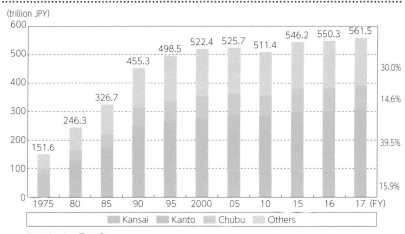

Kansai region: Type B

Note: Nominal figures. The calculation method was changed in FY1990.

Sources: Cabinet Office, *"Annual Report of National Accounts Statistics"* and *"Annual Report of
Regional Accounts Statistics"*

Figure 5   Trends in the GRP shares of economic sectors

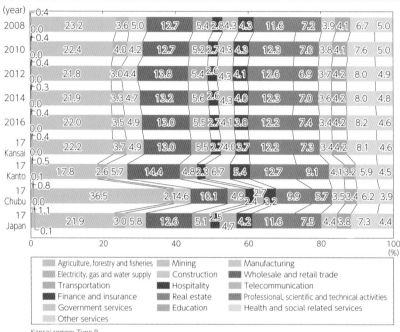

Kansai region: Type B
Note: The values used for the calculation of the shares do not include imputed interest. However, we used the
       GDP figures by industry to calculate the total GDP.
Source: Cabinet Office, *"Annual Report on Prefectural Accounts"*

Figure 6   GRP per capita

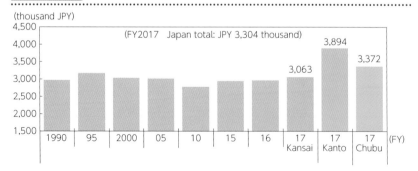

Kansai region: Type B
Source: Cabinet Office, *"Annual Report on Prefectural Accounts"*

Figure 7 — Kansai's GRP and sovereign states' nominal GDP (2018)

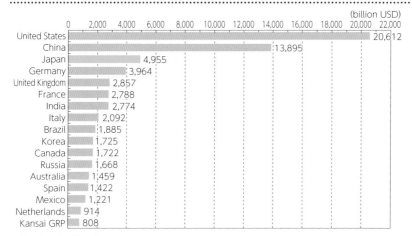

(billion USD)

United States	20,612
China	13,895
Japan	4,955
Germany	3,964
United Kingdom	2,857
France	2,788
India	2,774
Italy	2,092
Brazil	1,885
Korea	1,725
Canada	1,722
Russia	1,668
Australia	1,459
Spain	1,422
Mexico	1,221
Netherlands	914
Kansai GRP	808

Kansai region: Type A
Note: Nominal GDP in 2018. The figure for Kansai is based on its nominal GRP for FY2017 (April 2017–March 2018)
The 2018 exchange rate was JPY 110.43 to the US dollar.
Sources: UN, *"National Accounts Main Aggregates Database"* Cabinet Office, *"Annual Report of Regional Accounts Statistics"*

Figure 8 — Value of manufactured goods shipments

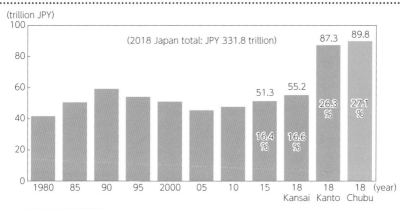

(trillion JPY)

(2018 Japan total: JPY 331.8 trillion)

year	value	
1980		
85		
90		
95		
2000		
05		
10		
15	51.3	
18 Kansai	55.2	16.6%
18 Kanto	87.3	26.3%
18 Chubu	89.8	27.1%

(16.4% appears on the 15 bar)

Kansai region: Type B
Note: Figures represent total values of manufactured goods shipments by firms with 4 or more employees.
Source: Ministry of Economy, Trade and Industry, *"Statistics Table on Census of Manufactures"*
For 2015, The Ministry of Internal Affairs and Communications and Ministry of Economy, Trade and Industry, *"2016 Economic Census for Business Activity"*

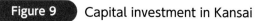

Figure 9   Capital investment in Kansai

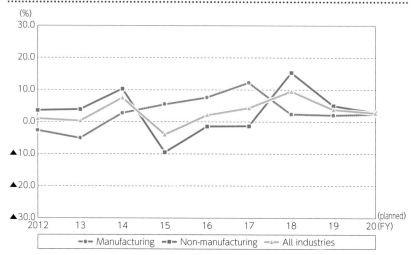

Kansai region: Type B
Note: YoY. Figures for FY2020 are the planned values as of December 2019.
      Includes investments in land, but does not include investments in software.
      Source: Bank of Japan, Tankan (Short-Term Economic Survey of Enterprises in Japan)

Figure 10   Capital investment in Japan

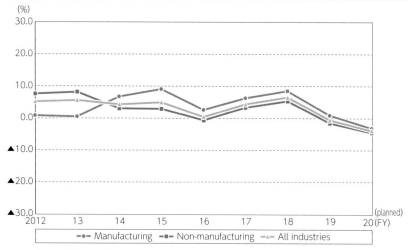

Note: YoY. Figures for FY2020 are the planned values as of December 2019.
      Includes investments in land, but does not include investments in software.
      Source: Bank of Japan, Tankan (Short-Term Economic Survey of Enterprises in Japan)

Figure 11 Index of industrial production (IIP)

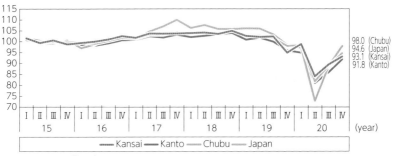

Kansai region: Type A
Note: 2015 = 100. Seasonally adjusted.
The Kansai, Kanto, and Chubu regions are under the jurisdiction of the Kansai,
Kanto, and Chubu Bureaus of Economy, Trade and Industry, respectively.
Source: Ministry of Economy, Trade and Industry, *"Production, Shipments and Inventories"*

Figure 12 Employment by industry (2020)

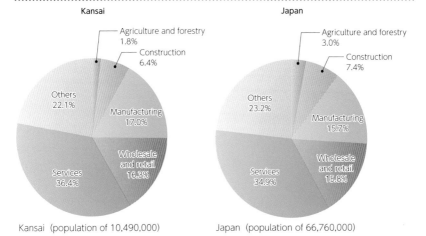

Kansai (population of 10,490,000)   Japan (population of 66,760,000)

Kansai region: Type A
Note: "Services" represents the total employment in the following industries: Hotels and Restaurants,
Entertainment, Health and Social Work, Education, Mixed services, and Other services(services that
cannot be categorized).
Source: Statistics Bureau, Ministry of Internal Affairs and Communications, *"Annual Report on the Labor
Force Survey"*

Figure 13 Exports by product category (2020)

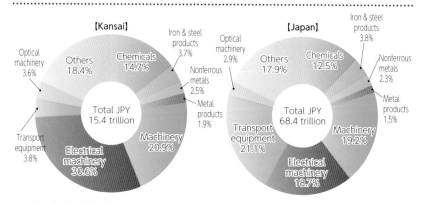

Kansai region: Type A
Source: Ministry of Finance, Osaka Customs, *"Trade Statistics"*

Figure 14 Imports by product category (2020)

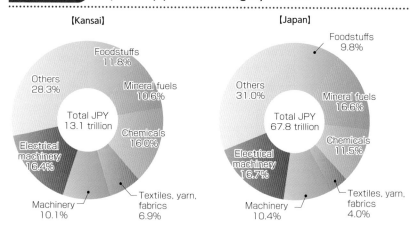

Kansai region: Type A
Source: Ministry of Finance, Osaka Customs, *"Trade Statistics"*

Figure 15   Destination of exports from Kansai

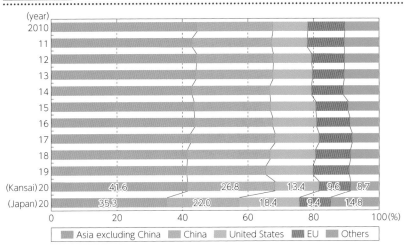

Kansai region: Type A
Note: The figure for 2020 are definite.
Source: Ministry of Finance, Osaka Customs, *"Trade Statistics"*

Figure 16   Origin of imports into Kansai

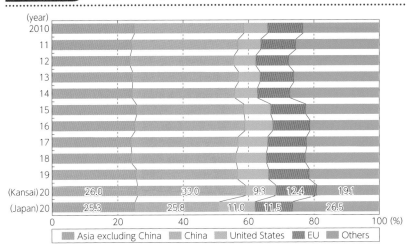

Kansai region: Type A
Note: The figure for 2020 are definite.
Source: Ministry of Finance, Osaka Customs, *"Trade Statistics"*

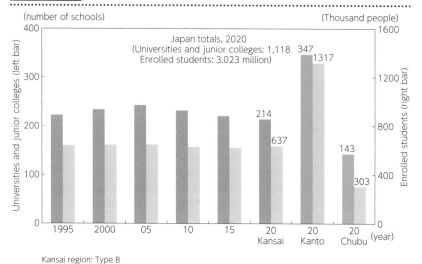

| Figure 17 | Number of universities, junior colleges and enrolled students |

Kansai region: Type B
Source: Ministry of Education, Culture, Sports, Science and Technology, *"School Basic Survey"*

| Figure 18 | Number of national treasures and important cultural properties(2021) |

	National treasures	Important cultural properties	National treasures, domestic share (%)	Important cultural properties, domestic share (%)
Fukui	6	114	0.5	0.9
Shiga	56	825	5.0	6.2
Kyoto	237	2,199	21.1	16.5
Osaka	62	682	5.5	5.1
Hyogo	21	470	1.9	3.5
Nara	206	1,328	18.3	10.0
Wakayama	36	395	3.2	3.0
Kansai	624	6,013	55.5	45.1
Kanto	335	3,746	29.8	28.1
Chubu	44	1,097	3.9	8.2
Japan	1,125	13,331	100.0	100.0

Kansai region: Type B
Note: Values are as of April 1, 2021
Source: Agency for Cultural Affairs

Figure 19 International overnight visitors

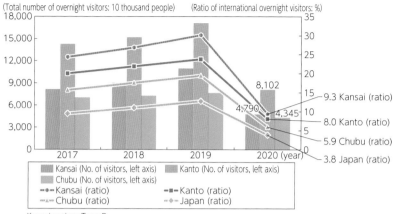

(Total number of overnight visitors: 10 thousand people) (Ratio of international overnight visitors: %)

Kansai (No. of visitors, left axis) Kanto (No. of visitors, left axis)
Chubu (No. of visitors, left axis)
-●- Kansai (ratio) -■- Kanto (ratio)
-▲- Chubu (ratio) -◆- Japan (ratio)

Kansai region: Type B
Note: Ratio of international overnight visitors = Total number of international overnight visitors / Total number of overnight visitors x 100
Sources: Ministry of Land, Infrastructure, Transport and Tourism, *"Overnight Travel Statistics Survey"* (The figures for 2020 are preliminary).

Figure 20 Visit rates of international visitors by prefecture

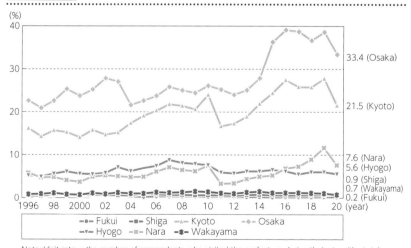

-●- Fukui -■- Shiga -▲- Kyoto -◆- Osaka
-▼- Hyogo -✕- Nara -✱- Wakayama

Note: Visit rate = the number of respondents who visited the prefecture during their stay /the total number of respondents (N) x 100
The figures of 2020 are average for Jan-Mar as the survey was cancelled after the onset of the COVID-19 pandemic in April.
Sources: Japan National Tourism Organization (JNTO), *"Destination Survey of Overseas Visitors to Japan"*. From 2011, Japan Tourism Agency *"Consumption Trend Survey for Foreigners Visiting Japan"*

Figure 21 Average expenditure per visitor by nationality (2020)

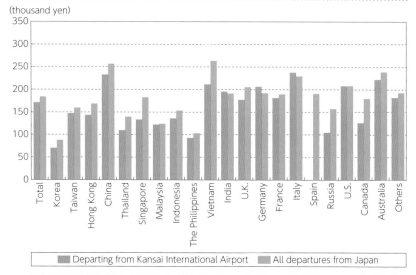

(thousand yen)

Departing from Kansai International Airport   All departures from Japan

Note 1) Travel spending per person departing from Japan. The figures of 2020 are average for Jan-Mar as the survey was cancelled after the onset of the COVID-19 pandemic in April.
Note 2) No data country shows no respondents.
Source: Japan Tourism Agency, *"Accommodation Survey"*

About Us
Organization Name: Asia Pacific Institute of Research (APIR)
Date of Establishment: December 1, 2011
Research Director: MIYAHARA, Hideo
Address: 7th Floor., Knowledge Capital Tower C, GRAND FRONT OSAKA
3-1 Ofuka-cho, Kita-ku, Osaka 530-0011 Japan

Kansai and the Asia Pacific
Economic Outlook: 2021-22

2022 年 4 月 28 日　初版発行

| 編　著 | ASIA PACIFIC INSTITUTE OF RESEARCH
（一般財団法人アジア太平洋研究所） | ©2022 |

| 発行所 | 日経印刷株式会社
〒102-0072　東京都千代田区飯田橋2-15-5
電　話(03)6758-1011
https://www.nik-prt.co.jp/ |

| 発売所 | 全国官報販売協同組合
〒100-0013　東京都千代田区霞が関1-4-1
電　話(03)5512-7400
https://www.gov-book.or.jp/ |

組版・印刷・製本／日経印刷株式会社

ISBN 978-4-86579-312-3　C0033